The Sin of Mother Mary

Drew O'Brien

For my husband, Scott, & all my mothers:
Toni, Kathie, Lori, Jessie,
and Mary

The Sin of Mother Mary

1.

The sun dropped to the edge of a violet horizon, a glowing, skinned plum. Its dying rays finally forgave Santa Monica Boulevard of its autumn heat, pulling the shadow of night west, over downtown Los Angeles, across the Hollywood sign, through the dingy window at the YMCA on Selma and Cole, and across the pasty white face of a sleeping young man. The shroud of night passed over his closed eyes. His lids crept open to reveal brown, angry eyes as they rolled in their sockets. A hand paled by years of protection from daylight reached up and combed through thinning strands of chestnut hair. He sighed and lit a cigarette.

For Danny, like any other prostitute, night brought absolution: no heat, no cops, and especially no good people. His world was back, and he was safe again among the odd and real. Taking a deep drag off the Marlboro, he looked up at the pencil drawing hanging over his bed. Its crinkled, yellowed edges framed a man's face that stared from Danny's past. With the breath of smoke weaving through his throat and sinuses, he considered ripping the drawing down and tearing it up. The same thought plagued his mind each time he looked at the drawing. It stirred up the pain, and the pain was a grudge, and the grudge was an icicle in his gut. *Reach for it. Shred it. Be done with the sketch and her already.* He reached but his resolve failed again, as it had for days and years past. He blew a lungful of smoke toward the familiar face.

Savoring the cigarette for a just a moment longer, he snubbed the butt into an ashtray, another relic from his past--a holy water wall font depicting Virgin Mary and Christ, a miniature replica of Michelangelo's Pieta with a recessed bowl at its base. Next to it was the bottle of Red Devils he had ready for his big day in March. He pushed himself up from

4

the bed, unaware of the dust and filth that whirled its way across the seedy room. Later, as he walked toward the corner of Formosa and the boulevard, he felt alive in night's shadow. The darkest recesses of his heart seemed to blend with the inky darkness around him, and the bruise time, when the black of night would be assaulted by the blue of dawn, was twelve hours away.

Danny yawned and bent over to tie his shoe. Brakes squealed and he looked up to see a midnight blue BMW. He paused to check out the driver but the other young man who stood a few feet away didn't, and he glided into the car's front seat. Gum wrappers and street grime flew into Danny's face as the car sped off, and he ran a hand through his hair -- this was happening way too much lately, and way too many fresh, younger hustlers were hitting the boulevard.

It would have been a perfect time for Danny to take a hit off a joint or shoot up some smack, but drugs weren't his thing. Not for any moral or health reason, but because he had always been afraid of them. Just like he feared daylight, he had his reasons for being afraid of drugs: '...too much crazy shit in my head...' he would tell the other hustlers on the street. He wasn't going to be another mental case burned out on acid, and no way was he going to tempt the insane gene that he knew lurked somewhere inside him. But most important now, no one was going to say next March that he did it because he was high.

He made his decision clean and sober, and once he did, he spent a lot of time at the Hollywood Library reading up on the most efficient and least painful ways to kill himself. He would stay especially away from the messier ones some movie stars chose. Quick and painless was what he wanted, and no mess. He had always practiced safe sex to avoid the plague, and he had become particularly more careful now since making his decision. No, he wasn't about to waste away and die a gasping, lingering death. Easy and effective was his goal, and barbiturates were the answer.

Since he turned twenty-two, he thought about his death plan twice every day: when he got up at sunset, and when he ran to get to his bed at the Y before sunrise. Standing here now, though, watching the BMW turn left on Cahuenga made him think he shouldn't wait till next March. The chirp of a Toyota's horn made him jerk his head around. A rust-streaked Lincoln Town car that must have once been an elegant navy blue, cut past the Toyota and halted at the curb in front of him. Danny had one thought as the door creaked open: please don't let him be a talker. Not a confessor, please.

A little man with red-brown hair combed forward into bangs darted his head like a nervous bird, then slapped the burgundy leather front seat and nodded to Danny. Before, Danny would have just ignored a trick

5

like this, but with the BMW still on his mind, and the glint of a gold bracelet on the little man's left hand in his eye, Danny slid into the seat and closed the door.

The leather seat was as cracked and worn as the little man's tanned, mid-50's face. Stale cinnamon gum and what smelled like an old, wet washcloth hit Danny's nose. He noticed the man's pencil-thin mustache that vibrated with each nervous chew. Because all of Danny's tricks were now either sleazy leather bears or married fathers who 'never do this', Danny hoped this little man would be different. Just as long as he didn't 'want to talk' it would be okay. Thirty seconds crawled by before Danny's nerves sat on edge.

"Yeah. So what are you into?" Danny asked.

The little man stared at the steering wheel, with his head bowed like he was praying, and said, "I've never done this before." Here it comes, Danny thought.

"Let me tell you what I do, don't do, and what it'll cost you."

"Wait a second. You don't have a cold, do you?" the little man asked.

"No. My voice always sounds scratchy like this."

Danny glanced down at a business card that read 'Harrington Davis Clothiers' and reached for it. The little man sprang to life and snatched the card up before Danny could get to it. He slid it into the pocket of his suit jacket.

"So what do you want me to do?"

"I don't know. Not sure. Can we talk a second?"

Great, Danny thought. Twenty bucks to listen to how normal this guy is, that he's not a fag or anything, blah, blah, blah. Danny sighed and slid back in the seat.

"See. My wife doesn't understand me, and I'm not sure..."

"Bless me, Father, for I have sinned," the reedy woman's voice said as if she couldn't get the words out. Father Michael Halloran wanted to say 'Relax, Mrs. Casebolt, I know it's you.' He was also pretty sure that the sin she was about to confess would be the same one she confessed two weeks before: gossiping about her neighbor. It wouldn't be worse than her sin a month ago about a fantasy involving Ricardo Montalban and a can of Reddi Whip, and it wasn't going to be any worse than the sin she would be confessing two weeks from now. One sin as garden variety as another, and this same sinner today would be dunking a glazed doughnut with him Sunday in the parish hall after mass. There weren't any new sins to Halloran because from 1965 to this dry, August day in 1985, he had heard them all.

Halloran pulled his collar away from his neck because it was pressing his Adam's apple as Mrs. Casebolt finished her confession. His football player's neck was always too tight against his collar and he wondered if the rectory housekeeper would ever stop shrinking his collars. But if his transfer makes it through, he thought, no more pinching collars. Just a sweatshirt and the Varsity team at Servite High to coach, no more ineffective penances, no more repeat confessions. The dark closet he sat in became cloying as Mrs. Casebolt's perfume choked his nostrils with the scent of Casablanca lilies.

"Father? Father? Are you still listening?"

"Oh. Of course," Halloran lied. "Your penance is three Our Fathers and one Hail Mary."

Mrs. Casebolt prayed the Act of Contrition and Father Halloran's mind wandered off. How bad was the traffic going to be to the USC ticket office? Where was Father Beauchamp? Time was wasting.

"Amen. Father, Amen!"

"Yes, Amen. Now go in peace and sin no more," he said as automatically and disinterestedly as the kid at Jack-in-the-Box said 'Can I take your order, please?' when he stopped for lunch earlier today.

"Thank you, Father," she said and then the door of the confessional clicked open. The only thing new about this session of confessions was the whining miniature fan overhead that St. Joan's had finally been willing to install at Halloran's insistence.

As he waited for the next confessor to get settled, Halloran thought about how much he hated the pretense of giving penance in Jesus' name. He wasn't wise and he was far from holy. That's why the transfer made so much sense. He wanted to see the direct result of his work, watch the ball run into the end zone, and teach young people that to work is to pray, and how God, in the form of victory, rewarded effort. It was proof that his life was having any damn effect on anybody that Halloran wanted. So he would patiently take the 'confession orders' today, and hope that his transfer would be approved tomorrow.

Another penitent shuffled into the confessional, and as Halloran slid the gauze-covered screen aside to start again, he thought, 'Welcome to St. Joan's. May I absolve your sin please?' A loud knock on his confessional door startled him and made the person on the other side gasp in surprise.

"Father Halloran? You need to open up," the high-pitched voice of Father Beauchamp insisted.

"Big line out here," Halloran said as he cracked the door. "What took you so long?"

Father Beauchamp paused to catch his breath, holding his open palm to his chest with a feminine gesture. His chest heaved under his thick hand. He raised his hand to indicate he almost caught his breath.

"What's the big rush, Father?" Halloran asked.

"It's stuffy in here. They want you up at Queen of Angels in Hollywood," Beauchamp said.

"I can't make it up there today. I got things to do."

"You have been ordered to go."

"Why?"

"To administer Viaticum to Bishop Crawford."

Halloran leaned back and folded his arms, rolling his eyes with disinterest. He looked at his watch again.

"Why not a cardinal or a high Church official?"

"It's a Los Angeles Diocese tradition that a bishop receive Viaticum from the pastor of his former parish."

Halloran exhaled through his clenched teeth, puffing out his cheeks in an exasperated breath. He shrugged and gathered up his Bible and scapular.

"What choice do I have? I'll get out of here as soon as possible."

Father Beauchamp paused. He sniffed the air like a suspicious cat. He waved his arm broadly to fan the bothersome odor from the confessional.

"Kind of musty in here."

"If we could get some air conditioning, maybe it wouldn't feel like a locker room after every confession," Halloran responded.

"It's not going to be any fun for me, either," Beauchamp said, slapping his fat stomach. Beads of sweat percolated down on his temples. "Drive carefully up there."

Halloran stepped off the elevator on to the third floor of The Queen of Angels Hospital. The soles of his shoes, polished to a shining ebony, slapped against the tile floor. He glanced down to notice the reflection of his shoes and legs from the impeccably polished tile floor. Fluorescent light reflected a green haze as Halloran rubbed his nostrils, already on fire from the dry Santa Ana winds, but now stinging with each waft of rubbing alcohol and bleach. As he made his way down the hall, faintly aware of his palms moist from anxiety, a familiar rhythmic murmuring struck his ear.

Following the hushed voices, Halloran paused at the doorway of a waiting room. The brown vinyl and wood chairs that lined its gray walls were empty, but a group of nuns and priests knelt in the center of the room, cushioned only by gray, flat carpeting. In their habits, they formed a black and white huddle, their hands each interwoven with rosaries that dangled and slipped forward as they completed each prayer. Halloran paused to listen to their calming recitation of the Lord's Prayer, and then continued down the hall. As he proceeded further, he noticed priests in habits similar to his own, others in long cassocks, and still others in the crimson cassocks of higher church officials. He nodded to the priests as he passed.

A youthful priest stopped Halloran at the door of the Bishop's room. The priest's long, brown Franciscan robe flowed around his wiry frame. That robe makes him look like 'Dopey' the dwarf, Halloran thought. His face was sparsely whiskered, and when he stopped Halloran, his brown eyes widened with nervousness.

"His Eminence is to receive no more visitors," he said through a voice that almost cracked with puberty.

"I'm Father Halloran. I'm from St. Joan of Arc's Parish."

The young priest frowned with distrust as he shrugged and held out his arm to prevent Halloran from entering. He stared up at Halloran who stood a full head taller. Halloran grabbed the young priest's arms and thrust them down to his sides.

"I repeat. I'm from St. Joan's."

"Well good for you. I'm Brother Gilman. From St. Athanasius Friary. What do you want?"

"I was summoned to perform Viaticum for Bishop Crawford."

Gilman's eyes squinted with confusion. He glanced down the hall and tapped his sandaled foot nervously. He folded his arms.

"All right, then. Wait here."

Gilman opened the door quickly and slipped in. As the oak veneer door closed, it fanned a draft of rotting yeast, carnations, and the smoky, soapy scent of frankincense. Halloran waved his hand in front of his face to clear away the odors. He opened his leather bag and removed his scapular, placing the fine, violet silk ribbon around his neck and kissing the embroidered silk crosses on its ends. The door opened once again. As he stepped into the room, his shoes squeaked on the floor that was more pristine than the tile of the corridor.

Bishop Crawford lay in the hospital bed clutching a worn leather book. The bed was raised enough to support his head and shoulders, or as Halloran saw it, what was left of them. The Bishop's head was mammoth compared to his neck that did not have more diameter than a memorial candle. And his pale hospital gown hung from the two knots of his shoulders, its neck open to show his clavicles standing out clearly above his top ribs. What made his head look extra large was his thick growth of white hair. His eyes were aquamarine jewels set in black caves. The sharp cliffs of his cheekbones jutted just below. The skin of his face was taut as a desiccated mummy, a blue-gray in the hollows of absent cheeks, and a waxy white everywhere else.

Opaque blue tubes brought pain reliever to his left arm and nutrition into his right. His chest pumped rapidly with each shallow breath, nearly in rhythm with the monitor that beeped quietly with each pulse of his heart. The blue, the white, the gray, along with the bright light of the day, and the white sheets on the bed, made the Bishop look like some sort of ghost in a phantom chariot. In contrast to all the white, two priests in black habits stood to his left, while Cardinal Manning in red robes sat to his right. Next to the Cardinal sat a slight, middle-aged woman in a gray wool dress. She dabbed at her deep-set eyes as she plucked the dead petals off a long stem red rose. Carnations and roses lined the room, interspersed with red votive candles and a small, smoking pot of frankincense. Gilman kneeled in a dark corner of the room, whispering a prayer as he passed his rosary through his fingers.

Halloran approached the edge of the Bishop's bed. The Bishop slowly turned his head toward the side of the bed. His eyes flared with anger. In a deep and strong voice that seemed oddly out of place in the wisp of a man in the bed, Bishop Crawford addressed Halloran.

"Who are you?"

Halloran dropped to one knee at the foot of the Bishop's bed and bowed his head. "Father Michael Halloran of St. Joan of Arc's Parish."

"Oh," replied Crawford. "I suppose I know why you're here."

Halloran looked up to the Cardinal and glanced at the woman next to him. The Cardinal called Halloran over to him. Halloran rose, his knee cracking as he did.

"A retired athlete, huh Father?" Crawford said from behind.

Halloran nodded and smiled. When he reached the Cardinal, he again took a knee as the Cardinal held out his left hand and presented his ring. Halloran lightly took his hand and kissed the ring, and he could feel blood rush to his cheeks. Some church customs still embarrassed him. The Cardinal stood, his vestment rustling crisply against the vinyl hospital chair.

"Father Halloran, this is Mrs. Hammerly."

"How do you do," Halloran said.

"Mrs. Hammerly is Bishop Crawford's sister. She understands why you're here, too."

Mrs. Hammerly's eyes welled up and she dabbed them again. She wiped a thin stream of mucous from her nose. She began to whisper something, thought better of it, and shook her head. "First he gets AIDS from that blood transfusion a few years ago," she sobbed. "Now, he's refusing to accept ... or ... prepare for ..." Mrs. Hammerly stood and wept loudly into her handkerchief. A sonorous blow of her nose interrupted her gasps and tears.

"Quit your blubbering, Sis. I'm not going anywhere," Crawford offered.

Mrs. Hammerly sat down again. She folded her handkerchief and tucked it into her purse. She began to pluck dead petals from a lavender tea rose. Once he was satisfied that the Bishop's sister had calmed again, the Cardinal leaned forward to address Halloran quietly.

"Starting that whispering again, huh, Manning? You Church officials and your little secrets," Crawford said to Halloran's back.

"Bishop, please remember your respect for Mother Church and the hierarchy," the Cardinal said.

"I don't understand, your Eminence. Am I here to perform Viaticum or not?" Halloran asked.

"Yes. But while you were on your way, Bishop Crawford made an unusual request."

"I'll tell him, Thomas," Crawford said.

The Cardinal shrugged and rolled his eyes. He gestured for Halloran to return to Bishop Crawford's side. Halloran turned and walked to the side of the Bishop's bed. The Cardinal sat, lightly patting Mrs. Hammerly's shoulder. Halloran leaned toward the Bishop.

"I know I'm dying, Father. I just need to confess before I do."

"Do you prefer to confess to the Cardinal? We can step out," Halloran offered.

"No."

"To me?"

"No. Not yet. I need a Murphy first."

"A who?" Halloran asked.

The Bishop held up a worn ox blood-red leather book, which made his fingernails appear a cadaverous gray blue. Halloran glanced at the book and shook his head. He reached for it but the Bishop pulled the book to his chest.

"It's Mary Murphy's diary. It's my confession, too. I have to hand it to a Murphy."

The Bishop's arm dropped from fatigue, making the diary bounce toward the edge of the bed. Halloran lunged to catch the book, but it landed safely between the edge of the bed and the side handrail. Halloran stepped back and adjusted his jacket awkwardly.

"Who are the Murphys?" Halloran asked.

"A family that was in my -- sorry -- your parish."

"I don't recognize the name."

"You'll have to get parish records. Go through the old books."

"If I can't find them?"

"There were seven Murphy children. Someone must still be

around."

Halloran looked at the Cardinal who pursed his already tight lips as he arched his eyebrows. The Cardinal shrugged. He glanced at Mrs. Hammerly but she just shook her head. Halloran rolled his lips for a moment before speaking.

"A Murphy can't offer you Absolution," Halloran said.

"Really, Father Halloran, I'm still a bishop. Don't you think I know that?"

"No offense, your Excellency."

"I'm not just concerned about my soul. The Murphy children must know what happened."

"Your Excellency, how can I convince one of these Murphy children to come?"

"Tell them it concerns their mother," Crawford answered.

Mrs. Hammerly jumped up, her face looking like a glistening, red tomato as tears burst from her eyes. She waved her handkerchief toward her brother. "Gregory, there isn't much time. Please, just let the Father hear your confession and perform the rites." The Bishop folded his arms over the reed that was his body and rolled away from his sister to face Friar Gilman.

"Holy Mary, Mother of –"

Gilman's prayer halted as he dropped his rosary, startled by the Bishop's stare. The Friar snatched up the beads and kissed the crucifix. Bishop Crawford folded his hands and whispered.

"Blessed Mother Mary," he said. "Get me a Murphy and I'll give up my spirit."

2.

Halloran's phone rang the next morning and jostled him awake. Though his instant thought and most private hope was that the Bishop had died, the Cardinal reassured him that the Bishop was stabilized. The Cardinal wanted to know how the search for the Murphy children was going. Halloran scratched at his chest through the v-neck T-shirt he wore.

"I'm driving to Orange County, today, your eminence. The second Murphy child, Louise, lives down there with her family. I'm sure I'll be able to persuade her to help us. I got her name from the doctor treating the schizophrenic sister. Yes, those two both moved to Minnesota. No. That one slammed a door in my face. No, she's the suicide. If Louise won't help, there's still one child after her— a boy. I'll let you know."

Halloran hung up the phone and lay back in his bed. He stared up at the ceiling, then to the crucifix on the wall. He could smell fresh coffee and frying bacon, and his paunchy stomach growled with hunger. As he stood and stretched, his arms and legs cracking, he heard a soft tap at the door.

"Father Halloran," the soft female voice said. "I heard your phone. Would you like some breakfast?"

"No, Agnes, I won't have any time today. Just a cup of coffee."

Halloran felt the car window and sensed it was cool enough outside to roll it down. As he drove the street that was shaded by a line of old eucalyptus trees acting as wind breaks for the orange groves dotting the land between housing developments, a cool breeze flushed out the stale air of the car. Halloran crinkled his nose for a minute when he caught scent of the trees. Smells like cat pee, he thought, and almost rolled the window back up but the fresh, comfortable breeze stopped him. It soon didn't matter, because he turned into one of the housing developments and parked in front of a two story, Mediterranean house that couldn't have been more than a couple of years old. He confirmed the address once more, and then walked up the flag stone path, past the manicured lawn and garden, and paused at the front door.

Halloran stepped back when he saw the mezuzah. "I must have the wrong house," he said aloud. He turned to walk back to the car when he heard the door open behind him.

13

"Can I help you?"

Halloran turned back around to see a redheaded woman in black slacks and cornflower blue silk blouse. Small in stature, her gray-green eyes flared as she noticed his habit and collar. She grabbed the doorjamb.

"Oh, God, who's dead?"" she rasped through her high voice.

"I'm sorry, Ma'am. I was looking for Louise Murphy, but I—"

"I was Louise Murphy. Now I'm Louise Murphy Schwartzman."

"Mrs. Schwartzman, I'm Father Michael Halloran. From St. Joan's Parish."

"St. Joan's? I haven't thought of that place for years."

"If I could beg a little of your time. I'm on a mission on behalf of Bishop Crawford."

"I thought he died. Cancer or something."

"No. He's still with us. Though he is gravely ill. And that's why I've come."

"All right, Father. If you have to."

Mrs. Schwartzman led Halloran through the front entry, her low heels tapping on the blonde marble floor. Halloran glanced at the curved staircase and the bronze bust of Beethoven placed at its base. Faint violin music grew louder as Mrs. Schwartzman led Halloran into a sitting room painted eggshell with white damask furniture, beveled glass tables, and a white baby grand piano. Mrs. Schwartzman gestured for Halloran to sit on a Louis XIV accent chair.

"Mrs. Schwartzman, my car is awfully dirty and I wouldn't want –"

"Don't worry for it. We get the furniture cleaned once a month. Don't worry about it. You like Perlman?"

Halloran sat lightly on the chair. He went to lean his hands on the chair arms, thought better of it, and instead folded his hands in his lap. Mrs. Schwartzman fluttered past him, darting about the room looking for something. She lifted a small crystal chest that sat at the center of the table and picked up a minute remote control.

"There it is."

She aimed it at an infrared light on the wall and depressed it. The violin music faded quietly into the background. The whirring hum of a ceiling fan was now all that could be heard. She placed the remote down and stood behind Halloran.

"That's better. I love Vivaldi loud but not when I have company. Oy, that Perlman. Now what'd you say?"

"I don't really know much about classical music."

"A priest who doesn't know about music? Come on now."

"Well, it just wasn't something –"

"Coffee, Father?"

14

"Yes, please."

Mrs. Schwartzman left the room. Halloran's eyes wandered about the room: stark, pristine, accented by modern art on the wall, bronzes on pedestals in each corner, and a huge black and blonde marble fireplace. He noticed a silver tray with a silver menorah and other Jewish ritual equipment stacked neatly on the corner of a sideboard. Elegant, he thought. But it's cold; no photos, no memorabilia, no history of the lives in the house. Mrs. Schwartzman returned with a silver coffee serving set and bone china cups that tinkled with each step she took. She set the coffee service on the table before Halloran, and plopped down on the white sofa opposite him.

"I convinced my husband that white would be the predominant color in the house. It's so clean, pure, fresh, don't you think, Father? Cream? Sugar?"

White means forgiving, or forgetting, he thought. "Yes."

"Yes, for white? Or, yes for cream or sugar?"

"All three."

She leaned over and poured the coffee into white bone china cups that were colorless and pattern-less accept for an accent of gold on the rim. She handed the cup to Halloran and then poured one for herself. "So, Father, what can I do for you?"

"As I already said, the Bishop is dying. But he's made an unusual request."

Mrs. Schwartzman presented a tray of chocolate cookies to Halloran. He declined. She grabbed two and set the tray back down. She shoved an entire cookie in her mouth and began to chew rapidly. Realizing that her mouth was filling with crumbs and that they were about to spill out, she slurped from her cup of coffee. "Sorry, Father," she said as she swallowed. "Chocolate macaroons. From Canter's. Go ahead."

"I was called to the Bishop's side the other day. To administer the Last Rites."

"Oh, God, he's that far gone?" she said. She chomped into the other macaroon.

"Yes."

"What's he got again?"

"The Bishop has... He had a transfusion a couple of years ago during open-heart surgery. He got tainted blood and has AIDS."

Mrs. Schwartzman set her cup and saucer on the glass table, the porcelain and glass making a sharp clink. She wiped the corners of her mouth with her thumb and index finger, and then dusted her fingertips off onto the table. "That's just awful. No one should suffer like that."

Mrs. Schwartzman glanced down at the glass table and saw the

15

crumbs from the cookie. She reached out with her index finger and, using it like a magnet, she plucked up the crumbs then sprinkled them into her coffee cup.

"I hate a mess."

Halloran nodded and set down his coffee cup. He folded his hands and leaned toward Mrs. Schwartzman. "Before accepting his Last Rites, the Bishop wants to talk to a Murphy."

"I'll bet," Mrs. Schwartzman said.

"He requested that we locate a Murphy child so that he could make his last confession to one of you."

Mrs. Schwartzman stood up. She picked up the coffee pot and extended it to Halloran who declined. She poured herself another cup. "If I remember correctly, only a priest can hear a confession."

"That's right, normally. But he is the Bishop and we have to honor his request, don't we?"

Mrs. Schwartzman picked up another macaroon from the tray. She did not extend it to Halloran this time. The cookie snapped in her mouth. "What is it you want from me, Father?"

"Mrs. Schwartzman, I was hoping you would grant the Bishop his request."

"I can't."

"He said you would consider it if I mentioned that it pertains to your mother."

"I'm sure it does, Father. But I have two reasons why I won't. First, you are sitting in a Jewish Orthodox household. My husband's family required that I convert in order to marry him. Don't look so shocked, Father. I lost my Catholic faith a long time before. I believe in God, but that's about it. So I wasn't sacrificing anything important to me. But because I believe in love and love my husband, I converted. I could never hurt him by participating in any Gentile ceremony." Father Halloran nodded and stood. He straightened his jacket.

"Father, there's the other reason." Mrs. Schwartzman sat as if something unseen pushed her down and she let out a sigh as she sat. She patted Halloran's chair to get him to sit again. "I've worked very hard to forget about my past. I don't have one before I met my husband as far as I'm concerned. If Andrew and Mary ever pop into my head, I just think about something else."

"Andrew and Mary?" Halloran said.

"My parents."

"They were that awful that you put them out of your mind?"

"Let's just say I've never forgiven them and leave it."

Halloran bent over and took a sip of his coffee. He glanced

around at all the white: the walls, the couch, the picture frames, and the flowers. His eyes almost burned. "How about your brothers and sisters, then?" He asked.

"I haven't seen any of them since my sister's funeral three years ago. I get a birthday card from my youngest brother every year but I don't even write back. I can't go listen to the Bishop and have a bunch of old stuff stirred up. I can't do it."

"Mrs. Schwartzman, you've made it very clear you can't help me. You have your reasons. You were my last hope." Halloran turned and walked toward the front door. Mrs. Schwartzman stood.

"Father, wait a sec, please."

Halloran paused at the front door. Mrs. Schwartzman ran up the stairs, her heels making sharp clicks against the blonde, marble steps. Halloran folded his arms and sharply exhaled. A ray of sun struck the crystals of a large chandelier and it sparkled like a flare. The light reflected onto the staircase wall, and Halloran could see the light broken into a prism of six colors. Mrs. Schwartzman stepped back down the stairs, her shadow breaking the rainbow of color down into one violet band. She waved an envelope toward Halloran.

"Father," she said, handing him the envelope. "Take this. It's my last birthday card from Danny, my little brother. The return address is in Hollywood. It says the YMCA."

"YMCA?"

"He's been in Hollywood since he dropped out of UCLA. He's been trying to sell a screenplay, I guess. Who knows, he might be willing to help you out. I doubt he's very busy."

"Thank you, Mrs. Schwartzman."

Halloran followed the hilly curves of Sunset Boulevard east through Beverly Hills, past the expansive green lawns and the manicured gardens. Through his open window he could smell cut grass and the star jasmines, gardenias, roses, and musky olive trees that were planted everywhere. Occasional screeching brakes and engines that sounded like grinding gravel were the only reminders that he was on a city street. Otherwise, he thought, the lawns and gardens, the pristine sidewalks and curbs, with the wrought iron gates of the secluded larger mansions interspersed, made a picture of perfect suburbia and a surreal serenity.

The traffic clogged up as he crossed into West Hollywood. He had been looking for a gas station since Beverly Hills because he had no idea where to find the address on the envelope. Darting his eyes about to see what was ahead of the crawling line of cars, he could only make out storefronts. His eyes burned from the smog and exhaust that drifted into his open window and he reached up and rubbed them. About a block ahead on the right, he noticed two young women standing near the curb and a space where he could pull over.

Horns blared and cars sped past Halloran as he moved the car to the right and stopped. He waved toward the two women and depressed the control button that rolled down the electric window on the passenger's side. One of the two women stepped forward, and as she did, Halloran for the first time saw that she wore a pink tank top that fit her too tightly, and a black skirt that just hovered above her mid thigh. Her breasts vibrated with each step she took toward the open window, making Halloran blush. She folded her arms over the open window, allowing her breasts to fill the window briefly before she slid her shoulders low enough to greet Halloran.

Her black hair was pulled back into a thick braid and her face was creamy white, fresh scrubbed and lightly made up. Halloran estimated her age at no more than seventeen and when she spoke to him, she blinked slowly, causing her long eyelashes to rest like two delicate feathers over her deep brown eyes.

"What's up?" she said. But before she could croak another sound out of her husky voice, she saw his habit and collar. She started giggling.

"I didn't think you guys liked girls."

"Miss. I'm trying to find an address and I was hoping you could help me."

The woman nodded, then leaned back and looked cautiously in both directions down Sunset. She leaned her torso into the car and pulled aside her top, exposing her left breast. Halloran started back, pushing his body against the driver's side door. She slowly covered her breast again, dropping her head back in. Halloran saw nothing since his eyes were pinched shut.

"Did I scare you or something? What's the matter?"

Halloran opened his eyes. He relaxed back into his seat but he did not look into the woman's eyes when he spoke. Her flowery perfume mixed with the gasoline fumes of the idling car.

"I just need directions, young lady. Or better yet, if you could tell me where the nearest gas station is."

"So you really are a priest?"

"Yes."

"Sure you don't got some kinky Catholic school girl fantasy you wanna make come true?"

Halloran leaned over and released the parking brake. He put the car into drive but hesitated long enough to bless the girl with his right hand. "Find peace, young lady."

"Hold it, Father, I get it. You really do need directions. What's the address you're looking for?"

Halloran slid the transmission back into park and handed her the envelope. She grabbed it from him and her ebony-black nails curved like claws scraped the paper. "Hold it a second."

The woman stepped back over to her companion. Halloran noticed with each step, her firm buttocks flexed and stretched the tight, black material. Her naked thighs made a tan, brown muscular line to her knee crease. "Forgive my sin, Lord," Halloran said.

Both women were now pointing and apparently discussing the best directions to offer Halloran, nodding occasionally and then shaking their heads. Halloran glanced around to see that this particular section of Sunset Strip was lined with crystal and china shops, high fashion clothing boutiques, and what to Halloran appeared to be upper scale restaurants with valet parking. The shop lights were flickering and flashing on as dusk began to fall. He could not understand how prostitutes fit into this boulevard of luxury. Just another luxury? he thought. The prostitute stepped back over to the open car window.

"Yeah, okay, Father. This YMCA is on Santa Monica Boulevard, just off Cahuenga. Ever been there?"

"No."

"It's pretty sleazy there. Lot of low-lifes. Anyways, stay on Sunset till you get to Highland. You'll be right by Hollywood High. Hang a right. Go down two blocks to Santa Monica Boulevard. Hang a left. Three blocks down or so is Cahuenga. That's your street. Probably a right. Got it?"

"I think so."

"Did you need anything else, Father?"

"No. Bless you."

"Thanks for the blessing, again."

Halloran released the parking brake and checked his mirrors. As he pulled into the traffic, he heard her yell: "Watch out for the low-lifes!"

The YMCA stood exactly where the young prostitutes had said: on the corner of Santa Monica and Cahuenga. Halloran easily spotted it because mounted on the southeast corner of the three-story brick building was a dark blue sign with blazing neon letters that read 'YMCA.' The sign itself looked to be forty or fifty years old, and as Halloran parked the car, he saw that the faded brick building was adjacent to two decrepit sound stages which must have once been a small film studio. Blue jeans, T-shirts, and towels draped down from open windows devoid of screens on the second and third floors. Halloran stepped up to the double glass doors and noticed blue spray paint that formed the outline of a body on the door stoop. The words 'BASH VICTIM' and the date '12-07-84' stood out in red paint near

19

the head of the figure.

The glass door whined on its rusty hinges as Halloran passed through, baying at his back as it returned to its regular position. One overhead fixture cast a yellow light that was absorbed by the brown walls. The flecked tile floor felt sandy under Halloran's feet as he stepped to the reception counter. A ceiling fan created a draft that smelled of stale cigarettes and a locker room, while a single light bulb in its base threw a small halo onto the counter. Halloran saw the rubber soles of two sneakers crossed on the dingy green Formica counter. His eyes followed legs clad in blue jeans down to the open sports section of the Los Angeles Times. Two sets of brown fingers clutched the pages.

"Excuse me," Halloran said.

Neither the newspaper nor the feet moved. Halloran cleared his throat and paused a moment to allow the person behind the newspaper to respond. He glanced at a small section of the wall behind the counter that contained cubbyholes. A pool ball snapped to initiate a game somewhere in a nearby room.

"Could you help me, please?"

Still no response. Halloran, unaccustomed to being ignored, reached over the counter and yanked down the newspaper page. Clear cocoa brown eyes glared at him, the face containing them a smooth coffee complexion that sparkled under the fan's light bulb. The eyes sized up the insolent intruder but immediately softened when they saw Halloran's collar. A young black man of about twenty dropped his feet off the counter and stood to assist the priest.

"Yeah?" the young man said.

"I'm looking for Danny Murphy."

"He in trouble with the law again?"

"Again? Oh, no. This is a family matter."

The young man scratched his head as he assessed the priest's statement. He leaned his muscular upper body on his elbows.

"You sure you're not here to cause trouble?"

"I'm sure. I just need to talk to Danny a couple of minutes."

"Well, sorry. You can't."

"Just wait a second here. I'm a priest. You can see—"

"Don't get excited, Reverend. He ain't here right now."

Now it was Halloran's turn to slump onto the counter. He pushed up his sleeves and propped his chin up with his elbows.

"Any idea what time he'll be back?"

"Not till tomorrow morning. He works nights. Sometimes he don't ever come in."

Halloran perked up. "Where does he work? I'll talk to him there."

The young man laughed under his breath and scratched his head again. He plopped back down in his chair. He picked up the newspaper and started reading. Halloran slammed his hand on the counter.

"Don't ignore me. Just tell me where to find him."

The young man did not lower the paper. As he spoke, his breath vibrated the newspaper page.

"You didn't hear it from me."

"Okay."

"He works out on Santa Monica, just a couple miles from here. Right by the Warner Hollywood Studios."

"What's the name of the company?"

"Just go there. You'll see him whoring around."

"Excuse me?"

"Forget it, Father. Just go up the boulevard a ways. Turn right and park near the Formosa Cafe. He'll turn up."

As Halloran turned to leave, he heard a familiar click. He glanced back toward the sound and saw a round wall clock with two large hands but missing the minute hand. Every classroom he ever sat in had one of them, and the last click registered seven-thirty. Thrusting his wrist toward his face, he realized the time was correct. He nodded to the young man behind the counter and bolted across the gritty floor and the glass door that whined and bayed at his back.

Approaching La Brea Avenue, Halloran saw two young men, these he judged to be seventeen or eighteen. One leaned against a warehouse wall, and the other walked a few steps then stood at the curb as if he needed a ride. Both were shirtless, one in corduroys, the other in torn blue jeans. Both had physiques that looked like Greek statues and both smiled toward Halloran as he passed. He smiled back and waved.

A few blocks past the young men, a building painted brick red jumped out from the shadows on Halloran's left, and as he approached it, he saw a green-striped awning, and the words painted on the side of the building in bold white: Formosa Cafe. He darted his eyes up to the corner street sign and it read Formosa Avenue. He turned left and parked. As Halloran folded his hands and closed his eyes to pray for help finding Danny, a tap at the window disturbed him. Halloran opened his eyes to see a young Latino who could not have been older than fifteen. The boy smiled until he glanced down to see Halloran's collar. The boy pushed away from the car and began to run. Halloran threw open the car door and caught up with the boy. He grabbed the boy's shoulder and turned the boy to face him. "It's okay. You don't have to run."

The boy's eyes were wild with fright. He struggled under

21

Halloran's grip.

"What's the matter?" Halloran asked.

The boy dropped his head and closed his eyes. "You are a holy Father. Are you here to take me back to my Papa?"

"No. What's your name?"

The boy still would not look up. "Leo, sir."

"Leo, I'm looking for Danny Murphy."

"Yes, sir."

"Do you know him?"

"We both live at the Y. He hangs out at this corner."

"Have you seen him?"

"He went on a date about a half hour ago. He should be back anytime."

"A date? What do you mean?" Halloran asked, hoping that what he was thinking and fearing would not be the truth.

"You know, sir. A man picks him up, then they –"

"Oh. I understand," Halloran said, maintaining a calm demeanor so as not to traumatize the boy who now shook slightly.

"Leo?"

"Yes, sir."

"Were you raised Catholic?"

"Yes, sir."

"Does your mother know you're here doing this?"

"Mama is muerto."

"I don't speak Spanish."

"Dead."

"I'm sorry. Leo, did you feel ashamed when you saw me?"

"Yes, sir. You reminded me of days when Mama was alive and we all went to St. Margaret Mary's Church."

"Do you still believe in God?"

Leo reached into his shirt and pulled out a small gold cross on a chain. He kissed it and held it up to Halloran.

"Yes, I do. But I will always be a sinner because I'm queer."

This cut Halloran short. He reached into his pocket and pulled out a ten-dollar bill. He handed it to Leo. Leo shook his head. "Leo, I want you to take these ten dollars and get some food. When you eat it, I want you to remember me, and just think about a better plan God may have for you."

"Father, no matter what, I'm always going to be queer."

"Maybe. But the first step out of your sin is to take care of yourself by using the gifts God gave you."

Leo nodded and took the bill. Halloran noticed that his small

22

hands had extraordinarily long fingers.

"Thank you, Father."

"Leo, I also want you to take this," Halloran said handing him a card. "That's my phone number at my parish in Lomita. You call me anytime you need help."

"Gracias, sir."

"You don't have to live like this."

Leo nodded. He shoved the ten-dollar bill into his pocket and ran off. Halloran returned to his car. He folded his hands and said a silent prayer for Leo. As he prayed, he heard a car drive up to the corner. He watched a young man who looked ten years older than Leo step out of the front seat of a Buick Sky Lark. The young man, dressed in black jeans and a white T-shirt with the sleeves removed, leaned into the car and nodded to the driver. Halloran could just make out the profile of a heavy man wearing a fedora. He saw the man wave a flabby arm that ended in fingers that sparkled with jewelry. The young man slammed the passenger door and as the car drove off, he turned in Halloran's direction. He leaned against a street lamp that cast a dirty orange halo about the young man. The young man pulled out a cigarette from a package that bulged in his left T-shirt pocket. He struck a match and lit the cigarette, keeping his eyes trained on Halloran. The young man's thick brow caused his eyes to be black sockets.

The young man approached Halloran's car. As he stepped up to the passenger window, the streetlight reflected off the car and cast a strip of light across the young man's eyes. Halloran noticed both the odd, almost horror film quality of the light and the young man's dark, staring eyes. Halloran was accustomed to the confrontational stare of a rebellious teen football player, but something more shown in this young man's eyes. There was male hostility but something more. Rancor? The young man broke his stare and glanced around suspiciously. He ran his hand through his wavy chestnut hair. He turned again to Halloran as he smoothed the back of his hair and nodded. Halloran nodded back. As he approached the car, Halloran was able to see two slight crescents of flesh where his tucked white T-shirt met the waist of his black jeans. He crouched down to meet Halloran at the open driver's window and again, ran a hand through his hair. His hair was thinning at the crest of his large forehead and small lines flared from his large, hazel eyes. Halloran noticed his high cheekbones and sharp jaw. Taken together, the elements of his face made him quite handsome in a boyish way, and yet Halloran also saw that the young man was strangely haggard.

"Fifty bucks. One half hour. Kink is okay, but nothing unsafe," the young man said with a medium voice that sounded slightly hoarse and dull in emotion. He blew a puff of white smoke over his left shoulder. His eyes wandered down to Halloran's collar and his thick eyebrows rose in surprise.

"Another priest. Two in a month!" He exclaimed.

"That's not what I'm here for," Halloran mumbled.

"I don't need a confession today so what's up?"

"Are you Danny Murphy?"

The young man sprang to his feet, pushing off the side of Halloran's car causing the metal panel to pop with a dull thud.   He started to walk off when Halloran threw open the car door and rushed for him. Halloran darted in front of him and blocked his way, his body a mountain compared to the shorter young man.

"You mind, I got things to do," the young man said.

"If you're Danny Murphy, I've been trying to find you."

"Trying to get me back to church? Fuck the Pope and all the saints."

The young man tried to step around but Halloran's thick hand clamped his slight shoulder. The young man wriggled free and rubbed his now sore arm.

"What the hell kind of priest beats up on people?"

"The kind that used to play football. Roughly. Now let's try it again. Are you Danny Murphy?"

"Maybe."

A convertible blue Camaro with four young men whirred past, horn blazing. One of the men yelled: "Hey, Father, go for it!" while the rest hooted and catcalled. Halloran laid his hand gently on the young man's shoulder. "Would you mind coming back to my car so that we can talk a little? Privately?"

The young man ran a hand through his hair and glanced at his fingers where two loose hairs wove through the digits. He quickly reached back and smoothed the back of his hair again, prodding the terminus of his right-hand part and fluffing it, his burning cigarette now dangling from the right corner of his mouth, favoring his full lower lip. Halloran now noticed that he wore small gold earrings in each ear. "Danny. I assume you're Danny."

"Dan. Get that straight. You don't call a guy who's only five-seven Danny. Makes him feel even shorter."

"Fair enough. Dan. This is about your mother."

"Is that supposed to matter or something? I got money to make, dude."

"Just give me a second to explain."

"You going to kick my ass if I don't?"

Halloran folded his arms, inflating his chest. Danny looked over

24

Halloran's thick build and gave in.

"Okay, let's get this over with."

Halloran gestured toward the car and Danny walked to it, his shoulders sloping in an obvious hunch. Halloran glanced around himself, now concerned that someone might misinterpret his presence. Shrugging, he surrendered to his God's will and slid into the driver's seat, slamming the car door. Danny took one last drag from his cigarette, a deep, rattling breath sparking the tip of the cigarette into an orange torch. He dropped the butt onto the curb and stamped it out. He jerked his door shut.

"I'm going to leave the windows open because we'll probably roast if I don't," Halloran said, though it was more because of the stale stench of Danny's cigarette. Danny shrugged and gazed out the windshield.

"I'm not gonna be here long enough to find out."

Halloran smiled with relief as he relaxed back into his seat. He felt an uneasy stiffness in his lower back until he pulled the seat catch and adjusted it to a slight recline position. "That's better. I've been in this friggin' car all day."

Danny shifted in his own seat and Halloran thought that he might be a little self-conscious. Danny flipped down the windshield visor.

"No mirror?"

"Yeah. Just pop up that smaller panel."

Danny popped the smaller panel and saw an oversized reflection. He drew back in his seat, then dropped his head and played with his hair. When he had it adjusted to his liking, he popped the mirror panel shut and leaned back. The car was beginning to warm up.

"As I said. This apparently has to do with your mother."

"What about her?"

"I don't know exactly how it has to do with her. I'm not even the one who wants to talk to you so badly. The Bishop does."

"Well tell him to drag his holy ass out to Santa Monica Boulevard. I'm sure he knows the way."

"He's dying."

"Then wheel him here."

"Isn't that a bit harsh given his situation?"

"Lots of people die. Everyday, believe me."

"He wants to talk to you before me makes his last confession."

"He asked for me? A prostitute?"

"His dying wish is to talk to a Murphy. We've tracked down everyone in your family we could and no will help."

"You talked to everyone?"

"Except for the two in Minnesota and the one in Camarillo State Hospital."

"You gotta be kidding. You even asked Louise?"

"She gave me your address."

"That was big of her. That's the first she's used it."

"She wasn't willing to help either. Because of her husband and all."

"Oh, yeah. Old Doctor Jew. She'd never stand up to him. For anyone."

"She had even less interest when I told her it had something to do with your mother."

"Big surprise. Mom showed us what she felt about us a long time ago."

"Forget about your mother then. Would you just be willing to show up? That should at least get him to give his final confession."

"You priests used to scare the shit out of me with confession. Sitting in that pitch-black closet, then the voice booming in outta nowhere."

"When was your last confession?"

"When I was eight. My first and last. I was so scared I just made something up so I could get outta that dark closet."

"In this situation, you would just sit by his bedside. He needs to tell you something and give you your mother's diary."

"A diary? But wait--he's in the hospital?"

"Yeah. Queen of Angels, not far from here."

"I'm not going to any hospital. He can keep her diary, too."

Danny started to laugh. He pulled open the passenger door and dropped a foot onto the curb. Halloran reached over and grabbed his arm. Danny struggled a moment, his hair flying out of place and revealing its thin spots at his temple.

"Wait. Please," Halloran said.

"Hey. Ease off the arm there. I gotta go make some more cash. It's been swell talking with you."

"How much do you make in a day?"

Danny relaxed a moment. He ran a hand through his hair.

"That depends. I used to make four or five hundred, then I wouldn't have to work for a week or so."

"Now?"

"Two, no, make that three hundred. Why?"

"I'll make a deal. You come with me to the Bishop, and I'll make sure you get three hundred."

"To walk into a hospital? No way."

"All right. Four hundred."

"That's a little better. Like four tricks for me. What the hell's he got, anyway?"

"AIDS."

"Oh. Shit. I told you he probably knew his way around the boulevard."

"It was through a transfusion he had during heart surgery a few years ago."

Danny pulled his foot back into the car. Halloran let his arm go. Danny flipped down the visor and fixed his hair.

"I just had my six month test. I've been negative up to now." Danny said. "I only do safe stuff. A couple of my friends died of the plague and they got really skinny and barfed all the time. That's too bad for the old fart." Danny flipped the visor back into position and pulled the car door shut. He turned to Halloran.

"Okay. I guess, since you're paying and all, I'll go."

"Just one thing, Dan."

"Yeah?"

"Let's keep your job -- especially our little deal -- to ourselves."

"Cool. It's not like I talk about every trick, anyway. That'd get pretty boring, you know?"

Halloran and Danny traveled silently down Santa Monica Boulevard toward the hospital. Danny regarded Halloran's hair a moment, then reached out and ran his hand quickly through Halloran's full, wavy hair that was flecked with gray. Halloran jerked his head away. "What do you think you're doing?" Halloran said.

"I'm not hitting on you. I just can't believe how much hair you got for someone so much older."

"Your hair looks okay."

"Nope. It started thinning last year, right after I turned twenty-two"

"It happens."

"I'm not ready to give up my job yet. I lose my hair or get fat, it's over. I got receding hair and love handles now."

"You will get older. It's a fact. What are you going to do then?"

"I don't gotta worry about that -- I got a plan. I'm not like the rest of the dudes out on the street. I don't spend my money on drugs and shit. That's what everybody ends up doing if they don't die. Pushing and doing drugs."

"You're different somehow?"

"It'll all be different in March. I got plans."

"That's not very long from now."

"I don't worry about that. I'm okay right now. That's all I care about. Today could be the last day of my life, you know?"

"So what happens in March?"

"Sleeping pills most likely, but slit wrists aren't out of the running.

27

I haven't decided yet."

"Suicide. That's a great plan."

"Nobody's ever given a shit about me one way or another. I'm sick of this whole thing."

"Why March?"

"I got my reasons."

As Halloran pulled the car to a stop at a signal, a large billboard's lights flickered on. Danny rolled his eyes and laughed quietly. He poked Halloran.

"Check out the sign."

Halloran glanced at it. The billboard was black with an AIDS ribbon plastered in the center. It read: GET SAFE. GET TESTED. Halloran's mouth twisted into an ironic frown as he looked back at Danny.

"What are you looking at? I told you I just did my six month test," Danny said.

"Why do you even care?"

"'Cause I die when I say so, and it ain't gonna be gasping for air in a hospital."

Halloran slowed the car as he pulled into the parking lot of the Queen of Angels Hospital. The name of the hospital blared in a white halo on top of the fifteen-story, art deco building. Halloran and Danny got out of the car, Halloran again clutching his leather doctor's bag. The hospital parking lot was quiet except for the traffic on the nearby freeway that filled the dry night air with a mechanical duplication of pounding surf. Halloran paused.

"Is that the freeway?" Halloran asked.

"Yeah."

"Almost sounds like waves hitting a beach."

"Sounds like crappy traffic to me. Course, I hear it all the time."

"Dan, I appreciate what you're doing. I will pray for your soul."

"Whatever. What's in the bag?"

"Ritual equipment for the Last Rites."

"You really believe in that crap?"

"With all my heart, mind, and soul."

"The only thing about church that was good to me was those powdered sugar jelly donuts and the fruit punch we used to get to have after. You serve those?"

"In the Parish Hall. Every Sunday."

"I can still taste the raspberry jelly and fruit punch. I eat doughnuts all the time but never get any like those."

"Come to the church and get some."

"Yeah right. Go listen to all that bullshit? Become another person looking out for his own soul and forgetting about everybody else's. Or else being good only because it will get me something in the end. Religion makes people selfish. I know why so many people believe in it."

"Why's that?"

"They're afraid. They gotta believe in something. The truth is too scary."

"And what is the truth?"

"This is all there is. When we die, we die. And for your whole life, no one's looking out for you but yourself."

"I'm sorry you feel that. Let's go on in."

"I'm sorry for you, too. You need something else so badly that you believe in a big fairy tale somebody dreamed up a long time ago because they were scared. I'm not saying that most of the ideas of the Bible aren't good to live by, but the supernatural stuff is crazy. A father in the sky, how childish can you get? No one can handle the idea that this is probably all there is."

"We are quite unimportant, desperate things, then?" Halloran asked.

"Quite."

"Could you be wrong?" Halloran pressed.

"I might be. What about you?"

Halloran ignored the question and stepped through the glass doors. Danny ran a hand through his hair and followed behind. Halloran's soft-soled shoes made a squishing sound against the floor. Danny's boots clicked and clomped. As they made their way down the hospital ward corridor, squishing and squashing, clicking and clomping, Danny grabbed Halloran's shoulder and stopped.

"I can't do this," Danny said.

"Come on. What's the matter?"

"The smell in here."

"It's just antiseptic. Floor cleaner. Some alcohol."

Danny leaned against a wall and dropped his head back. A nurse in a white uniform glanced toward him with a look of concern. Halloran now clutched Danny's arm and nodded toward the nurse. He pulled at Danny's arm.

"Come on. Didn't you ever visit any of your dying friends?"

"No way. I can't."

Danny folded his arms and leaned on them. His face grimaced.

"I gotta find a bathroom."

"You going to be sick?"

"No. I just get the crampy shits when I'm nervous."

29

Halloran stood outside the bathroom as Danny emerged. Mopping his forehead and face with a paper towel, Danny held his hair back with his left hand. Halloran could now see large patches of pale scalp and the deep receding harbors at the young man's temples. Danny noticed Halloran's glance and dropped his head to let his hair fall forward, then ran his hand through it to smooth it out.

"Okay?" Halloran asked.

Danny inhaled and forced the air out through his distended cheeks. He leaned once again against the wall, folded his arms and rolled his eyes.

"Let's go."

Halloran walked off, leaving Danny against the wall. Danny rolled his eyes once more, then followed. As Halloran approached the Bishop's room, several elderly priests and nuns who all wore glasses and who looked like chubby dolls in black and white clothes greeted him. They fluttered about Halloran, almost jovial at his return. He pointed to Danny and their chubby faces, already pale green from the fluorescent light overhead, now pursed up in confusion. Halloran gestured toward Danny as he stepped to the door of the Bishop's room. Danny passed through the huddle of nuns and priests who stared at him. One of the nuns with a face as full as if she stashed apples under her cheeks parted her lips for a partial smile. When Danny smiled back, she cast her eyes to the floor. The huddle moved off and left Danny and Halloran. Halloran tapped on the door.

Friar Gilman opened the door, and Danny took a step back, the stench of rotten breath and mothballs almost stinging his eyes. Friar Gilman, who was probably no more than twenty-three, let his eyes move from Danny's head, down his body, and back to Danny's face. Halloran interceded.

"Friar Gilman, I am here to fulfill Bishop Crawford's request."

Gilman stared at Danny as he spoke to Halloran. "Of course. Wait here a minute." He closed the door and Danny exhaled.

"What the hell is that? Rotten eggs?" Danny asked.

Halloran shrugged. Friar Gilman opened the door again and Halloran stepped into the room. Danny followed closer on Halloran's back as if he was a shadow. As they moved further into the silver light of the room, Danny stared at the mottled tile floor. His bashful attempt at entering the room behind Halloran was betrayed by his noisy boots. The Bishop lay asleep or unconscious, Halloran could not tell which, but the oxygen tube was still attached beneath his nose. His chest rose and fell steadily as each breath moved through his body with a deep rumble. A wispy cloud of frankincense hung in the air, and as it passed the fluorescent light panel above the Bishop, it glinted like a fish breaking the water's surface. More roses, lilies, carnations, and Gerbera daisies created a floral forest despite the silver gloom that stunted their colors. The Bishop's sister was again seated near the bed, and the Cardinal sat stiffly next to her.

Danny stayed back near the door, reaching for his cigarettes then pausing as he looked around the room and caught himself. Gilman moved back into the darkest corner of the room and kneeled, never taking his eyes off Danny. As Halloran stepped toward the Cardinal and bent to kiss his ring, the Cardinal's eyes darkened into slits behind his black horn-rimmed glasses. He pulled his hand away from Halloran and sprang to his feet, his red robe rustling across the chair and billowing.

"Father Halloran, what is the meaning of this?"

Halloran rose, his knee popping. He leaned and stretched his back as he straightened his habit jacket.

"Your Eminence, I answered the Bishop's request."

"I never heard him ask for a... rock-n-roll heathen."

"This is the youngest Murphy boy."

"He cannot remain in here. You," he shouted to Danny, "Out!"

Danny stood with his back pressed against the door, his left leg shaking with nerves. But when the Cardinal bellowed at him, his eyes turned to wet glass. Halloran stepped in front of Danny. "Your Eminence, he's the only one in his family that consented to come."

"Halloran, this is an outrage. I will not allow that dirty, little heathen to soil Bishop Crawford's Viaticum. This is a sacred time and —"

"Oh, Tim, shut up and sit down. You woke me up with all your belly aching," Bishop Crawford yelled.

The Cardinal turned toward the Bishop, pointing toward Halloran and Danny. The Bishop's face flared a hint of pink beneath its gray pallor and his clear blue eyes shone beneath his tousled, wild white eyebrows.

"You haven't seen who Halloran has brought to hear your confession," the Cardinal said.

"Obviously not Mother Theresa, by your hollering. Father Halloran, let me see who it is."

Halloran stepped away from Danny. Bishop Crawford lifted his neck, his face screwing up from the pain. Gilman flew to the side of the bed and depressed what looked like a remote control, causing the mattress to rise at an angle to meet the Bishop's head. The Bishop squinted. "Well, step into the light so I can see which of you it is."

Danny stared at Halloran, bewildered. Halloran nodded and Danny stepped to the foot of the bed. The Bishop's eyes moved like synchronized sapphires, studying Danny's upper torso and face. The anemic earthworms that were his lips creased into a slight smile as he extended a hand that looked like gray flesh sagging off wire. Danny touched it quickly. "Well, it's Daniel Thomas Murphy. Number seven.

The miracle baby, I believe your mother said of you. Eight-pounds-seven-ounces. Please sit down."

Danny glanced around and Halloran nodded toward a worn, mustard yellow chair that sat next to the Bishop's shoulder. Danny sat on the edge of the chair. The Cardinal glared at Halloran then flopped back into his chair. Halloran shrugged, stepped over to the dark corner, his shoes squeaking and sticking as he did, and sat. Gilman kneeled nearby, whispering a prayer and threading his black onyx rosary beads.

"Your mother told me once that your father wanted you to be named after Danny Thomas -- a good Catholic -- in honor of his dedication to Saint Jude. She told me she was just happy to find both names in her book of saints," Crawford said.

Danny's eyes narrowed.

"I recognize you," Danny said. "I've got a drawing of you from when you were younger."

"Oh. Your mother had it that you would be a priest," Crawford said. "Obviously, that didn't come to pass. What do you do?"

Danny ran a hand through his hair and glanced at Halloran who shifted in his seat and cleared his throat so loudly that it startled Gilman out of his prayer. Gilman looked up at Halloran with a start, but quickly resumed his prayer that had taken on the rhythm of a chant. The Cardinal leaned back in his chair, folded his hands, but extended his index fingers to form a steeple. He arched his eyebrows in curiosity.

"I write," Danny said.

"A writer, eh? Don't think anyone planned on that one. Still, poetry and fiction are noble pursuits, if you can support yourself. Which is it for you? Poetry or novels?"

"Neither."

"Short stories, then?"

"No."

"You're not a blood-sucking reporter, are you?"

"No."

"What, then, do you write?"

"Movies."

"Hmm. Your mouth sounds dry. Don't be nervous. There's a pitcher of water there and plenty of plastic cups so you won't catch anything." The bishop chuckled a bit.

Danny reached over to the side table and poured himself a cup of water from a stainless steel pitcher that was dotted with condensation. As he gulped the entire cup down, his throat gurgled with relief. He refilled the cup and swiped his forehead with the back of his hand, absorbing the perspiration that had accumulated in sparkling patches.

32

"You were always a high strung boy. Your mother was so concerned about your stomachaches that she took you to the doctor. Nervous stomach, I think she said."

Danny jumped up and stood behind the chair. He eyed the door and considered bolting for it. He wasn't here to have his head shrunk by this holy old fart. "What is this? Who the hell are you?"

The Cardinal glared at Halloran. Halloran stepped up behind Danny and placed himself between Danny and the door. He put his hand on Danny's shoulder.

"I thought you said you recognized me," Crawford said.

"I do -- from a drawing I got in my room," Danny said.

"Who drew it?" Crawford asked.

"My mom."

Crawford nodded and dropped his head a moment. He looked back up and tears had begun to build on his lower eyelids. He waved both hands weakly, gesturing for Danny to sit back down. "I was the pastor at St. Joan of Arc's when you were a child," Crawford said. His voice cracked on the word 'child.'

"I'm out of here."

Danny pushed past Halloran. He felt the old, familiar wringing in his lower gut. As he grabbed the door handle, Crawford spoke again.

"Come back here and sit down, Daniel."

Danny opened the door and turned toward Halloran. His eyes filled with tears of rage. "I don't like this old fart. Would you give me a ride home?"

"Don't you want to know why?" Bishop Crawford asked.

"Why what?" Danny snarled.

"Why she did it."

"Who?"

"Your mother, Mary."

Danny's hand dropped from the door handle. The door clicked softly shut. He turned to face Bishop Crawford. "How do you know anything about her?"

"When I was pastor, I got to know your mother and family quite well."

"What? You screwed her?"

A collective gasp echoed through the room. Halloran dropped his head, afraid to look toward the Cardinal. The Bishop paused for a moment. A wispy, reedy sound rose from his throat and alarmed Friar Gilman who jumped to his feet. The Bishop shook his head and raised his hand toward Gilman. He laughed.

"You were always a panic, Daniel."

"I don't want to hear about her, okay?"

"Daniel, please. You have a full life ahead of you and deserve to hear the truth. I'm dying, and I need to tell you what I know."

Danny leaned his back against the door and dropped his head. He folded his arms and his leg began to shake again. Except for the Bishop's deep breaths, the room was silent and all eyes waited for his response. He kicked the door with the sole of his boot and stepped back over to his seat. His body went limp as he shrunk into the chair.

"Okay. Talk."

The Bishop rolled onto his side to face Danny, his broomstick of a body barely wrinkling the white hospital bedclothes. Intravenous tubes in both of his arms stretched back toward their bags and made the Bishop's arms look like a marionette's. He adjusted his head on top of his pillow, causing Gilman to pause on his rosary and jump to the Bishop's side to adjust it. Bishop Crawford handed the diary to Friar Gilman.

"Here, Friar. Take this."

"Your Eminence?" Gilman said.

"You've been at that rosary long enough. I need you to do something more constructive right now."

"Your Eminence, you want me to read this?"

"No. Just hand it to the boy."

Friar Gilman turned the book in his hand. He fumbled with his rosary before kissing the crucifix and tucking it into his robe. Danny glanced over as Friar Gilman made his way around the Bishop's bed. Friar Gilman handed Danny the diary.

"What is this?"

"Your mother's diary," the bishop answered.

"This thing's as thick as the Hollywood White Pages. What did she write— her whole life story?"

"Daniel. All my life I've striven to do the work of the Lord. To follow his path. To know his wisdom, as I acted with what I believed was compassion and good works. I failed in winning souls on occasion, or failed in my duty to perform an enlightened sermon. But those failures pale in comparison to how I failed your mother. She came to me to make a confession; her final one as it turned out. She gave me her diary instructing me to read it and keep it in trust as part of her confession. I have read it and understand the part I played in the tragedy, and that is what I want to confess to you. You need to understand why she did what she did. For the sake of my soul, and yours, please read it. Forgive her. Now, Halloran, we can proceed with the rites. I'm prepared."

Father Halloran nodded toward the door. Danny shrugged and held out his hand. He didn't come here for a diary he wanted his money.

"Give me twenty minutes or so and I'll take you back," Halloran said.

Danny stepped back into the hallway and sat in a vinyl chair. He placed the diary on his lap and tapped his fingers against it. His heart began to pound a bit and he realized that somehow, he was actually afraid of the diary. No way was he going to read it. The alcohol hospital smell and glaring fluorescent overhead light added to his nervousness. His dad came into his mind, and he remembered those visits to the hospital. As if to stop any further recall, he began to thumb the pages of the diary. A nervous cramp soon took over his lower belly and he darted his eyes around and down the hall, looking for the nearest bathroom.

Halloran emerged from the room a few minutes later and they drove down Santa Monica Boulevard without speaking. Danny figured that it must never have been easy to pray with a dying person. Halloran slowed the car and pulled into a Bank of America parking lot. Danny watched him at the ATM and thought that after all, he wasn't a bad looking guy. 'Wonder how much more I could make tonight' he thought for a moment. 'That's it, if there was a Hell, I just reserved a room in the boiler room.'

Halloran slid back into the driver's seat and handed Danny the four hundred dollars they had agreed on. Danny never had that much money in his hands at one time and he began to daze.

"It's all there," Halloran said. That snapped Danny out of his daydream.

"You pull this from the collection plate?"

Halloran didn't respond. They drove the last few blocks again in silence and pulled up to the front of the YMCA. Danny didn't know what to say so he grabbed up the diary and threw open the passenger door. When he went to close the door, Halloran raised his hand. Danny paused.

"Did you ever read 'Les Miserables'?" Halloran asked.

"Nope."

"Fine. I hope this money bought you some time to pause and reflect about your mother. And about yourself. God has a better plan for you, believe me."

Danny shrugged and shut the passenger door. Halloran drove off. When Danny walked through the YMCA lobby, he saw that it was just past three-thirty in the morning. By the time he got to his room though, he realized how tired he felt. He tossed the diary across the room where it landed on the floor with a distinct thud. As he crawled into his bed, Bishop Crawford's face seemed to bear down on him from the drawing. He closed his eyes and fell asleep immediately.

When Danny woke up the next night, his eyes landed on the diary. As he stretched, he remembered the four hundred dollars. He checked his

501's draped over the chair to be sure the money was still there. The crisp edges of the bills tickled his thumb. He didn't have to go to work that night. The four hundred dollars could last him close to three weeks so he could take a vacation. The sounds of the street and the dark night tugged at him, but he really didn't feel like sex. He lit a cigarette.

He turned on his hotplate and boiled a couple of eggs to distract him from the night's temptation. As he peeled the eggs, he stared again at the diary. Again, his stomach twisted with nervousness and fear. That's when he looked up at the drawing of the bishop. He must be dead by now. What did the bishop mean by all this? No, I don't want to read this crap. But the bishop's face, stared back at him, taunted him.

"Jesus, you're a pushy bastard," he said to the drawing.

He shuffled over to the diary, picked it up, and opened it.

3.

Okay, so the doctor tells me I have to write down everything I can remember so here goes. This is when the trouble started. The Minnehaha creek was pretty low this particular day. Usually, it made a lot of racket as it clanked along the granite rocks, but in the spring and summer, it sometimes was barely stronger than an electric percolator. I kneeled down and the moss and leaves felt like a wet sponge against my skin; I was glad I was wearing my shorts instead of my dungarees, I'll tell you. I had one pair of each and if I went home with stains on my dungarees, my mom would've let me have it – 'Those pants make you look like a skinny boy, anyway. Now you go and get 'em stained. What man's ever gonna want a tomboy, Mary?' I unscrewed the rusty lid on the mason jar my Dad gave me and dunked it into the creek.

That jar was a special secret between Dad and me. My mom put up raspberry jam every year from the surplus raspberries our next-door neighbor gave us. She used the same jars again and again and she told us kids that if any jar ever broke, there'd be hell to pay because it's the Depression and no one can afford broken jars. None of the kids ever broke one. Dad swiped one once and brought it to me.

"Here, honey. Use this for your paint water and make somethin' pretty," he said one day.

"Mom'll kill me if she finds out."

"Don't worry about Mom. You just keep it hid and I'll take care of her."

When Mom went to put up her raspberries awhile later, she called the three of us kids in. Irma, my older sister, was thirteen and she came into the kitchen brushing her thick, chestnut hair -- I ran a comb through my straight red hair in the kitchen one time and Mom smacked me and said it was a dirty thing to do in the kitchen -- Mom just let her brush and brush her wavy mane. Little Jimmy was seven then and he came running in, his two little hands cupped together. I was already sitting on a chair, clicking my worn out brown shoes together and watching Mom. Raspberries sputtered and rolled as they boiled in a big iron pot behind Mom, and the steam they sent up made Mom look like smoke was coming out her ears.

"I got a prize for you, Irma!" Jimmy said.

"What did you bring me?"

He opened his hand to show a gray puff of a baby mouse that ran a small circle in his palm. But it suddenly fell over on its side. I jumped back and looked at Mom whose face was twisted into an impatient frown.

"I think he gots a broken foot," Jimmy said.

"Oh, Jimmy. He's so cute," Irma said. "You know I can make him better."

Irma reached out with her left hand and the mouse hobbled into it as if he knew her. She held the mouse up to her face and the mouse stood on its tiny pink back feet and sniffed toward Irma.

"He's just a baby. Ain't he cute?" she asked.

She held the mouse out to me and I jumped back. Everyone, including Mom, laughed at me.

"Don't be so scared, Mary. He's just a little guy and can't hurt you," Jimmy said. "A hawk dropped him and that's how I got him. He can't hurt nobody with his broke foot."

Irma puckered her lips and made kissing sounds toward the mouse. She plopped the mouse right onto the top of her head. He peeked his head that was no bigger than a thimble from under her hair, his dark eyes kind of staring at me. Irma giggled as she cupped his little body and pulled him out of her hair that was now a mass of tangles on the one side.

"What are you gonna do if Dad starts a dairy farm? There'll be animals all over," Irma said.

I didn't have an answer for that because the idea of having all those animals around made me feel sick. Mom and Dad already knew that I was allergic to cats, and the stray mutt Irma rescued when I was four that bit me didn't help. Cows, goats, pigs, and whatever else may be on a farm were all mysterious beasts to me. I liked what grew in nature -- flowers, trees, plants -- but animals scared me.

Mom clutched her fisted right hand with her left hand so hard that the thick creases and cracks that were brown and pink from work now looked white. She started rocking slightly and reached down and wrapped her hands in her stained lace apron. She stared at each one of us and when she got to me, her fat face looked flat and her gray eyes didn't blink. A few strands of her brown and gray parted hair that was normally pulled back into a bun clung to her sweaty, thick forehead like broken spider webs.

"That's enough about animals. Who broke the jar?"

I stopped clicking my heels and shrugged up at her. She shifted her eyes to Jimmy and his lower lip quivered open like a pink comma in the middle of the brown mess of his face.

"Jimmy?"

Jimmy shook his head and two tears made streaks through the dirt on his cheeks.   Irma's brush strokes made a tearing sound as the raspberries hissed and popped and began to boil over. Mom reached for the stove and turned down the flame making her thick arm jiggle as she did. When she faced the stove, I noticed that her body was almost wider than the whole stove. She dropped a lid on the pot and turned back toward us.

"Irma?"

Irma shrugged and stroked the mouse. Dad leaned against the rusted porcelain sink and watched. I think it was the first time I noticed how small and thin he was, especially next to Mom. As he dried his hands, his eyes were blank and I knew this look on his face meant he was trying to figure out something important. He reached up and scratched his head, lost in thought, and wandered into the middle of the kitchen. Mom cleared her throat and Dad now realized he had stumbled into the middle of something. He looked at the three of us kids, but paused on me when I looked up and smiled at him. His soft blue eyes sparkled a moment and then he turned his face, tan and gaunt, toward Mom.

"There a problem or something?"

"One of these wild comanches broke a jam jar. I'm trying to find out who. You can go back to work."

"Hang on there, Martha."

Mom rolled her hands into fists and rested them on her wide hips. She turned toward Dad and towered over him and around him. "If I need your help, I'll ask for it."

"Just a sec. I broke the jar."

Dad glanced at me and I dropped my head. I thought for sure Mom was going to wallop him for it. Instead, Mom's big arms fell to her sides and she rolled her eyes toward the ceiling.

"Them jars don't grow on trees, Ernest."

"I know, Martha. They come from the beach."

Mom shook her head and went back to the raspberries on the stove. She turned the burner back on and said over her shoulder, "What wild tales you spinning now, huh?"

Irma knew the meeting was over and she stomped out as soon as Mom went back to the stove, her heavy footsteps caused the wood floor to creak. Jimmy and I looked up at Dad who had broken out into a broad smile. I wanted to know what Dad meant, too.

"It's no wild tale. Glass comes from sand. Sand comes mostly from the beaches along the big oceans in the East and the West."

"You hear that, kids? Another useless fact from your dad," Mom snorted.

Jimmy wasn't even paying attention anymore. But I didn't think the fact was useless. I didn't know how sand became glass but I thought it was fascinating that sand could be turned into something as useful as a jam jar. Anyway, Dad gave me the jar and took the blame for it. That was all a long time back and right now, I didn't care if my bare knees were getting soaked as I dunked the jar. I got a chill from the water that was so cold that it burned, and from the birches and aspens that made too much shade over the creek.

The spring sun did break through the shade to make ribbons of light and warmth, but I had to get back to a spot up on the grass bank where the sun had no obstacles. I held my mason jar of water in one hand and my big sketchpad, watercolor tins, and brushes in the other. It wasn't just the sunshine or the dry spot I could sit on without staining my white shorts that coaxed me back to the spot; I had been sketching a cluster of pink lady's slippers that blossomed on the bank near the name tree.

The name tree was an old birch whose gray and white bark had initials carved in it by everybody. There were hearts with initials carved in them, high school initials, initials with dates. The trunk of the tree was so huge that the carving didn't seem to hurt it. I practiced my artist's signature on that tree and I glanced at the four scrapings I had made previously: Mary; Mary Benton Hellman; Hellman; M.B.H. I signed my projects with all those different names and still hadn't decided which one I liked best. Anyways, I sat down in the sunny spot right near the name tree.

I glanced at the cluster of flowers once more, then opened my sketchpad and looked at my sketch to make sure it was okay. I don't know how many erasures I made to get the image of the little flowers that look like ballet slippers to look just right. I scraped up a lot of the textured white paper, too, and I didn't even know if the paint would blend right.

I laid out my watercolor tins and dipped a medium brush into the creek water that smelled musty, dropping a small pool onto each tin. The water made the tins look like primary colored gems. Pausing a minute to slip off my brown school loafers, I evened out my white socks so that they both sat at the middle of my shin. As I worked on the socks, the sunshine highlighted the blonde hair on my legs that had grown so much denser recently. I didn't like how it looked like gold wire so I stretched my socks back up to knee length.

Picking up the brush again, I dipped it into the creek water and rolled it across the red tin that was now soft. I applied the first touch of soft red and watched as the paper surface, ragged from my mistakes, absorbed the color unevenly. A quick brush of water softened the color but the paper still absorbed the water unevenly, turning my sketch into blisters of uneven color. If I was going to get into high school honors art, I had to complete this nature assignment almost perfectly. I paused in frustration and could now hear the afternoon traffic beginning on

40

Minnetonka Avenue.

Brakes screeched and horns honked on the street just beyond the bank where I sat. The Minnehaha creek follows Minnetonka Avenue like two friends until they separate at Minnehaha Falls. As spring becomes summer at this time of the year, the creek is low and the falls nearly quiet. But Minnetonka Avenue on Friday afternoon revs the life into sleepy downtown Hopkins for a few hours. I liked the electric feeling of that time of day and I could close my eyes and imagine I was painting along the Champs Elysees in Paris. Somehow, the sounds of Hopkins just made me want to paint. I picked up the brush again, rolled it generously in the red tin, and lay the color on, this time without worrying. The blistering page didn't matter. Some water, color wash. Blend. Blend. Blend.

"Hey, Mary!"

I turned around and saw Alice Johnson -- or Yonson, as her mother pronounced it -- waving at me, her white blonde hair pulled back into a pony tail that seemed to pull her shoulders into a perfect posture. Her boobies that were too big for her body bounced as she waved.

"We're taking a bus to the city!"

I then noticed that Alice led the large group of thirteen-year-old girls known as the Gals Club at Hennepin Grammar School. The group paused to see who Alice hollered to, then moved on past her. Alice persisted.

"We're going to see 'Gone With The Wind.' "

"That movie with Clark Gable?" I asked like I knew who he was. I only knew his name because Irma went to the cinema in Minneapolis every Saturday she could, spending money she earned baby-sitting.

"Yeah. It's six hours long and we have permission to stay for the whole thing. Come on"

"No thanks. I gotta get an art assignment done." I also thought that movies filled Irma's head with stupid ideas about romantic love.

"That's all you ever do. Come have some fun for once."

I shook my head and she waved once more and ran up to join the group. If I eventually wanted to get into the Minneapolis College of Art and Design, I was going to have to present a strong portfolio. I didn't want to risk it. Besides, I wondered if the big group of mostly stupid girls knew the Minnehaha Creek was one of the sources of the Mississippi; that the very creek they walked past everyday fed right into the river. My Dad told me that and he knows a lot of different things. Who needs to go see a movie about the south when we got the source of its great river right here in Hopkins? I didn't need to, anyways.

As I picked up the brush again, I heard the wind as it sliced through the tall aspens, causing their branches to chatter and sway. I lifted my head to catch the breeze and thought I could smell the burning hay or alfalfa, whichever it is that smells like burnt peanuts. But the breeze was coming from the south and west, from the big farms down there. I rolled the brush into the red tin once again, and felt a strange moisture building on my legs. I glanced down, thinking that I must have sat on a mossy spot, and there was what I first thought was red paint on my inner thighs. The redness came from the area of my shorts where the legs met, and I felt dizzy: blood! Blood seeped through my white shorts and down my thighs, a sticky, warm flow.

I'm bleeding! I'm bleeding! I must be dying! What's wrong? I thought. I sprang to my feet and spattered the blistered painting with drops of blood. I grabbed up my mason jar, my paint tins, and sketchbook, dropped them in my knapsack and ran up the bank toward home. I'm dying. I'm dying. My shorts are ruined!

These thoughts all jumbled up inside my head as I ran along Minnetonka Avenue. I thought maybe I should run straight to Doctor Anderson's, but I changed my mind and ran past. The alfalfa winds were blowing against me as I darted through the rich part of Hopkins where all the houses have two stories, fresh paint, and gardens. It's the Catholic section of town where most of the Irish and Bohemian families lived. Just past those streets, the town becomes small fields and patches of land. As I ran past the fields, I saw the spire of the Lutheran Church and even though I had only gone to church a few times in my life, it was to that one. I had the feeling that maybe I should run into it and pray, but now the blood on my legs was beginning to dry and I thought that maybe I wasn't dying yet. I ran across the railroad tracks and then up a dirt road. Now the fields were even bigger but the farmhouses were smaller.

My feet kicked up whirls of dust and my white socks were caked with dirt as I saw the familiar rows of thorny raspberry bushes on the wooden fences the Darlana's called trellises. I slowed down and stopped to catch my breath. Looking down at my thighs as I hunched over, I saw that the blood had mostly dried. After I caught my breath, I walked past the last row of the bushes and turned onto our small lot. We did not have an expansive field of rich raspberries but in that moment, even our small dirt patch of weeds and old tires felt safe. I saw Dad in the garage and, dropping my knapsack, I ran through the weeds of our yard and straight toward him.

He was dabbing his brow as I lunged for him and threw my arms around his waist. I cried into his dirty work shirt and the musky smell of his old sweat made me feel better. "Darlin', what's the matter?"

"I'm dyin', Daddy, I'm dying!"

"What?"

"I'm bleeding everywhere."

He held me out and looked at me, his thin face twisted with fear. He shook his head and knitted his brow as he looked me up and down. 'You don't look hurt nowhere.'

"Look."

I turned one of my thighs to him and he bent his head to look. He squeezed my arms lovingly, and then let go. He reached to dab his brow but I saw that his cheeks turned a little pink under his tan.

"You ain't dying, darlin'."

"But it's blood. Lot's of it."

I reached for him again, but this time he did something he never did before: he pushed me away and held onto my shoulders. He stared down at my face and started to say something, but it's like he tripped on his own lips. He took my hand, lifted it to his lips that the winds caused to look like two shedding snakes, and kissed the top of it as if we were now strangers. Patting it, he let it go.

"Darlin', you're a young lady now."

"What do you mean?"

"That's all I can tell you. You're okay. Your Ma's gonna have to tell you the rest."

Dad turned around and walked back into the garage. If he said I wasn't dying, I knew I was okay. Still, I was going to catch hell for the mess I made of my shorts. The back porch screen was caked with dirt and creaked as I opened it. Mom was baking gingerbread and the kitchen was filled with moist, hot, spicy air. I didn't know how I was going to tell her so I walked slowly into the room. She sat at the kitchen table and the pine chair pushed against her back, causing a balloon of flesh to bulge under her tea rose-patterned housedress. As I came around to her side, I saw that she was resting with her eyes closed, her forehead propped up by her fingertips and elbows. A small stack of yellow and white pieces of paper lay in front of her.

"Mom?"

"Yeah."

When she looked up at me, her gray eyes were ringed by wetness. She wiped them with her thick palm, and then tucked a few of her loose gray hairs back on her head.

"I got a problem."

Mom's face softened. She tapped the table for me to come and sit next to her. The pine chair scraped across the wood floor as I pulled it out and sat.

"What's wrong?"

"Dad told me I need to talk to you about it."

If I had reached out and pushed her with all my strength at that moment, I could not have forced her into the position she shifted into. She looked rigid, her face once again going thick and composed. "So you talked to him already."

Like you ever have any time for me, I thought.

Mom stood up and dabbed her face with her apron. She grabbed up the sheets of paper from the table and dropped them in her apron pocket, and then crossed over to the white enamel stove and pulled open the oven door. The blast of heat and baked cake aroma filled the room as she closed the rusty metal door. She was going back to her baking and I was bleeding. I stood up.

"Mom, look!"

I turned my thigh toward her and tugged on my right short pant leg. Her eyes shot down at the bloodstains and back up to my face.

"It's about time."

She reached under the sink and pulled out two clean dishcloths. She handed them to me.

"Put one of those inside your BVD's today. Tomorrow morning, take it out and put the other clean one in its place. Wash the dirty one out back and use bleach. Just keep going back and forth for the next few days till you stop."

"Why am I bleeding, Mom?"

"What'd your Dad tell you?"

"I'm a young lady now."

"He's right, for once. This is going to happen to you every month till you're my age. You're making eggs now and when they don't get fertilized, you'll lose 'em through your blood."

"How would they get fertilized?"

Mom picked up a potato and scraped a knife over it, dropping the brown skin into the sink. She turned the potato slowly in her hand as she peeled it. I stood at her side, my arms folded. When is she going to answer, I thought. When she had peeled it half way, she answered.

"Don't worry about that. Pretty soon, every boy you've ever known is going to want to show you how. That part of your body can bring you pleasure, or pain, or joy, but never all three. It'll be your fault if you make the wrong choice."

"How will I know?"

"You have to learn, but take it from me. Don't mess with boys like I did. Just wait for the right, strong man who's going to marry you and take care of you. When you get married, he'll show you how."

"How will I know who the right man is?"

"Don't worry about that, either. You're always asking so many

44

questions. You just use all your brains and talent to make yourself pretty and desirable and he'll come along."

"Is that how you and Daddy met?"

Mom's head dropped a moment. She reached into her apron and toyed with the papers that now crackled. She raised her eyes with a strange smile again.

"You go get yourself and them shorts cleaned up."

4.

I didn't sleep much in those days and Mom said it was probably because my body had new juices going through it. I lay in my bed on this one night and watched the thin lace curtains wave in and out as a very cold breeze blew from the raspberry field right near our bedroom window. If the wind was strong enough, you could sometimes hear the leaves on the bushes rustle. I was always sure it was a wolf or a coyote stalking the house, and Irma was always sure it was a raccoon with its paw caught on a raspberry vine. Tonight, though, Irma lay next to me, snoring away like an exhausted bull, drowning out any of the night sounds. A half moon shone in and made the petals on the daisy wallpaper glow.

My grandmother died in this room, and when my mom got the house after, we couldn't afford to change the wallpaper so she made it the girls' room. Even though I didn't believe in ghosts or anything like that, I always felt good in our room like Grandma was there with us. This night wasn't just sleepless, I also felt anxious. Then I got the urge to paint and I knew I could do some touch up on my lady's slipper painting. I lifted my legs quietly off the bed and felt the cool wood floor on my feet. As I crossed our room to get my knapsack, I heard the console radio in our sitting room begin to murmur softly. I snuck out into the hall and looked around the corner.

Dad sat in his big chair that was so old and worn out that no one could remember what cloth it was made of. Mom had crocheted a gold and blue afghan that draped over the back of the chair but it was soiled from years of sitting. Dad scribbled on a yellow pad, paused to glance at the radio, and then jotted more notes on the pad. A maple table lamp with a frayed shade cast a yellowish pink light on him and some radio drama that came on late carried on like a separate conversation. Dad's newest contraption--some sort of gopher trap--lay on the floor next to him.

I snuck back into my room and Irma snored away. I grabbed up my knapsack and my sketchbook, slipped them under the arm of my flannel nightgown, and crept back out. Dad looked up as soon as I crossed the rickety threshold into the sitting room and he pulled the top of his frazzled terry cloth robe over his v-neck undershirt.

"What you doing up at this hour, darlin'?"

I sat down on the floor rug that Grandma left, its thick braids pushing into my skin. I spread out my art supplies.

"Tomorrow's a big day and I couldn't sleep."

"What's going on?"

"I have to show my portfolio to the art teacher at Minnetonka High. She has to accept me for honors art."

"That's a real important thing. You should be sleepin'."

I shrugged and picked up the gopher trap. "This the new thingamabob?"

The thing was a metal tube not much bigger around than an egg and it had a small door with a spring hinge that I flicked with my thumb. As I turned it in my hand, I saw a hole on top and another small door that I had to twist open. The hole on top confused me.

"That's for the sugar beet or potato bait," Dad said. "You stick it in on top, and then pull back the spring door like this. When the critter crawls in for his treat, the door'll spring shut and you got him."

"So what happens once you got him?"

Dad set his pad down and crossed his hands. Leaning forward, he spoke softly like he was afraid someone in the house would steal his idea.

"I make enough money on this thing early on and I buy us a truck. I go round to all the sugar beet and potato farms and pick up the gophers, say once a week. Then I drive the little nuisances out to the hills next to the Pillsbury Mine and I set 'em free. They ain't gonna do no harm out in all those iron mines."

Turning the trap in my hand, the metal felt cool. I fingered the spring door again and it snapped back and almost caught my thumb. I handed it back to Dad and he started talking in a way that made him sound like a salesman.

"Your sister started me off on this one. You know how she's always nursing a sick baby sparrow, or taking care of strays, nurturing 'em. She said that even though gophers are ruining this county's potato and sugar beet crops, they still deserve to live. She got me thinking. Probably a lot of people feel like that, so here's the solution."

I had heard my dad say those words -- here's the solution -- so many times with so many different things he tried to invent or schemes he tried that I was bored. I twisted off the lid of my mason jar and dabbed drops onto my paint tins. Dad's chair squeaked as he leaned forward to see what I was working on.

"Those lady slippers sure look fine. If this trap takes off, we're gonna be the richest people in the county and you won't have to worry about no scholarship to go to the art college."

"What are you doing up yourself?" I asked.

"Got some figuring to do before I go see Mr. Snelling at the bank.

47

He has to lend me some money to get all the traps made."

"Will he?"

"If I cut him in on some of the profit, I don't know how he could refuse."

The upper edge of one of the lady's slippers was fuzzy because of the marred paper. Red and soft blue bled together in a real amateurish way. I rinsed my brush and rubbed water on the area to lift some of the lousy color.

"Umm - hmm," I said. But I wasn't really interested.

"If it takes off, I can finally get your mom a couple of new dresses, and those new dishes she saw at Woolworth's."

I scrubbed and scrubbed the color. Blend. Blend. Blend.

"If it doesn't go, I don't know what ... Darlin', you listening?"

"Yeah, Daddy. Just getting crazy from this one part of my painting. I'm lucky it's just a nature painting -- I could never get away with what I'm doing on a portrait."

"You gonna start painting people now?"

"I hope so."

Dad jumped out of his chair and creaked across to the fireplace. He reached onto the mantle and picked up a framed sepia photograph. Staring at it with that expression that said he was thinking about something important, he sat down and held the photo out to me.

"Think you could make this your first portrait?"

It was a photograph of Mom when she was young and thin. Her short hair just peaked out from under a sequined hat that crowned her face. Rouged cheeks, softly shadowed eyes, and painted lips made her white teeth stand out in a pearly smile. I glanced at the photo and smiled at my dad but he still wore his important thinking expression.

"This photo was taken just before I tried to get my first patent. You just wouldn't believe what a dancer she was. The Charleston, the Jitterbug. She could move like no one else. Her body was long and thin like your own. I was the one who got her and I thought I was on top of the world."

"It'd be a tough photo for me to paint. The hat and all."

Dad set the photo on his lap and ran his index finger over a layer of dust.

"Might be at that. She deserves it though. She's sure been patient."

Dad leaned back in his chair as a radio commercial about anthracite coal broke in. He stared at the radio.

"When we get to portraits, I'll give it a try," I said.

"I know you and your Ma don't see eye to eye very much. But that

woman stuck it out with me even when my first patent failed and I had to
go to work at 3M. She followed me to the Mesabi Mountains when I went
to mine gems and everyone else got rich on iron ore. Irma and you was just
little babies then. Then came the farm -- do you remember it?"

"That where Irma's dog bit me?"

"Yeah. Scared us all but at least it wasn't on any part of your body
that's gonna show!"

I blushed crimson.

"Dad!"

"Anyways, I couldn't get the artichokes to grow and everybody said
I was a fool to try. But they was and still is a delicacy and if they had grown
... Thank goodness your Grandma Benton came through and let us live
here. God rest her soul."

"I need to get on to my painting now."

"You go 'head. Just remember: I was a lucky young fool to ever
get to dance with your Ma. And all that art talent you got? Comes from
her side. She's Bohemian -- her Grandma was from the old country, some
sort of princess. I met her once and she was cold as Lake Minnetonka
mud. I guess she missed her country and never made any friends here. She
was some sort of artist and that's where you get it."

He sat back in his chair and I could see two teardrops clinging to
his left, lower eyelashes. As I dipped my brush in to refill it with water,
Dad got up with Mom's photo in his hand. Small threads from the tattered
edge of his robe tickled my forearm as he stepped around me. He clicked
off the radio.

"Don't stay up all night."

I did stay up long enough to see the sunrise orange and pink
against the thick cumulous clouds that hung like cotton batting. I finished
the lady's slippers painting about an hour before, still unable to relax, and
the thick feeling in the air that always comes before thunderstorms didn't
help. When I crawled back into bed next to Irma, she had taken up my
whole side. I kicked her and she rolled over grumbling in her sleep. At
least I knew that we didn't have to get up for school. Other than chores, all
I had to do was meet with Miss Hogrebe at two o'clock. I dropped off.

Miss Hogrebe wasn't running on time that afternoon but I was
actually glad; what I called my portfolio was all my work that I carried in an
old potato sack I tied up with twine. I don't know why, but I thought it
made me look real amateur. I untied my bundle and laid it all out on the
teacher's desk in the middle of the classroom. The oak that had been
scarred and marked with ink, and pencil made the white and beige pages of
my work stand out. Paintings to the left, drawings to the right. That's how
I set them up. I rolled up the burlap and sat it on one of the student chairs

along with my art knapsack.

I paced around the room and the dried dirt under my loafers scratched the tile floor as I tucked my sleeveless blouse into my plaid school skirt. I shot my hands up to the tortoise shell barrettes my mom and dad gave me last Christmas; my thin, straight hair didn't really need them, but they did add a touch of amber color to my red hair. They were even. I walked over and cranked open one of the windows. Warm, moist air blew out the stuffy air smelling of old glue and chalk. Dust had settled all over the student desks already even though school had only been out for two weeks. I heard the click of a woman's heels that made a rhythmic clock sound as they approached. I sat down. The door burst open.

Spicy perfume like cinnamon hit my nose as a flurry of floral fabric seemed to spin into the room. Sticking out from the top of a caftan was Miss Hogrebe, her arms flailing as she spoke.

"So sorry. Please pardon me, young Miss."

A southern accent mixed with some sort of New York edge poured out of the woman's mouth painted with bright red lipstick. A mass of dark brown hair with a flourish of gray stuck out of the top of a floral scarf that was wrapped all the way around her head. It stretched across her entire forehead just above her thin, dark eyebrows. Dark eye shadow lay above false eyelashes that she batted briefly at me before she turned toward my work.

"Yes. Oh, yes. Umm - hmm, umm-hmm."

She flipped each painting and drawing, causing the fabric of her caftan to billow with each turn. I couldn't tell if the caftan was hiding a fat body but her long, pale face I saw in profile had deep hollows. I had never seen anyone like her in all of Hopkins. When she got to the lady's slippers, she paused.

"Paper problem. Some extra blending, I see."

When she said that, my stomach felt like it had collapsed. Of all my work, that one painting was the problem and I knew it. I wanted to grab up my work and run out the oak door, down the long flight of cement steps of the main school building, and all the way home. I had no explanation for that dumb mistake.

"Looks like you were experimenting with texture. Very risky."

She finished looking at my work and turned toward me, folding her arms, and staring at me with her large, dark cocoa eyes. Miss Hogrebe's gaze moved up and down my face and torso and I felt uneasy. I dropped my head.

"You have nothing to be ashamed of. Being poor is noble."

Quit looking at me, I thought. Just give me the bad news. I glanced up at her.

50

"Your pale skin and green eyes -- they're green, aren't they? -- make you beautiful in a wholesome way. Your work shows that."

What a loon. "Yes, Ma'am."

"First of all, it's Miss. Second, call me Lori. It's short for Leora but that's a long-winded Texas story you'll hear some other time. Tell me, Miss —"

"Hellman."

"Miss Hellman, what do you want to be?"

"An artist."

"How long have you wanted to be one?"

"My whole life -- as far back as I can remember. I've been drawing and painting all the time."

"Women don't make it as artists very often. I assume you're planning on getting married?"

Was I talking to my mother? "I don't even think about it. I just draw and paint."

Miss Hogrebe turned back to my drawings. She picked up a charcoal drawing I had done a few years ago. It was a miner tending a mining cart.

"You did this when you were ten?"

"Yes."

"Why'd you choose that subject?"

"My Dad was a miner. I pretended like that was him."

"And this?" she held up a pencil drawing of my dad sitting on a tractor.

"Dad again."

"He's a miner and a farmer?"

"He's been a lot of things. We've lived in a few different places."

"Oh."

The way she said it made me think she thought I'd only be another temporary student passing through with my itinerant farming family. I figured she wouldn't want to waste time on me if she thought that.

"But now we live in my Grandma's old house and it's permanent." I didn't have the guts to add: unless Dad's invention takes off.

"Umm-hmm. Such maturity in this work. How old did you say you were again?"

"Thirteen."

"My, my. You don't look it. I would take you for seventeen, or even eighteen."

She set the drawings back down and flipped through the paintings again. The clock overhead clicked its large hand to the six. Two thirty. Miss Hogrebe shook her head and sat, staring at me again.

51

"I'm not sure what we could do for you."

The force of her statement made my foot slide and make a skidding sound. My heart pounded in my ears as I stood up, unable to lift my head. I shuffled to the desk and began to gather up my drawings, my face growing red with embarrassment. Miss Hogrebe grabbed my arm with her left hand that was covered with brown age spots, its nails painted in the same red as her lips.

"You're misunderstanding me, Miss Hellman. What I mean to say is that I would be honored to have you in my honors art classes."

"What?"

"Your work is superior and I doubt that you're going to learn much from me. But you are more than welcome in class."

I grabbed the desk to catch myself as my heart raced. Miss Hogrebe patted my arm.

"You're going to be a very great artist one day."

"Thank you, thank you."

"You can go now."

"Is that it?"

Miss Hogrebe nodded. I reached for my burlap portfolio and threw it onto a desk, hurrying because I was sure she was going to change her mind. As I piled my work onto the center of the potato sack, Miss Hogrebe stopped me.

"What's that?"

"My portfolio."

"Huh?"

"Just a way to carry my work."

"So noble, so humble. Some day, that will be a Corinthian leather portfolio."

I didn't know what she meant, but I ran to the door, forgetting to tie the burlap. I pulled the door open and Miss Hogrebe hollered.

"See you in the fall!"

My feet couldn't move fast enough as I hopped down the gray steps of the school and started down the lumpy pavement of Minnetonka Avenue. Green leaves and white trunks flew past me and the sun caused my head to itch from its heat. I only paused when I realized the corners of a few of my paintings were sticking out from the untied burlap and I patted them back into place and wrapped the sack more snuggly. Each step I took seemed to be a reaction to my heart's pounding action -- I did it! I did it!

A truck horn blared and my feet crossed each other, sending my drawings into the air and my hands skidding against the asphalt. For a second, I thought it was a train bearing down on me but as the brakes squealed, I turned my head to see the rough rubber edges of a truck's front tires stop two feet from my nose. Burnt tire seared my nostrils. With that strange rubber impulse that happens when you trip in public, I snapped back to my feet. Brushing off my skirt, I could feel my barrettes dangling from my hair that fell onto my shoulders. But my attention focused on my work: most of it lay in a pile underneath where I fell with the exception of the lady's slippers that blew up and clung onto the street sign post, and the charcoal of my dad on the tractor that plastered itself under the driver's side tire of the truck.

"What the hell you doing in the middle of the street?" I heard the driver say in a voice pitched higher than mine and full of anger. I was about to answer but when he rounded the truck, I paused. His dark eyes that flared with anger when he turned the corner of the truck now softened like a baby deer's. I couldn't help but stare at his high cheekbones and sharp chin. He seemed to become awkward as he ran a hand through his wavy, dark hair. He looked to be only three or four years older than me and not much taller than me, either.

Now I felt awkward and I reached down and scooped up my portfolio, fumbling to get the burlap back around the pages. He leaned over to retrieve the drawing of my dad and his arm muscle bulged like a sand dune from his white undershirt. As he stood to hand me the drawing, I saw that his chest and shoulders were also developed but the rest of his body looked like a reed in his blue jeans. His voice now dropped to a medium, gentle level.

"You hurt?"

I shook my head, still too embarrassed to say anything, though it was more him than my fall that embarrassed me. My blouse stuck to my back from perspiration that had started bubbling from my skin as I stood there.

"You an artist or something?"

His front teeth were bright white and slightly buck so that when he spoke, they rested on his bottom lip, giving him an involuntary grin. I nodded to his question and my barrettes tapped against my temples. My face must have gone bright red as I smoothed my hair back into place and clipped them back into place.

"Your hair's okay. Real pretty. I never saw you at Hopkins High," he went on. "You go there, Red?"

"That's not my name. I gotta go now."

"You need a ride somewhere?"

He leaned against his truck and I stepped back, clutching my portfolio to my chest with both hands, and glancing down. I couldn't walk away and I didn't know why. When I looked up again, he had a half-smoked cigarette in the corner of his mouth and the smell of burning skunk

53

drifted past my nose. He noticed my grimace and shifted the cigarette to the opposite side of his mouth and away from me.

"Sorry. I think they call 'em Camels because they smell like camel dung."

I smiled and he flashed a smile back, never blinking his dark eyes. He darted his eyes away from me and pointed toward the street sign.

"Think you lost something."

The lady's slipper painting was wrapped around the metal street pole. I shrugged at him. 'Well,' I said.

My feet now felt like cement, but I got them moving and crossed to the Minnetonka Ave and New Ulm Street sign pole. As I freed the painting and slipped it back into my portfolio, I glanced back toward him and he was snuffing out his cigarette with the tip of his shoe. He noticed me, flashed his smile again and waved. My arm was a slave as it waved back. What are you doing? I thought.

He jumped back into the truck that I now saw was loaded with cabbage and lettuce. As it pulled away, a sign on its side read: Murphy Wholesale Produce. Murphy. One of the rich Catholic families? Is he a Murphy or does he just work for them? What would Mom say to a Murphy being interested in me, and not in Irma for once? Why did I really care one way or the other? I'm one step closer to my college art scholarship! I picked up my pace again.

As I crossed our yard, I saw Dad in the garage. He waved at me and then stepped into the garage that was black as a cave in the afternoon sun. My feet kicked up dust and a foxtail lodged in my sock as I ran toward the garage -- Dad had to be the first one to know. As I stood in the garage door, my eyes had to adjust because of the sun. Dad was just sitting, flicking the metal parts of a gopher contraption he had made, his arms folded over his work shirt. I ran to him and threw my arms around his neck but he returned the hug weakly.

"I did it, Daddy. I'm in honors art."

He looked up from his gopher trap for a moment, his face having his important thinking expression. He nodded and smiled.

"Good, Darlin', I'm proud of you."

I hugged him a little longer, hoping that he would react more to my news. He pulled his arms away and patted my shoulder.

"Go on in and tell your Ma. She needs some good news."

Dragging my feet to the back porch door, my ears echoed with a dull thud as the top of my head suddenly stung and a small pinecone bounced to the ground. I rubbed the sore spot and looked up to see my little brother Jimmy perched on a thin limb of the old pine tree that grew next to the back of our house. He must have been thirty feet in the air and the branch bowed under his weight.

"Jimmy!"

"Sorry, Mary."

"Get down from there. You're gonna hurt yourself."

Jimmy scampered like a monkey back to where the thicker part of the branch joined the tree and sat, leaning his back against the trunk. He flashed the 'okay' sign at me but it wasn't all right with me. I glanced back at Dad who was now taking the gopher trap apart, either unaware or oblivious to where Jimmy was. Mom was in the house so I knew she didn't have any idea what Jimmy was doing.

"Jimmy, get down!"

He shook his head and crossed his legs like he was the casual king of the tree. Jimmy didn't listen to mom and dad and he sure wasn't going to care what I said. I gave up. I couldn't understand how mom and dad let Jimmy climb a fifty-foot tree or 'go exploring' for half a day, but would yell in a panic at Irma or me if we were out of sight for longer than five minutes. I rubbed my head again because it was tender and because I didn't understand why we were treated so different.

But the smell of homemade bread, yeasty, ripening crust and the slight sour smell of wet dough, took my mind off my aching head as I walked into the kitchen. Mom and Irma stood with their backs to me, both of their wide rear ends swaying as they kneaded bread dough at the counter. Lacy splotches of flour powdered their rear ends and upper thighs and they made me think of dredged turkeys. Gyrating in unison like a high school drill team, Mom reached to dust her loaf with flour and Irma followed. Mom flipped her dough to work it, and Irma did, too. With her hair pinned back exactly like Mom's, I thought that I could have been looking at Mom when she was young.

"Mom?"

Mom didn't turn around. She rolled the loaf on the counter and a small cloud of flour puffed from it.

"Yeah."

"I got some good news."

Irma picked up her wad of dough and slammed it on the counter. Mom smacked her shoulder with the back of her hand.

"Not so hard. You'll bruise the yeast."

I set my portfolio and art knapsack on the table and Mom cast a sideward glance at it. Irma turned to look at my knapsack while she picked dough from between her fingers.

"I got some news, too. It ain't good," Mom said.

"Real bad," Irma added.

Mom turned toward me and I saw the wetness around her puffy

eyes again. She dusted the excess flour off her hands and began to pick globs of dough from her fingers. She didn't look up.

"Them bastards at Three M did it again."

My mouth dropped open. Mom never used curse words.

"They got some sort of poison that kills the gophers right in their holes. Won't hurt the soil, either. Mr. Snelling at the bank said that your dad's trap wouldn't be worth the risk because no one's gonna want to trap the gophers and have to set them free when they can just kill 'em and be done with it."

Mom's eyes flowed with tears and she lifted her apron to dab them away. Some of the flour mixed with the moisture on her face and it left a pasty streak on her right cheek. Irma and I looked at each other because we never saw her cry before and when Irma stepped toward her, Mom pushed her away. She sniffed a couple of times then turned back to her loaf of bread.

"What you got to say?" she asked me over her shoulder.

Irma turned toward me and folded her arms, her eyebrows arching as if to tell me that Mom's crying would be a tough act to follow. I didn't doubt that.

"I got into honors art. I start in fall."

Irma rolled her eyes and blew air through her cheeks. She turned back to her loaf. Mom stopped kneading and laid her hands flat on the counter, addressing me again over her shoulder.

"It's a bad day around here and you don't need to brag. Besides, you ain't got no more time for art. You gotta give up that girlish stuff and start becoming a woman."

"But Mom."

"Don't but me, Missy. Don't ya' think I know what I'm talking about? You keep fooling with all that art, and you're gonna wind up like me."

"The art teacher just told me —"

Mom turned and stepped toward me like she was about to hit me. She plunged her thick fingertips into her shoulders as she spoke.

"Look at me. I was a dancer, the best, the absolute best. No one could move like me, no one. They said I'd make it in vaudeville, on stage, if I stuck to it. But the great men, the rich ones, the right ones never went to see dancers. Now look at the queen of the flappers, fat as an ox and worried whether she's got enough pennies to buy flour."

"If I stick to it and work hard, I might be different."

"What you gotta do is learn how to fix your hair and make yourself presentable so you can find yourself a man who will take care of you. Just look at your sister here. She knows how to attract the boys and she's

56

getting practice for the babies, too, with all those animals she nurses. And it won't hurt you to start pitching in with the cooking around here, either. You want to keep him once you got him, don't ya'?"

"Who says I can't be a good cook and a good artist?"

"Don't take no tones like that with me."

Mom reached out with her thick, floury arm and grabbed up my portfolio and art knapsack. The knapsack burst open and my tins of colors splattered onto the floor as the mason jar exploded into sharp hunks and shards. Mom bent over and snatched up the broken neck and lid of the jar and flailed it at me.

"You little thief! Who told you could take one of my –"

"I did."

Dad jumped between Mom and me, his little chest inflated and his arms making triangles on his hips. Mom's face tightened up like a dried apple.

"You just leave her alone, Martha. Someone's got to do something special in this family. She may be the one." Mom waved the broken jar at him.

"Just what we need. Another failure in the family."

Dad reached up and rubbed the back of his sunburned neck like a mosquito bit him. He stared at her without blinking.

"I'm outta hope, Ernest. Fresh out."

"Mary's got to try."

Mom dropped the mason jar fragment into her apron pocket. Her feet made a gritty shuffle as she turned her back, went to the counter, and started kneading again. Irma and I just stared at each other because we had never seen Mom and Dad fight.

"If Mary's going to use my mason jars, it's going to be to put up raspberry jam. Not for nothing else. Mary, get this mess cleaned up in a hurry. Irma's boy is due here in about an hour."

Dad glanced at me and smiled. He picked up my portfolio and handed it to me, then dropped his head and walked out of the kitchen. Mom added over her shoulder:

"You get yourself cleaned up, Mary. He might be bringing his younger brother, too."

I cleaned up my paints and went into my bedroom. I started to brush my hair, and I actually didn't think so much about Dad's failure, or Mom's anger at him, and her fears that we would starve. I didn't think about Irma and her boyfriend, either. What popped into my mind was the boy in the truck. With each stroke of my hair, I thought about him telling me that my hair was pretty. Even though I had more chores to do before Irma's boyfriend arrived, I couldn't help it: I pulled out my sketchbook and picked up a pencil. The lines and shading scratched onto the page and in seconds, I had a drawing of a boy standing next to a truck, and scribbled-in circles that would later become heads of cabbage and lettuce. And for the first time in all my years of drawing, I titled a sketch: 'New Ulm Street.' I couldn't wait to paint it.

5.

Irma dated a lot of boys, and Mom was happy that she did. She met boys in school, she met boys in town, and she met boys when she went to the movies on Saturdays. Irma would tell me that after two dates, she knew the boy was wrong and she'd move on. And if any of them got frisky, well, like Mom had said to me once, Irma never 'messed' with any of the boys. She was looking for men. During my whole first year of high school, when I did almost nothing but my honors artwork, Irma dated. Just after Irma graduated from Hopkins High School in June of 1941, she invited another boy home.

I sat on a stool in the garage working on a technical sketch for one of my assignments. Ever since he had given up on his gopher trap, Dad had taken up doing handyman repair work and his work bench that used to be a junk heap of greasy, jagged metal parts now looked like a factory conveyor belt. I took a break from my drawing and picked up an electric iron with a frazzled cord that looked like a haystack and read the label Dad had tied to it. I set it back onto the workbench next to three other appliances. Dad fidgeted with the base of an electric fan that was a pinwheel of black and red wires, his temples dripping with sweat in the wet summer heat. He snapped the base into the fan then wiped his brow with the back of his dirty shirt cuff.

"Okay. Let's give her a whirl."

He inserted the round metal prongs into the plug on the light socket over head and the white bulb faded as the fan whirred into life. Dad smiled as he pulled a rag from his pocket and wiped his hands. As the stagnant air of the garage began to cool and flow past my legs, the breeze carried a faint smell of engine oil and paint. If Dad ever noticed it, he didn't say, but as I sat on the stool, I kept extending and crossing my legs while I drew. I was hoping he'd see that I had shaved off all the gold hair from my legs. Except for a couple of nicks, my legs were now soft and smooth. I shifted one more time hoping he'd say something, but he didn't. He just kept tinkering.

Dad next slid Mrs. Viker's toaster to the edge of the bench. As he leaned forward and stuck a finger into the toast slot and depressed the spring, I could see his perplexed face reflected in the shiny chrome. He manipulated the pop-up mechanism that squeaked like a sick mouse each time. The sound of an automobile engine approaching rumbled the garage and Dad stopped toying with the toaster. He glanced up at me and I shrugged. The rumble grew louder as the car drove closer and Dad scurried over to the open door. I plopped down and stood at his side.

"That can't be a '39 Ford," Dad said.

"What's so important about a '39 Ford?" I asked.

"It sure is. A convertible, too. Is that your sister in the front seat? That ain't so safe with the roof down."

"Look how shiny blue it is. What are the gray seats made of, Dad?"

"I'd say suede."

The car rolled to a stop in front of the garage, its brakes screeching and tires kicking up dust and pebbles. Irma jumped up and flashed a huge smile as she waved and pointed at the driver. The young man jumped out of his seat and over the driver's door like an Olympic hurdler, dashing around to the front of the car to the passenger's side. He caught my gaze and touched the cap of his flat leather hat that looked like a pancake. As he pulled open Irma's car door, a bright purple silk scarf he wore around his neck burst from his leather jacket and billowed toward us making a kite tail. Irma stepped out of the car, holding her skirt regally.

Dad yanked out his hanky and wiped his right hand quickly as Irma led the young man by the hand to meet us. His eyes, green as corn leaves, sparkled over his long, narrow nose and his mouth was a full, pink smile embraced by dimples. The young man shook free of Irma and held his keys out to Dad.

"Here are the keys. Park the car carefully and there'll be a big tip in it for you!"

Dad's face wrinkled with confusion and when I looked at Irma, she beamed with a smile. The young man stepped back, looked at Irma, and then spit out a huge guffaw. Irma joined him in their huge laugh. Dad glanced at me and I shrugged. The young man reached out and tapped Dad on the arm.

"Just kidding."

Dad cracked a slight smile but his eyes were still distrusting slits. Irma stood back and her eyes shifted down to my bare legs. She screwed up her face and nodded toward the house, obviously wanting me to go in and change. The young man caught sight of her twitching head.

"You having a conniption or you going to introduce me?"

Irma's mouth smiled but her eyes still glared at me. It was the first time any of her boyfriends even acknowledged me and I liked the feeling.

"Dad. This is Benjamin Augsburg."

Benjamin reached out his hand and Dad shook it briefly.

"Ben. Please call me Ben."

"I don't recognize your last name. You from around here?" Dad asked.

Ben looked at me and smiled. His eyes tracked the same path as Irma's, but he didn't nod for me to go. He held out his hand.

"Wisconsin. So you must be Mary."

I smiled and nodded, just tapping his extended hand.

"What town?"

"Durand, Sir."

"Hmm. Don't know it."

"Well if this don't beat all. Ernest, you ever seen an auto as pretty as this?" Mom hollered.

All of us turned toward Mom who was running her hand along the side of the car. She wore her housedress with the roses on it that she had specially washed and ironed. Her hair was piled on top of her head instead of pulled back into a bun and even her apron looked white and clean. Mom stood back from the car and shook her head with amazement when she saw her reflection on the shiny blue panel. Ben skipped around the three of us and held out his hand to Mom.

"I'm Benjamin Augsburg, Ma'am."

Mom held out her hand and Ben bowed down and kissed it. Mom's head fell to the side and she began to giggle like a coquette. She's acting like a schoolgirl, I thought with amazement. Why? He's just another in a long string of boys.

"I'm Mrs. Hellman."

"Mrs. H. -- can I call you that?"

"I don't see why not."

"Mrs. H. And Mr. H. I brought you a little gift from my family to you."

Ben stepped to the side of the car and pulled out a box. It wasn't just any box, though. It was wrapped in gold foil paper and had a gold foil bow edged with lace sitting on top. Ben presented the box to Mom and she leaned slightly as she took the full weight of it. Dad stepped to Mom's side and grabbed the box as Mom shook her arms in relief.

"Seems awfully heavy," Mom said.

Dad scrutinized the box then looked at Ben. "Why'd you go and bring us a gift?"

"That's pretty rude, Dad," Irma said.

"Seeing as though you folks have invited me for dinner, and gone to the trouble of preparing it, I thought a little gift would show my appreciation."

Mom nodded in agreement, her mouth turning down and her

61

eyebrows arching. Dad just shook his head.

"Mr. Hellman, you'll insult me and my family if you don't accept it."

Irma stepped to Ben's side and grabbed his arm in a show of support. She glared at Dad, which was nothing new for her.

"Well, why don't we go on to the kitchen table," Mom said. "Dinner's ready anyway and we can open the present in there."

Dad shrugged and stepped toward the back porch. Ben jumped ahead of everyone and skipped to the top of the stairs and propped open the screen door with his arm. Dad nodded to him without looking at him and stepped in. Mom followed on dad's heels, laughing and patting Ben on the arm as she passed. Irma followed and as I passed by Ben, I thought I heard him inhale sharply. I paused and he smiled, strangely, as he let the screen door slam back into place. Jimmy came scurrying out of nowhere, kicking up dust, and threw open the screen door and ran right past Ben.

"That's little Jimmy," I said.

Dad was already seated at the head of the dark pine table on which Mom had placed a tatting tablecloth and lace napkins. Mom handed Jimmy a plate of supper and sent him to his room, then directed everyone to their respective seats. She went into the kitchen and clinked and clanged pots and pans as she put the food into serving dishes. I sat next to dad and Irma sat next to me. Ben picked up one of the jonquils in the bowl at the center of the table and handed the bright yellow flower to Irma who stroked it against her cheek like it was a puppy. Ben reached for a second flower and handed it to me. Irma glared at me again like it was my fault.

Between Mom acting so strange and Irma putting on her show, the only person I recognized at that table set with blue and white china was my dad. The way he stared at the bright gold present, you would have thought it held a bomb.

"Mr. H."

Dad looked at Ben and his eyes were glazed over. So now even Dad was acting strange.

"Sorry. Mr. Hellman, it's probably a good idea to open that before dinner. I mean, it goes with dinner and all."

"Martha!"

"I'm busy, Ernest."

"Ben here wants us to open our gift now."

"Oh. Just a second."

Mom walked over from the stove, wiped her hand on a dishtowel, and tossed it over her shoulder as she leaned over dad. She rubbed her hands together lightly as if she wanted to clean them off, and then slid her fingers under the wrapping that crinkled and crackled. I sat forward in suspense. Irma was on the edge of her seat, too. I glanced over at Ben and he sat back, smiling. A cardboard box with a purple, green, and yellow family crest peeked out from the wrapping.

"My family crest," Ben said.

Mom's fingers reached between the box flaps and something jostled inside, tinkling like glass. She paused.

"Sounds like crystal."

Ben's smile broadened. Dad folded his arms and leaned back in his chair. Mom pulled open the box with a popping sound. Her brow wrinkled as she looked down.

"Bottles?"

"Not just any. Pull one out, Mrs. H."

Mom reached in and pulled out a brown beer bottle, still capped. She held it to dad to see a label that had the same family crest as the box sported. Dad's jaw dropped.

"Oh. How nice. Beer," Mom said.

"Twelve bottles of our family's reserve brew. My dad has made a fortune on that batch."

Mom strained an enthusiastic smile but Dad jumped up from his seat. Irma dropped her head in her hands.

"I forgot to change my shirt," Dad said.

Dad left. Irma raised her face from her hands and her cheeks were blushing. Mom tapped the table nervously and glanced back toward the backside of the house. I curled my lips under and Mom glared at me.

"Don't start into crying, Mary. You always overreact to situations."

In this situation, I was holding back a laugh. I couldn't believe that this guy was so stupid that he would give my father beer. Didn't Irma ever say anything about alcohol not being allowed in our house? Or that there could be a problem with Ben's father owning a brewery and dad's father being a violent drunk who killed his wife? She was so stupid.

"Ben. Your gift was very nice, it's just that we don't drink in this house," was all Mom could manage before she went after Dad. Irma slumped in her chair and Ben leaned back in his chair and rolled his eyes.

"Your old man a drunk?"

"No. He's just irritating. Ignore him."

"That ain't true, Irma." I couldn't believe she would call him irritating. She was so stupid.

"Now don't you two pretty ladies go get yourself all upset."

He reached over and picked up the box of beer, the bottles clinking against each other again. Ben headed for the door. Irma stood up.

"You ain't going are you?"

"No. I'm starved. I'm not going to let this go to waste, though."

Ben never let any beer go to waste as I saw a couple months after that disaster dinner. Sitting on the bank near the name tree, it was late afternoon in late summer, which meant the shadows cast by the aspens and birches were extra long. I wasn't working on a nature painting then, but pulled out 'New Ulm Street' that I hadn't touched since I sketched it. The grass tickled the back of my legs and a soft afternoon breeze brought alfalfa to my nose and a whipping, jerking sway to the tops of the aspens that were just beginning to go to yellow for fall. The wind's roar overhead and the sharp skids and dull horns of the traffic on Minnetonka Avenue below the trees made a noisy symphony in my ears. So much so that when the male voice yelled from behind, I didn't recognize it.

"Come on, Mary. It's me."

I turned and saw Ben. He propped himself against a tree and waved, his face and eyes making a goofy smile. Walking toward me, his black leather boots slid sideways on the riverbank, and he was just able to catch his footing and avoid a tumble down the grassy slope. I closed my sketchbook and pulled it close to me. He arched one of his muscular shoulders that stuck out from his bright red tank top and pointed to the ground next to me. I shrugged and scooted aside. His khaki pants scraped as he plopped down and his thick blonde hair fell in his face.

"You working on something you don't want me to see?"

A smell like camphor or the medicine I had to take when I had chickenpox blew toward me as he spoke. And I thought I smelled perfume. I leaned away from him.

"You sick?" I asked.

He slid closer so that his hip now rested against my thigh. I tensed my leg and separated the contact.

"No. I feel great."

"What are you doing here?" I asked.

"Just looking for your sister."

"She's at home. You know that."

"I'm just having a little fun in town."

"But you live in Wisconsin."

"Who are you? Charlie Chan or something?"

Ben put his arm around me and the fine hair on his forearm tickled the back of my neck. I was only fifteen and this was the first time a boy ever got so close to me. I felt warm and my back felt like an electric tingle.

"We're gonna be real close, you know that?"

I grabbed his hand and threw it off my shoulder. It made me feel dirty to have him touch me.

"I've got to get back to my work."

"Don't you even have a second for your future brother-in-law?"

64

If I just heard that my mother was going to have another baby, I couldn't have been more surprised. I cranked my shoulders toward him.

"You and Irma are getting married?"

He nodded but his head dropped and his blonde hair fanned across his face. From under this golden veil, he spoke like he was sharing a special secret.

"I gotta marry her."

"I have to go now." I jumped to my feet.

"No. No. No. Sit down."

He pulled me back down next to him. Now he whispered into my ear and I didn't know if it was his breath or his lip grazing my lobe. Again, the electricity shot down my back.

"My father says she'll make a man out of me. My mother knows the real reason."

"What's the real reason?"

"Forget it," he said.

I shrugged. I didn't know what he meant. Ben turned my face to him.

"So you see, we're gonna get real close."

Ben pushed his mouth against my lips and I felt his wet tongue try to pry them open. I jumped up and wiped the back of my mouth with my shoulder.

"Are you sick or something?"

Ben rolled onto his knees and looked up at me.

"I don't know why I did that."

"I'm gonna tell Irma."

He grabbed my legs and restrained me, now looking up like a beggar.

"Please. I love Irma. I do."

I twisted my thighs to loosen his grip. He held on like a dog.

"Please. You gotta trust me. This is life or death for me. My money and maybe Irma's, too. I have to get married and my dad says Irma's the one. Do you understand?"

"Then why aren't you with Irma right now? 'Stead of here. I smell that perfume, too. I think you been messin' around."

Ben pulled away from me and tucked in his shirt. He looked back at me, shook his head, and smirked, just like mom or dad did just before they would say 'you're too young to get it.'

"It's a big thing, getting married," he said. "I had to build up the courage."

"By messin' around? You probably even been necking. I'm gonna go tell Irma."

Ben pulled a black velvet box from his pants pocket. He opened it and a gold ring with a diamond as big as my thumbnail sparkled like the North Star in a moonless night. I reached out and touched the stone and as Ben turned it for me, it caught the sun's rays and I saw all the primary colors. That would be a beautiful thing to have, I thought.

"See," Ben said. "I really mean it."

I was in a daze as I stared at the diamond. Ben snapped the lid closed and looked at me, his eyes seeming to beg.

"Okay," I said. I gave in because I realized if they got married, she'd be out of my hair.

"I won't tell Irma."

His face relaxed as he stood and brushed off his pants. He looked like he was about ready to go back to mess around a little more. I stood up.

"You have to come now and propose to Irma," I said.

"I got something else I have to do."

"She's my sister. I care more for her than almost anything." Could he hear the lie in my voice? I just wanted Irma to leave home because I didn't need a second mother anymore. Maybe Mom would be nicer to me, too, if there weren't as many kids around. Hmm. Too bad Jimmy was too young to get married.

"Okay," Ben said. "I know Irma'll say yes. It's your dad I'm more worried about."

"Irma talks too much. He's not a bad man. He's very understanding."

Ben picked a couple of foxtails off his pant leg and I noticed some green grass smudges near his knee. He smoothed back his hair and I saw that his green eyes swelled with pink. He rubbed them.

"I look okay?"

"Yeah, I guess."

"Want to come with me? I'll give you a ride in my convertible."

"Go by yourself. I'll be there in a little bit."

Ben swayed slightly with each step back up the bank. He paused when he got to the sidewalk on Minnetonka Avenue, and for second he looked like a coyote with his foot caught in a trap. He hollered at me.

"Thanks, Mary."

The way he said it made me feel like I should say 'I'm sorry.' But anyone that thought Irma was such-a-much didn't deserve my pity. I nodded to him and he walked off. Why did he smell like medicine, anyways? And what about that perfume? Did he love Irma or not? I tapped my fingers on my sketchbook because these questions bothered me and I didn't know what to do.

Should I tell Irma about his disgusting thing with his tongue?

66

What if he tries it on her? More questions flew through my head, but I knew something right there: love is stupid, and so was Irma, and Ben was really stupid. I strummed the brown cardboard cover of my sketchbook, and I knew I had something better than stupid love. Art. No stupid boy was ever going to change that. I scooped up my sketchbook and knapsack and set off for home. Now I just had to hope that mom and dad would say yes to Irma.

As Ben and Irma marched down the aisle at the end of their wedding at Durand Lutheran Church weeks later, and while the twenty-person choir in green satin gowns belted Handel's Alleluia Chorus, I could smell the musky sweet white carnations in her bouquet that she waved toward Mom, Dad, Jimmy, and me. The smell of the bouquet, the soaring height of the church's beams, and the choir that boomed from the loft gave me goose bumps. It was beautiful and I lost myself in it. We only went to church when it was a funeral or maybe a baptism, and Dad always said that we were Lutheran-ish, which meant that we only went for a special occasion. Mom didn't hold much store in Jesus and all that, but she did have us pray to God whenever there was a crisis in the house. She rarely mentioned her own dad who she called the 'cheatin' preacher who left us' and when we moved in with Grandma Benton, Mom said we could never say anything about him in front of Grandma. This church made me think about Grandma's funeral, and I was glad we were there for Irma and Ben.

Irma and Ben, though arm-in-arm, nodded toward the opposite sides of the church. Irma's face was tired and her smile was frozen flat. Ben's eyes, usually so mirthful, were tense slits over a tight-lipped smile that must have been forced.

It was sort of embarrassing because other than us, and a few of Irma's school girlfriends, the only other guest on our side of the church was my crazy great Aunt Clotine. She was my Grandpa Hellman's seventy-six-year-old sister, our only living grand relative, and she was let out of the state mental hospital in St. Paul just for Irma's wedding. Her hair was cut into a short, white page boy that made her look like she was wearing a bathing cap and her blue cotton hospital dress smelled like moth balls. She sat on the other side of Dad and when we stood up to watch the newlyweds pass, she sat whispering to herself. At least she wasn't partaking in her favorite hobby of sticking straight pins into her chin and then laughing as she would taunt one of us kids, saying '*Push it in…I dare you…*'

But it wasn't great Aunt Clotine or her mumbling that embarrassed me as we stood there. It didn't help that Mom, whose eyes gushed from the start of the wedding to the end, burst into an inconsolable sob when the reverend asked in his reedy voice if anyone objected to the marriage to please speak. She didn't, of course, but Dad's lip started quivering then and continued until we stood. What was embarrassing was that across the aisle in the church, an army of Augsburgs filled the twenty-five oak pews. Where Dad wore his gray seersucker that had small moth holes in the elbows, Mr. Benjamin Augsburg the first (our Ben was the second) sported a satin black tuxedo with a satin cummerbund like most of the rest of the groom's male guests.

Mr. Augsburg sat upright in his pew, a full head taller than anyone sitting near him, his gray-gloved hands folded and leaning on a black walking stick that was crowned with a gold talon. When he reached up and adjusted the monocle that sat below his gray, bushy eyebrow, touching his thick mustache as he brought his hand back down, he looked like the king of England. Sitting next to Mr. Augsburg, a barely visible, delicate branch next to the oak stature of her husband was his wife. An intermittent glance by Helga Augsburg, a tight-faced, thin-lipped woman with gray-blonde hair and small eyes she tried to enlarge with false eyelashes, didn't help -- she cracked a small smile each time I caught her eye but when she turned her attention back to the wedding, I could see the crepe paper, pink edge of her upper lip curl with disgust. What was she looking at us for? Was she interested in Mom's pink chiffon dress she made for the wedding? But she wore a white satin, ruffled dress that looked right out of a Gainsborough painting. After she looked about ten times, I realized that she was not looking at our simple clothing but looking at us. Evaluating us, studying us, maybe even mocking us. Somehow, her way of looking made me feel very self-conscious.

After the gray chiffon and black tuxedo parade of the wedding party passed, the pews began to empty, and the murmuring of the guests began to drown out the choir. The Augsburgs led the exit. Through the whole ceremony, neither Mr. nor Mrs. Augsburg changed their somber expressions and as they followed behind, they might as well have been tailing a funeral line. I glanced back at the reverend and his two attendants, costumed in white satin vestments, as they stood back near the altar that was covered with pink and white carnations and white day lilies. The attendants began to snuff out the white tapering candles, and they, too, somehow looked sullen. Mom, Dad, Jimmy, and I now followed the procession, and Mom and Dad looked as sad as they did at Grandma's funeral. I didn't understand what could make such a joyous occasion filled with flowers and candles and that music that was a heaven's choir seem so sad. I would find out later.

When we got home from the wedding reception that Dad said was nothing more than a 'beer hall bash' because of the endless flow of Augsburg Beer and the toasts that went on forever, Dad took off his suit and went out into the garage. Mom took Jimmy to bed and I went into my room. It was stuffy with violet perfume and pancake makeup and as I went to open the window, I stumbled over a couple of white cardboard boxes from which spilled white tissue paper. Remnants of Irma's bridal preparation were also strewn on the bed. The window slid open bringing with its wood-warped creak the rustling raspberry bushes and a balmy late summer breeze.

I turned back to the room and realized that Irma couldn't boss me anymore. I kicked off my shoes and hopped onto the bed, the springs squeaked and moaned as I jumped like a grammar school kid. Irma had packed up all of her keepsakes, and as I jumped, I saw a room with an oak desk, a dilapidated oak dresser, and walls with holes and clean marks where Irma's movie photos once hung. Each leap and responding thump against my feet from the old mattress I jumped on reminded me that my life would be different from now on. Space, freedom, hope. Let Irma be the suck-up and get married just like Mom wanted. Heck, she could have ten kids for all I cared. It just meant more space for me to spread out my pads, pencils and paints and practice the art that I just knew would make me famous some day. Irma was so stupid.

"What the heck you think you're doing, Mary?" Mom yelled.

I stopped jumping and stood on the bed. The springs were still vibrating underneath the soles of my feet. Mom stood at the open door, still wearing her pink chiffon dress, and I thought she was going to let me have it, but she just looked around. She reached out to a spot on the wall, pulling a piece of tape and a remnant of a dried flower stem along with it. Irma had hung her first school dance corsage there, right next to a spot on the wall that was the exact shape of one of her 4-H ribbons. Mom held tight to the scrap in her left hand, then reached up and wiped her puffy, red eyes with the handkerchief in her right. She turned and as she walked out the door, said:

"Don't stay up too late, Irma."

I was going to correct her, but she closed the door too quickly. Why was everyone so weepy? Irma got what she wanted. So did Mom, I thought anyways. Ben wasn't happy either. Why? What's wrong with everyone?

Paint it! The impulse hit hard. I stepped off the bed and pulled out my burlap portfolio. Opening my sketchbook, I paused on 'New Ulm Street.' I couldn't paint it yet because I had a problem with perspective on the truck. But I had the young man just right, his tight forearm and bicep leaning just right on the hood. Miss Hogrebe hounded me about it all last year and she didn't even know that I couldn't paint it until the drawing was perfect. I flipped the page gently and allowed one more page before I started. This was going to be my second painting with a title. On this one I would use only the cool colors of blue, violet, indigo, and green.

6.

"Mary, you're coming along nicely on this one. The composition is wonderful. It feels so sad. What's it called?"

"Irma's Wedding."

Miss Hogrebe held up my drawing and regarded it. She brought the center of it to the tip of her nose and her eyebrows wrinkled. I knew something was wrong.

"His head. The groom?"

"Yeah?"

"It's too large. You have to fix the proportion. The cool colors create a sad mood for a wedding. The background elements and foreshortening are ... genius."

Miss Hogrebe set the drawing down and glanced over the shoulder of her caftan. She rested her thick chin for a moment and the maple leaf pattern of her dress made a fall color beard. Students shuffled in, all carrying real portfolio cases, not burlap. Miss Hogrebe flipped back the burlap leaf of my portfolio as she reached for the next drawing. She paused.

"Still carrying the potato sack, huh? I had hoped to see you on this first school day with a portfolio case that suited your talent."

I shrugged. Miss Hogrebe turned the onionskin page and it rustled as it revealed the next drawing.

"Oh, Mary. Aren't you ever going to finish New Ulm Street?"

"I think I finally got the drawing right."

Her face tensed up like she just bit a lemon. "You have until the end of this semester. It will go down as incomplete if you don't finish it."

Students mumbled as desks creaked and scraped. Miss Hogrebe turned toward the class, scratching her bright orange headband. The bell screeched to start the first period art class. Miss Hogrebe's shoes shuffled as she moved to the classroom door. Kicking up the doorstop, she released the door and it flew back.

"Ouch!" came as the door thudded against a lagging student. Miss Hogrebe's eyebrows arched as she regarded the door. In a single flash of force, the door swung open and slammed against the wall. Miss Hogrebe folded her arms and all eyes went to the door.

71

In walked a boy who must have been my age. He glanced at the door that now stood open with its doorstop fallen back into place. He shrugged his slight shoulders that were covered by a white shirt with billowing long sleeves ending in tight cuffs. The bright red vest he wore on top of the shirt was embroidered with thick designs in gold thread and hung askew. He almost looked like a pirate. He reached up and straightened the vest with his right hand. In his left hand, he clutched a red velvet portfolio that looked soft as deer fur.

His hazel eyes crowned by black eyebrows that were stitched together by hairs in the middle of his broad nose bridge fixed on Miss Hogrebe. Miss Hogrebe's eyes scanned the new boy, starting at his head on which was cocked a green beret, and stopping on his mouth and chin. Sparse but thick black hairs formed a mustache and Van Dyke beard that would someday make him look striking. At his age, though, they were a downy attempt at eccentricity. Miss Hogrebe cracked a smile through her burnt umber lipstick.

"Sorry," he said in a soft east European accent.

"You are?"

"Artie Janek." He pronounced the 't' in his first name like a 'd' and the 'j' in his last name like 'ch.' He reached into his portfolio and pulled out a wrinkled piece of paper. He handed it to Miss Hogrebe. Her eyes darted over the paper quickly, then back to the boy.

"So you're a senior from Urbana High School."

"Yes."

His accent reminded me of that scary Bela Lugosi Irma took me to see at the movies once. This boy's accent seemed nicer, though.

"Is that Chicago?"

"Yes."

"Where you from originally?"

"Excuse, Mrs.?"

"Miss. What country?"

"I American. Born Chicago. My parents do be from old place."

"Where's that?"

"Now is Czechoslovakia. Once it was Bohemia."

"A land of great artists."

Artie shrugged. "May I sits now? Don't like all this seeing at me."

"In a second. Did you really pass all grades in Urbana speaking English like that?" Miss Hogrebe asked.

"Yes. Can read and write English real okay. But speak only Bohemian at home so English I speak bad. Can sit now?"

He gestured toward the class that was all eyeballs on him. I couldn't blame anyone though because I couldn't take my eyes off him

72

either.

"Take a seat up front here."

Miss Hogrebe pointed to the desk next to me. Artie walked so that his suede boots made only a soft sound against the tan tile floor. As he sat down, he glanced at 'New Ulm Street' that was still on top of my desk. He dropped his portfolio and stood up, his eyes darting from my drawing to my face, then back again to my drawing. My cheeks prickled with heat.

"Miss Hogrebe, my art no good like that yet."

Miss Hogrebe's face twitched with irritation. She stepped over to Artie's desk, her brow furrowing with impatience.

"I'll be the judge. Let me have it."

Artie nodded and sat. He handed his portfolio to Miss Hogrebe, but kept stealing glances at my drawing. He caught my glimpse and his eyes locked on mine. Almost bronze in color, they seemed to glow with gold-green highlights. He smiled at me and I saw that his front teeth crossed slightly. Miss Hogrebe slid back into her chair behind her desk, turning the portfolio back and forth like she was examining a Christmas goose. She didn't open it right away. Instead, she toyed with thick tassels that corded it like bands of gold, running her fingers along embroidered gold piping that bordered the book.

"Where'd you get your portfolio?"

Artie's transfixion with my drawing was broken and he looked up, shrugging and seeming not to understand the question. Miss Hogrebe pointed to his portfolio.

"This. Where'd you get it?"

"Art book?"

Miss Hogrebe nodded.

"Grandmother made. She did art paintings once."

Miss Hogrebe's eyebrows arched and she cracked the book open. Her eyes flared as she gasped.

"Is wrong? No good?" Artie's voice sounded like the cry of a nervous puppy.

Peeling up a page that looked like cloth, Miss Hogrebe held up Artie's painting. The class erupted with a sharp inhale. I stared at the painting of thick, purple grapes, ochre cheese, and a green wine bottle with a graceful neck. Water drops sparkled on the grapes and the cheese reflected a mirror image on the wine bottle. I could almost reach out and snatch the plump fruit, and its beauty made me hunger somehow.

"Class. The medium here is oil. On canvas. Why it's not mounted and framed, I don't know."

Miss Hogrebe next lifted up a canvas that depicted a light brown loaf of bread, golden rolls, and a crock of butter. The food again looked so real that I thought I could eat it. Another painting of a silver coffee set with a slice of cake emerged. Artie's work looked like photographs, as good as the still lifes of the Dutch masters.

"Miss Hogrebe, is okay? Do I stay in class?"

"Yes, Artie. You may stay."

Artie still stood and now folded his arms. He glanced at my drawing and tapped his foot.

"Something else, Artie?" Miss Hogrebe asked.

"Can't make people like her."

"That's Mary, Artie."

His eyes locked on me again and he smiled. I felt warm and my back tingled with sweat suddenly.

"Hello," he said.

He smiled again and that, along with his paintings, made me shrug my shoulders and nod a greeting. I feel so strange, I thought.

"Why did you choose these subjects for your work, Artie?" Miss Hogrebe asked.

"All things that make life good. Food and wines and good things like that."

"As long as you challenge yourself." Miss Hogrebe glanced at me when she said the next thing. "And finish what you start, the choice of subjects is up to you. Welcome to class."

My dad and his garage inspired Artie's next choice of subject. Just a couple of weeks after that first day of class, Artie and I began working on our art together after school. He had been to our house a few times, and because Mom didn't take to him, we started working in the garage with Dad.

"You call this one Papa's Bakery, huh?" Dad chuckled when Artie first showed him his work.

Because of that reaction, I think, Artie got the idea for his next painting. We were finishing class projects in the middle of October. The aspens were on fire with their yellow leaves, and the sunlight that entered the open garage had an orange glow as it cast long shadows. Dad had fixed up an old radio for us and Glenn Miller's orchestra blared 'String of Pearls.' Dad was soldering a wire in the base of an electric coffee pot, making small puffs of smoke that smelled like burning caramel.

Artie and I sat next to each other and sketched. I don't remember when it started, but lately I'd watch Artie sketch when he wasn't looking. It wasn't for technique or for what he was drawing; his long fingers moved liked graceful snakes, each turn of his wrist causing his forearm muscle to inflate and bulge out a vein. The scratching of his pencil on the paper and the rhythmic movement of his arm hypnotized me. He looked up and caught my stare. He smiled.

"You liking the sketching I do?"

I blushed at being caught.

"Yes."

"It bore me. I want to do something different."

Artie glanced around the garage that was in its usual state of clutter. Dad clamped the base of the coffee pot together and set it on the workbench. He pulled out the soldering iron plug with a pop. Artie watched him and his face became entranced. Dad threw the soldering iron next to the coffee pot on the workbench and wiped his hands. He caught Artie's stare.

"You okay there, Artie?"

"Mr. Hellman, may I?"

Dad nodded. Artie set the soldering gun at an angle to the coffee pot. He grabbed one of Dad's wrenches and crossed it in the opposite direction. Dad and I just watched. Artie looked around the workbench and paused on a coil of silver solder. He picked it up and set it in front of the coffee pot. Dad scratched his head and knitted his brow. I sat with my arms crossed, not understanding either.

"Mr. Hellman, may I paint your work bench with tools as are?"

Dad curled his mouth as he considered it. "I'm going to have to get that pot back to Mrs. Darlana tomorrow."

"I need only for sketch. I do today. Painting, I don't need for."

Dad glanced at me, smiling and shaking his head. He shrugged his work shirt into blue wrinkled epaulettes on his shoulders.

"Long as you can get your sketch done today. It's all right with me."

"Yes. Thank you, please."

"You're sure a wormy boy, Artie," Dad said with a smile.

Artie looked down at his chest and pulled at it in a panic. He thrust his arm at his face, inspected it, and then looked at Dad in confusion.

"He just means you're funny, Artie." I said. "Different."

"Oh." He looked relieved.

"What you going to call this new painting," I asked.

"Dad's Tinkers."

Dad laughed and tossed his rag under his workbench. He started to walk out, but paused at the doorway.

"Stay for dinner, Artie?"

I nodded at Artie and he shrugged. "Why no? Okay." he said.

Just before Mom called us to the table an hour later, Artie scratched out the last of his sketch. I hadn't touched mine since he began. He glanced at my sketchbook.

"Why you not worked at all?"

He smiled and grabbed my hand. Lifting it to his lips, I felt his mustache tickle my fingertips.

"This hand is gift. Don't let no work."

He kissed the tips of my fingers and I felt my spine tingle. A cool sweat erupted on my neck as I allowed him to press his tender lips against my fingers once more.

"Mary. Dinner!" Mom screamed.

I pulled my hand back, and, never looking at his face, I stepped down from my stool. I shifted my sketchbook and pencil to my left arm, and then gestured toward the house.

"Dinner's this way."

Since Dad's repair work had picked up, our dinners now had rolls or corn bread as a side dish every night. Tonight, a beef stew full of carrots and potatoes in a thick gravy sent steam up from my bowl. Dad sliced thick hunks of cornbread from a cast iron skillet blackened by years of burned grease and hot ovens. The fork he used to serve it clinked against Artie's plate. Jimmy, who was now ten and all arms and legs, scooped and slurped his stew. Mom dipped her spoon delicately and only looked up out of the corner of her eye to see if Artie was eating.

"Artie here's gonna do a picture of my workshop, Martha. How 'bout that?"

"Hmm," Mom muttered.

Dad arched his eyebrows toward Artie and I, and then dunked his spoon into his bowl. Clinking spoons against stoneware was all we heard through most of the meal. Mom kept her head bowed toward her bowl like she was praying.

"Stew's sure good, huh?" Dad interjected.

I nodded and Artie smiled. Jimmy stood up and wiped his mouth with the back of his sleeve. He pointed at his empty bowl.

"Can I be 'scused?"

Mom raised her eyes for the first time during the meal, saw Jimmy's empty bowl and plate, and then nodded. Jimmy bolted for the back door.

"Not till your homework is done," Dad hollered.

Jimmy blew air out of his mouth in frustration as he stomped off to his bedroom. "Martha. Can I get a second helping? Sure is good."

"Why don't you ask our guest if you can have his, seeing as he don't like my stew."

I blushed and couldn't believe she said that. Dad's eyes darted to Artie's bowl. When I glanced down at it, I saw that cubes of moist beef still filled the bowl, though all the potatoes and carrots were gone. Artie lifted his napkin and dabbed his mustache and beard as delicately as if he was

76

applying paint to canvas. He raised his eyes to meet Mom's, and I thought I could see an expression of hurt as he looked at her without blinking for a moment before he spoke.

"Mrs. Hellman, stew is too good. I don't eat meat now because vegetarian."

"Huh?" Dad mumbled.

Artie's eyes slid to Dad and I saw now that they sparkled with a grin.

"Just eating things that grow in ground. No meats except for fishes."

"Fish are meat, ain't they Ernest?" Mom hissed.

Dad shrugged.

"Why are you doing that, Artie?" Dad asked.

"Don't want to eat flesh of earth animal. Animal spirits get into human and make baddest things."

Dad sat back in his chair and rubbed his chin. Mom stood and yanked Artie's bowl away, then grabbed Dad's and mine. She stomped to the sink.

"Thanks you, Mrs. Hellman."

Artie's not afraid of her, I thought. He stands up for what he believes. I wish I could do that. Artie stood and wiped his mouth once more. He twisted the corners of the red checked napkin as he bowed to Dad. "Mr. Hellman, thanks you for dinner. I go now."

It felt like a hammer struck my stomach just then. I wanted him to stay longer and I stood up -- to stop him? I don't know why, but I stood. Artie didn't seem to notice me as he turned toward Mom.

"Thanks you for stew, Mrs. Hellman."

Mom waved over her shoulder and grumbled. Dad stood and shook Artie's hand, then picked up his bowl.

"It was fine to have you Artie. Anytime. Can't wait to see the picture of my bench. 'Scuse me -- got more stew to eat."

Artie stepped to the back door, his footfalls barely audible on our wood floor that made elephants out of mice. Wiping my mouth, I dashed off behind him and was hit by a crisp autumn wind that made the aspens chatter and my cheeks burn with cold. Artie stopped near our pine tree and turned toward me. My hair floated across my face, tickling my cheeks. Artie stepped toward me and my body seemed to float forward of its own will as the light from the house made his eyes shine like gold. His full, long lashes closed on them as he leaned forward.

My eyes had already closed as I leaned toward him and the first thing I felt was his soft whiskers against my lips. His breath caressed my nostrils with a warm, sweet fragrance and our lips touched. He pressed into me and my mouth opened slightly as we kissed. I felt wet velvet tap against my teeth and I realized it was his tongue. Opening my mouth wide, his tongue rubbed mine and I let it answer with a soft embrace. Shivers and sparks shot through my body while our tongues and lips moved as if in a dance.

The kiss ended, and when Artie pulled away, I felt groggy, like I had just waked from a nap. Artie reached down and picked up my hand. It was a limp, moist, warm sponge. He brought my fingers to his lips again, kissed the tips, and said, "This hand is gift. Don't let no work. Always make beauty in world."

He ran off and as I walked back into the house, I felt as if I never had seen the sitting room before. Dad sat in his chair, the radio hummed with 'Amos and Andy,' Grandma's rug lay where it always had. Somehow, it all looked fresh and new.

"I don't want him hanging 'round here anymore, Mary," Mom said.

Mom sat on the couch, knitting and looking at me over rolls and pleats of blue yarn. Dad just furrowed his brow.

"He's an artist, Martha. They're always excitin' and different."

"He'll come to no good, you mark my word."

"Mom. That's no the way to talk about the boy I'm going to marry," I blurted out.

Mom dropped her knitting needles and her ball of yarn rolled off her lap. She glared at Dad who smirked and chewed on his pipe.

"What'd you say?" Mom said.

"Just kidding, Mom."

I had been thinking about Artie being the right boy for me for a while, but it was the first time I ever said it out loud. I liked how it sounded, and especially how mad it made Mom.

"What kind of girl we raising who jokes like that, huh, Ernest?"

Dad said something back to her, but I really didn't listen. They talked, but it was like I was inside a jam jar looking out at them; I felt sweet and warm and no matter what they were saying, it didn't matter. Their voices became a murmur and I almost felt sleepy.

"Mary, you listening, girl? You're staring off like you're in one of your dazes."

Mom's voice shattered my protective jam jar. She leaned over the back of the chair and thrust her face toward mine. Coming out of my daze, my first thought was mom wanted a kiss. The anger of the moment pushed that out of my head right away, though.

"I hear you, Mom."

"You just act like you don't know him at school, you hear? Mary?"

I nodded and looked at Dad. He shrugged, looked at Mom as

78

always, and then nodded in agreement with her. He slipped his pipe into his mouth, closed his eyes and leaned back in his chair. Mom stepped away from my chair and picked up her knitting again. She rubbed the needles together so fast that I thought she could start the yarn on fire.

You don't like him, I thought. I'm going to marry him.

That first kiss felt strange and good, but especially exciting. It was exciting how my body did funny things like send shivers up my spine, and then turn the ends of my breast into small rocks like I was cold. Each time we kissed after that, I would see my Mom's face and how much she hated Artie and that made our kissing somehow more exciting, too. As we stood outside Artie's house on the front lawn that was turning brown from the late October sun, near the small bed of petunias that poked three fragrant blue eyes from a tumbleweed of dead stems, I pulled away from his kiss. I thought I saw a woman's face poke out from behind a dark curtain in front of his house. The aromas from the roast beef and dumpling dinner Mrs. Janek had made special for me was still in the air.

"We shouldn't do this right in your parent's front yard."

Artie laughed and pulled me to him, his breath a small breeze of licorice and cinnamon. His body was thin but strong against my plumper frame. Mr. and Mrs. Janek threw open the front door and waved.

"Thank you. Thank you both."

"Bye, bye, Maaarrey."

"My parents, they still think they in old country," Artie said. We were now at the corner of the Darlana's field and our front yard. He pulled a leaf from one of the raspberry brambles and the branch snapped in response. "My country is U.S.A. and no need that old place." Artie reached out and pulled me to him, but I stepped back toward the bushes when I saw the light on in our parlor.

"Don't want Mom to see us together."

Artie complied and stepped to me, his breath sending up a fog in the chilling night, fall air. We kissed and our movements made the raspberry bushes rustle. Pulling apart, I thought about the crystal ball I almost knocked over in his parent's parlor and I was curious.

"So did your Great-Grandmother really see you in that crystal ball?"

"Mama says she did."

"Does your Mother really know how to read palms or was she kidding me?"

"She used to do a lot, till she find out Church thinks sin. Now she do only for fun."

"Do you do any of that stuff?"

Artie stepped back and picked up my hand, holding it between his.

He looked at me like he was ashamed, and then dropped his head.

"What's the matter?"

Artie didn't lift his head.

"I'm afraid you may not like me anymores if I say."

"You can tell me. Whatever it is."

"What you say your religion is?"

"Dad says we're Lutheran, but we really don't go to church or anything."

"Guess okay, long as not Catholic."

A shadow passed by the sitting room window of our house and I couldn't tell if it was Mom or Dad. I grabbed up my portfolio.

"I gotta go now. Hurry up and tell me."

"Tomorrow night, tell Mr. Hellman you paint with me. Then I show you what I do, okay?"

The door on our porch creaked open and I saw Dad peering toward us. I leaned over and we kissed once more, quickly.

"Gotta go. Dad's looking for me."

Artie took two steps back and he moved like an anxious puppy. His face was bright.

"Meet here tomorrow. Then I take you!"

I nodded and he scurried off.

"Mary, darlin', that you?" Dad yelled.

I dashed around the raspberry bushes and the dirt and rocks of our dead front yard crunched under my feet.

"Hi, Dad!"

As I got to the porch, I could smell the cinnamon and caramelized sugar of baked apples, but my stomach was tight as a fist from all the Janek's food. A bitter flavor of Kirsch and buttery pastry still lingered on my tongue and I wondered if Dad would smell either the Kirsch or the Hungarian wine on my breath.

"Your Ma said you'd be painting with Artie and probably eatin' with him, too. Did ya' have a nice dinner?"

"Yes. Mrs. Janek cooked like it was Thanksgiving or something."

"Doesn't surprise me. Sometimes the immigrants are the wealthiest people in town, with all their goods and valuables from Europe. Mary, I want to tell you something."

I just wanted to get to my room, fast, but I didn't want to act suspicious. I turned toward Dad and I could see his eyes were misty.

"What's wrong, Dad?"

"I like that Artie. I really do. If he makes you happy, and helps you with your art, I think you really should think about marrying him, if he ever asks you."

80

"He hasn't asked yet."

"You both got school to finish, anyway. What would you say if he did?"

"Yes."

Dad stepped back and opened the front door for me and as I passed, he grabbed my shoulder. God, he smells the wine on my breath, I thought. Instead, he regarded me a moment, then pressed his lips against my forehead.

"You're growing up, girl, you surely are. My artist girl."

The weight of my burlap portfolio suddenly doubled as a shock wave of shame and guilt over drinking wine hissed through my body. I smiled and nodded, and as I passed into our sitting room, the plainness of our house, the flat gray, the lack of any beauty at all struck me. No wonder Mom is so grumpy all the time, I thought. She has no joy to remind her of life. Dad gets no special fun at all, except for that tired radio.

"'Night, Dad."

I creaked across the barren sitting room, keeping my eyes from seeing the moth-worn couch and curtains. I dropped my portfolio in my room and collapsed on my bed. The crescent moon shined in the sky and the way it glimmered through my window, it reminded me of the Janek's crystal ball. I wondered if the moon looked the same in Paris right then. Sweet Paris and its night. A gentle wind began to stir the raspberry bushes outside, making them sound like restless mice. I rolled the flavor of Kirsch and buttery pastry around in my mouth and I could still smell Artie's licorice and cinnamon kiss. I drifted off to sleep.

A stronger wind whipped the aspens the next night as Artie and I ran hand-in-hand into the woods near Minnehaha Falls, just on the edge of town. Yellow aspen leaves turned ghostly white by the faint moonlight spiraled around us. The falls roared nearby as we crunched and sunk into the spongy ground. Orange light burst through the black trunks of aspens and birches. Artie halted to catch his breath and I noticed what looked like a small shack between two birches. There was something sinister about it and I clutched Artie's arm.

"What is that?"

Artie glanced toward the shack. He smiled and rubbed my shoulders.

"Hunting lean-to. For hunters to camp."

I pulled away from him.

"You're not taking me hunting!"

He laughed.

"No. Almost where we want to be, though. They already started."

He pointed to the orange light that I now saw was a bonfire, smoky and musky with burning wood. Yellow and orange sparks spiraled with thermals toward the tall tree tops as human figures seemed to dance in rhythm about the bonfire. Was that a drum beat I now heard? It was low and steady, like a heartbeat as we approached.

We stood at the edge of a small clearing and the heat from the fire grazed my face even as the cold night air still tickled my back. But I was not concerned about my temperature in that moment; a group of ten people, all looking my age, stopped their dancing when they noticed us. The boys in the group were naked except for a short cloth around their waists, and the girls were naked from the waist up, wearing knee-length skirts made of something like deer fur. Large feathers that looked as big as Mom's carving knife stuck out from beaded headbands they wore around their heads and their painted faces reflected the orange firelight making them into phantoms. Indians! I thought and turned to run. Artie grabbed me as I heard shrieks of laughter over my shoulder.

"Is okay, Mary. These are friends."

My heart pounded and it was Artie's firm grip that made me turn around. Some of the dancers were still laughing, but one of them stepped toward us. As she reached us, I saw that her thick, black hair hung low enough on her chest to hide her naked breasts. She reached up and wiped away trickles of sweat that dripped like icicles down her painted cheeks.

"Hi, Artie," she said with no accent.

"Gopher Foot, this Mary. She here to see how we worship nature."

Gopher Foot squinted and then her eyes brightened in recognition.

"Mary, it's me, Alice from Home Ec."

My shoulders relaxed.

"Alice who brought the corn cakes last week?"

"Yep."

She pointed over her shoulder.

"Everybody here is either from Hopkins High or North Star High."

Some of the dancers now waved and I saw two boys sitting cross-legged and beating short drums that looked like Boston Cream Pies. Now I thought this was another new fad I missed because of my artwork.

"Mary, Gopher Foot here and all others are part or full-blood Ojibwa. They come here to worship nature spirits and to cure sick."

While Artie spoke, I couldn't help but look at Alice's -- Gopher Foot's -- almost naked body. The flames of the fire caused the smooth, tight muscles in her brown legs to stand out firm, and I thought about how stupid my own white toothpick legs would look just then. Her stomach was flat as one of the drums that began to beat again, and I felt the slight pressure of my stomach against my skirt waistband.

"Mary? You hear me?"

"Oh. Yeah."

A tight feeling gripped my throat and it only subsided when I saw that my breasts were bigger than hers. I took a deep breath and arched my shoulders back. But my victory was short-lived.

Artie was slipping off his shirt and he handed it to me while Gopher Foot reached into a pouch on her skirt and pulled out a wood bowl fashioned from a walnut. The heat of the fire on my face couldn't match the burn of embarrassment and something new that flashed through me when I saw Artie's body. Gopher Foot dipped her fingers into the walnut shell and a white, thick goo clotted on her finger tips.

She better not be, I thought. She is! She's going to touch him! No wonder they call her Gopher Foot -- she's sneaking in on Artie.

Running her index and middle finger straight down Artie's torso, she traced parallel white lines down the middle of his chest and I saw two slight muscular mounds around his nipples, each sparsely covered with fine hairs. I almost lost my breath. More hair circled his belly button then continued down to the waist of his pants as Gopher Foot's fingers finished tracing. Artie's body looked like Minnetonka Avenue as he slipped a headband and feather onto his head.

"I going to dance with everyone. You watch, okay?"

I'll stay around just to make sure she doesn't touch you again, I thought. I nodded. As Artie joined the ring of dancers, the drums began to beat, and they all melded into a glowing ring of vibrating bodies, each drum beat now echoing its rumble in my chest. The dancers began to chant in a language I didn't understand. Gopher Foot broke from the group and began flailing her arms. She crouched down on all fours and darted her body back and forth, and for a second, I thought she moved like a mountain lion. She jumped back into the line and resumed the group step. Next, a young man broke from the dancers and jumped and pawed at the base of a nearby birch, his hands slapping against the trunk with dull thuds. He looked like he was going to climb the tree, and then he jumped back into the dance.

More dancers took turns away from the line, and each time they moved like different animals. This one a hawk, that one a deer. Another a horse. The chanting became a chorus of human animal calls each time a dancer broke loose, then resumed the steady rhythm along with the drumbeat. Aspens swayed overhead and the wind sucked up more of the fire's embers that swirled yellow before the twinkling aquamarine, fall constellations. The steady drums, the rhythmic chanting, and the swaying bodies began to make me feel lightheaded, and now my shoulders and hips began to move on their own. Everything in the sky, all the trees around, and these Indians all felt connected, and I felt part of it, too.

Artie slithered from the dancers, growling and stalking, his shoulders hunched like a wolf on the prowl. I didn't understand why these Indians would allow him to join them, but as my own body drunk up the feeling of belonging, I sure understood why Artie wanted to be with them.

Pretty soon, we started showing up every night for the chanting dances and we were always welcomed. After two weeks, I was now invited to join in. Gopher Foot walked up to Artie and me this one night and offered me a feather and a leather headband.

"Mary, you're learning the way of nature spirits. Dance with us."

"But I'm not an Indian."

"Neither is Artie, is he? As long as you respect our ways and learn them, that's all that matters."

I slid the band onto my head and it squeezed my scalp like a rubber band. The quill of the feather scratched my scalp.

"Ouch."

Gopher Foot reached out and adjusted the quill. Her brown arm smelled like cooking oil and rosemary. Reaching into her skirt, she withdrew the walnut shell and extended it out to me.

"Use this to make three lines on each of your cheeks, like mine. Then help Artie with his lines."

She turned and stomped off to join the dancers. A waft of smoke from the burning birch wood logs passed by my nose as I dipped my fingers into the shell. A cool paste coated my fingers and as I drew lines across my cheeks, I could smell mint and something like chalk. I turned to Artie.

"How'd I do?"

He nodded while he peeled off his shirt, and then extended his chest and abdomen toward me. I dipped two fingers as I had seen Gopher Foot do, and then touched the base of his throat. His skin was warm and soft against my touch as I drew my fingers down his torso. A tingle began in my fingertips then shot through my body as my hand creeped toward his belly. Artie grabbed my wrist and nodded toward my body.

"If you want to dance, should look like other girls."

I glanced around at all the girls who were naked from the waist up. Artie plucked at the collar button on my blouse. The orange glow of the fire and the rhythmic foot stomping nearby made me want to draw a deep breath. I looked down at my open collar and shrugged at Artie.

"My fingers are gooey. Would you help?"

He popped open the other buttons on my blouse and pulled it off my shoulders. The night air prickled the skin on my chest, but Artie's body

84

gave off warmth. He stared at my bra, and then nodded again. I looked around once more, nervously rolling the thick paint between my fingers. Artie must have seen the look of fear in my eyes.

"We dance for nature together. We do it as natural as we can."

With that, he unbuttoned his trousers and dropped them to the ground with a whoosh sound. He wore light-colored boxer shorts like Dad's I'd seen in the wash loads at home, but the legs were cut much shorter. The hair on his upper thighs reflected the firelight. He reached for his underwear.

"No, Artie. Don't take those off."

His eyebrows furrowed in confusion as he pulled the shorts higher on his body.

"Just needed to pull up. You okay?"

"Yeah."

His eyes shifted from his body to mine, then looked at me hopefully. His eyebrows arched as if to say 'well?' I handed him the walnut shell and gestured for him to turn around. With his back to me, I unclasped my bra and dropped it onto my blouse and his pants. The cold air now stung my nipples and I tore the barrettes from my hair, pulling my hair down over my breasts as far as I could. My hair covered most of each breast, but the large undersides showed from beneath and they must've looked like two halved honeydew melons.

"Okay."

Artie turned around and smiled, glancing quickly at my breasts.

"You worship for me. I so happy."

He thrust the shell back into my hand and finished applying his stripes. Artie grasped my hand and we joined the circle of dancers. I followed step as best as I could. But I realized that legs were flying independently from arms that would thrust into the air with no step repeated. I relaxed, closing my eyes, feeling the drums beat in my chest. Each leaping step we took in the circle felt so easy, so free. My head grew heavy and lolled of its own accord, while all the time Artie's tight hand grasp sent electricity through me.

My head now grew light, and it felt as though my body was floating off somewhere. I felt myself leap from the dancers, my arms moving in a feeling of flight. Owl, eagle, hawk, the birds of the night and day flashed through my mind, even as my arms fluttered as if in flight. I am free. I am alive. I am nature. I am God. The drums stopped and so did the dancing. I snapped my eyes open and saw all the dancers staring at me, their faces half dark, half orange. I dropped my hands and felt silly. Artie was at my side.

"You okay, Mary?"

"Yeah. Why'd the drums stop?"

"You act crazy. You pretend like bird for long time."

"What do you mean?"

"For whole hour, you're bird."

"An hour?"

Gopher Foot stepped between the dancers and walked up. She looked at me, a curious expression in her dark eyes.

"Mary. You were in a spiritual trance. Did great wisdom come to you?"

My body quaked. With cold, from the embarrassment of still being stared at, and from hearing that an hour had passed when it seemed like only minutes. Crazy Aunt Clotine and her straight pins popped into my head. A surge of dread welled up in me and for a second, I felt like I was slipping into a tunnel, out of everyone's reach. I sat.

"I really thought we just started dancing."

"No. Much longer," Artie said. He grabbed my elbow and began to help me up.

"Wait a second, Artie."

"No. Need to go now."

He pulled at my elbow to force me up and now I was furious. I shook loose his grasp. His eyes widened.

"I want to dance some more."

Gopher Foot intervened.

"Come back tomorrow, you guys. We'll be dancing for the fertility god."

Now she was telling me what to do. Were they in cahoots or something? I glared at her.

"Are you telling me to go?"

Gopher Foot took a step back, her face looking uncomfortable.

"After a spiritual travel, it's best to relax and wait for the message to become clear. Come back tomorrow, you guys."

"Why does everyone think I'm tired? I'm not."

"Let's go draw, then," Artie offered.

I waved away the idea. If I couldn't dance anymore, I wanted to go home. The last thing I felt like doing was drawing or painting.

"You've still not painted 'New Ulm Street', Mary. I expect you to finish it over Thanksgiving," Miss Hogrebe said the next day.

"Okay," I answered.

Miss Hogrebe paced in front of her desk the next school day. She reached up and scratched under her canary yellow headband, her eyes boring into me from under the shadow of her false eyelashes.

"You haven't started anything new since the semester started and

86

here it is already the end of October. An artist who doesn't create will always destroy. Either himself or someone else. There is no in-between."

I didn't know what Miss Hogrebe meant.

"I've done all my assignments."

"That's not what I'm talking about."

"I haven't been inspired lately. So what?"

"You better start finding some inspiration. Your portfolio as it stands now is sorely incomplete and won't get you into the art college."

"Maybe I don't need art college."

"If you want to be an artist in Paris some day, you better plan on more study and a stronger portfolio."

"Who cares about Paris now? I got the bears, and the eagles, and the earth. They'll help me with my art."

Miss Hogrebe squinted in confusion and folded her arms. Her eyes now darted around my face and stopped on my hair.

"Ever since you changed your hair, you've seemed a lot less interested in your art."

I drew my hand down each rise and dip of my braided ponytail. I was surprised that Miss Hogrebe would have said anything at all about my hair or dress.

"It's got nothing to do with my hair."

"It's because of Artie, isn't it?"

"No."

"Well, in case you haven't noticed, he's still completing assignments and producing auxiliary projects."

"Maybe 'cause we work together."

"Then where's your work?"

"I'll get some done."

"You have till Thanksgiving break. I want to see New Ulm Street finished and some new project underway. Effort and results."

I ran home, not thinking much about Miss Hogrebe's threat. A raspberry vine, brown from fall, snagged my skirt with its spindly finger as I turned into our dead yard. I could hear the clank of Dad's hammer as he worked in the garage, his work now backed up. For some reason, more and more people in town had a little extra money to repair things. I was glad he was so busy that he could only wave when I passed by the door. Now, only if Mom was out back washing clothes or sweeping the porch, I'd be able to get to my room without an argument. Every time we talked now, it turned into an argument. 'God of thunder and rain, please make her be somewhere else,' I thought as I stepped through the kitchen door. The long autumn shadows made the inside of the kitchen dark as twilight.

Mom stood at the sink, a single light bulb casting a dull yellow highlight on her gray hair. Her fleshy arms jiggled as she peeled carrots, each stroke making a metallic jingle as it scraped the skins. Jimmy sat at the kitchen table, practically in the dark, pulling out thick strings of seeds and flesh from the top of a pumpkin. Mom glanced over her shoulder at me, and then tossed a carrot into a pot with a thud. Here it comes, I thought.

"Well, if it isn't our little Indian squaw."

"I'm not married, Mother."

Another carrot dropped into the metal pot, this time sending a sharp pop and an echo.

"You could'a' fooled me. I thought you and the Czech had tied the knot or something. Cripes, I been expectin' a papoose."

She laughed at her own joke, a few loose hairs on her head vibrating as the caustic giggle rumbled through her. Now I expected her to make fun of my hair, just like she did when she saw my cowhide skirt last week. I pounded past her on the way to my room, hoping to avoid any further jabs, but her next insult stopped me.

"Why you're dressing like that, I'll never know. Wanna look like trash or something?"

"Artie says I look good."

"That why? When'd he become a fashion expert? Why you even still messin' with him?"

Did she think Artie and me were doing more than kissing? Why'd she say 'messing' with him?

"We help each other. That's all."

"You just better find yourself a real husband like Benjamin."

Benjamin! He's been cheating on Irma and they hadn't even been married for six months. What was wrong with Mom? I suddenly got the urge to tell her what we were really doing in the woods; she hated Indians, all Indians. 'Just American trash' she said once. If she knew I was dancing with them that would be it. But sometimes she really made me want to lay into her with the truth.

"I only care about working on my projects with Artie. Nothing else."

"You're wasting time with him. Other boys probably think you're engaged already."

"I don't care what other boys think."

"You better start. You ain't gettin' younger."

I'm a nature god, I wanted to scream; I'm part of the sky, and the trees, and tonight I'm gonna dance the fertility dance! I don't need to worry about boys, or getting married. I had Artie for that if I wanted. I have Mother Earth now. That's all I care about. I wanted to scream it all at her, but instead, I turned my back and spoke over my shoulder.

"Artie and me are going to work on more projects tonight."

"You been out every night for the last two weeks. That's it."

I turned back to face her and she stood facing me, a half-peeled carrot in one hand, and the peeler in the other.

"You know I'll fail if I don't finish."

She waved the vegetable peeler toward me like it was a knife.

"It don't matter whether you can paint a pretty picture or not, don't you get it? Sides, you got to vacuum Grandma's rug and dust the sitting room."

"I can get those chores done before I go."

"No. I don't want you wasting no more time with him."

I kept hoping that Dad would walk in, but his hammering kept a steady beat. Besides, he hadn't come between Mom and me since his repair business picked up so much. Mom went back to her carrots and I turned and walked out. Three more carrots plunked into the pot as I walked into the living room and I thought that if those carrots were Mom's tears, I would run to her and tell her I'd be good and she wouldn't have to worry. But I heard a hissing chuckle as I closed my bedroom door.

When I opened my eyes that night, as the birch smoke burned my nostrils and the fire warmed my face, Gopher Foot shook her rattle made from a brown gourd, and the drums stopped. She held up two dried stalks of corn plants and looked toward the sky.

"We now thank the god of rain and the god of the sun for making Mother Earth grow fat with children. Let's dance for the blessing to be passed to each of us."

The drums resumed above the crackle of the fire, sending sharp, rapid echoes into the dark woods. Our bare feet sunk and squished into the cold sponge of wet leaves and bark as we danced around the jumping flames. Gopher Foot did not join us, but instead marched around us in the opposite direction, stopping at each person and brushing him or her with the dried corn stalks. She drew the corn stalks down each dancer's bare torso, speaking an Ojibwa chant as she did. She then lowered the stalks to each person's private area, waved them back and forth, and chanted till she screamed.

When she reached me, she brushed the stalks over each of my breasts. A dried herb odor, like thyme, attacked my nostrils as the dried leaves made my bare skin itch. She brushed my vaginal area, covered now by a much briefer buckskin skirt on which was attached four feathers. Her movements made me think of dusting.

My eyes closed by themselves and I swayed with the rest of the dancers, each drumbeat again echoing through my chest. As happened whenever I danced, my mind flew far away, the eagle then the hawk taking turns to guide me. I felt a rush of electricity that swirled in my belly as Gopher Foot touched me with the stalks.

When she stopped, my eyes popped open. She now caressed Artie with the stalks. The fronds moved down to Artie's private area that was covered only by a loin cloth made of the same buckskin as my skirt. Artie wriggled and shifted his shoulders, now thrusting his pelvis toward the corn stalks. His face was a tight fist of beard and sweat. Circling shoulders and thrusting pelvis, his body movements made me feel hot with embarrassment. Was it me, or was Gopher Foot lingering on Artie?

As my heart pounded with anger, I heard what sounded like the slurp and pop of two people kissing. I jerked my head to the right and saw Johnny Red Eagle practically swallowing Nancy Laughing Bear's lower jaw. Stepping back in surprise, I now saw that all the dancers Gopher Foot had touched paired off. They writhed in deep kisses, looking like pairs of inchworms. Boys pushed toward girls who prodded back while the drums beat like frantic horses. Soft whimpers and breathy growls replaced chanting, and the firelight made the lusty inchworms glow as they clutched and pawed each other.

Disgusted by the acts that soiled the reverence of the aspens and stars overhead, I turned to Artie to ask him to take me home. But Artie and Gopher Foot were wrapped in a deep embrace, their faces joined at the mouth, and Gopher Foot's proud corn stalks were now limp husks hanging behind Artie's back. My throat knotted and my heart pounded against the tightness.

Throwing back my head to scream, I saw the aspens that were naked skeletons sway in the wind. Clouds bore down onto the treetops. The stars disappeared. I yanked up my skirt and blouse from a rock nearby and raced into the woods. Dark tree trunks made black columns I had to dodge, and as my frenetic heart and rapid breaths clogged my ears, a cool mist began to moisten my face. Each time my foot met the moist loam, I was stuck for a second and had to press with all my weight to land the next footfall. In that moist darkness, my left foot sunk in the ground and snagged on something underneath the soil. A tree root? A boulder? I couldn't tell.

The mist became thick drops of rain and it was warm compared to the crisp night. Grabbing my left calf, I pulled but my foot was still stuck. It didn't hurt, but it did scare me to be stuck in the darkness. I twisted my shin to the left, and then pulled again. Still no good. Twisting my leg back to the right and pulling with a big tug, I fell back and felt something grab me from behind. Adrenaline burned my body as my throat let loose a screech.

"Is okay, Mary. Okay. It's me."

90

I shook loose when I heard his voice, the extra adrenaline now feeding my rage at him. My clenched hands became fists and I beat at the darkness, my body feeling like a coil of anger. The metallic twist of a flint cigarette lighter burst forth a spark, and then a small flame, and I paused my shadow boxing: Artie stood a couple of feet away from me, his face a soft, yellow cameo. Raindrops clung to the tip of his nose and to the edges of his eyebrows. He reached out and grabbed my shoulder with his free hand, his touch sapping the energy out of my fight.

"Mary. My Mary. Why you run?"

Tears swelled on my eyelids as raindrops cascaded down my nose to meet a thin stream of mucous. I wiped my nose with the back of my hand, inhaling sharply, not taking my eyes from Artie's wet face. The rain crackled on the bushes and trees.

"You kissed her."

"Mean nothing."

Another adrenaline pump pulsed through me making my hands clench again.

"Is that what you feel when we kiss?"

"Oh, Mary."

Artie popped the lid of the lighter closed. He clutched my shoulders but I pulled back from his grip just as the moon poked through a break in the clouds. Artie faded into a silver-edged silhouette.

"You kissed her, Artie. Our special way."

I could just see Artie shake his head and by the way his voice tone changed, I could tell he didn't take me seriously. His humor at my expense now added frustration to my anger. Who did he think he was?

"That just part of fertility dance."

A chill shot through me making me feel naked. I wrapped my skirt and blouse around my shoulders. They felt like wet blankets, but it was better than standing naked in front of Artie. My foot stuck again as I tried to go.

"Don't go, Mary."

Mud slithered down my leg as I freed it and I could smell the wet, decayed leaves that clung to the mud.

"You just go back and do some fertility dancing. I'm sure that sneaky Gopher Foot will want to."

I don't know why I said that and I knew if he turned back toward the bonfire and Gopher Foot, I would die. Goose bumps erupted on my skin. Artie's arms enveloped me and he kissed my neck, his wet whiskers tickling my flesh.

"Let's go get out of the rain."

The urge to run from him, to scream at the god of the trees to uproot an aspen and heave it on his head, weakened as he held me. His body that was always warm soothed the inner and outer chill that shivered through me. Our lips met in a soft kiss. He pulled me to him and I felt for the first time his shirtless body. Through the rain, my fingertips felt his warmth and my hands shifted in the embrace, the subtle rise of his upper back muscles leading to a firm narrowness in his waist. His body was a wet statue, firm and classically proportioned as my palms covered it in circular motions. He leaned into our kiss, and as I pulled him closer to me, the rain made our bare torsos adhere. Off in the distance, rustling feet and laughter punctuated the night as the rest of the dancers broke off and ran towards town.

Artie's mouth prodded and scooped at the tender flesh of my throat, each touch firing a corresponding shock down my spine. Still vibrating from his touch, he led us squishing through the muddy woods back to the hunter's lean-to, which looked like a square, black cave in the moonlight that filtered through the clouds. He crawled in ahead of me. Reaching out, he pulled me off my feet and into the lean-to. My rear end thudded against the ground and I was surprised it felt so dry. Artie giggled as he curled up on his side next to me. In all the times we had kissed before, we always stood outside one of our houses or sat in a private part of the school grounds. It felt odd to have him lying next to me. That and the smell of dank wood mixed with old campfires made me jerk forward to support myself against my elbows. Rain ricocheted and pelted the wood planks over our heads, and I wondered if it was going to hold when I saw two small streams of water percolating like tears from the sides of the lean-to.

I glanced up to see the moon duck behind thicker clouds, causing our shelter to grow darker. Artie's hand glided around my waist and became a warm snake as he tugged at me to lie next to him. My wet skirt and blouse hung from my shoulders like soggy epaulettes and I pulled them down more securely over my naked breasts, resisting Artie's pull. He had already seen my breasts during the fertility dance, but just then, I felt more naked. 'Don't mess with boys' I heard my mother say in my head and another chill went through me. It wasn't the night air or being wet; I wanted to go home.

"We should get going soon," I said.

"Lots of rain happens. Should wait or else we get more wet."

He was right: the rain swelled into a deluge as the wind whipped the trees, causing them to propel wads of gathered rain onto the lean-to that rattled like it was being bombarded by walnuts. Artie's arm tightened and pulled on my waist. I stiffened my arms against his prodding, but then felt a tickle as Artie kissed up and down my right forearm. The sensation made me giggle, but it also made me uncomfortable.

"Should relax till rain stops. Come down next to me."

"I'm not going to lay on the ground," I said, but it was a hollow statement. The rain seemed to fuse with Artie's voice and it all seemed to taunt me. What do I want? I didn't know. What should I do? I didn't know again. Should I let Artie go back to Gopher Foot, and then go quietly back to my art? What about Paris? What about our kisses? We are going to get married, anyways, aren't we?

"Mary, you okay there? You staring off into the night."

"I'm just thinking."

"I put shirt and pants on ground for you. You won't get dirty."

Too late, I thought. Every time you touch me, something strange goes through me and I feel bad. My body liked being touched and I hungered for the affection ever since Dad stopped hugging me when I started to bleed. 'Don't mess around with boys' Mom says again, almost like she's saying it in my ear. Artie's no boy, Mother, and he touched me like you never did. He's an artist, a man, a real man. My husband. My husband. My arm started to relax as these thoughts played through my head. Artie placed his hand on my shoulder and guided me to the ground. The wet clothes stung my back with cold and I started to shiver. I rubbed my elbows with my hands, but Artie pulled my hands to his face and kissed my fingertips.

"Mary, my master artist, Mary. Don't be afraid."

Artie stretched his bare leg over me and began to rub my legs with it, the soft hairs on his thigh and calf caressing my skin like a fine sable brush. My hands began to warm as he turned them outward, kneading them with his fingertips and working them as if they were clay. They no longer were just a part of me, but they were a part of Artie and me as I let them stretch over my head. 'Don't mess with boys. Don't mess with boys' I heard, but my arms, and my neck, and my shoulders convulsed with pleasure as Artie's soft mouth painted them with kisses.

Both of his legs now stroked mine, and in a moment, he lay on top of me. My back arched toward him as he kissed my breasts and now my body was a canvas stretched before him.

"Oh, Mary. Mary," he whispered softly.

My arms and legs pulled his body closer as his hands sculpted my flesh into moments of chilling pleasure. His breath was hot against my skin. When he reached down to my most private place, I heard the rain and smelled the rotten camp fire again. My heart pounded with fear and my body clenched in a frozen panic.

"Why are you doing that?"

"Mary. I bring you best feeling now."

Don't mess with boys. Don't mess with boys. His body was tense against mine and I felt something swollen against my thigh.

"No. I'm scared. Something's wrong."

He kissed my neck and rubbed his cheek against my face.

"All is okay. Think of our art, and beauty, and Paris."

"And getting married?"

Artie was kissing my belly. Did he say it? Did he really say 'yes'? Paris. Art. Love. Marriage. This is how it all begins, I thought. This is creating love. My body relaxed and Artie's hands touched me lightly, and in a moment, my flesh was searing. I clutched his body as tears streamed down my face. Is this how a masterpiece begins?

"Why you no start new picture, then?" Artie asked me a few days later.

I shifted on the stool in the garage, the unseasonable warm fall day making my skirt stick to my thighs. Dad stood at his work bench and pounded away at a crooked brass hinge while Bing Crosby's voice crooned 'The Nearness of You.'

"I haven't felt like it," I answered.

That was true, but what I couldn't tell Artie was that since we did it, I wasn't able to do much except for think about him. Just the night before, I woke up at about two in the morning, my stomach actually aching when I thought about Artie. I wanted us to be close like we were that day. Close in that way again.

"You gonna get in troubles with Miss Hogrebe," Artie said. He scraped a pink eraser across one section of his drawing of a cello and a clarinet and when he flicked the particles off the page, they landed on my arm and looked like burnt hairs. I raised my arm to his eye level.

"Sorry."

As his fingers dusted off the erasures, my chest constricted a breath. My face flushed with heat.

"I'll finish my one painting she's been hounding me about, don't you worry. Why don't you stop for a minute?"

I reached under the workbench and presented Artie with a basket covered by a checkered red cloth. He glanced at it and rolled his eyes.

"Now what you make me?"

I folded back the napkin to reveal a pile of oatmeal cookies that swelled with raisins.

"Take a break."

"You gonna gets me fat with all these cookies, and pies, and rolls you been making. No wonder you do no more pictures."

Dad looked up and saw the basket of cookies. Scratching his head, he asked if he could have one. I held the basket out and he snatched up a cookie and took a bite. His eyebrows arched in approval of the flavor. He elbowed Artie.

"Hey there, Art. I'd say she's gonna make someone real happy with her baking."

"Father already best baker. Don't need another."

Artie took a cookie and set it on the workbench. He brushed off his drawing once more and held it up.

"What you think?"

"Pretty as always, Art," Dad offered.

Tensing his face up, Artie pointed the drawing directly at me.

"I think it's better than the Indian drums and corn stalks," I said.

"Don't care about that. Need to know if composition is okay."

I nodded. Artie slammed his sketchbook shut and jumped down from his stool. He seemed real irritated.

"Got to go. Thanks you, Mr. Hellman."

Artie walked out and Dad looked at me as if I knew what was bothering him. I shrugged and took off after him. When he heard me pounding behind him, he stopped.

"Artie, what's wrong?"

He crossed his arms and glared at me like I should know already.

"If you no get enough work in portfolio, can no come with me."

He stomped off, keeping a fast pace and kicking up dust as his feet pounded the ground. I couldn't keep up with him and just as we passed the Darlana's raspberry vines, I screamed at him.

"Where do you think you're going? Paris is full of Nazis!"

Artie stopped and whirled towards me. My feet were still moving and I stopped just before I smacked into him. A grin floated across his face then faded.

"New York. Can be artist and make lots of moneys there."

"How would we get there?"

"Father and Mother says they'll help me with money for a little while."

"You know my family doesn't have any money. I don't even get an allowance. Guess that's it for me."

"I find way to help you. Once there, you stay with me where I live."

"I could only do that if we were married."

Artie's brows tensed so much that the creases they made in his forehead looked like a triangle.

"We no have to do that. We can be free artists in New York."

My body heaved with disappointment. I dropped my hands to my side and my stomach felt like someone just punched me.

"You don't want to marry me?"

"I want to make art with you."

"Don't you love me?"

His sketchbook flopped onto the ground. Artie pulled me to him.

"Mary. I love you. I love what beautiful pictures you make. We gots to do lots more art. We gots to have pictures to show galleries in New York and then have others we can sell. That's what we need to do now."

He leaned to kiss me but I felt like a limp balloon inside and I turned my cheek to him. I felt his whiskers brush my skin.

"You want to walk with me home?" he asked.

I shook my head and Artie paused, not seeming to know what else to say. He touched my shoulder and walked off. He stopped once more, and I thought he was going to change his mind. He's going to run to me, pick me up, and tell me he wants to marry me.

"Mary. Sunday we work on your painting you gots to finish."

Disappointed again, I didn't really listen to what he said. My eyes followed his footsteps, each step grinding more leaves into the mosaic of yellow, orange and brown that had built up on the ground. Naked aspens and birches made spindly silhouettes against the orange sun that warmed my face even as I felt cold inside; I couldn't go with him to New York if we weren't married, and he wasn't going to marry me. A stranger feeling pulsed below the feeling of cold: a feeling that I was guilty and bad. Bad because I did that with him. You thought you were going to get married. The thought didn't make me feel any better now that I knew we weren't. As I began to walk toward home, the Darlana's raspberry vines looked like a hoard of big, brown spiders.

Just above one section of the vines, a cloud of brown dust swirled up and flared with a crimson highlight from the setting sun. An engine sputtered and coughed as the top of a dark truck peeked out above the raspberry vines. I paused as the truck pulled up to the end of the Darlana's dirt drive, and when I saw the driver, I froze. He flashed a smile toward me and I recognized the teeth that jutted slightly over his bottom lip. An arm shot out from the open truck window and waved. My heart pounded as my feet broke into a thumping gallop, and as I cut the corner of the Darlana's drive, I raced through two raspberry bushes.

7

"You okay there?" he nodded toward my knees.

I looked down and saw that long gashes crisscrossed my shins all the way around to my calves. Globules of blood formed on the edges of the cuts and tiny burgundy trails began to streak my white legs. I didn't care about the scratches, or that my legs began to sting and itch.

"Must've been the raspberry thorns."

He pulled a handkerchief from the back of his dusty denim overalls and handed it to me. I looked at it for a moment.

"Don't worry, Miss Dainty, I haven't blown any snot into it."

He broke into short bursts of guffaws that sounded like the machine guns I heard in the movies. It made me feel a little awkward.

"Thanks."

I wadded the hanky and dabbed at my legs.

"You should've gone 'round the bushes, 'stead of through 'em."

The way he said that made me think of my Mom somehow, but when I looked up at his dark eyes and sharp features, I stopped thinking about my Mom right away. He's so beautiful, I thought. My heart raced in my chest, making my breaths short. He leaned against the open truck door.

"What are you doing here, anyways?" I said, each word vying for my nervous breaths.

"I could ask you the same thing. Last time I saw you, it was downtown."

He remembered. I thought my heart was going to beat out of my chest.

"I live here."

Before I had time to blink, he popped a cigarette into the corner of his mouth and lit it, blowing a gray puff of smoke toward the sky. He shifted his weight to his right hip and his left leg vibrated like a butter churn. He moved fast, I thought.

"You a Darlana?"

"No. I live next door."

"They got a ton of raspberries coming in the spring. I'm here to pay an advance on the crop."

I glanced at his truck and saw the Murphy Produce sign that I had worked so hard to duplicate in my 'New Ulm Street' drawing. He must have seen me regard the sign.

"That's my Dad."

"So you're a Murphy?"

"Last time I checked. Andrew's the name. You want to stay on my good side, don't call me Andy. A guy who's no bigger than five seven don't want his name shortened, too."

His eyes darted up and down my body and I thought that maybe my legs were bleeding again. They weren't and when I noticed the slight smile that crossed his face, I felt awkward.

"So what's your name, Red?"

Heat stung my face. Don't blush, I thought. My face grew hotter. A breeze caught my skirt and I reached to keep it down just as my left thigh peeked out.

"Mary."

"You got nothing to be shy of, Mary. Not someone pretty as you."

"Hellman."

"What?"

"That's my last name."

Another breeze kicked up and this one sent a chill through me. I rubbed my arms from the blast of cold air. Andrew reached into his truck and tossed me a jacket.

"Here. It's getting kind of cold out here."

The navy blue jacket of heavy felt had leather arms that were the color of butter. As I slipped it on, I could smell musky hair oil. A familiar embroidered capital 'h' on the left breast made me pause.

"You went to Hopkins High?" I asked.

"Yep. Graduated last year."

"What'd you get the letter for?"

"Varsity baseball."

"You were on the champion varsity baseball team and you're still hanging around Hopkins? Why aren't you playing at one of the big colleges?"

"For one thing, I ain't all that good. For another, I'm sick of school."

Andrew lifted his left hand and as he ran it through his wavy, dark brown hair, I saw that his fingers were long and well manicured. Even though they were so neat, they looked thick and strong.

"Did you ever try out?"

"Nah, why? I got myself a good job at my dad's grocery. I'm okay for now."

The raspberry vines scratched out a rustling noise and some of the last leaves on the aspens came twirling down the street. Strands of my hair suddenly covered my face like an itchy net. Andrew reached out and lifted my hair from my face, stopping a moment to run his fingers through my hair. I blushed again.

"I gotta go now."

Slipping his jacket off, the leather and felt massaged my skin and I caught one last waft of his hair oil. I handed it back to him, then grabbed tight to my skirt that was beginning to billow.

"You just gonna disappear again for another year?" he asked.

I shrugged, but inside, I had the urge to leap into his arms.

"This Sunday, we play our last softball game with our league. Come and watch me play. If you think I'm good enough, maybe I'll try out for a college team."

"Really?"

"No. But I thought it sounded good."

I laughed.

"Okay. Where?"

"The baseball diamond at the high school. At noon, just after church lets out."

Artie and New York flashed into my mind and I guess Andrew could see the hesitation.

"What's the matter? Need more time after church or something?"

"No. I'll be there."

Andrew's face broke out into a smile that was so wide it divided his face in half. He tossed the jacket into the truck and hopped in after.

"I'll see you then, Mary Hellman."

I didn't know much about softball or baseball and didn't care about them, either. But that Sunday, despite winds that howled in from Canada, Andrew's team played its last game. My legs and arms shivered as I sat on the faded green bleacher. When his team was in the field, Andrew played that spot between second and third base. Most every hit in the game bounced or flew in his direction and every time, his lanky arm scooped up the ball and catapulted it to wherever the batter was headed. One out the umpire called. Then another, and another through the whole game.

By the end, Andrew's team was already ahead by five points when he got up to bat. Each time he batted, he glanced at me and smiled. But this time, he stepped up to home plate and swung at the air a couple times before letting the bat rest against his shoulder. The pitcher wound up, but Andrew stepped out of the batter's box and the pitcher paused. Andrew took off his cap and bowed to me. The few other kids in the bleachers with me bundled up against the wind and threatening gray sky, whistled and cheered.

Andrew stepped back into the batter's box. The pitcher fired the ball like a cannon shot, and Andrew swung his bat and connected the ball with a sharp crack. The softball soared over the infielders, the outfielders, and then the back fence. Cheers and whistles erupted around me again as Andrew tossed his bat aside and strolled onto each base. When he got to home plate, he tapped it with his toe and threw me a kiss. All the players in the dugout and the ones on the field descended on Andrew, while slaps on the back and handshakes flew in all directions.

Andrew stepped away from the crowd and walked to the backstop. Weaving his fingers through the gray chain links, he leaned back and stretched his arms and legs.

"The guys all want to go get some burgers and beer. You wanna come?"

"I can't drink beer."

He rotated his head toward the ball players, then gazed back at me. Sweat shined on his temples and narrow nose bridge.

"You don't have to order beer."

I knew he wanted to go be with his friends but I was disappointed. I wanted some time just with him.

"Why don't you go have burgers with your buddies? We can do something else some other time."

Andrew must have seen the disappointment in my face or else he could tell from the tone of my voice that I really didn't want him to go.

"Nope. I'm gonna spend the rest of the day with you. Go on over to the truck and I'll be there in a couple of seconds."

A short time later, we were inside Andrew's truck on our way through town. It was then that I discovered he wasn't much of a talker and I felt so strange riding in his truck that I couldn't say much either. Even though both side windows were rolled down, the cab of the truck smelled like old potatoes and brown apples mixed with stale sweat. I shifted my body against the cracked and faded brown leather seat, snorting a deep breath of the fresh dusk air.

"Sorry 'bout the smell in here. Me and my dad can't figure how to get rid of it and I'm sort of used to it."

I leaned back toward Andrew because I thought I would hurt his feelings if I kept trying to get fresh breaths. An ivory white statue of a veiled woman sat on his dashboard and she looked familiar to me.

"Who's that statue of?"

Andrew's face crinkled up and it was the first time I saw anything but a smile in his eyes.

"You gotta be kidding." His voice tone sounded irritated.

"I recognize her but I can't remember who she is."

"The Virgin Mary. Jesus' mother." The words hissed out of his

100

mouth and sounded mean.

"I know she's Jesus' mother. I just never saw a little statue of her like that one."

Andrew shook his head and exhaled through his clenched teeth, making a 'shh' sound. He glanced at me sideways and his face started to soften.

"You're not Catholic, I guess."

"No. Lutheran. We don't even go to church that much."

He put his hand on my knee and it felt dry and warm. I pressed my knee against his palm on impulse even though I knew I should pull it back. His hand tightened and closed like an eagle talon.

"You might as well know now. I was born and raised Catholic. I pray to the saints and the Virgin Mary to protect me."

What did he mean by 'know now'? My heart skipped and raced.

"Whatever you believe is fine. For me, the spirits in the earth and sky are all that matter," I said.

He could have been a bank robber and I wouldn't have cared right then. Not the way he made me tingle.

"Huh?" he said.

"We can talk about all that some other time."

But his face was creased with confusion. He cleared his throat.

"So how'd you like the game?" he asked.

"You were amazing. It seemed like every point scored or every out had something to do with you."

He slammed on the brakes and turned toward me. His eyes looked like a frightened child when he spoke, his hands moving like airplane propellers.

"You really think I'm that good?"

"I don't know enough about it."

"'Cause I been thinking about trying out for the Twins. Everybody says I should do that in Spring." His left hand chopped the air for emphasis.

I shrugged then said, "I'm trying to get into art school and everybody thinks I should. It doesn't mean that I'm sure of myself."

Andrew's brows knitted and a strange smile crossed his face.

"Baseball's a little tougher than art, come on. I seen your drawing and it's good and all, but it's nothing like someone who can throw a knuckle ball or score a triple."

Andrew started the car back onto the street, but I had the urge to leap out of the cab; that was the second time Andrew said something that made me think of my mother and I didn't like it.

"You look kind'a pouty."

101

He seemed to be able to read my feelings again, and I was taken aback by it. I raised my face to him and his deep brown eyes sparkled with humor.

"I'm okay."

"Here's Svenhard's. Let's eat."

My family had never eaten at a restaurant as far as I could remember, let alone at Svenhard's, Hopkins's best smorgasbord. People at school sometimes talked about Svenhard's and its huge variety of foods. As Andrew and I made our way past the steaming steel pans of meatballs, potatoes, vegetables and breads that combined into a spicy, yeasty cloud of aromas, I understood why people jawed about it so much.

The other thing that made the place so great was that you could go back for as many helpings as you wanted. I didn't know if I'd do that as I scooped a piece of rare roast beef onto my plate next to a small mound of baby potatoes, but I was sure that Andrew couldn't possibly go back for seconds when I saw his plate heaped so high that it looked like a green bean, white potato, and pink ham mountain. His upper arm muscle bulged under the weight of his servings.

We took a seat away from the serving table, in a quieter corner where the din of clanking stoneware plates and clinking flatware died down to a soft hail. At this distance, the aromas of food seemed to meld into the scent of buttered, cooked cabbage. Andrew smiled at me silently, then crossed himself as Catholics do, folded his hands, and closed his eyes. A whisper of a prayer caught my ear, mostly because each 's' he spoke thrust through his front teeth. He crossed himself again, picked up a glass saltshaker dulled from greasy hands, and dusted his mountain of food.

I was still unfolding my napkin when Andrew crammed three forkfuls of food into his mouth. The sides of his cheeks bulged on either side of his thin lips that cushioned the white tips of his protruding teeth. His eyes were closed as he took deep breaths, obviously pleased with the flavors in his mouth. He shoveled in two more bites before he swallowed the others without ever looking up at me. I was struck by the innocent, almost child-like way he concentrated on his food, and how his front teeth rested on his lower lip as he chewed. He probably didn't realize they looked like piano keys and I guessed he never even thought about them. Not with food in front of him, anyways. 'He's a baby' I thought.

But he didn't eat like a baby; I was still picking at my roast beef when Andrew returned with a second plate full of chicken, vegetables, and biscuits. As he sat down, his belly bulged out slightly from his lanky frame, spilling over his belt like a roll of pretzel dough. He licked his fingers.

"Did you ever see so much good food?"

I shook my head as he raised his plate to his nose and took a deep breath.

"Here. You gotta try some of this chicken."

Andrew sawed off a piece of moist looking chicken breast and held his fork out to me. I felt funny taking a bite off his fork so I reached out for the morsel but Andrew stopped me.

"I don't have anything catchy."

I nodded and leaned over to take the bite but stopped again. I was going to have to touch his hand to steady the fork so that I could take the chicken. He must have noticed my hesitation because he nodded at me. I grabbed his hand and a bomb seemed to explode inside me. The chicken slid into my mouth and Andrew's head bobbed up and down, his eyes flaring with enthusiasm as I chewed.

"That is good," I said, but it wasn't the tender chunk of chicken in my mouth I was thinking about. "Everything here has been good."

He smiled and scooped more food into his mouth. Andrew ate fast, like it seems he did everything, and even though he scooped in several bites of food at a time, he still chewed with his mouth closed, except for the tips of his front teeth. He dabbed at his mouth with a wadded napkin.

"You know, when I was six and seven years old, my dad's grocery was losing money and we sometimes had to skip dinner. I never starved so much in my life like I did then." Half of Andrew's plate of food had been devoured when he said that.

"We had my Mom's biscuits for dinner a lot back then,' I said. 'I think even my fat sister Irma lost some weight."

"Sister's fat, huh? Is she as pretty as you?"

My face went hot with embarrassment, but Andrew didn't seem to notice.

"What about you?" I asked. "You have a fat sister or brother?"

"Just an older brother, John. He's fat 'cause he sits around all day in his big office in Philly counting his money."

"He rich?"

"He's getting there."

"What's he do?"

"Buys little companies then sells 'em to make money, I guess."

"That what you want to do?"

"No. I want to go to school."

"To study what?"

Andrew wiped his mouth with the back of his hand, and then leaned forward like he didn't want anyone else to hear.

"Maybe to be a doctor. I got decent marks in chemistry and math. I'm not sure yet."

He finished his second plate and stood up.

103

"You can't be wanting more?" I said.

He shook his head, rubbed his stomach that now looked like a bicycle tire, and stretched his arms over his head.

"No. Gotta get some of that dessert."

A couple minutes later, Andrew came back with another stoneware plate, but instead of meat and potatoes, this one had a piece of chocolate cake, a chocolate éclair, four sugar cookies, and a slice of apple pie mounded on it. A grin stretched across Andrew's face as he sat the plate down between us.

"You should'a seen how mad they got when I grabbed this plate instead of one of those little dessert ones," he said. "I couldn't of fit a piece a cake on one of those. What's the matter?"

I set aside my dinner plate and leaned back in my chair. My stomach was full and I couldn't think of eating anything else.

"That's an awful lot of sweet stuff."

"Come on, Mary. It's for both of us."

Andrew wiped off his dinner fork with his napkin, then sliced into the chocolate cake. His eyes closed again as he released the bite into his mouth and rolled the cake around. He released a deep breath.

"Mmm. You gotta try this."

With Andrew's moans and groans of pleasure, I knew I wouldn't be disappointed. I again steadied Andrew's hand, and again the bomb exploded inside me as I took the bite from his fork, but this time, our eyes locked and I saw Andrew's brown eyes grow darker as his pupils dilated. A shiver went through me as the morsel slid off the metal fork, and Andrew tipped the fork slightly to help it in.

"Don't forget the frosting" he said as he pulled the tines back over my lips. My mouth tightened and scraped off the creamy glob as the fork slid out.

Andrew's eyes brightened with that same food excitement he had over the chicken, and the bite of cake became a mud of chocolate in my mouth. It was a chocolate flavor I recognized, and as it floated over my tongue, I remembered the chocolate candy Mr. Janek served before dinner. Adrenaline burned through me. I jumped up.

"Oh God!"

The fork clanked onto the table as Andrew dropped it with a start, slamming back against his seat.

"What? What!" his light voice now falsetto with alarm.

"Artie. We gotta go. Come on."

I ran out the door of the restaurant, brushing crumbs off my skirt and straightening my blouse. Embarrassment pulsed through me, then a hollow feeling of betrayal. Why was I there with Andrew? Artie, my Artie.

104

I saw his face as it collapsed in hurt. What about New York? But I don't want to leave now. Andrew is so beautiful. So funny. Maybe Artie forgot our art date. Yeah. I hope so.

Andrew burst through the door, shoving the white lining of his pocket back into his pants as his keys jingled in his hand. His face was white with fright.

"Someone dead or something?"

"No. Everything's okay. I gotta get home."

"Wait a second, okay?"

I folded my arms in frustration as he ran back into the restaurant. He emerged with folded napkin that looked lumpy. Holding it out to me, he unfolded the edges and there sat two cookies from his dessert plate.

"I didn't want you to miss dessert."

I grabbed one and shook my head as he led me back to the truck, his mouth working furiously on his cookie.

Two chunks of cookie, gold and brown, remained in my hand as we pulled up in front of my house. The porch light burned bright as both mom and dad rushed through the front door and looked suspiciously toward us. As I got out of the truck, they folded their arms and their expressions went from curious to stone. I jumped down and my skirt stuck to the seat from behind, raising it up to my thighs. Dad looked away but Mom stepped to the edge of the porch. Her eyes darted from me to the side of the truck and back to me, her brow folding over with confusion.

"Mary, you're real late, girl," she said.

Andrew's truck door screeched shut and before I could say anything, he ran ahead of me and extended his hand to Mom.

"Andrew Murphy, Ma'am."

Mom's face softened and a smile creeped between her thin lips. She yanked the gray dish towel from her shoulder and wiped her right hand.

"You one of the produce market Murphys?"

"Yes, Ma'am." Andrew reached out for dad's hand but Dad only nodded.

"Mr. Hellman," Andrew said.

Mom tossed her dishtowel back over her shoulder and stepped past Andrew, the steps of the porch creaking under her weight.

"Nice truck," she said.

"If you like farting away gas," Andrew said.

Dad's face glazed in shock, and Mom's eyes narrowed into slits. My stomach knotted. But Mom burst into a laugh. She lay a hand on Andrew's shoulder and Dad stood with his own arms folded tightly.

"Well, can I take a look? We ain't had a good vehicle for years," she said.

Andrew glanced at me and I shrugged and nodded, not really sure why Mom would be so interested. They walked over to the side of the truck and I kept my eyes on them. Mom laughed again. I dropped my eyes away from Mom and Andrew and kept them aimed at the ground -- I couldn't bring them to Dad's face -- and stepped up the porch steps.

"Artie sure missed you," Dad said quietly.

My stomach twisted like a dead balloon and my shoulders became lead. A deep exhale seemed to come from out of nowhere in my body.

"So he didn't forget."

"Nope. He's a good boy, that Artie."

Dad's eyes never left Andrew and Mom as he said that.

"He's okay."

"He cares a lot for you and I think you should mind who you're foolin' with."

Now I looked up at Dad, my heart pounding with anger. But the worry in his eyes took the wind out of my rage.

"Andrew's no fool."

"Any boy who keeps a girl out till night without meeting her folks first ain't no genius."

Andrew's laugh fired off in short bursts and Dad's eyebrows went into their doubtful arch.

"Dad, I watched his game at Hopkins High today. I'm the one who told him I wanted to eat after the game and when it got so late, it was my fault."

I stepped past Dad as he began to scratch his head. Mom's laugh erupted and she sounded like a dying moose behind us.

"Artie says he came by to help you 'cause you're having trouble in your art class," Dad said over his shoulder. It was almost a whisper but it brimmed with disappointment.

If a tornado blew out of nowhere right then, I couldn't have felt more knocked back. I leaned against a porch support.

"He told you that? He shouldn't have." Now I was doing the whispering.

"You should'a been here like you said you would. You listen, girl."

Dad's voiced slipped into a deep rumble that was almost a growl. Grabbing me by my shoulders, he turned my face to his. His eyes pierced through me.

"Don't go wasting your talent. You wanna be an artist and you got somebody who's helping you with that."

I shook loose from his grip and he stepped back like he thought I was going to hit him.

"Maybe I need more than art."

106

Dad looked at the porch like he was ashamed of me, and he tapped a loose porch board with the toe of his boot.

"Stick with him, Mary," his voice cracked.

I stepped toward him and touched his arm.

"Dad."

"I like him a lot."

Mom and Andrew walked up and I couldn't believe that they were arm-in-arm. Mom dabbed at the pink corners of her eyes that were wet from laughing.

"This boy's got a wit, Ernest. You should take a listen sometime."

My head whirled with confusing and conflicting feelings. Mom liked Andrew? How could she? Dad liked Artie? Guilt. Ecstasy. Embarrassment. All the feelings tore at me, making me feel dull.

"Andrew. Whyn't you come in for some coffee?" Mom said.

But Andrew must have seen the torment in me again. His eyes began to soften and moisten on their edges. I shook my head slightly.

"No. I gotta go. Can I say bye to Mary?"

"Only if you promise you'll come again," Mom said.

Andrew's eyes looked at me with a hope and a plea and when they sparkled into a smile, I knew he had read the desperate 'yes' in my own.

"Yeah. I will."

"Well, then, Ernest, let's leave these two alone."

Mom's face broke out into the biggest smile I had ever seen on her face. She threw open the screen door and scampered into the house. Dad hesitated and stared at both of us.

"Ernest!" Mom screamed from inside the house.

Dad backed toward the door like an anxious watchdog, never taking his eyes off us until he pulled it open. He went in.

"I don't think he likes me much," Andrew said.

He took me by the arm and led me to the driver's side of the truck. His face twisted with concern.

"You never told me why we rushed out of Svenhard's. Who's Artie?"

My throat closed up because at that moment, I didn't really know. I rubbed my arms and Andrew reached out and pulled me to him. His hair oil, his musky body, and his strong grip flushed all other thoughts out of my head. From deep in my stomach, I felt a rush of warmth and chills at the same time. He brought my face to his and kissed me gently on the cheek. The fountain of energy surging through me caused my hands to grab his face in reflex, his wiry whiskers tickling my fingertips as I guided his mouth to mine. My tongue reached eagerly for his lips, and he collapsed into the kiss like a lion in surrender. He breathed and I exhaled, I exhaled and he breathed. We were one in our kiss.

That kiss made my lips tingle every time I recreated it in my head and the day I sat down in Miss Hogrebe's classroom to finish 'New Ulm Street,' it was like that kiss drove me to finish it. I wanted more than anything to show it to Andrew, to have him see that even though baseball was harder like he said, my art wasn't easy. Orange, yellow, and red lit up my pallet as I dipped and smeared my brush to load it. Streaks of warm colors brightened the gray of the pencil, making a hot summer day emerge as my brush glided across the page. My brush felt like it had a will of its own and I felt free and unlimited as I dipped and spread more color.

"Why you work so fast? Losing good details of drawing," Artie said.

"I want this to feel impressionistic." I couldn't tell him that a kiss from the subject of the painting spurred me on, and right then, I didn't want to. He still smarted from my standing him up last Sunday, and I sure wasn't ready to tell him that Andrew and me had been to the movies and to the smorgasbord one more time since Sunday.

"You make mistake by missing details. Details make picture like life."

Something in his tone made me look up. His eyes were unusually wide open, his pupils like black beads, and his mouth was a tight line between his mustache and beard. The black beret and black vest he wore ever since reading Dostoyevsky in our literature class added to his dark mood. Artie's face was framed by the window behind him through which I could see the edge of the campus field and a spindly, leafless aspen that looked like a claw reaching for thick gray clouds that spilled frozen rain.

He's sad and he thinks something has changed, I thought. But it hadn't: I still loved his mind, and I still wanted to do my art with him. Maybe even marry him if he asked me. Why couldn't I tell him about Andrew then? Because Andrew made me feel things I never felt with him before. Just being near Andrew set my whole body on edge and I felt both enticed and ashamed.

"I don't care so much about the details right now. I want the feeling to be captured."

Artie's eyes narrowed and I thought he looked at the drawing with suspicion.

"What is feeling trying to capture, anyway?"

If I could only answer that for myself, I thought. The classroom clock clicked onto the hour and I looked up to see that it was four o'clock. I glanced around the empty classroom, at the jars of paint that smelled like starch, then at the piles of colored pencil's with their wax and cedar smell, and at an easel crusted with drops of paint on which sat Miss Hogrebe's sample charcoal drawing of a nude woman. A breeze whirred into life outside and scattered frozen rain against the window like pebbles.

"I'm glad Miss Hogrebe let us stay after to work, aren't you?" I said.

"Especially 'cause your Mom told me no come over no more."

That's because of Andrew again, I wanted to say. She likes him more than you.

"So what is feeling?" Artie asked again.

"I guess it's summer. With all its sun and warmth."

He nodded but I could tell he didn't believe that. He dipped his own brush into a small jar and stirred it, sending tendrils of turpentine into my nose. Artie's eyes darted toward my painting, resting on Andrew a second before he spoke.

"Think I know way to get you money for New York."

New York! I hadn't thought about it for a week, and never had two syllables sent such a shock wave through my body as they did at that moment. New York, art galleries, fame. New York. No Andrew. Three syllables that stung as I thought of them. I swirled a dab of purple on my brush, then picked up a hint of green and stabbed the leaves onto my painting.

"Mary. You go crazy with colors."

"So, what."

My chest tightened with anger, but I didn't know why. I whipped my brush into my water cup to rinse it, the color leaping off it like it was afraid. I drove my brush into orange and then brown, and spanked the colors onto my drawing.

"Mary, you still want New York, don't you?"

Yes. I wanted New York. I wanted Artie. I wanted Andrew. Slamming down my brush, I looked at 'New Ulm Street.' It looked more like a palette than a painting.

"I've gotta fix this. It's gotta be okay."

"'Cause this first time we together in over week and half."

I looked over at Artie and he now sat with his arms folded. Another gust blew more frozen rain at the window.

"Mary? New York?"

I didn't know what to say; I didn't know what I wanted.

"Yes."

Artie let out a big sigh -- was it relief? I didn't know. He started painting again.

"Oh, yeah, Mary. Three weeks is the Thanksgiving. Mama want to see you then. Can come?"

I could see the platters of meats, baskets of bread, trays of pastries that Mrs. Janek was bound to prepare. They made me think of the smorgasbord, and Andrew going back for thirds on the fried chicken.

"We'll see, Artie."

The next night, I hadn't given Artie a thought. As I tucked the hair comb over my right ear, I glanced in the mirror one more time to make sure my dress sat evenly on my shoulders. The mother-of-pearl buttons made a line from the base of my throat to the middle of my chest, looking like a broken necklace against the pine green cotton. My hair flamed red against the green of my outfit. I turned in the mirror and made the gathered material of the dress billow and turn below the cinched waist. Swaying my hips from side to side, I held myself as if Andrew and I were dancing. I never went to any of the school dances before, and now I was Cinderella. My prince, my prince I said to the mirror.

A knock at the front door burst my fantasy. I dashed to my bedroom door but paused when I saw 'New Ulm Street' sitting against the wall. All the time I was getting ready, making sure that every strand of hair or spot of rouge was just right, I hadn't thought about whether or not I wanted to show the painting to Andrew. It was an experiment in a different style, and I wasn't sure. I snatched it up.

"Let me see my Andrew," Mom said. Her gray eyes sparkled as she bounded into the sitting room. Dad was stretched out in his chair. He nodded and rubbed his arms when I let Andrew and the twenty-degree, November night air in the front door. Mom threw her fat arms around Andrew, making them jiggle, then held him out and regarded his black jacket.

"This leather?"

"Sure is, Slim."

Andrew used the nickname he gave my Mom a few nights before, and I couldn't believe he said it right to her face. Dad looked up at me, his eyes looking like he was ready for Mom to explode. I stood still. Mom slapped Andrew on the side of his jacket, making a popping sound. She put her arm around his neck and turned him toward Dad.

"You ever think Mary would'a' " landed someone so comely, Ernest?"

Dad shrugged.

I agreed with Mom, though. Andrew wore that black leather jacket over a gray, button down shirt. His thick hair was slicked back with pomade and he smelled spicy. He slipped his long hand into mine and I could feel the pulse of his heart through the thick warmth.

"She ain't so hard on the eyes, either," Dad said.

"I guess she's an okay substitute for you, Slim."

Mom yanked her apron up to her face and snorted a laugh into it.

Dad shook his head, reached for the radio, and then sat back as the opening music to 'Sergeant Preston of the Yukon' romped from the set. Andrew glanced down at 'New Ulm Street.'

"What you got there, Mary?"

I turned the painting toward Andrew. His expression shifted from genuine interest to sincere puzzlement.

"It's sure ... colorful."

All the breath pumped from my body in a single contraction, making me light headed while my face burned with embarrassment.

"I call it 'New Ulm Street'," I said.

He shook his head and shrugged.

"Where we met the first time."

He looked up at me and I could see a smile force on his lips.

"Oh. Well, I don't know much about art. It looks like a doozy, though."

I let 'New Ulm Street' drop to my side. Mom stepped between Andrew and me.

"So where you taking my Andrew, girl?" Mom asked. "Oh. I meant my girl, Andrew."

"There's a dance over at the VFW post in town. We're gonna go there and cut a mean rug."

Mom's face brightened like someone turned on a light switch. She grabbed Andrew's hand with her left, and lifted her housedress just above the knee with her right. She stomped and jerked her legs and hips.

"A little Jitterbug," she said.

Andrew followed each of Mom's stomps and jerks, gyrating like a Jitterbug champion himself. Mom threw aside Andrew's hand. Dad's brow furrowed and a smile crossed his face, but it almost looked like he was getting ready to cry. Dad sprinted to the radio and rotated the dial until he found a raucous old song from the twenties.

"This one's too old for you to know," Mom said.

Mom raised her elbows and flattened her palms, stepping back and forth and pounding the floor with each dance step. Photos in wood frames of Grandma and Granddad rattled against the sitting room wall. Her jerking movements made me think of the way the flag in front of Hopkins High flapped when the wind roared in from Lake Minnetonka. I wondered if that's why they called some ladies from the twenties 'flappers.'

"This one's the Charleston," she hollered.

Mom grabbed Dad's arm and yanked him to his feet.

"Come on, Ernest. Let's show 'em."

Dad's legs and arms jerked as stiffly as if he had sat in his chair for a week and he was a slow shadow to Mom's frenetic pace. Andrew laughed and swayed his shoulders to the music, but I was paralyzed and dumb struck: I never saw my Mom dance before, and I had never seen her display so much joy. She switched between Dad and Andrew and a sweat began to build on her forehead. The song ended as a sponsor's voice boomed in. Mom stopped and bent at the waist to catch her breath, dabbing her brow with her apron. She glanced up at me.

"Mary, you little stick in the mud. You gotta learn to dance."

Dad stepped back to his chair, his chest bellowing a bit, but he touched my shoulder gently as he passed. Andrew straightened his leather jacket. Mom took a deep breath and said through a smile:

"Andrew, you listen to me. This girl's too serious, thinking about her art and such all the time. You take her out and show her how to have some fun."

"You can count on me, Slim."

Andrew did keep his promise at the VFW dance. A thirty-piece band blared big band hits of all kinds, and we danced both slow and fast. On the wooden dance floor that echoed and rumbled under our dancing feet, we were surrounded by dancers of mixed ages: some as young as Andrew and me, others looking as old as their late twenties. When 'Rum and Coca Cola' started, Andrew stopped dancing and led me to the refreshment table. Three men in uniform, with three young girls decked out in taffeta dresses, stood by the punch bowl.

"Army," Andrew said as we approached.

Just as I reached for the silver ladle that sat in the cut glass bowl that was as big as a bathtub, one of the soldiers plucked it out, never even glancing at me as he made a fervent point to his friends.

"Hitler is like Napoleon. His next stop is gonna be the U.S. We're gonna have to get involved."

The other two men in uniform scoffed at him as he scooped up a ladle of the red punch, clanging it against the side of the bowl and filling two cups. He handed the cups to the two ladies and they disappeared into the crowd. I glanced at Andrew.

"You think that soldier was right about the war?"

"It's in the Lord's hands. Whatever happens, it's His will."

The punch coated my tongue with a cherry syrup glaze that only quenched my thirst because it was cold, and I paused before my next sip. Andrew downed his cup and the punch gave him a red mustache.

"Good, isn't it?"

"It's kind'a sweet."

"I know. That's why I like it."

He ladled himself another cup but just as he was about to bring it to his lips, the last dance was announced. Andrew grabbed my cup of punch, stacked it inside his, set the cups on the table, and yanked me back onto the dance floor. I was relieved when the slow rhythm of 'Moonlight Serenade' began, because Andrew had snickered at me during all the fast dances -- I didn't inherit my Mom's dancing talent, I guess. But during the slow ones, Andrew seemed more uncomfortable, holding me out from him at arms length and touching my hand without holding it.

This last dance, he held me out even further, his forearms making two stiff rafters as if I smelled or something. He pulled me along and my feet plodded between his, but my arms started to grow sore from reaching so far for him. As we turned, I planted my left leg tighter around his, throwing him off balance a moment. I fell into him and pulled on his waist for support, which brought us so close that his mouth rested against my ear. His breath whispered past my ear and a chill shot through me as I felt him so close.

"Not so close," he whispered.

My chest felt like an iron was pressing it. Did he think I looked ugly? Was my dress too plain for him? I looked away and saw the other couples dancing close and felt left out. But Andrew laid his cheek against my hair and the pressure of his cheek against my head blotted out any disappointing thoughts. I turned my face toward his and our lips brushed.

"No. It isn't time," he said.

His cheek was now against my lips, his whiskers abrading my lips delicately. That, taken with his firm, dry grip on my hand and the strength of his body pressing against mine made my head feel like bubbles. My heart pounded and a picture of my father and mother kissing flashed through my head. Throwing my head back, I again met his lips and this time, I pushed my mouth against his. The music faded and we stood alone. Quiet laughter from gawking dancers broke the spell of our kiss.

As we drove home from the VFW hall, the spell of that kiss had not left me. We didn't speak a word and as Andrew drove the truck along Minnetonka Avenue, the headlights made the naked aspens into gray, lacy phantoms through the frost that framed the windshield with a sparkling sheen. I wished I had a pencil right then to sketch the gray figures, but when I glanced at Andrew's beautiful profile, I stopped thinking about drawing. The night air poked at my cheeks with electric jabs. Andrew reached out and grabbed my hand and a wave of heat flashed through my body.

"Do we have to go home now?" I asked.

"It's kind'a late, Mary."

Those words fell on me. I didn't want the feeling I had to end and I wasn't ready to say goodnight. I may not have been Cinderella but I also wasn't ready for pumpkin time, either. Just up the street I could see a storefront I had walked past before. Now I had a strange feeling of almost owning it.

"Isn't that Murphy's Produce coming up?"

"Yep. That's our place."

"Can we stop?"

"For what? You got a sudden urge for a rutabaga or something?"

"Pumpkin."

"Huh?"

"I've never been inside. I just wanna look around."

"All right. But it's just a bunch of old fruit and vegetables."

Moments later, Andrew's key thumped the door lock open. We walked in, our shoes scuffing against the concrete floor, and I was overwhelmed by fresh and rotten odors. Oranges? Rotten cabbage and mushrooms? Fertilizer? The scents played a sick and sweet game with my nose. Andrew popped on the light and wooden bins mounded with fruits and vegetables lined the walls and made three long rows. A bin of potatoes was swollen with brown tubers, but right next to it, a bin of onions looked picked over and shabby.

"'Cause we're late in the harvest of a lot of things, our stock is kind'a seedy right now."

Andrew said this with a tone of voice I had never heard him use. It was as if he was trying to sell them to me, and his attitude was absent of feeling. He stood near me with his shoulders so stiff behind him that he looked like a scarecrow.

My heels tapped as I walked up one of the rows and glanced at each bin. I never had seen so many different kinds of fruits and vegetables and all the bins seemed full to my eye. A bin at the end of the row was loaded and exploded with color; red apples reflected the yellow light overhead like a pile of rubies. I stood at the bin and the scent of sweet apple wafted up. Andrew walked over to two large sliding doors that looked like washboards and rapped on them with his hand, making them rumble and clang like a broken church bell.

"We get shipments Monday through Saturday from all over the country. All deliveries are made through these doors."

He still spoke with his salesman's tone, but his voice also cracked like he was nervous. As he stood next to the door with his arms folded, he looked like a frightened boy and I didn't know what scared him. I need to take care of him, I thought, and I walked over and lay a hand on his face. He turned his face away as I rubbed his cheek.

"Over there's where we do the counting and weighing."

I slipped my arms around him and lay my head on his chest. He kissed the top of my head lightly.

114

"I gotta get you home now."

He stepped back and took my arms from his waist and pushed me away, causing a few strands of my hair to stick to his chest like a web. I swiped them back into place.

"No. This night isn't over."

"Yes it is."

I grabbed his face with both of my hands and his eyes shut in reaction to my touch.

"Mary. Stop it. Don't tempt me, please."

My fingertips found the flesh just behind his ear and I traced the line of his hair. His skin was tender and slightly oily. He jerked my hands forward and held them in front of his face. He whipped his mouth around and kissed my hands.

"Your hands make me feel so good. I love your hands."

My face reached up to his and our lips met as if they never had touched before, melding and folding over each other with greed. Andrew's arms enveloped me and whatever resistance he had now withered into a frantic cascade of lips against flesh.

"Forgive me. Forgive me," he whispered.

Under the gold light of Murphy's Produce and Grocery, sometime before midnight, the last thing I saw before closing my eyes and lying back was the bin of ruby apples.

"Mary, take the apples out of the oven," Mom hollered Thanksgiving afternoon a couple weeks later.

The heat and aroma of apples baking in cinnamon, along with the rich aroma of a roasting turkey filled my nostrils as I pulled the oven open with a creak. Mom was darting about the kitchen, more frantic than usual as she prepared our Thanksgiving dinner. She thrust a jar of raspberry preserves in my face as I set the apples on the counter.

"Stick a finger in and tell me what you think."

The grainy raspberry jam rolled on my tongue and burned with sour flavor. My face must have screwed up from the tartness.

"Perfect. You gotta always remember about raspberry jam, Mary. No matter how much sugar you add, you still get the burn of the sour berries."

Mom had been handing out her kitchen tips ever since she met Andrew. I guess she figured that I had a lot to learn if I was going to be a good wife.

"I wish to heck I knew where your sister Irma and Ben are, since you didn't manage to invite someone special."

"Andrew's not been around, Mom. I don't know why."

"Well, it's gotta be something you done. You best figure it out before you lose him. It's three o'clock already. Don't anybody have any respect for Thanksgiving anymore?"

On this particular Thanksgiving, I didn't have much respect for it, either. I had been avoiding Artie for the last two weeks, feeling guilty about Andrew and all. And ever since that night two weeks ago in the Murphy Produce and Grocery, Andrew hadn't come by. I missed him so much that my body ached for him, and I even walked to Murphy's one day after school. The manager, Mr. Nilsson, said he wasn't around and didn't know when he'd be back. I left Andrew a note and I never heard from him.

When I woke up this morning, I was sick to my stomach again and I thought it was because of Andrew. As the sour raspberry flavor rolled in my mouth, I needed to upchuck again so I ran out of the kitchen. When I walked back in, Mom stood next to the oven, her arms rolled up on her thick sides.

"You still not feeling good?"

"It's just my stomach. Probably nerves, like you said."

"I don't need no more problems today."

She turned back to the stove because the sweet potatoes boiled over, causing butter and sugar to smoke with a burning caramel smell. She yanked them off the stove and cursed at them under her breath. The inside of my head fluttered like a butterfly was caught in it and I had to sit down. Mom whirled around when she heard the chair scrape across the floor.

"This ain't no time to sit, Mary."

"I'm a little dizzy, Mom."

Mom's eyes narrowed like she was suspecting something. Folding her arms, she leaned against the counter and stared at me. My head was too light to care what she was doing at that second and my stomach made me irritable.

"What?" I asked.

"You in the middle of your cycle? That what's wrong?"

Another wave of nausea bubbled up toward my throat, and I closed my eyes to steady my head.

"I haven't had it yet this month. I think this flu or whatever has plugged me up."

Her voice became dry and flat as a cracker.

"How long?"

"I guess about twelve days."

Mom stepped across the kitchen, each step heavy enough to rattle the dinner plates on the table. Towering right over me, she grabbed my hair and yanked it back. My scalp seared with the tension.

"Stop it. It hurts!"

"Who?!"

116

My eyes wrung with tears from the pain.

"What?"

"You're pregnant."

For a moment, I didn't feel the tension on my hair. My body seemed to collapse in on itself and I felt flatter than rolled biscuit dough. How could I be pregnant? I was only sixteen.

"Who'd you mess with? Who?!"

She pulled harder on my hair and my head made a shelf against my neck. Mom's nose jabbed against mine, and her breath was all sage and black pepper as she grunted her breaths. Images of Murphy's Produce and the hunter's lean-to flashed into my head as the electric feeling of realization shook me. The turkey sizzled and popped in the oven.

"What the hell?" Dad hollered. Mom's grip released and my head snapped forward, as my scalp pulsed with sharp pain.

"You crazy, Martha? She's not a little girl anymore."

Dad dropped Mom's hand and she stood back at the stove. Running a hand through her own hair, her body heaved with each breath.

"No kidding, Ernest."

"What's going on here?"

"Just ask her what special treat she's got in her oven," Mom said. "Happy damn Thanksgiving."

Mom threw a dishtowel across the kitchen and stormed out. Dad, his eyebrows angled back and his forehead a wrinkled dough of worry, slumped into the chair next to me. He looked at my face for a moment, and I could see him fight back the flood of disappointment building in his eyes. He said one thing.

"Is it Artie… or Andrew?"

His voice rose with Artie's name, and fell with Andrew's. It was obvious in that terrible moment what he wanted me to say. The shock of being pregnant, and the shame of having no idea which one was the father made telling the truth impossible. One or the other, I had to choose. My thoughts wandered. The Eiffel Tower. The Chrysler Building. Rubens. Rembrandt. Apples. That jaw line. Laughter.

"Mary, girl, you're dazing again. Who's the father?"

Mom walked back in and her eyes were puffy red. She almost never laughed in front of us, and never cried. But I could tell she had been crying. Her voice wrenched with anger.

"It better be who I think," she growled.

Artie's painting of his father's bakery flashed into my head. He had a life of art ahead of him. Andrew made me tingle, and I trusted him. The decision became clear.

"Andrew."

117

A slight smile waved across Mom's face and she turned away and creaked open the oven to check on the turkey. Dad's mouth tightened, and he stood so slowly that I thought his legs had frozen up. He barely spoke.

"Go get your coat, Mary. We're gonna take a ride into town."

Those were the last words Dad said to me and as we rattled along in the 1931 Ford sedan Dad had fixed up to run again, I was glad to have the wheeze and swish of the old engine to fill the silence. We pulled up to St. Anthony's Catholic Church and the car vibrated to a stop. As Dad hopped out, the engine kept sputtering and shaking the ratty leather front seat. Dad walked over to the two story, brick house right next to the church and knocked on the front door. Dad spoke quickly to a skinny, bald priest in a white apron who leaned on his broom handle with one arm as he gestured toward the street with the other.

Dad got back in the car, said nothing, and we drove on. Going down Minnetonka Avenue, I felt my stomach twist again but not with the nausea I felt before. Instead, my stomach felt like lead as we passed Murphy's Produce and I saw a sign painted in red letters that read: 'Fresh Washington apples, 15 cents a pound.' Somehow, the sign made me think of my 'New Ulm Street' painting and that sinking feeling dissolved into a yearning. Andrew. My Andrew. A pang of joy bubbled up in me as Dad slid back into the car: I'm going to see my Andrew.

When we pulled up to the house that must have been Andrew's by the way Dad glared at it, a load of cars lined either side of the street and snaked up onto the dirt and grass driveway. Dad grunted and parked us up the street. We walked back to Andrew's house but Dad stayed well ahead of me, the maple leaves crunching under his feet and his hands plunged into his red and black, checkered wool jacket. He never raised his eyes as we passed by the two story Victorian houses that looked just like they were made of gingerbread. Odors of roasting turkey and baking hams floated from stovepipes that stuck out like black eyes from the tops of the rounded shingle roofs. Each smell of food made my stomach flip a little and I was glad we were outside. Curtains were tossed back as we passed two of the houses but I couldn't see who was looking at us. Even worse, I couldn't figure why. Dad stopped at the red brick walk in front of Andrew's and nodded for me to step ahead of him.

The beige house had a powder blue trim that was flattened by the gray afternoon sky. Scraping my heels against the worn brick that must have been red once but now looked brown, I could hear voices murmur from inside the house and a sharp peel of laughter screeched as I stepped onto the long porch. Dad stepped up next to me and he jerked away when our shoulders brushed. Pulling open the screen door that whispered against its oiled hinges, Dad lifted the brass knocker that looked like a bust of an

English knight in armor. It fell heavily against its plate, clanking like a blacksmith's hammer. I noticed then that the knocker plate looked like a shield and I could just make out the engraved old English letters. It said: 'Murphy.'

The murmuring voices inside the house died down like the crickets in the raspberry patch did whenever Irma and I yelled at each other at night. Women's high heel shoes clicked above the softened voices as they approached the door. Metal grated as the door latch opened, and a woman who was four or five inches shorter than me peered up at us through the door that she kept suspiciously cracked. Her brown eyes, their whites pink from some sort of problem, narrowed and sent a jolt through me. 'Andrew's eyes' I thought, stepping back as the woman's small face, made up with red lipstick and peach rouge, folded in on itself with a snarl.

"Yeah, what?" she said with a reedy, strained voice.

Her ears are sparkling, I thought. Diamonds?

"Ma'am, I'm Ernest Hellman. This is my daughter, Mary. We need to talk to Andrew."

The woman's eyes dropped like a sneering waterfall as she scanned Dad, but when they whipped toward me, I felt an icy dismissal and a loathing. Her eyes darted back to Dad. He shifted then cleared his throat as a soft tinkle broke the silence. The woman raised a deeply cut tumbler to her lips and the ice jostled against the glass making the amber fluid sparkle as she sipped. She swallowed loudly and exhaled as if the amber stuff burned her.

"We don't work on Thanksgiving. Try us at the shop tomorrow."

Her breath smelled like old shoe polish and it must have bothered Dad, too, because he leaned back. The door slammed shut and the little woman's heels clicked away. Dad looked at me for the first time since we left home and his eyes widened like he was scared. 'Tell me this is all a joke,' they seemed to say. He dropped his head again, and then pounded on the door.

This time, a deep male voice rumbled with a laugh as the door pulled open. A man all in black, who must have been well over six feet because he made Dad look short, leered down at us. A white collar peeked out from under his black jacket and I could just see a thick brush of white hair on his head as he pursed his face into a question.

"Yes?" he said.

"Reverend, I'm --

"*Father* Haggarty, sir," the priest corrected Dad in his thick Irish accent.

"Oh. Okay, Father. The lady we were just talking to —"

"Mrs. Murphy." The priest folded his arms.

119

Andrew's Mom, I thought. Ice spears shot through me.

"Mrs. Murphy didn't give me a chance to explain," Dad said.

"It's no wonder. She's seeing to Thanksgiving dinner and all, as I think every good Christian is doing right now." The priest now sneered at us.

"My wife's getting our meal together, Father. I didn't come out in the cold with my girl here to chew the fat about godly ways."

"What is it you need, then?"

"We need to talk to Andrew. It ain't regarding work, either."

Dad spoke forcefully like I never heard him before. The priest seemed to understand because his face softened. He stepped aside and invited us in. The voices that murmured outside now roared and echoed off the tall, dark wood walls of this first room. A glass case full of china, crystal, and silver glared from chandelier light overhead and I almost needed to cover my eyes. Two doorways stood on either side of the room, and both were surrounded by dark, deeply carved wood. Through the one on the left, I could see a group of men sitting in a fog of smoke while they talked and sucked on cigars between gulps of beer. Women scrambled about through the other door, wearing aprons and holding tight to steaming pans and bubbling crocks. I craned my neck to look for Andrew.

"I'll see if I can find him. He's been at the church so much the last couple weeks, I wouldn't be surprised if he was praying on the stone steps right now."

Dad shrugged and the priest went into the room with the ladies. Two children in navy blue jump suits burst in from a dark hallway, paused to look at Dad and me, giggled and bolted up the stairs in front of us, their foot steps on the burgundy carpet sounding like footfalls in soft snow. Dishes clanged and spoons scraped as a concentrated aroma of turkey and cinnamon with browning butter floated around us. I leaned my head back to take in the smell of the cigars to drown out the smell of the food that made me queasy. I looked at the chandelier overhead. Spikes of crystal spilled from a heavy center bowl, bouncing and reflecting rays of light like an exploding sun, filling my face with warmth. Spring. Summer. Bright pink lady's slippers.

The bright light went out as the tall priest stood in front of us again. I lowered my eyes to see Mrs. Murphy and another tall man who pushed his black-rimmed glasses back onto his nose that was purple and red on its tip. They stood to either side of the priest.

"Mr. Hellman, this is Mr. Murphy."

Mr. Murphy, his expression glazed by confusion, reached out and took my dad's hand. He glanced at me and the way his eyes paused on my body, it made me blush. Mrs. Murphy winced as if she was chewing on a

120

lemon as the men shook hands.

"What do you want with us?" she blurted.

"This business concerns your boy, Andrew. Any way we can talk to him?" Dad said.

"Mary?" I heard over the wall of people in front of me. Father Haggarty stepped aside and I saw Andrew on the bottom stair. His hair was mussed as if he had been sleeping, but when I saw his eyes, a jolt of electricity seemed to shoot up my spine and my scalp now tingled.

"What're you doing here?" he asked.

Father Haggarty glared at us while Mr. Murphy's soft, confused expression didn't change. Mrs. Murphy's face twisted in confusion and something else. 'Panic?' I thought. Dad stepped through the wall of people and looked directly at Andrew.

"Son, we got a problem."

The following Thursday, December fourth, the first snow flurries of the winter caused problems by knocking out power all over Hopkins and St. Anthony's Church, lit by a few altar candles, was as dark and gloomy as an abandoned barn and smelled as wet and mildewed. Feeble gray sunlight caused the narrow stained glass windows of the church to look like tarnished silver tears. The church was empty except for the Murphys who sat on one side of the maple pews and mom and dad who sat directly across from them. Andrew held my hand gently as he slid the old diamond ring his mother gave him onto my ring finger. It stuck at my second knuckle because my fingers were so much bigger than Mrs. Murphy's. Andrew slid it off and tried to push it on but it was no use. After a very awkward silence, Andrew shrugged and gave up and ring looked like a diamond garter on my finger. Father Haggarty mumbled the final blessing and presented us to our parents.

Mrs. Murphy thrust her face onto Mr. Murphy's massive shoulder, bawling and snorting. Dad stared past us toward the statue of Christ on his cross that hung behind us. Andrew cleared his throat and took my hand. No one moved for a moment until Mom stood up, her face a giant smile, and rushed to us, throwing her arms around us. I don't know why, but my sister Irma's wedding flashed into my head right then. 'This is worse,' I thought.

"I'm so glad you stopped in. You feeling any better?" Miss Hogrebe said the next day. I nodded.

"Miss Hogrebe, I got to –"

"Good. I've got something for 'Irma's Wedding.' Well, for all of your work."

She cut me off and whatever she was up to, I just wanted to say what I had come to tell her and get out: a simple 'thank you' for all her

121

support over the years, and the harder one, 'goodbye.' She wasn't making it easy.

Miss Hogrebe opened her bottom desk drawer and pulled out a large package wrapped in green foil and crowned by a red ribbon. She thrust it toward me, the bracelets on her right hand jingling.

"I don't give Christmas presents to all my students. Actually, I'm just giving one to you and Artie this year."

"Artie?" I said as casually as possible but inside I panicked. The last few weeks had become such a daze that I hadn't even thought about needing to talk to him.

"Yes, Artie. He's been real worried about you since you've been out. Anyway, open it."

The foil was smooth under my fingers as I slid them under the wrapping and began to tear it.

"Mary, don't forget the card. Wait a minute. What's this?"

Miss Hogrebe grabbed my left hand and held it to her face. Her brows knitted as she looked at the diamond ring perched on my first knuckle.

"What's this? You going steady with someone?"

"I'll tell you in a second."

I really wanted to just grab up the present and run. Using both hands, I tore back the foil and a rich, brown chocolate color greeted my eyes. Pulling the rest of the paper and card off, a leather portfolio complete with a belt and brass clasp lay before me. Miss Hogrebe flipped it over and pointed at the gold lettering near the top of the case. My initials shone against the leather.

"See. Next semester, there's no question who this case belongs to."

I held it up, regarded the initials and couldn't speak. A lump bellowed from my stomach and twisted in my throat. I threw my arms around Miss Hogrebe and my body shook and twitched. I'm not going to cry. I'm not going to act like a baby. I scooped up the portfolio and its wrapping paper and the last thing I heard her say as I ran into the hall was:

"Get some more rest. Don't forget to read the card."

The portfolio had grown heavy in my arm late that day as I turned past the last row of the Darlana's brown raspberry vines. Dad was hammering away on something in the garage and as I crossed the weeds and stones of the front yard that looked like frosted lace from the snow the day before, I saw a shadowy figure stand up on the porch. The figure stepped into the gray sunlight and I recognized Artie.

"Maaarry ..." he hollered.

Artie's face was as thin and hollow as an Egyptian mummy, making

122

his beard and mustache stand out like black brushes from his face. His eyes were fire from the dark recesses of his sockets as he waved and ran toward me. His thin arms grasped me so tightly that my new portfolio thudded to the ground next to me. The bristles of his mustache tickled my cheeks as he kissed my face over and over again. I stepped back from his embrace.

"Mary. You no feel so good still?"

"No." I saw Dad glance around the edge of the garage door, drop his head, and step back in.

"Is lots of days you missing school. Have ammonia?"

"Huh?"

Artie chewed on his lower lip as he hunted for the right words, and I slipped deeper into myself because I wasn't ready yet to talk to him.

"Sickness here?"

He tapped my chest lightly.

"Oh. Pneumonia? That what you mean?"

Artie nodded and smiled.

"No. I'm not that sick."

"Good, 'cause I bring something for you."

Whatever it was, I didn't want it. My leg muscles twitched and I had to clench my shoulders to keep from running. To where, I didn't know. From what? Everything at that moment.

Artie pulled a plain white envelope from his pocket and handed it to me, his face breaking into a deep grin. I held the envelope a second, its dry, weighty girth making me feel even more afraid.

"Open. Open," he insisted.

A sigh squeezed from my lungs as I slid my fingers under the envelope's lip. Inside was a load of ten and twenty dollar bills. I jumped back, never before having seen anything bigger than a five-dollar bill or a few ones at a single time. I ruffled them then looked up as another lump crept into my throat.

"What is this?"

Artie's face smiled with full self-satisfaction as if I missed the punch line of a joke.

"Now, you and me, we going to New York. You just gots to pack your bag."

"Where'd you get all this?"

Artie pulled out a round form of pewter shaped into leaves. I recognized it as he handed it to me.

"Pawn guy say not worth much. But we keep base till can buy back crystal ball from him."

"Artie, you sold your Grandma's crystal ball?"

"Yes."

123

"But she saw your birth in it."

"Just pawn it. Will get back as soon as we gets money from New York art."

I folded the envelope closed and handed it back to Artie. As I set the pewter base in his hand, I saw his bright eyes turn dark.

"You not want New York?"

"I can't go, Artie."

His hands dropped to his sides and his big smile now fell, pulling his eyes down in its collapse. His voice grew quiet.

"Not want to do art anymore?"

"Artie. I'm married."

I held up my left hand and his chin now followed his face in the avalanche of pain.

"Mary. You no tell me you don't love me no more. Why?"

"Artie, I do."

"Why you married then?"

"I can't tell you. Just -- never mind. I can't go with you."

I snatched up my portfolio and ran into the house. Collapsing on my bed, the lump in my throat began to twist into tears, but my Mother's words flashed into my head: 'You gotta give up that girlish stuff and start becoming a woman.' The temperature in my room felt like it suddenly plunged and the cold of my Mom's voice and the cold of the air smothered any tears I could have cried. I pulled the maple leaf quilt over my head and slid into the warmth and darkness of my bed.

I slept that entire Saturday away and don't remember any dreams. Sunday morning burst me awake when Mom barged into my room.

"Time to pack you up, girl."

By eleven fifteen that morning, Mom rummaged through my mostly empty closet and I set the portfolio with the green foil still clinging to it on top of my trunk and bag. The unopened card from Miss Hogrebe fell from the folds of the torn paper. As I reached for it, Dad burst into the room.

"America's been attacked! We been bombed!"

Mom ran from the closet, two old cable knit sweaters of mine still hanging from her arm.

"Where? Where we been bombed?" Mom screamed.

"Pearl Harbor!"

"Where the hell's that?"

"Somewhere in the Pacific Ocean."

"Oh, Ernest, cut the crap. I thought Minneapolis or New York got hit."

"Come on, Martha. Let's go get the whole story. It's all over the

124

radio."

Mom and Dad sat and stared at the radio as the announcer boomed about the Japanese, the U.S.S. Arizona, and Hickam Field. The way they listened, you would have thought the world was ending. I excused myself and went back to my room. Pulling the envelope off the wrapping paper from Miss Hogrebe, I paused and looked at it for a long time, unsure whether I really wanted to read the card. Just over my line of sight as I considered the card, I saw the dead raspberry patch, thorny and brown. I realized at that moment that I wouldn't be hearing them shuffle in the wind or hear the raccoons scurrying through them in the summer. Those observations compelled me to open the envelope.

Inside was a hand-painted card, a diffuse blend of watercolors that layered over each other to form a rose. The card read: 'Mary, Always remember that you are an artist, whether you choose to paint or not. Your life is a creation of something bigger, and your talent is a mere expression of that universal power. To know the creator, keep aligned with your own creative force. Miss H.'

I wasn't sure what Miss Hogrebe meant, but at that moment, it didn't feel like life had anything to offer but destruction. Sighing, I slipped the card back into its envelope and dropped it into the portfolio.

8

Danny noticed the dawn making a halo around the closed window shade and realized he had been reading all night. He reached over and tore a page from an old issue of the Hollywood Reporter, folded it to make a bookmark, and placed it in the diary. Closing it, he slid it gently to the foot of his bed. As he lay back and closed his eyes, his mind raced from one thought to the next:

Grandma Hellman, what an old-fashioned bitch.

Grandpa Hellman— he was a failed inventor.

Mom wasn't always bat-shit crazy he knew that now. In fact, the same way he would obsess on ideas that he had to capture in paragraphs that sometimes grew into scenes of a screenplay, his mom would do the same thing with her drawing and painting. Different from her, though, he wouldn't allow his imagination to ever go too far. The same reason he didn't do drugs. He was sure if he did either, his mental trolley would fly off its tracks. Was fear keeping him from his talent? Was he any different from his mom in the way she let herself be distracted from her art?

And it was Dad, and that Artie guy that did it. Mom let herself be sexed up, a slut, sort of like him. He didn't love any of his tricks anymore than she loved his dad. She should have just stood up to Grandma Hellman and run off with Artie.

But I would never have been born, he thought. So what.

'Hail Mary full of grace...' why the hell did that old Catholic prayer pop into his head? Wait. His mom really was full of grace, creative, artistic grace that she gave up on. That's it. I got to stop reading this, he thought, because it's stirring me up and pretty soon, I may go bat-shit crazy, too. The thoughts swirled and raced through his mind until he slept.

The next night, again with the sounds of Santa Monica Boulevard beckoning, he lit his cigarette, boiled a couple eggs, and tried to prevent himself from plunging back into the diary. He let out a sigh and picked up the diary.

9.

Later that Sunday afternoon, Minnetonka Avenue, which should have been filled with shoppers and strollers, was empty and gray as a churchyard. We sat at a stop sign with the truck rumbling like a restrained, anxious horse and with the smell of rotten cabbage floating through the cab. Andrew's eyes darted to the rearview mirror. My trunk and cedar hope chest, together with a few pieces of spindly, ancient furniture from my bedroom, had shifted in the truck bed.

"Everything okay?" I asked.

Andrew nodded. He hadn't said a word since picking me up and I hadn't felt like talking to fill the dead air, either. We passed Hopkins High School and I had the insane urge to leap out of the truck and run into Miss Hogrebe's art classroom. Why? I couldn't say, but my head felt dizzy as I thought about just a month before being a sixteen-year-old student anxious to get on to my next semester of honors art. Could that really only be a month ago? Time is strange the way it snags you in its net and sweeps you along.

The truck lurched to a stop in the Murphy's driveway. As Andrew pulled the brake into place, the small statue on his dashboard shook loose and fell to the floor. Andrew scooped it up, brushed it off, kissed it, and set it back in place before he slid out the truck door. In a few seconds, Andrew untied my belongings, dropping the rope that secured them into the truck bed with a thud. He stepped around to my door and wisps of his warm breath in the frigid air made him look like he was smoking.

I slid out and the air tightened my cheeks with a frosty chill. Andrew supported my elbow and as my feet touched the ground, my lower belly flared with burning pain. My knees were stale biscuits that crumbled from the pain and I fell to the ground. The gray afternoon light snapped off.

When I opened my eyes, a yellow orange light burned them. I blinked a couple of times and saw a table lamp with a round, glass shade that had thistles painted on it. Raising my head, which wasn't easy because it felt like it was filled with potatoes, I saw my legs stretched out in front of me. How'd I get in bed? I wondered. White sheets with lace edges and a crocheted quilt in oranges, whites, and greens covered me. Where's my maple leaf quilt? Was this my bed? The stale fruit and peppermint smell of

127

mothballs, along with pungent eucalyptus leaves, filled my nostrils and my blurry vision could just make out a figure kneeling at the foot of the bed. Mom? Rhythmic whispers vibrated my ears as the figure seemed to drop a chain of black beads one at a time. Concentrating on the figure's hands, my vision cleared enough so that I recognized the hands.

"Andrew?" my tongue fought a thick and dry war with my teeth.

The figure kissed the beads in his hand then slid up to meet me. Now I could see Andrew's face and the skin of his forehead folded with worry.

"What am I –" my throat seized shut.

"Don't try to talk. The doctor said he gave you something to help with the pain."

When he said that, I remembered the burn of the belly pain, but I didn't feel it just then. The potatoes in my head began to dissolve and my eyes cleared up, too. Andrew laid his head on my shoulder and I could see dark, carved wood furniture and faded violet and green wallpaper. As I surveyed the old room with its rich but worn furnishings, my eyes landed on two pill bottles sitting next to the glass lamp on a night table.

I pressed with extra force to open my throat and get some words out.

"Andrew, am I sick?" I heard myself faintly whisper.

Andrew lifted his head and kissed me on the cheek. Were those tears near his eyes? I wasn't sure.

"Doc said you almost lost the baby."

When Andrew said that, his eyes bore into me with an anxious, worried look. But all I thought about was his tears. I reached up and cupped my hand around his face and his eyes closed. He turned his face to kiss my hand and brought his hand up to support mine as he did. The black beads I saw before wove through his fingers and looked like inflated watermelon seeds. A small, silver cross dangled from the end of the beads.

"What's that necklace you have?"

Andrew's eyes popped open and he sat back with a smirk on his face.

"You don't know what this is?"

I shook my head. I had seen them before, but I never really knew what they were.

"It's called a rosary. We use them to keep track of our prayers."

I shrugged. Andrew kissed the cross and slipped the beads into his pocket.

"You'll find out what they mean later."

I saw a cross above the bedroom door that looked like stone engraved with a geometric pattern. Andrew followed my glance.

"That's a Celtic cross."

I glanced around the room and each corner had a wood curio cabinet filled with crystal or porcelain figurines. I thought it was my eyes not being adjusted yet, but then I realized that each wall of the room, with its dark, grape-patterned wallpaper, was covered with paintings, or mirrors, or candleholders. Small pieces of furniture, chairs, or vases crammed the floor along each wall. The room was filled with scads of stuff like an expensive garage. Metal shined in one corner and I could make out a suit of armor in the shadow. Sitting up, my head felt a little dizzy and I pointed to the armor.

"Is that what I think it is?"

Andrew rolled his eyes and sighed.

"Does it bother you?" Andrew asked.

"No."

"My dad is a nut for Irish history so he collects all kinds of old Irish junk. I call him my Old Mick."

"The room's sure filled." It felt more like a closet than a room to me. It made me feel claustrophobic. I felt like I was getting in the way of all the things.

"Everything that isn't Irish in here is my mom's. She collects, well, everything. It's some sort of hobby she has for expensive stuff."

I pushed back the blankets and shifted my legs toward the floor.

"I gotta get a closer look at that armor."

"Hey. You ain't supposed to –"

As soon as my feet touched the floor, the room began to whirl. I lay back to catch myself.

"The Doc says you gotta stay in bed for the next three months or so. You can't just get up like that or you could start bleeding again."

"Bleeding?"

"Yep. Doc says you got high blood pressure, too. The baby's in a real delicate way right now."

Andrew guided me back onto the pillows and began to pull the sheet and blanket up. The heavy oak door flew open.

"I hear voices in here. Andrew, you better not be messing up my Irish linen."

Andrew hopped off the bed like a little boy caught being bad. Mrs. Murphy stood at the open door with a service tray. Essence of rose water filled the room.

"I can come in, can't I?" she said.

Andrew nodded.

Mrs. Murphy, her shoulders and head sticking just above the tray she carried, crossed to the foot of the bed, her little feet clicking against the wood floor like a scurrying raccoon. She set the tray at my feet and when she did, I felt like I had to pull the blankets up. But when I did, Mrs. Murphy reached over and grabbed them from me and pulled them taut as she placed them over my chest.

"We have to be careful, dear, not to snag the imported lace. Of course, I wouldn't expect you would completely understand, coming from where you do. Andrew, let's have the tray for your little wife here."

Mrs. Murphy said the word 'dear' like it had a 'y' in it, more like 'dee-yer.' When she addressed me, it made me feel self-conscious, like I had done something wrong.

Andrew set the tray on my lap and Mrs. Murphy removed the cover from a porcelain bowl. Grainy oatmeal sent up a thread of steam.

"Oatmeal, Mom?" Andrew said.

"You never mind him, dear. That's genuine Irish oatmeal, filled with good things to help you with your condition."

"Thank you, Mrs. Murphy."

Mrs. Murphy folded her tiny arms and turned toward Andrew, and it was obvious where he got his small body frame.

"This isn't going to do at all," she said.

"What?" Andrew said.

"Her calling me Mrs. Murphy. There's gotta be something better."

"How about Mom?" Andrew said.

"No. No, I don't think so."

Mrs. Murphy turned back toward me as I lifted the first spoon of oatmeal to my mouth, startling me. The oatmeal spilled down my chin and luckily the spoonful had cooled enough so that it didn't burn. I reached up and pushed it into my mouth with the index finger of my left hand, glancing at Mrs. Murphy just long enough to see her grimace.

"'Daisy'. You can call me 'Daisy', dear. That's short for my first name, Desiree."

Daisy grabbed Andrew by the arm and began to lead him out.

"Come on, son, let's let the dear get used to her room and eat in privacy."

Andrew pulled away.

"I'm going to stay with her."

"Fine. If you want to watch her eat."

"Not just now, Mom. We're going to share this room, ya' know."

"She has to rest for three months, son. It will be better for her and the baby to do that privately."

"We're sharing a bed, too, Mom. We're married."

"Don't I know it."

Daisy shrugged and scurried to the door. As she pulled it open,

130

she added: "Andrew. You get her trunk and stuff out of your room and bring it in here as soon as you can."

Daisy started to pull the door closed, and paused again.

"And dear, try not to get any of your food on the quilt. Mr. Murphy brought it back from Ireland last year and he would be livid if his Irish colors got stained by oatmeal."

Daisy walked out. Andrew watched Daisy leave, but his face twisted into a sour expression.

"Hang on a second," he said, then stepped to the door. He pushed the door causing the heavy wood to slam against its threshold and the brass doorknob tumbler to rattle. He sat down again on the bed at my side.

"She didn't close it all the way."

"Why?"

"Who knows with Mom. She probably wanted to discourage us from any 'bad behavior' in the house."

I set my spoon down and Andrew sighed.

"You don't have to stop eating. Mom's got her weird ways and you'll figure out when she's joking."

"I'm not that hungry anyway."

Andrew reached for my hand and leaned forward. As he did, the black beads in his pocket rattled.

"Mary, you gotta eat. You passed out a long time ago and you missed lunch and dinner."

"You make it sound like I was on a booze bender."

The one bite of the oatmeal coated my tongue with such a thick sweetness that my stomach twisted shut. I didn't want to eat. Reaching into Andrew's pocket, I pulled out the black beads that felt like smooth stones and held them up.

"So what do these do, anyway?"

Andrew pulled the rest of the beads out of his pocket and set them in my hand. The silver cross on the end of them had a small figure of Christ on it. Where the hands attached to the cross, a thin, dark film that looked like dirt or grease filled the space.

"Do you like how it feels?"

I shrugged. It feels like beads, I thought.

"I like the feeling of the beads between my fingers."

Andrew said that softer than anything I ever heard him say before. He sounded like a little boy proud of his toy train and his eyes seemed to sparkle with wonder. I wanted to throw my arms around him and kiss his face. Not that I wanted him close in that way, but more like the way Irma used to kiss and kiss the cheek of a puppy or chick. I guess I wanted to just take care of him. The dirt or grease on the cross aroused my curiosity.

"You had these beads for a long time?"

"Yep. They were my Grandpa's, then my dad's, and now they're mine."

"They're sure dirty."

Andrew plucked the beads out of my hand and kissed the cross. He dropped them into his pocket.

"Whyn't you just eat some more."

He stood up and turned his back. I didn't know why he was so mad all of a sudden.

"Don't go. Stay with me."

He didn't turn around right away and I could see his shoulders sway like he wasn't sure what to say next. He stepped toward the door and stood just below the Celtic cross.

"I'm gonna go get your stuff."

He started to walk out as the potatoes pounded in my head again. Daisy's rose water perfume left a scent cloud that cloyed my nostrils. I dropped back onto the pillows and Andrew was at my side. He yanked the bed tray with the oatmeal off my chest then grabbed my shoulders.

"Mary. You okay?"

I was okay, just tired. I nodded and Andrew's lips brushed my forehead. My head lolled to the right and the orange and green of the quilt became a fuzzy pumpkin patch.

'I won't mess it up' echoed through my head as I used my last breath to whisper it.

I slept constantly for the next few days, always aware of the quilt with the Irish colors. The day Andrew and his dad, Gerald, moved the double bed into the room, Andrew's dad nodded a welcome and didn't say anything else. Andrew walked out of the room softly, but Gerald stayed a little longer and stared at me. I felt uneasy and pulled the blankets up around my neck and smiled. I fell asleep again. Daisy began that day to trade off with Andrew to bring me food. Daisy attended to me during the day, Andrew took care of me when he got home from work at night.

One morning, the sun broke through the gray clouds and burst through the burgundy drapes of the dark room, casting a golden light throughout. Daisy knocked but didn't pause as she walked in. She only waited for a 'come in' when Andrew was home with me. A breeze of rose water filled the room. The food tray Daisy carried to the edge of the bed clinked until she set it on my legs.

"Andrew had to go over to Woolworth's to sign up for the Draft before work."

"The draft? What's that?"

"We're at war with the Japs, don't you know that?"

132

"Well, yeah."

"Where you think they get all the men from? Everyone's signing up now."

"What does that mean? Is he going off to war now or something?"

Daisy heard the desperation in my voice but instead of comforting me, she taunted me.

"It just means they can call him up anytime -- we never know."

She turned to go then added as an afterthought: "Young girl like you shouldn't become a war widow and a mother at one time." She closed the door and I heard her hyena laugh fade away. In a moment, she came back in.

"Room needs a little light today." She walked over to one of the windows.

A hunger pang struck me. This particular morning was the first time in the two weeks I lived with my in-laws that I actually was hungry and didn't need to sleep all the time. I hoped that Daisy had brought me something better than oatmeal to eat; whenever Andrew wasn't around, that's all she brought me. I told Andrew and he said that I was wrong and that it must be my sickness that was tricking me. He said it would upset Mom if she heard me complaining. I lifted the cover on the bowl and there was a steaming serving of the gray cereal.

Daisy pulled open the drapes to let in the sun and I thought I saw her glance over her shoulder, her little face smirking when I lifted the bowl cover.

"You know, Andrew is such a natural organizer. Gerald says he's got the horse sense to be a rich businessman someday."

She spoke over her shoulder while she tied the drapes back. When she turned back toward me, the sunlight made the whole right half of her body, from her gray-brown short hair to her knobby knee that stuck out from her floral house dress, glow like an angel's halo. And the left half of her body was darker than the dark side of the moon.

"I had been meaning to ask you. You don't mind if I sit a minute with you?"

She was already sitting on the edge of the bed with her arms folded when she asked. I could see her short legs dangling off the side of the bed as she kept her glance focused toward the left wall.

"Go ahead," I said. I took a spoon of the oatmeal and it had the rummy taste of molasses. I lifted another spoonful as my stomach gurgled with appreciation. Daisy cranked her head toward me and I thought she heard my stomach growl. But instead, she began to stare and after looking at me for what seemed like an hour, a smile crossed her face. Oh, no, I thought. Here comes a joke about me or a criticism camouflaged by a laugh and a 'just kidding, dee-yer.' Oatmeal, eat more oatmeal. I broke off eye contact with her and dropped my eyes down to the bowl.

"You're sure pretty, dear. Gotta hand it to you there."

Pretty was the last thing I felt. My stomach bulged like a hot air balloon at the country fair. But worse, my body, which had always felt tight and narrow, now felt swollen and thick from lying in bed all this time. I didn't know how to respond to Daisy. The hair on my neck tingled like a spider was crawling on me.

"The oatmeal is good today," I said.

Daisy continued to stare and now folded her arms.

"Andrew's never said much about you to me."

"What do you mean?"

"Well," she said. She turned her shoulders toward me and straightened the sleeves of her dress like she was uncomfortable or preparing for attack.

"You like to shop?" she asked.

She asked that like she was trying to throw me off scent or lure me into something. I might have been kooky with my art and all, but I could always pick up someone being mean or crafty.

"We never had much money so it's not something we did very often. My sister, Irma, would sometimes spend babysitting money at Nickolet's. I was never very interested in shopping."

"I shop a lot. Find great buys all the time. I haven't been able to find a Madonna and Child, though."

"A what?" I said between bites.

"The Virgin Mary with baby Jesus. I've looked everywhere for a statue, or a painting. I can't find one. Can I ask you something personal?"

"I guess," was all I could say.

"Who did you date before Andrew?"

"Huh?"

"Boyfriends. Pretty as you are you must have had one or two before Andrew."

I can't explain it but the way she said 'pretty' was not a compliment but an accusation. Unsure what she was getting at, I just shrugged. She leaned toward me on one elbow and it was the first time she was within three feet of me since our wedding photo.

"Let's be pals, dear. Tell Daisy about the boys."

She must know something about Artie. The thought sent the spider shiver down my neck again. But what she knew right then she could only have thought she knew. It would take me to confirm or deny it. The spoon handle made several metallic clinks against the bowl before I realized I was tapping it.

"It's a simple request, dear. Just curious, don't worry."

If she really wanted to get to know me so much, why didn't she ask about my art or what I felt about my mom and dad? Daisy interrupted my thoughts but I decided I wasn't going to tell her anything. Besides, the baby was probably Andrew's so what did it matter to her who I liked before?

"Andrew's my first boyfriend."

I wasn't lying; Artie never called me his girlfriend and he even told his mother that we were just friends. What I felt didn't matter then and it sure didn't matter now.

"Really? Your first?"

Daisy's mean smirk was now accented by arching eyebrows. She winked with her left eye.

"Andrew's the first."

I never heard the word 'first' sound so nasty or dirty in my life.

"Yes. He's the only one for me."

The spoon handle rolled off my fingers and splattered into the oatmeal. Grains of cereal and drops of molasses sprayed onto my pink flannel nightgown but missed the sheets and quilt.

"Just seems hard to figure," Daisy said. Her eyes darted to the comforter to verify I hadn't spilled on it.

"What?"

"A pretty girl like you. Andrew being your first fella and ending up in your predicament."

Dabbing at the cereal on my nightgown, the napkin stuck a moment as I wiped up the molasses.

"I'm in no predicament, Daisy. I love Andrew with all my heart. I know he loves me. So whatever else happened just got us together faster."

Daisy stood up, the pink rose print of her housedress sticking to her thighs and making them into chair arms. She reached out and withdrew the material from between her thighs and straightened the hem. Her little dark eyes flattened into slits.

"I know a lot of people in town; did I ever tell you that? They call me the wild Irish Rose, even though I'm American."

A grin stretched across her face as she stepped toward the door and paused.

"What nationality are you, anyway?"

"Mostly Bohemian, I guess."

"Oh. Those Bohemians grow big men and women. 'Course, you already know that, don't you? Nice getting to know you."

She walked out the door. The oatmeal had turned to a transparent slime as it cooled in the bowl. I dropped the spoon.   I lifted the tray onto the side table and a chill shot through me. I pulled the quilt up tight to my neck.

I don't like her.

"She's ain't so bad. I like her," Mom said a couple weeks later when she and Dad came to visit me for the first time just before Christmas. Daisy had just left the room to get some tea when Andrew pulled one of the chairs from the wall and set it down for Dad. He sat very lightly in the dark, cherry wood chair and I wanted to tell him not to be so nervous because the material that covered the cushion was so worn that it looked like a frayed peach. Dad's eyes darted around the room, and he shifted in the chair as if a doctor were about to give him some bad news. He reached out for my hand and as our palms touched, he appeared to calm down. That's when I got the first chance to see his face and noticed he looked gray as ash and rough like sackcloth. A bolt of guilt flashed through me: I was the one who caused him to look so sad and ill. A dark cloud of self-doubt overshadowed my joy at seeing him.

"You get a load of this thing here, Ernest?" Mom said. Standing by the suit of armor, Mom's hair was done up under a violet felt hat that spilled small netting just over her brow. She almost looked like an iris as she flitted to one of the curio cabinets. She leaned over and shook her head and when she turned to look at us, her face glowed like she found a diamond mine. Andrew lifted another chair and started to cross the room, but Mom stopped him and pointed to the curio cabinet. It was then that I noticed she wore white Easter wrist gloves.

"That stuff in there all real?" she asked.

Andrew nodded and rolled his eyes. He looked embarrassed.

"Yeah. My mom doesn't like anything that's phony."

"She's got an eye, I can say that for her."

Andrew patted the chair and Mom nodded, but she continued to move around the room like she was inspecting it. If she wasn't shaking her head in amazement, she craned and strained her neck to take in every detail. Mom wouldn't have understood the closed-in feeling all the stuff gave me, especially now that a lot of it was covered with hollyhock and red metal garland. With just the two chairs moved over by the bed, it felt like everything was about to tumble down on top of me. Mom wouldn't understand and I think that if she had a house with a room like this, and the money, she would be filling it up, too.

"This is what you call a real Victorian house, I'll say that." Mom sat down next to Dad but her eyes still wandered about the room. Andrew came and sat on the bed next to me, keeping both his feet planted on the floor.

"How you feeling, girl?" Dad finally spoke.

136

"She's doing great, Ernest. Just look at this room. Why, she's just about a princess, far as I can see," Mom said.

"Doc says she is doing great," Andrew said. "Thinks she may be up on her feet in about a month."

I was glad everyone was answering for me right then because I was ready to explode with the truth about the baby, about not knowing who the father was, about everything that was making Dad look sick. The dark clouds of guilt swirled into a storm of confusion inside me.

"You do gotta move, Mary. Exercise is good for the baby," Mom said.

Daisy walked in carrying a silver service that made her appear as if she wore a sterling shield. The scent of ginger and cloves wafted in behind her. A pile of powder-sugared cookies filled one side of a silver tray and little slices of cake with gems of candied cherries and lime filled the other. Glancing around to figure her path in the new geography of chairs in the room, Daisy looked a little irritated. Mom stood up and extended her hands to help. Daisy paused a second and then handed her the tray. She shook her head and looked toward the wall. The sparse sunlight in the room reflected off the silver and cast a light halo on Mom's smiling face.

"Don't you agree with that, Mrs. Murphy?"

"What?" she answered over her shoulder as she stood by the wall. Daisy bent over and lifted a small, round table, carried it over and set it between Mom and Dad. I saw that it was inlaid with a pentagram pattern. She grabbed the silver service back from Mom.

"Exercise is good for the baby," Mom said.

"Oh, yeah," Daisy replied.

From my position in the bed, I saw Daisy sneer at Mom's big rear end for a second before she added a comment.

"From what I can tell, it may even be more important for Mary."

That was the first time Daisy said my name, and it felt odd. No one would have been aware of that, least of all Mom. She just nodded in agreement with Daisy about her exercise remark as she sat down with a deflated look of confusion. But Mom bounced back fast when Daisy handed her a plate and offered the tray of cookies. Mom first pulled the white gloves off her fingers as if they were oxeye daisy petals, snapped open the dully-worn, brass clasp of a faded clutch purse, and dropped the gloves into it. She then took the plate and placed it on her lap as delicately as if it was made of silk, and she used only her fingertips to select one cookie and two cakes. I couldn't believe that Mom actually extended her pinkie as she lifted the cakes from the tray. She nodded a 'thank you' as Daisy poured her a cup of tea, again that pinkie stuck out like a flagpole. Had Mom's hands been delicate, manicured, and painted, she might have been able to pull off this bizarre fantasy of sophistication. But her thick stubs with chafed creases and worn nails had the effect of making her look like a chambermaid at a rich child's tea party. You can be sure none of this escaped Daisy's notice. After a delicate sip, Mom paused.

"You must tell me what you put in this tea."

"Just mulling spices," Daisy said.

"Huh?"

"Some cloves, a little ginger, some cinnamon. That sort of thing."

Mom nodded like she understood instantly, but I knew she had no idea what mulling spices were. A rivulet of tea sputtered into another cup as Daisy poured Dad some tea, then handed him the cup that chattered against its saucer. Mom took another sip and looked up over the gold edge of her porcelain cup.

"Ernest, I saw some contraptions in that parlor out there. Why don't Andrew and you go take a look at them and give us ladies some time to chat."

"Who is this woman?" I thought.

She caught Dad as he lifted his cup to his lips, and he paused before he sipped.

"Martha, I ain't had any tea yet."

"Take your tea with you."

"I haven't even got to say anything to Mary except hello."

Mom cast a glance at Daisy and offered a stiff smile of discomfort. Daisy's eyes narrowed and watched.

"Ernest, there'll be plenty of time."

Dad looked over at me and I shrugged. Andrew stood up.

"Come on, Mr. Hellman. I'll show you the copper Irish still and the loom Dad brought back on one of his trips."

Dad looked at me and his bright eyes were dull as his skin. "Go, Dad. It's torture looking at you," I thought.

"Ernest." Mom's tone was firm.

Dad started to stand and as he did, his leg wobbled. Andrew flew to his side and held his arm.

"Mr. Hellman, you okay?"

"Yeah, just give me a second. My leg just fell asleep."

Dad stood up again and he winced as he put weight on his leg. He looked back at me with his dull eyes.

"Darlin', I'll be back. Don't you worry none."

Andrew kissed my forehead and the two men walked out, closing the door behind them with a thud. Daisy sipped her tea, dragging the sip out to a deep slurp. Mom picked up the powder-sugared cookie and bit the edge of it with her front teeth in a most lady-like manner. Crumbs

138

powdered her lower lip as she rolled the morsel around in her mouth.

"What kind'a cookie is this?"

"Pfefferneuse."

Daisy let out a sigh and rolled her eyes about the room. Mom finished the cookie with a second bite and a new flurry of white crumbs dusted her chin. She smiled toward Daisy and I glared at her, dusting my own chin with my fingertips. Mom looked over at me, her face screwed up in confusion. I now poked my chin with my forefinger, hoping that she'd get it. Daisy thrust a small linen napkin toward Mom who took that hint and wiped her mouth.

"So, Mary, did you know Irma's home?"

With Dad and Andrew out of the room, I felt the storm become a flat shower inside. Both tension and enthusiasm drained from me.

"You mean for Christmas?" I said.

"We're not real sure yet. Oh, Mrs. Murphy. Sorry. Irma's my older daughter. She's having some marriage trouble."

Daisy's eyes that had been wandering now stopped and bore into Mom.

"More tea, Mrs. Hellman?"

"Please. Call me Martha."

'Someone get me outta here,' I thought.

Mom, relaxing a bit more, took a big bite from one of her cookies. Her gloves were off and he appetite was healthy. Daisy just smiled at her and I wanted to know what was behind the smile.

"So your sister left Ben. Do you know the Augsburgs of Durand, Mrs. Murphy?"

"No, I don't."

"Well anyway, your sister says that she knows Ben has been messing around with a couple of the local floozies."

"Mom!"

"It's okay, Mrs. Hellman. You can go on," Daisy said.

I wasn't bothered by Mom's choice of words. It was more her choice of subjects. As she talked about Irma, somehow I felt naked in front of Daisy.

"Your sister says she'll never go back to him. That she can't forgive him. But I told Irma that some men need to play sometimes. Don't you agree, Mrs. Murphy?"

I couldn't stop Mom now. Daisy glared at me.

"Just like some women do," Daisy said.

'What is she getting at?' I thought. God how I wished Mom would just shut up.

"Only the kind of women he messed with. Anyway, I told her that rich men are like little boys and unless she wanted to be pregnant and divorced, she should look the other way and figure out how she can win him back. It's always the woman's fault, don't you think, Mrs. Murphy?"

Daisy raised her cup as if she were toasting Mom's wisdom. But her eyes narrowed as she looked over its lip directly at me. I got the feeling she was aiming a rifle right at me.

"Always," she said.

"Well, anyway, I think your sister understood because she's going home after Christmas to spend New Years with Ben. Isn't that a good story?"

Mom prattled on for the next hour, talking about all kinds of things that I guess she thought might interest Daisy. A smile eventually formed on Daisy's face and she nodded almost constantly as Mom spoke. Finally, there was a soft knock on the door and Andrew and Dad walked back in. After all the chatter, I was glad just to see someone else, but I saw again that Dad seemed to be moving slowly. Daisy stood and offered her chair to Dad and Andrew took the other chair. Mom's face melted into disappointment and she stood.

"You going, Mrs. Murphy? Mom asked.

"Lots of Christmas preparations to attend to, you know?" Daisy said.

"But I hardly got to know you."

"Don't be foolish, Mrs. Hellman. I got to know you quite well and after all, can anyone be more concerned about in-laws than the groom's mother?"

"Oh, yeah, I see what you mean," Mom said.

I didn't. What was she talking about? Just who were these women choosing sides about my life? My life.

"You three take your visit with your dear here. Andrew, call me if anyone needs anything."

Daisy stepped to the door and shut it lightly. Mom looked around, unsure what to do and then set down her teacup and cookie plate. She stood.

"Ernest, let's go. Mary really needs her rest."

Before Dad could answer, Mom threw open the oak door and walked out. Dad stood, wringing his hat in his hands. He leaned forward and kissed my forehead.

"Mary, you be a good girl. You do look well, considering all you're going through. We'll be back Christmas with a present for you and Andrew."

Dad offered his hand to Andrew.

"You take care of her now, you hear?"

Dad's shoes scraped across the wood floor as he walked out of the room. Andrew glanced behind and when the door shut, he climbed up into the bed and nuzzled next to me. His lips reached up and gently brushed my neck.

"Andrew, I'm a mess."

"It doesn't matter. You know how much I love you."

My resistance started to melt because whenever he said 'I love you,' his voice softened into a boy's. But I still took his hand and placed it on my stomach. Sliding his hand up and down the swelling beneath the pink and white flannel, I now spoke softly.

"See. I'm gonna be a mom and right now I hate how it makes me look."

Andrew leaned over and kissed my stomach, glancing up at me after he did. Tears started to form in the corners of his eyes.

"That's our baby and it just makes you more pretty."

Our, I thought. Now tears of guilt started to sting my eyes. Artie flew into my head, and my dad's sad face, and I suddenly wanted to tell him that I didn't know whose baby I was carrying. That I lied to him. That I didn't deserve him, or anyone.

"I'm not so pretty really, Andrew."

"You're my girl and you're a knockout."

"I feel bad."

But he didn't hear that. His mouth was buried in my neck and it tingled with the sensation.

"Andrew, I gotta tell you."

"Shh."

"Andrew. This is the third time today."

His hand moved from my neck down to my breast and my body shivered. Andrew slipped his hand under my nightgown and my head rolled back from pleasure. As Andrew moved on top of me, I thought I saw a crack in the door and a shadow behind it.

"Andrew! The door's open."

Andrew whirled around and jumped to the door, slamming it into its threshold and throwing the metal lock. I smelled a waft of rose water as he crawled back onto the bed.

"You smell that?" I whispered.

"What?"

"I think your mom was –"

"Make sure to shut the door next time, Andrew," Daisy hollered from the other side of the door.

Andrew jerked away from me and his face flushed as he ran his hand through his mussed hair. He looked at me then shrugged at the inevitable. Getting up from the bed like he had done so many times before during our weeks at his parents' house, he walked over to the small, cherry wood table radio near the knight's armor. The radio popped on with the Proctor and Gamble announcer leading into 'Guiding Light'. Alice Brady began to whisper something about her hidden passion to Richard Denning and Andrew turned it up louder. Putting a finger to his lips to stop me from protesting at the volume, he crept back over to the bed like a little boy ready to launch a water bomb, kicking off his shoes as he sat. He slid off his shirt and climbed under the blankets with me, and though my mom's big mouth and my dad's gray face played through my head once again, I kissed Andrew's shoulders and lay back.

Hours later, I woke up with a start when I heard screaming.

"You spend my money on all this crap. What do ya' mean you ain't happy, woman?" I heard a male voice boom through the bedroom wall. Andrew sat up, rubbing his eyes as the quiet sobs and muttering of a female voice barely made it through the wall.

"It's okay," Andrew whispered. "They been doing this my whole life. It only happens when they drink. Go back to sleep." He wove his fingers through mine and lay back down. But the adrenaline in my body made me too tense. "I never heard Gerald scream like that," I thought.

Daisy's muffled voice seemed to screech as she built up into another sob, but again I couldn't make out her words.

"That's because they're new-newlyweds!' Gerald screamed. 'Same as us when we star-arted."

Now my curiosity replaced the adrenaline. Gerald was slurring his words. What was going on? Andrew rolled over and wrapped his arms around my waist and his legs around my thigh. I could feel he was aroused again and I was about to push him away until I heard him lapse into a deep sleep.

"You're cold as ice, woman. Don't be blaming me."

Even though Gerald's words were aimed at Daisy who was no friend of mine, the meanness and roughness of his voice made me feel bad for her. And what about Andrew? Had he heard this whole life? Did he inherit this temper? I hadn't seen much temper in him yet, but I also had never seen it in Gerald, either. What about Daisy's nasty wit? Was that in Andrew, too? Who was Andrew really?

"I'm just so..." Daisy's voice screeched and broke into sobs. I heard Gerald's heavy foot steps and the back door crash shut. As I lay back, Daisy's sobs faded into whimpers. Andrew's breathing lulled into a deep snore that sawed through the dark night, and I pulled the blankets up to my neck, unable to sleep as I wondered about myself.

The next morning, Daisy trudged in with the tray of oatmeal

clinking in her hands and she didn't say anything as she set it down. As she bent, I saw that she wasn't wearing her floral housedress and the light makeup that made her look fresh and young for her age. Instead, she looked old and haggard, the lines in her face looking like canyons that appeared overnight. For the first time in my weeks of being there, she didn't smell like rose water but more like a rotted pine tree. Had she been chopping firewood or something? A dishtowel slipped off her shoulder and I reached to hand it to her.

"So the Bohunk Bloodsucker can move after all," she said as she grabbed it and turned for the door.

Normally, her jab would have hurt, but this time, I felt sorry for her because I knew she didn't have any idea that Andrew and I could hear their fight the night before. Her resentment of me, of my age, of the beginning of my new life, made sad sense. It was sort of embarrassing, too. But I didn't say anything as she walked out and slammed the door behind her.

The drunken rages happened weekly through the Christmas holidays and into the new year. Each morning after, Daisy brought my oatmeal and set the tray down silently. By the fifth month of my pregnancy, I was on my feet helping Daisy around the house, but other than basic instructions or requests about what needed to be washed or swept, Daisy didn't speak to me. We'd finish the chores, then she'd go off into town to look for a Madonna and child, and on the days after these fights, her arms would be full of packages and boxes but never the treasure she wanted so much.

It was around that time that I started a painting for Daisy. Because I understood her a little bit more, and also felt bad for her, I started a painting of a Madonna and child from a photo of a Da Vinci painting I saw in one of the dusty books in my room. Whenever she left, I'd hurry to pull my watercolor pad and paints from under the bed. My hands hadn't touched a pencil, paint brush or pad in so long that when I started to work, it felt like I had never done art before. But in a few days, I was comfortable with it again and saw that my work had improved over all the time I lay dormant. It was strange how the texture of the page and the flow of the color even made me forget about my swollen body and my breasts that had grown to be two painful mounds. I was glad to be working again, even though it was in secret. But that would make the surprise for Daisy -- a 'thank you' for helping me through my first couple of months of being pregnant -- much more fun.

The first morning in my seventh month, I was bent over sweeping musty dust into a metal dustpan, my stomach sticking out so far that I couldn't see my feet as I bent. A cuckoo clock kept a choppy rhythm as I

143

swept the oak parlor floor and the April afternoon sun cast gold highlights on the deep burgundy and cherry wood sofa and chair. The back door slammed shut and I heard the rustling of a paper bag. Creaking up slowly from the weight of my stomach, I saw Daisy standing in front of me with a strange smile.

"Well, dee-yer, I didn't find a Madonna and child, but look at what I picked up."

Daisy pulled two crystal candlesticks from the bag and let the bag drop on the floor. Where the sun struck the sharp cut edges, a sparkle and then a small rainbow burst from the beveled cuts.

"They're beautiful," I said and reached out for them.

Daisy yanked them back.

"They're antique Waterford. Don't ever touch them."

She turned and set them on a dark cherry side table that was dented with wear and gray where its varnish had faded. Rubbing her hands together in such a way that she looked like she was getting ready to devour a main course, she fixed her face into a staring smile. I felt awkward. Standing still, I towered over her and with all my weight from the baby, I cast a huge shadow over the deflated balloon of her body. Yet, I still felt nervous.

"Know where I got those?" she said.

"No." How could I?

"Lindstrom's Pawn Shop. That old Lindstrom's gotta have some Jew in him, because you should' a' seen how he tried to jack up the price on those. You'll never guess what else I tried to buy."

Her face almost puckered from the sour way she spoke, but that dumb know-it-all smile stayed on her face.

"I don't know," I said.

She turned back to the table with the candlesticks and rubbed her hand across it. The rays of sunlight made purple mountain ranges on the back of her veiny hand. Daisy nodded.

"It'd look wonderful right here. The way the light would hit it especially."

I shrugged, not really sure what 'it' was.

Daisy grabbed a tarnished silver box that must have been from the Orient by its ornate design. Setting the box where she would place the phantom object, she stared at the gap in the drapes for a moment. My hand with the dustpan started to twitch and I turned to go.

"Don't leave yet. I need your opinion."

I was impatient as Daisy slid the box into the path of the sun ray. She stepped back and folded her arms like she was considering a portrait.

"Yep. That's it. What'd you think?"

144

"If you tell me what it is, I might know better."

"I'd bet you already know. 'Course, you know what Mr. Lindstrom said?"

I wanted to scream at her: What are you talking about?

"No, I don't know what he said."

"I can't buy it."

My foot began to tap and I felt trapped by her strange game.

"Oh."

"Know why?"

"How could I know?" I exploded. "You haven't told me what it is."

Daisy actually took a step back and smiled. Was that approval at my anger or pride that she pushed me so far?

"Of course, dee-yer. It was the most gorgeous antique -- Lindstrom said it was from Eastern Europe -- crystal ball."

A jolt of adrenaline in me made the baby kick. I still hadn't gotten used to the feeling of the little thing inside me and whenever the baby kicked, it scared me. I rubbed my stomach.

"Your face is a little white, dee-yer. You wanna sit?"

"I need to dump the dustpan."

"Mr. Lindstrom said the crystal ball wasn't for sale. He promised the owner that he'd keep it till he could buy it back. Guess who the owner is."

My face flared with heat. I shrugged.

"A boy named Artie Janek."

She knows, I thought. My head felt light as my thoughts swirled. Now I did need to sit. I waddled to a Chippendale side chair and eased myself down against its creaking complaints and ignoring my back muscles that had become a pretzel of continuous pain. Daisy's little feet clicked across the floor and she now towered over me, still taunting me.

"Seems this Artie wanted the money so that he and his girl -- let's see if I can remember her name."

"I'm not feeling well, Daisy."

"I bet you're not. Just think how I felt when Mr. Lindstrom said 'Mary.'"

"Oh. Well, they're lots of Marys around."

"He didn't know her last name."

"Well you're making a mistake if you think it's me."

"No. You made the mistake, dee-yer. And I'm not going to let Andrew pay for it the rest of his life."

"I don't know what you're talking about."

Daisy grabbed the arms of the chair and leaned in my face. Her

145

nose and eyes squeezed into a growl.

"Don't lie to me. Doesn't matter, anyway. I got this Artie's address and I'm going over to see him."

The room felt like it was collapsing and the cuckoo clock turned into a banging drum of a heartbeat in my ears. Why is she doing this? Leave me alone.

"Why?" I asked.

"Because Father Haggarty told me today that an annulment based on adultery can be granted if there's proof of pre-marital sex. So what'd you think of that?"

More Catholic stuff again. I didn't know what she meant at all, except for the way she said it, I knew it was a threat.

"I don't really understand."

"I would imagine you wouldn't. Let me explain it, dee-yer. You seduced my boy and I'm sure he took you up on your offer. But that can't be his child and that's proof of adultery. And that's enough to end this joke of a marriage. As soon as I know for sure, then I'll tell Andrew. It's going to break his heart because he loves you so."

Adrenaline made the baby kick again. Rubbing my stomach, I creaked back onto my feet. To hide? To run? I really didn't know.

"It's Andrew's baby," I whispered.

"You think I believe anything you say? Your own mother obviously taught you to be a chiseler. Look how she sent your sister back to her cheating husband."

My stomach twisted when she said that about Mom. I had to defend her.

"My mom didn't teach us to steal, just to find someone to take care of us."

"It isn't going to be my son. You're not going to have that little heathen bastard under our roof."

I couldn't listen anymore. Plodding back toward the bedroom, I paused to pick up the dustpan.

"Don't bother," Daisy said. "I'll clean up the rest of this mess."

I nodded and turned.

"Oh, dee-yer."

Daisy's tone went from acidic hate to gentle, almost supportive. Now what, I thought.

"Father Haggarty said he'd help us arrange for you to stay at St. Agnes if you want."

"What does that mean?"

"If your folks won't have you back after they find out about your lying and slutting around."

146

"There's nothing to find out."

Daisy picked up the paper bag and crinkled it as she scooped up the dustpan.

"St. Agnes is a good place for unwed mothers. They'd get you started on your Catholic catechism, too. That is, if you still wanted to convert."

Daisy said that like she was Bob Hope talking to Bing Crosby. But it didn't make me laugh.

The following Sunday, I guess I got the last laugh when Andrew came in after church. His hair was slicked back and he wore his Sunday suit, the same gray, striped suit he wore at our wedding. I sat on the bed because I just had enough time to slide the Madonna and child painting underneath before he walked in. Not that I cared much whether anyone found out about it or not any longer. Leaning over, he kissed my face and a look of worry furrowed his brow.

"You're not feeling good again?" he said.

"I'm okay. As okay as you can feel seven months pregnant."

"Sorry we're late. Mom took us on this side trip to some house where these Bohemians live."

I'm dead. And he's toying with me now, too.

"Why'd you go there?" I asked.

"That's funny. Mom said to ask you what we went there for."

"I don't know what you mean."

"I guess it's Mom and her jokes again. The family who lived there moved to New York a month or so ago and neighbors didn't have a new address. Anyway, Mom said I should tell you and that you'd get a kick out of it."

My eyes dropped and I saw the corner of my watercolor pad sticking out. So Mr. and Mrs. Janek followed Artie to art school. That figures. I kicked the pad under the bed with my left toe.

"I don't know what she's talking about."

Andrew grabbed my hands and held them between his own. They felt a little cold.

"Mary, I need you to think about something carefully."

Here it comes. He does know.

"You've been back on your feet a long time now. Back then I really understood why you couldn't go to church with us."

My chest heaved in relief, and also a little in fatigue; we had talked about this a lot before.

"I think you could go now," he said.

"Andrew, I'm lugging around a lot of extra weight. I'm tired now all the time. Can't this just wait?"

147

He dropped my hands and stood up, running his hand through his hair the way he did whenever he was upset. Unbuttoning his shirt and loosening his tie, his face looked like it was about to flare with anger but then his eyes dropped down to my belly. I felt nervous the way he looked at it.

"When you're feeling better, we're gonna have to talk about this. It's real important to me and to the family."

I found out how important it was to Andrew on June 2, a Sunday that brought an early summer heat wave so full of humidity that the drapes in the room felt like steaming towels. I lay on top of the blankets on the bed, feeling the bristles of the wool yarn of the Irish quilt prick my bare calves. Staring down at their white flesh that made them look like fat summer sausages as they ballooned out from under my light blue cotton summer dress, I tried to remember how my legs looked just a couple months ago, before they swelled. Forget trying to remember their thin, girlish look just a year ago. An ancient fan wheezed air toward me as its blades, crusted by what looked like decades of gray grime, sent out a faint smell of the mechanic's oil my dad used. Wouldn't it be strange if he had fixed this fan sometime before. I'm sure he could never have guessed who that grimy beast would be cooling.

Andrew, Daisy and Gerald were still at church as usual while I daydreamed about the fan. But I got back to work quickly because this Sunday was different from all the other ones I spent alone in the house; I was finishing Daisy's Madonna and child. Even though she tried to get a hold of Artie to prove that Andrew wasn't the father, which she couldn't do because I couldn't even prove it, the fights with Gerald still continued. Maybe it was just the feeling of relief when I found out the Janeks moved to New York instead of my pity for her, or else just the pleasure of doing art again. Whatever it was, I wanted to finish the painting.

My brush flew across the top of the paper, blending a line of Prussian blue with water to make a graded wash sky behind the subjects. With that done, my brush stopped like it was tired of painting and I looked over the work. Gowns look good. Halo subtle on both. Colors unify subjects to background. Done. I picked up the painting and held it out to see if I could do anymore work on it. Comparing it to the picture in the book, I saw it had some problems; the Madonna's hand looks off in its foreshortening; Jesus' head might be too big. As a whole thing, it worked okay and if I didn't want to start it all over again, I had to accept that this was as good as I could get it. Something was missing in it, though. I surrendered the brush to my jar of water, and then dropped it with a clink into my metal paint box.

As I snapped the box closed, I looked at the photo of the painting

148

in a way I hadn't seen it before. I had only ever examined its parts, its proportion, and its composition. That's how I was able to draw and paint it. It was a thing I wanted to duplicate and except for the couple problems I noticed, I did accomplish that. But what was missing? All of a sudden, the Madonna's expression, the way her eyes looked like they were caressing the child, the expression caught me. Her hands curled around the baby Jesus' body in a way that they both clutched him in protection and upheld him in adoration. My eyes shot back to my work. Yep. There's the expression on her face, her slightly parted lips as she soothes the baby. Her hands look like the painting's, too. I had captured the painting, but somehow, my work looked like the paintings in a Sunday school book. Like a frozen religious moment. Da Vinci's painting captured a religious moment, but froze it with all of the subjects' human frailties; this wasn't the supreme mother of God, but a mother loving her child, regardless of what the child was going to be to the world. This was a mother's devotion, a mother's affection, and a mother's worry, all of it captured in flat, plain colors. All of the colors of my palette couldn't bring out these qualities and I guess I wasn't born with the deep talent to see and re-create them, either.

This realization, and my failure to capture all of the painting's feeling in my copy, caused a contraction of tears in me. I sweated from the heat in the room as thick tears coated my face with liquid heat. I slammed the book shut. Lying back and ignoring my painting at the end of the bed, I pulled Andrew's pillow from his side, and a waft of his hair oil goaded my pain. My chest heaved with a wail as I clutched the pillow to my fat belly. The baby kicked inside and I felt sorry for it being trapped inside me. A black wall of sleep rolled over me.

"Well, what's this, dee-yer?" Daisy's voice broke through the haze of my sleep. I sat up to find Daisy and Andrew standing at the foot of the bed, both regarding the Madonna and child.

"When did you do this?" Andrew asked.

I shifted on the bed and tried to wedge the pillows behind my back to relieve some of the ache but I was having more trouble than usual. Andrew, as always, jumped to my side and fluffed and molded the pillows into a firm support. My mouth was thick and dry from my sleep when Andrew kissed me hello. His face looked frazzled with worry.

"I didn't know you had this much talent, dee-yer."

"It's for you, Daisy. As a thank you."

"It's exactly what I've been looking for."

Her appreciation surprised me, but not her inability to recognize what I found to be the major problem with the work. Art was obviously a thing to her, not a feeling. She held the painting close to her face. 'Here we go,' I thought.

"What kind of paint is this?"

"Watercolor."

Daisy's face contorted with disappointment.

"Oh. That means it won't last as long as an oil painting, right?" she said.

"I suppose not," I said.

"It's still beautiful, dee-yer. Thank you."

Andrew wrapped his arms together in a tight package and his right leg that he had crossed over his left was vibrating like a nervous hummingbird. "What's the matter with him?" I thought.

"Mary, the painting's just great and all, but we got a real problem," he blurted. 'We just spoke with Father Haggarty, and he agrees."

By 'we,' I knew Andrew meant Daisy. Preparing for her part in this conversation, she quietly set the Madonna and Child aside, slid an armchair over to the edge of the bed on Andrew's right side, and folded her hands as if she was about to pray. Like twin gargoyles I had seen in photos of buildings in Europe, Andrew and Daisy leaned toward me and stared. My eyes moved between Daisy's narrow expression and Andrew's frown. I'm naked again, I thought. Whatever it was that was so important to Andrew, I wish he would have told me privately.

"Mary, now you know I've looked away all these Sundays when you haven't come to church with us," he began.

"I've been sick practically the whole time with the baby and all."

"I know. I understand that. But the time has come, with you being so close to having the baby."

"Son, spit it out," Daisy chimed in.

"Father Haggarty told me today that if you don't accept the sacrament of Baptism now, and you have problems -- he crossed himself -- both you and the baby are gonna end up in Purgatory for all time."

"You'll have to confess and renounce all your past sins. All of them, dee-yer."

Daisy emphasized the word 'all' with an icy stare. Andrew looked like he was ready to explode from all his tension and worry. I felt backed into a corner and I wanted to run from them.

"In order to be baptized, do I have to say I believe?"

A frantic glance from Andrew prompted Daisy to answer.

"As an adult, to be welcomed into the Church, you would need to acknowledge God, Jesus, and the Church."

"Come on, Mary. We can get Father Haggarty here this afternoon. Please," Andrew said.

"But I can't."

"Why?" Daisy roared.

"Do it for the baby, Mary," Andrew added.

"Why?" Daisy roared again.

"My dad told me don't ever to pretend to believe in something you don't believe. Believe it with all your heart, or forget it."

"What does that hick know?" Daisy said.

"Mary, you saying you don't believe in God at all?" Andrew asked.

I thought about all the Sundays I had been watching Andrew and his family go to church. It seemed so automatic that it almost felt like it was mechanical. Or phony. The priests who came to visit were real enough with their drinking and poker, but did they feel like God's messengers? Dad and his faith in science and invention seemed more truthful than anything the priests ever said. And what about Daisy and Gerald's fighting? That didn't convince me of the power of God in their lives, either. I just wasn't sure about it right then.

"I don't know yet, Andrew."

"Mary, does it make a difference if I tell you I can't go on loving you unless you convert?"

"A long time ago, you said you love me for who I am, and that if I _"

My stomach twisted in on itself and erupted with pain that felt like it was going to blow the top of my head off. Nerves seemed to shoot electricity through my arms and down my legs.

"Mary?" Andrew jumped to my side.

Another great surge of twisting muscle pounded toward my thighs. My breath left me in reaction to this second pain and my eyes felt like hard-boiled eggs. Pound, surge, pound, surge, and I could barely keep my eyes open.

"It's time. We gotta get her to the hospital," I heard Daisy say as if she stood in a cave.

Gerald drove us to the hospital, I think, but all I could see was the red and yellow of my stomach pain. Suddenly, I lay on my back with a man and a woman in white staring down at me as overhead lights flew by. We paused under a set of metal lights and a spongy cloth that smelled like turpentine was brought to my face.

"Inhale, please," I heard, and when I did, my breath was choked off and I gasped for air. The people leaning over me nodded and smiled, and the white of their uniforms, the green of the walls, and the red and yellow of the pain swirled into a multi-colored cyclone right in front of my eyes. Blackness hit.

A figure stepped out of the blackness and it looked like it came from one of the ghost stories Irma and me used to read: gauzy fabric made a hood, and flowed down the figure's arms, spilling into a gown tied at the

151

figure's waist. Bright blue and white light glowed from its face and as it floated toward me, I thought I recognized it.

"The Madonna?" I said. But the figure just kept floating toward me like a cloud on a northeast wind.

"Virgin Mary?" I said. Now my arms and legs shook with fear. The figure was so near that it seemed to throw its arms around me and the white light from its face burned my eyes.

"Mary?" a voice echoed. Ammonia burned my nose and my eyes stung as a flood of yellow light dissolved the figure away.

"Mary?" the female voice said again. With my eyes still aching from the figure's bright light, I looked around and saw a round metal ceiling lamp, and a woman in a white uniform leaning over me. Her head was upside down and she wore a white hat. 'A nurse?' I thought. A clock on the wall clicked its minute hand to show it was five minutes to twelve, but I didn't know where I was, or if it was even day or night.

"Mary, can you hear me?" the nurse said.

Her voice scratched like metal in my ear. My head felt full of cotton but I was just able to lift my stiff neck and nod my head. The bed vibrated underneath me and the ceiling started to move.

"I'm in the hospital?" I whispered, my breath a dry wind over the grit of my throat and the sponge that was my tongue.

"Umm-hmm" the nurse said through a smile.

Some sort of sharp edge poked against my cheek like a dress label sometimes does to my neck. Turning my head to see what it was, the nurse reached her hand next to my cheek.

"Don't worry. I'll tell you."

Still in too much of a daze to even know what I was doing in the hospital, and not feeling like I could even ask a simple question, I just stared at her.

"Hang on a second," she said.

The nurse turned the bed I was on to the left and the smell of disinfectant and rubbing alcohol burned through my dull nose. My weight started to shift on the bed and I felt my arm bump into a cold, metal bar but I couldn't lift my head enough to see past my pillow. Grabbing it, I asked the nurse what it was.

"Just a safety rail. Makes sure you don't fall off."

The bed came to a stop and the nurse yanked on the side of it, making the creaking sound of a folding ironing board.

"Let's get you on this one," she said. As she pulled the pillow from under my head, I saw the edge that had been jabbing me: it was a white index card with a safety pin holding it to my pillow. She walked around to the bottom of the bed I was on and lifted my legs onto the other bed.

"I can't feel. I can't feel 'me," I said.

My legs were dead logs hanging off my body and it scared me.

"That's just the Novocain. It'll wear off later. Boy will it."

Back at the top of the other bed, the nurse grabbed my arm and shoulder.

"You're gonna have to help me with this part."

With a count of three, she pulled and I pushed with my arms, and we both grunted as my body shifted onto the new bed. Just that effort by itself made me really tired. I wanted to sleep.

"Well, hang on a second," she said. She sounded kind of irritated with me.

The safety pin popped in my ear and the index card slid with a scratch from the pillow. The nurse must have been far sighted or something, because she held the card out from her face a full arm's length. She broke out into a grin.

"Look at that," she said. She held the card so that I could read it and I could just make out two crooked, typed words: 'Murphy. Boy.'
Sleep avalanched on me.

When I woke up again, my neck and head weren't as stiff. The rubbing alcohol and chlorine bleach smell from before was softened by the smell of flowers. On a table in the corner of the room I could now see was painted pale yellow, a vase of red roses stood tall next to a short bowl of daisies. On my left, I saw a window with its beige Venetian blinds drawn open. Daylight made the room feel like a sunny kitchen. The nurse from before passed by the oak door that was propped open and when she saw I was awake, she gestured for me to wait a minute. As she walked off with her shoes clanking against the tile floor, I thought, 'Where does she think I can go?'

My lower legs began to tingle and even though they hurt, I was glad that didn't feel dead anymore. Burning pain shot up my body as the muscles in my lower stomach area seemed to clench then loosen on their own under my skin that still felt dead.

"Was that a pigeon?" I thought when I heard gurgling and cooing all of a sudden just outside the door. But it also crackled and sounded like it was choking.

"What's a bird doing in the hospital?" the thought bothered me. The bird's odd sounds got louder, but in a second, I knew it wasn't a bird: Andrew walked into my room, a lighthouse beacon of a smile shining on his face.

He carried a bundled white blanket and from its folds, I could hear the bird sounds. But then I saw something else: a tiny, pink hand that reached and grabbed at the air like a greedy claw. Andrew pressed his lips

153

against mine, as he lowered the bundle into my arms. Over the folds of the blanket, a head that was no bigger but just as dappled as a pomegranate, lolled back and forth, its thin wisps of black hair sticking out in all directions. The baby's eyes were purple-edged, pink folds and his hands reached up with a jerk and touched his nose that looked like pink and amber wax. Two tiny lips smacked together as the baby suckled in its sleep. Andrew's mouth, I thought.

As the baby twisted and adjusted his sleeping body, I couldn't believe that this living thing came from me. His smacking mouth and his quaking hands seemed to reach through me, into my heart. I held him to me and could smell a delicate powder and his newborn skin that smelled like honeysuckle.

Andrew, who now shared the bed with us as he leaned on his elbow, pulled the baby's blanket back with his fingertips and stared at the child. A smile I didn't recognize took over his face -- was it fear or amazement? -- while a dew drop of a tear dangled on each of his lower eyelids. Andrew threw his arm around my neck and kissed my face and neck over and over.

"Thank you, Mary. Thank you."

A sense of alarm disturbed me.

"Andrew, are we still calling him Ernest Gerald?"

"Yeah. Yeah. That's a good name."

Ernest Gerald turned his tiny head and his lids parted just enough to show his pale blue eyes. The blanket flattened his nose as he fell to sleep. Andrew buried his face in my neck and I felt him vibrate as he cried silently into my shoulder. Suddenly, I knew that this is what my life must be meant for: to bring new life into the world.

154

10.

"You could feed the whole world with those things," Daisy said. She handed me a hand towel then left the room. She was right this time because my breasts had become swollen honeydew melons of milk for Ernest Gerald. I slid the shoulder of my housedress down and released what felt like an anvil. As Ernest Gerald clamped onto the raw nipple, I could still hear Andrew's brother, John, and Gerald grumbling at each other then bursting out with laughter. John was on a business trip from Philadelphia but stayed around to celebrate Andrew's nineteenth birthday.

"Hold on a second, Ernie," I said. At four months old, Ernie's little, toothless gums clenched my nipple like a vise. Pulling my breast away for a second, Ernie began to fuss and struggle to re-attach himself. The pain eased up and I brought him back to my breast.

"There you go," I said.

His mouth gulped and grabbed as he fed, but he didn't bear down this time. He knew what hurt me, I think. Ernie's suckling sounds were loud enough to drown out the wind and frozen rain that threatened to become October snow. The vanilla smell of his head that I had rubbed earlier with baby oil began to lull me. I needed to calm down right then because I really didn't want to miss any of Andrew's birthday party and I hated being isolated in our room like this. Andrew did not like to see Ernie feeding so he left me alone whenever it was time for the baby to eat.

Even though we had been having intercourse almost every day since Ernie was a month old, Andrew would not touch my breasts and insisted that I keep them covered. So here I sat with Ernie, his clicking and slurping sounds in between his moans of feeding satisfaction, the substitute for the jokes and guffaws going on in the parlor. A crisp knock on the front door caused everyone to quiet down. Daisy's little feet clattered to answer it.

"Wonder who else was invited?" I said to Ernie. He kept eating and I kissed his head. Daisy's voice shrieked and it startled me. Ernie's eyes popped open and he pulled away from me and started to whimper.

"Come on, sweetie. It's time to burp a little."

I turned Ernie onto my shoulder and began to pat his little back that felt firm and soft as a sack of flour. His flannel pajamas muffled the

155

hollow echo of each pat and his shoulders began to heave with hiccoughs. He clenched his hands into fists as he drove his lips into my shoulder, still trying to suckle. Murmurs and what sounded like an angry shout caused me to stand and go to the bedroom door. It flew open just as I got to it. Andrew stopped short from running into me as he waved a torn letter. Panic seemed to bristle his whole body.

"This is it. I can't believe they sent it on my birthday."

"What?"

"I've been drafted. I gotta be at Camp Roberts in ten days."

"What does that mean?"

Andrew reached out and wrapped his arms around Ernie and me. Ernie was still hiccoughing. "Mary, it means I'm going to war."

"How far away is Camp Roberts?"

He read the telegram again, and then dropped his arms to his sides. His face looked like it had fallen off his head. "California. I gotta go to California. In ten days." Andrew walked over and dropped onto the bed. I didn't know how to help him right then, but when Daisy burst in, I knew that probably wouldn't help much at all. Daisy's face was red and her eyes were blobbed with tears as she stood at the edge of the bed, her two hands holding crystal glasses with what looked like gin and ice in them. One was half empty and Daisy raised that one to her lips. She thrust the other toward Andrew.

"Your dad just poured this for you. Take it."

Andrew shook his head. He tossed the letter on the bed and reached out for my hand. Ernie cooed.

"Now's not the time to play Carrie Nation. This'll help you calm down."

"I don't want it, Mom. Save it for Dad."

Daisy took another sip from her drink then set the one she tried to offer to Andrew on the bed table. She snatched the letter up from the bed and read it again. She folded it and placed it in the pocket of her skirt.

"Case you change your mind. One drink ain't gonna hurt anything."

"Andrew, can't you tell 'em you got Ernie? He's so small and all, maybe they would reconsider," I said.

"You don't get it, do you?" Daisy said. "Every boy in town is already over there or getting ready to go. You want people to think he's hiding behind you and the baby? He's gotta go. We knew this was coming."

Andrew stood and snatched up the drink. He put his arm around Daisy and she leaned her head against his shoulder and started to cry. Guiding her out the door, he set the drink into her left hand and she

156

sneered at him.

"You should try the gin or something else, Andrew. It'd really help at a time like this." Andrew led Daisy out of the room. Once she was safely out, he turned and shut the door. He locked it.

"Mary, I need you."

Andrew's face looked frightened as he drew his hand through his hair. Walking over, he took Ernie, who was now sleeping, and set him in his cradle. The sour smell of Ernie's milk spit wafted past my nose as Andrew pulled the burping cloth from my shoulder. 'Please, I need you now.' Andrew slid his hand under the shoulder of my housedress. I slid back from him.

"Andrew, everyone's still out in the parlor."

But he didn't hear me. He pushed me gently onto the bed and slid the housedress up until it gathered over my breasts. Climbing on top of me, he began to kiss my neck lightly.

That day began a period of constant sex that seemed to replace any other communication. Even as Andrew packed his bags, did the final inventories at the produce market, or visited his baseball friends for a goodbye, he never talked about being afraid of going to war or leaving us. The only thing that showed he was worried during those last ten days that swept by us like minutes was his brow that was twisted like putty. But he didn't say anything. Instead, he'd come home, set Ernie in his cradle, throw the lock on the door, and then take me. Each of the last sex acts before he left, I could feel him pour his fear and anxiety into me. And always afterwards, he would hold me and not talk.

We rolled away from each other one afternoon. The sunlight that made it through the thick, early November snow flurry cast a silver and blue tint against the dark cherry wood of our room. The soft peach smell of his hair pomade mixed with the spearmint of his breath that lingered on my face. Unlike all last week, when our sex finished with a calm relaxed embrace, this time, Andrew tapped my leg with his barefoot, a nervous, soft drumbeat. He reached for his cigarettes.

"Andrew. Not while Ernie's in here sleeping. It'll make him cough."

He dropped the package back onto the night table, cleared his throat with a thick grunt, and then pulled the blanket up to his neck. Andrew stared at the ceiling and I could tell he wanted to say something but couldn't find the right words. I was anxious just to hear what he was thinking or feeling. 'I go in four days.' The thought of his leaving sent a searing shock through me as my stomach twisted.

"I know," was all I could get out.

"I've been thinking," he said. "No. Let me say it right -- I'm really worried about something."

"We'll be okay here with Daisy and Gerald." I said that soothingly, but I wasn't sure what he was getting at.

"I know you'll be okay."

A wind gust rattled branches against the window, causing Ernie to growl in his sleep. I tensed, waiting to hear him rustle awake. His steady breathing returned and I glanced up at the window. Through the rattling branches, I thought I saw a long veil. I sat up.

"You see her?" I said. Andrew turned his head to look around the room. He shrugged.

"Who?"

The veil now took the definite form of a person's head and shoulders. A woman, I thought. I suddenly recognized her: it was the Madonna from the hospital. I pointed.

"Look. There's a woman out there."

Andrew rushed to the window and looked out, the ivory skin of his back and bare rear end standing out against the dark wood of the wall. He leaned so that his head almost touched the windowpane, looking left, then right. When he turned back around, the Madonna in the window was gone.

"The sky's all silver and gray out there. Must have cast a mirage on the window or something," he said as he slid back under the blanket next to me. I lay back, but I could feel goose bumps on my arms. She was there, I know it.

"Mary. I got a chill. It must be twenty below outside."

"Sorry, Andrew. But I know I saw someone."

Andrew sighed deeply and crossed his arms behind his head. Staring again at the ceiling, his forehead was wrinkled pie dough.

"Andrew. Tell me what's the matter."

"I'm afraid I might die over there."

"Oh, please don't think things like that."

"That ain't it, Mary. It's just that if I die over there, I'm going to miss you in Heaven."

"In the first place, you're not gonna die. You're too smart to get killed. In the second, you shouldn't worry so much about what happens after you die."

"Every day I'm there, I'm gonna worry about you. About your soul."

"What is he getting at?" I thought and the thought made me feel anxious.

He went on. "And what if the Japs or Krauts bomb here? What'll happen to you?"

"Andrew, this is crazy talk."

158

He wrapped his arms around me and pulled my face to his so that our noses touched. His eyelashes looked like grass blades sprinkled with dew.

"Mary. Tomorrow's Sunday. I leave Wednesday. I need you to accept the Lord and the Church."

So that was it. The baptism and conversion stuff again.

"Andrew, not this again. I'm due on my cycle and if I leave the house I'm gonna have to wear protection."

"You gotta do it for me. Or all I'm gonna do is worry every single minute about your soul."

He pressed his nose against my throat and I could feel the warm trickle of his tears. What if I never do see him again after Wednesday? Or what if he gets an arm or leg blown off? Or his ... It wouldn't take that much to make him happy and I could always cross my fingers or something if they ask me if I believe in God and the Church. I saw no choice. He didn't need to be worrying about us while he was fighting. I gave in.

"Okay."

"Mary, really?"

His face was as happy as the day Ernie was born. He sat up in bed and tucked his pillows behind his back.

"Yeah. So what do I gotta do?"

"Mom'll have to talk to Father Haggarty. Probably you could be baptized after mass tomorrow."

"So you'll come and get me after mass and we'll do it?"

"No, Mary. You should go to mass tomorrow at Saint Anthony's so that Father Haggarty will see that you're a serious convert."

"Okay."

"It'll just take a couple of minutes. Remember how Ernie was baptized?"

"Yeah."

"It'll be the same way."

"Okay, Andrew. Okay."

"Thank you, Mary. Thank you."

"Deo gratias," Father Haggarty sang without the organ.

"That means Thanks be to God," Andrew whispered while we stood next to each other, one pew behind Gerald and Daisy. I sat right behind Daisy and admired the small square of beige lace that looked like a hanky she wore on her head. Father Haggarty had just walked in, his white and red satin sleeves billowing like shiny clouds. He held his hands up toward the ceiling like he was hugging the air. I had only ever seen him at the house in his black jacket and black pants and I almost didn't recognize him. Sunlight made his robe burn with shiny color and the three little boys

159

that stood behind him in bright white and black looked like the baby skunks Irma found in the back of the garage one day. Bright red poinsettias climbed and cascaded around the gold cage that sat in the middle of the altar. The gold cage was draped with red and white satin.

"In Italian or something?" I asked but I was barely interested in the answer. All the colors and forms bewitched me.

"No. Latin."

I rocked Ernie on my left shoulder and didn't really care what language it was because the sound of Father Haggarty's singing voice was rich and beautiful to my ear. Looking up past the altar, two narrow, stained glass windows allowed rainbows of colors to flood the beige walls behind the altar, making a graded wash of hues that I suddenly wanted to paint. A wood carving of Jesus Christ hanging on the cross in rich mahogany hung right between the windows and seemed to radiate the color from its sides. Father Haggarty sang another phrase in Latin and his velvet voice, coupled with the array of colors and textures of the ornate altar, made me feel like I was standing in a Rembrandt painting. Candles flickered on the altar and they cast sparks of light on the gold cage. All the photos of Europe and its art treasures I had seen couldn't match what I was looking at now. Ernie cooed like he knew how gorgeous everything was, too.

"Mary? Mary!" Andrew said harshly.

Andrew's voice startled me and when I looked over to him, he was now kneeling. I heard what sounded like Daisy's sigh and when I looked toward her, she and Gerald were kneeling, too. Suddenly, I realized that the whole congregation was kneeling but I was the only one standing. My face heated up when I saw Father Haggarty glare at me from the altar. Andrew pulled my arm and I kneeled.

The kneeling, standing and sitting went on and on and I had no idea why or what, because the singing Latin stopped and the speaking Latin began. Everyone seemed to understand what Father Haggarty was saying but I didn't care. I was uncomfortable because I was due to start my cycle the day before and I didn't want to have it happen on this important day. So I wore my towel, and its dry edges pushed against my sensitive skin as the wooden pew forced it harder against me while I sat. With all the standing and sitting, it shifted out of whack and it irritated me no matter what position I was in.

Some relief came whenever the organ and choir jumped in at different moments. All the times I heard about the choirs of heaven, I now knew that this is where that idea must have come from. The voices with the organ seemed to make the walls vibrate around me and my chest quaked from the music. After what seemed like an hour, Daisy, Gerald and Andrew stood up to join a single line that led up to Father Haggarty who

160

was now laying little white wafers on people's tongues.

"Time for communion," Andrew said.

I only knew that it was the end of the church service when the steeple bell began to chime and it sounded like that Big Ben clock in England. Chills shot up and down me when I heard it. Father Haggarty raised his arms and said something else in Latin, and then people started to file down the center of the church. I now saw that all the women wore lace veils of different lengths as they passed by us, every now and then one of them would nod to Daisy and Gerald. As Daisy and Gerald moved into the flow of people, Andrew nudged me to step in behind them. But I had to get one more look at the altar and the mahogany ceiling that soared over my head and at the narrow windows that let in the gray sun that seemed to brighten the church's beige walls. Glancing over my shoulder, the pipes of the organ in the choir loft were a pewter and platinum forest. God, did I want to paint it all right then. God, did I want to paint anything.

"Let's hurry, Mary. We have to meet Father Haggarty in the baptismal room."

Andrew pushed me a little harder and when I joined the people filing out, a strong smell of lilac almost choked me. Someone had bad taste in perfume, I thought. My shoes scraped along the granite tile floor and when we got to the paneled oak doors that led to the outside of the church, Andrew nudged me to the left. I recognized the narrow door and as Andrew pulled it aside, it creaked on its hinges. Ernie was now riding my arm like it was a pony and as we passed into the dark baptismal room, Daisy snatched Ernie from me.

"I'll hang on to him till we're finished, dee-yer."

My eyes had to actually adjust in the room that was more like a vault with three stained glass windows that weren't more than six inches wide each. Father Haggarty stood next to the granite baptismal font that I remembered from Ernie's baptism. Andrew joined Daisy and Gerald to the side of the font and he patted and kissed Ernie who was now riding Daisy's arm, a big smile that was dividing his face was ready to become a giggle at any second. That was one of the only times in his six months of life that Daisy actually held him for longer than a second and it warmed me to see that he was okay in her arms.

"Mary, welcome. Can you take off yer hat, please," Father Haggarty said. I pulled the felt hat that was adorned with cherries and cherry blossoms from my head and Andrew reached out to take it from me. One side of my hair fell from the knot I had wrapped under the hat and I reached to tuck it back up.

"You're in the sight of the Lord, Mary. You don't have to be perfect," Father Haggarty said.

161

Glancing at Andrew and feeling a little embarrassed, I let the piece of hair fall back down. Father Haggarty waved me to the edge of the font.

"I need to ask you a couple of questions before I can baptize you."

"Okay."

"First, are you willing to renounce all your past sins, and to renounce Satan and his minions?"

Andrew had warned me that this would be one of the questions and he instructed me to say 'yes,' even though I still wasn't sure what anyone meant by it. I looked over at him and I could see in his eyes the look of worry. I wouldn't let him down, not now, not ever.

"Yes."

"Do you understand that this is the beginning of your catechism, and that you agree to pursue all the teachings of Christ and the Church in order to receive all the sacraments?"

Uh-oh. This one Andrew didn't mention before. I glanced at him and he nodded. Daisy stared icily at me.

"Yeah, okay."

"The final question, Mary. Do you accept the Lord Jesus Christ as the only Son of God, and acknowledge that the only true church of the Lord is the holy apostolic Catholic Church? That He is the light and the truth of the earth and universe?"

I glanced again at Andrew who looked like he was ready to jump out of his skin. Daisy's face pursed as if she was waiting to hear my lie, too. The colors of the altar, the pounding of the organ, the peal of the bell flashed through my mind. Something with all this beauty can't be wrong, could it? *'Believe it with all your heart,'* Dad seemed to whisper in my ear. Pressing my hand against the base of the font and stepping to the side to block it from everyone's view, I crossed my index finger over my middle finger. This is for you, my Andrew, my lord, I thought.

"Yes. I accept the Lord and his Church."

Andrew stifled a sigh or a cry, I couldn't tell which. Father Haggarty placed his hand on the back of my neck and it felt rough but warm. Guiding my head just over the water that had a stale, flat odor, he pushed my head toward the bowl until the tip of my nose was just touching the surface of the water. "Mary, turn your face toward me, please." I craned my neck so that I got a sideways view of Father Haggarty.

"Mary Benton Hellman Murphy, I baptize you, in the name of the Father, the Son, and the Holy Spirit."

Father Haggarty scooped up a handful of the water and poured it over my forehead. It cascaded down over my hair, and it percolated gently back into the bowl. "Amen," I heard Andrew say like he was relieved, Gerald say like he didn't care, and Daisy say like she just lost the war with

162

the Japanese. Father Haggarty handed me a small cotton cloth for my forehead and as I dabbed at it, the towel shifted in my underpants again and it felt as moist as my head and hair. I turned to Andrew.

"We have to go now. I got a personal problem."

Once we got home from the church, I checked my towel and I hadn't begun my cycle yet. Monday all the way into Tuesday, the day before Andrew was to leave on the train, I hadn't started. By that night, I was four days late on my cycle, and I wasn't sure whether I should tell Andrew or not. After all, he had a lot more on his mind than my moody body. I was being stupid, anyway. No one gets pregnant six months after having a baby. Your body has to have time to recover from it and nurse the new baby. It doesn't have time to send down a new egg. So why bother Andrew with it?

"Mary, I need you. Come over here," Andrew said. He lay in bed with his green and orange plaid flannel pajamas. I had just finished rocking Ernie to sleep and bent over and kissed his little warm head. Stepping over to Andrew, I pulled up the bottom of my pink flannel nightgown, and then climbed on top of the covers. I figured we would be doing it again, the third time that day, the umpteenth time in the last week. Andrew rolled over and kissed my bare knee, then pulled the nightgown back down. Throwing back the covers, he slipped down to the side of the bed and kneeled. He patted the bed for me to join him and I was confused.

"Mary, I need you to pray with me."

I slid down next to Andrew and pulled my nightgown back down, sort of embarrassed now that he was getting ready to pray. I folded my hands and leaned them on the bed and our shoulders touched. He crossed himself and began. "Dear Lord," he said. "Please send your angels to watch over my Mary and Ernie. Protect them while I'm gone, and provide your blessings to them. I pray that you watch over me, too, and get me home as quick as possible to take care of my wife and boy."

That prayer led into a multiple number of requests, followed by prayers to every saint and angel Andrew could think of. We spent half the night on our knees until Andrew's voice became hoarse. When we finally climbed into bed, Andrew rolled over onto his side and curled his arms around me and we fell asleep.

The morning hit hard and Ernie's cries that sounded choked by saliva and mucous woke us up just before the wind-up alarm clock clanged its tin bells. Our room was still dark as night even though it was seven-thirty in the morning. Glancing out the window, each pane a fog of thick frost, I could see that a light snow covered the ground and the sky was black and thick with more water, heavy as lead. The house was unusually quiet.

163

Daisy prepared a breakfast of fried eggs, bacon, and French toast fried in cinnamon and butter, Andrew's favorites, and the dark cherry dining table sparkled with crystal and china. But the clinking of tines against porcelain and the gurgle of coffee being poured into cups were the only sounds as we all sat as quiet as if we were at a wake. Daisy picked at her plate and would touch the corners of her mouth with the sharp corner of her red linen napkin and I didn't know if anyone else noticed as she dabbed at her eyes before dropping her napkin back into her lap. Andrew ate without looking up, and he held my hand with his left hand through the whole meal. After finishing three eggs and six pieces of French toast, and what seemed to be a side of bacon, he glanced at his watch and stood up.

"Train leaves in an hour. Gotta get going here."

Daisy dropped her fork and stood as Gerald slurped the rest of his cup of coffee. Daisy followed Andrew back to the bedroom and when he came back out with his two bags in his hand and his thick coat over his arm, she followed behind. Andrew stopped and placed his bags at the front door and again, Daisy stayed right behind him like a lost puppy. I grabbed up Ernie from his blanket on the floor and joined them at the front door. Gerald came up behind me and I could hear his arm slide into his wool jacket.

"I guess this is it," Andrew said.

Gerald stepped around us and pulled open the front door and an icy gust made us all shiver. "I'll get these bags into the car and get it warmed up," he said. Gerald stepped out.

"Dad, wait."

Andrew grabbed his jacket. Daisy helped him slide on his jacket and she began to button it up. "Mom, I can do that."

"Shut up," her voice cracked. "From the time you were Ernie's size, when you went out to play, or when you went out for Halloween trick-or-treating, or went to school in the morning, I always buttoned your coat. Just let me do it." She buttoned the top button, and then pulled his collar up around his ears. I don't think he realized it but as she finished with his coat, Andrew held his arms out like a little kid. He all of sudden looked so young to me. Daisy slipped both hands over his face and held it for a second.

"You be good, Andrew. And you come home just as quick as you can."

She kissed his left cheek, then his right cheek. As she pulled away, her eyes were black circles of running makeup. Andrew reached out and threw his arms around Daisy. "I love you, Mom. I'll make you proud, I swear."

Daisy pulled away and reached for Ernie. The way she took him

164

from me was like she was grabbing a sack of potatoes out of obligation. I didn't like that. "Whyd'nt you go with them to the train station?"

She turned and carried Ernie off to the kitchen. I wanted to grab him back, but then Andrew's sad, wet eyes flared with a smile and I ran and grabbed my overcoat.

Gerald had to drive slow through the light snowfall and when we pulled up to the train station, two trains sat side-by-side, their underbellies both bursting and blasting with steam while conductors and men in engineer uniforms were running all over the place. When we got out of the car, the snow had stopped but it felt colder than when we left the house. Gerald grabbed Andrew's bags and turned away when Andrew tried to take them from him.

Inside the small station that was no more than three benches and two ticket windows, Andrew took the bags from Gerald and walked up to check in. The station smelled like old cigars and worn leather. A woman in a tight skirt and fancy stockings grabbed a child by the hand and walked past Gerald and me. Gerald's eyes followed her plump rear end in its gray wool skirt. I looked over to Andrew who hadn't noticed her and watched as the cashier nodded and pointed to his left. Andrew ran back to join us. "Train leaves in five minutes. We just made it."

"I'm gonna go and start the car and keep it running," Gerald said. "I'll let you two have some time."

Gerald turned quickly and started to walk away. Andrew grabbed his shoulder. "Dad." Gerald turned back around, and his face that was usually just a flat expression of boredom looked puffy and red. 'He's been crying,' I thought. Andrew stood facing Gerald and it looked like neither of them knew quite what to do. Gerald looked around, and then put his hand out. I was sure Andrew would throw his arms around Gerald, but instead, he took his hand. As they shook, Gerald wrapped his other hand around their intertwined fingers.

"Lord bless you, son. Your Mom and I love you. Come home safe."

Gerald released his grip and turned toward the door. As he pushed the scarred wooden door, I saw him pull out a handkerchief and bring it to his eyes.

"Last call for Hopkins to Denver nine-thirty-five" the cashier roared.

"Let's go," he said.

I followed Andrew out past the platform, to the steps of the car he would be riding in. He threw his arms around me and kissed my neck, then my face. He pushed his cheek hard against mine and I knew I couldn't talk because a lump rolled up my throat. He couldn't, either.

"My love," he whispered. "My Mary. I'll be home soon."

But my eyes were fountains of heat and water and my mouth filled with a thick pain. Deep inside my chest, my lungs and stomach contracted and pulsed, pumping tears over my cheeks.

"Last call, nine-thirty-five!" someone yelled.

Andrew pulled away and stepped back onto the car's steps. The conductor stepped in behind him and threw a metal arm across the small doorway. The train blasted and gushed, and its metal wheels screeched against the frozen rails, sending up the smell of burnt engine oil as it pulled away. The snow began to fall and I could feel my tears freeze on my face.

"I'll write, everyday. I love you with my life," he said.

The train picked up speed and Andrew's face became a blur. But I stood there and watched the train and as it got farther away by each mile, my stomach felt like someone was reaching inside me, pulling and stretching my intestine right along the train track. I didn't know how I would be able to do anything without Andrew, and when the train disappeared like a gray bubble popping against the far horizon, my stomach felt like something snapped. Each minute from that point on felt like a year as I waited to hear from him.

That night, Gerald and Daisy drank more than I ever saw them drink before and at about three in the morning, their yelling voices woke me. Ernie had not been disturbed and I could hear his steady breathing in his cradle. For some reason, their voices were even crisper than usual, like they were standing right outside the door. But this time, it wasn't Daisy who was crying. It was Gerald.

"There's nothing to be done about it," Daisy said. Her voice was as cold and flat as when she spoke to me.

"My son, my baby boy," Gerald seemed to gurgle out through a wail.

"We can only pray and have faith that Andrew's got a good head on his shoulders," Daisy said. "Now stop your crying."

I couldn't believe it, but I thought I heard Gerald break into a sob. I also couldn't believe that Daisy talked to Gerald like that. Who did she think she was talking to anybody like that, let alone, her husband? I was sure Gerald would scream back at her. But he seemed to just keep crying.

"Here. You're gonna wake the kid up and then none of us'll get any sleep."

Gerald's sobs muffled. Daisy must have handed him a pillow or something. They stopped talking, but the worst part of what I heard was Gerald whimpering for the next hour or so.

That next morning, I couldn't get out of bed because every time I thought about Andrew, I felt my whole body sink. I kept Ernie next to me

166

the whole time. Somehow, he made Andrew feel close to me. Daisy burst into the room around ten o'clock.

"Get out a bed already, dee-yer. You've slept enough."

"That isn't it. I just wanna hear from Andrew."

She must have known what I meant. But she kept after me in her usual, mean tone.

"Listen, dee-yer. You're not the only one worried and hurting over Andrew. Let me tell you, no one's happy today. So get up and do some chores and get your mind off of it."

Two days later, I still hadn't heard from Andrew and I woke up with a stomachache that was so bad that when I stood up, I had to upchuck. Daisy had already been taking care of Ernie that morning. She called Doc Anderson out and he stood over me now with his hands on his hips.

"You don't have a fever. Did you say you had any body aches?"

"No," I whispered, afraid to even turn my head because the nausea choked me if I moved at all.

Doc Anderson scratched his blotchy pink forehead right under where his white hair grew like a thin forest. His eyebrows that were wild gray and white weeds sticking over his bifocals arched all of sudden, like he knew what was wrong. Pursing his gray lips, Doc Anderson leaned forward and spoke quietly.

"Young lady, you had your cycle yet this month?"

A wave of Bay Rum floated past as he leaned over me. His quiet tone and the grin that began to turn up the corners of his gray lips made me feel stupid somehow. Course I hadn't had my cycle -- I was sick.

"No. But that's because I'm sick."

"No, Mary. That isn't quite it."

Ernie whimpered somewhere off in another part of the house and my shoulders jerked to get me off the bed all by themselves. But the movement of my body made my stomach, empty as it was, twist and heave.

"You need a bucket there?"

I shook my head and as soon as I lay back, the wrenching nausea stopped. As the wave of nausea passed, a soft sense of relief began to take hold. Until I realized what the doctor must have been getting at. My throat closed with the very idea, but I managed to speak.

"What does all this mean, Doc?"

"Well, girl, it means little Ernie out there's probably going to be somebody else's big brother."

He patted my stomach and his grin widened into a smile. Inside me, a wall of ice collapsed; I couldn't be pregnant again. I couldn't go through all that again: my swollen body that still felt lumpy from Ernie; the

167

tender tips of my breasts that ached all the time; his crying and my sleepless nights, as well as my own crying that joined his like a sad harmony. I was just over the strange sadness that had crept over me just after he was born and had hung around like a dirty thundercloud. No. I couldn't be pregnant again.

"Doc. Are you sure? I thought I wasn't fertile till Ernie was a year old or so. Isn't it too soon?"

"No, Mary. It isn't. To be sure, I'll need some of your urine. But I tell you now, I know a pregnancy when I see one."

Doc Anderson pulled a glass cup from his leather bag and set it on the night table. He nodded toward and patted my shoulder.

"Whyn't you do your business in that cup there and make sure you snap the lid on tight. I'll go out and get one of Daisy's oatmeal muffins and let her know the good news."

He snapped the leather bag closed and crossed to the door, his footsteps dragging. As he opened it, a waft of baked muffins, smelling like burnt molasses, made me feel dizzy. I reached for the cup and all at once, its foggy sides made me think of my mason water jar. When was I ever going to paint again? For the last five months, it seemed like the only colors I ever worked with were the pale white of my milk, or the brown and yellow of Ernie's dirty diapers. Brown, yellow, pale white, and the pink of Ernie's skin; these were my colors now, my limited set of hues. Daisy's Madonna was the last thing I painted and just when Ernie was sleeping through the night and maybe I could start a project, along came this news. Yeah, Doc, I'll fill this cup with yellow for you because I already know what it means.

I grabbed the cup and I slid my feet onto the floor. As I pushed up from the bed, my head swirled with a fog and I could feel my hair was flat from its oil. My legs dangled off the bed and they were puffy and lumpy like they were hanging off a stuffed scarecrow, while my feet were plump pink and blotchy pork roasts. The door burst open and Daisy stood at the foot of the bed.

"Where's Ernie?" I asked.

"Doc's with him out front. They're eating muffins. So. On the nest again, huh?"

She almost spit the word 'nest' at me. I inhaled deeply to beat back my nausea and Daisy's screeching voice didn't soothe my aching head.

"Doc'll know after he checks my pee. I need to get it to him." I waved the cup at Daisy and eased to the edge of the bed.

"Just wait a second, dee-yer."

I wasn't going anywhere too fast right then, that's for sure. I leaned back.

"Yeah?"

"Gerald and me been talking, and since all the boys have left town for the war, he needs help at the market."

"I'm sick, Daisy. Can't this wait?"

"You been waiting long enough to help out around here. How long you think we were going to let you mooch?"

Screeching, nausea. Screeching, nausea.

"Anyway," she went on. "Now with this new one on the way, you're gonna have to earn your keep for all of you."

"What am I supposed to do?"

"Soon as this morning sick crap finishes up, you'll be helping Gerald out at the market."

"I never worked anyplace before. I can't do anything there."

"Sure you can. Stocking. Cashiering. You're a clever girl. Gerald'll figure some use for you. You'll be able to do enough to cover room and board, anyhow."

Yellow, brown, pale white, pink, and the rainbows of fruits and vegetables added in now played through my mind. But I was also afraid to work outside the house and I didn't know why.

"I was really laid up with Ernie the first four or five months. I might be with this one, too."

"I already asked Doc and he said that usually doesn't happen with a second child."

Colors, stomachache, swollen stomach, tender breasts flew through my mind. I really just wanted to give Doc my pee and lay back down.

"Daisy?"

I held the pee cup out to her again and nodded toward it to let her know I needed to get it done. She smirked.

"Oh yeah, all right. So I'll tell Gerald it's all set."

She didn't even wait for a nod from me but walked off, her little feet clicking out the door. It almost sounded like she was dancing as her steps faded. Peeing in that cup was all I could think about.

The next day I was feeling better as I nursed Ernie, and I heard Daisy's footsteps again clicking like a tap dancer as she flung the door open. Ernie's left eye popped open when Daisy ran in, but he kept right on nursing.

"A letter from Camp Roberts! Andrew wrote you!"

She held the envelope out but as I reached for it, she realized I had only one hand. Her thumb was already sliding under the lip of the envelope.

"May I read it aloud?"

"Daisy, it's probably real private, and it might even be—"

169

But with a flip of her wrist, she had the letter out of the envelope and folded open like it was a Japanese fan. Her eyebrows arched as she held the letter far enough so that she could read it.

"My Dearest Mary,

'I just got my first chance to write so I hope you don't feel like I broke my promise to you. I won't be able to write everyday because they got us marching, and climbing, and you wouldn't believe how much they got us working. We're up everyday at five and we aren't dismissed from training till four. Then we got to scrub floors, or dig ditches, or sometimes even clean toilets in the barracks. I'll try and write a couple times a week for now and we'll see what happens once they ship us out.

'How's my Ernie boy? Tell him to be good, and that I expect him to be the man of the house till I get home. I love him so much and I miss him.

'Are Mom and Dad doing okay? I'm sending them their own letter. If this comes first, tell them I love them.

'Mary, I can't believe it's only been a week since I seen you last. It feels like a year, I swear. I just dreamed about you last night but can't tell you about it because all our letters we write get read before they're sent. It's some sort of security thing and I don't want anyone reading personal stuff like that. I'm dreaming of you when I'm awake, too, till we can hold in each other in that special way.'"

Daisy cleared her throat and looked at me, a little embarrassed. She read on:

" 'Anyways, you wouldn't believe the weather here in California. Right in the middle of November, it's seventy-five. Down south, near Hollywood, they got these winds -- Satan's winds, someone told me -- they're so hot and dry that you can barely breathe if they blow. When the war's over, I'm bringing you here for a special treat. I love it.

'We stay here six more weeks, and then we ship out to the South Pacific. Get this: they said that we'd probably be transported on a luxury ship that's been converted. Either the Lurline or the Queen Mary. How about that?

'I gotta go now because it's lights out in five minutes. (They give us a bedtime -- I feel like a kid again.) I gotta get my prayers done. Hey. Have you started catechism yet? I bet you'll do your first confession, communion, and get confirmed before the war's over.

'They gave us each an assignment, some guys are paratroopers, and some are gunmen. Guess what I get to be? A medic! So, I'll kind to get to be a doctor after all, won't I?

'I'll write again soon. Write me back while I'm here.

'I love you, Mary. I miss you with all my heart.

170

'Love, Andrew."

Daisy folded the letter up and stuffed it back into the envelope. Her face puckered in such a way that she almost looked like she just sucked a lemon. She dropped the letter on the bed able.

"Well, that sounded cheery enough," she said. "I'd like to know where our letter is."

Daisy said 'our' as if she expected Andrew to write her more than he was going to write me.

Ernie pulled away and began to hiccough. I laid him on my shoulder and patted his back.

"Since you're feeling better, and since it's Friday, we figured you could start at the market Mondayish."

"What about Ernie?"

"I'll take care a him."

Her version of taking care of him was leaving him on a blanket on the floor and ignoring him unless he cried. But I wasn't about to bring that up as a reason why I wasn't ready to work. I tried something else.

"Hold on. You can't feed him."

Daisy crossed her arms and tapped her tiny toe as if I just asked for a million dollars. She blew air out of her cheeks.

"We'll get a hold of a breast pump for you. Bottles, too. That'll take care of it."

"I'm not sticking my booby into no machine. You crazy?"

"It's not a machine. It's real simple. I'll show you after we get it -- it'll take two seconds for you to learn how to use it."

11.

The glass cup that looked just like the end of Bennie Goodman's clarinet on the record cover felt cold as I pressed it against my nipple on Monday morning. Per Daisy's and the pump's instructions, I squeezed the pump's pink rubber bulb and half expected to hear the 'aw-ooga' of a horn. Instead, the glass horn latched onto my breast and as I pumped it again, it made a gushy sound like a flat tire as a needle-thin stream of pale milk trickled into the jar screwed onto its bottom. Even though the pump attached around my nipple in a way that didn't irritate like Ernie's mouth grip did, with each pump I began to miss Ernie's pressure.

As the jar filled to the halfway mark, the thought that I was doing this so that I could leave Ernie made my eyes well up. If Daisy had only given me a choice. Each pump now reminded me of the thud of Ernie's tiny heart that I always felt when I held him to me to nurse. I can't leave him, I thought. I just can't.

I stopped pumping and held the jar up to see that it was full. It would have to make up for the two feedings we were going to miss together. Gerald blared the horn out in the driveway and I heard Ernie's thick cry in the kitchen and my heart sank down to my stomach. Each of his thick wails pulled on me like a rope and I just stood there, the jar of milk in my hand and my booby hanging out. I felt like I was standing in the Darlana's raspberry field in January -- I was frozen and couldn't move. Cry. Honk. Cry. Honk.

"For crying out loud, Gerald," Daisy screamed. "Give her a second to get ready."

Daisy's voice broke through my paralysis. I capped the jar of milk and tucked my breast away. I ran for the kitchen, making my brown leather loafers that were gray and cracked on their edges clomp across the entryway into the kitchen. Burnt toast and coffee filled the air as I stepped in to find Daisy patting Ernie's back while she ate a muffin. I held the jar of milk out to Daisy and she nodded toward the icebox. I just wanted Ernie so I slid the jar in and slammed the icebox door. I turned and grabbed Ernie from her. He started to fuss.

"Oh, and I had him calmed down to Tuesday. Why'd you have to jostle him?" she said.

As Ernie whimpered, I pressed my lips to his soft cheek and kissed

172

him. Again and again I kissed him, and he grew more and more cranky. I squeezed him to my chest and tears welled up again.

"I love you, baby boy."

He cooed and rolled his dark eyes to me. 'Artie's eyes' I thought and I was struck cold. Gerald honked again and now Ernie broke into a scorched cat of a wail. Daisy reached for him.

"Great. Now I gotta go and get him settled again. Let me have him."

I kissed his cheek three times and the baby oil on his head clung to my hands like a perfume. Grabbing up my overcoat, I ran to the car. A chilling November wind practically froze my tears as I hopped into the front seat next to Gerald.

"About friggin' time, girl," he grumbled.

"Sorry. The pump took longer. Sorry."

"It's okay, girl," he said. He reached out and patted my knee and he rested his hand just before he shifted the car into reverse.

"Your mother-in-law thinks you're trouble. But now I'm taking care of you so you don't go worrying about her anymore."

I would find out later what Gerald meant by all that but right then, my attention was focused on Minnetonka Avenue. I hadn't been out of the house very much since Ernie was born and two things struck me as we drove: the number of store fronts that had been fixed up with paint and such, and the gobs of women that were walking along the street. As we pulled up to Murphy's Produce Market, I didn't understand why the only man I saw on the entire avenue was an old man with a white beard and a cane.

"Where'd all the boys go?"

"All off to the war, same as Andrew. All the shops in town, even the hay and feed store, and gas station, are being tended by ladies."

"What about their kids? Who's taking care of 'em?"

Gerald was already out of the car and his keys jingled as he slipped them into the front door of the market. It creaked on its hinges as Gerald opened it, reached around, and yanked the cord of a dirty shade. He flipped a 'closed' sign over to read 'open,' then waved for me to follow him. The air inside felt like a wet closet filled with horse manure and rotten cabbage. Gerald clicked on the light and I saw the bins I had visited with Andrew so long before now all covered with burlap sacks. Gerald pulled an apron off a hook and handed it to me. I stopped and looked at the brownish green smears and rusty red blotches.

"Well, put it on. It's just old vegetable and fruit stains. This ain't no beauty contest."

He watched as I slid the apron on and tied it around the back. I

173

paused for him to check me out and make sure it looked right. He shook his head.

"Looks better on you than on stupid Nilsson, that's for sure."

Gerald slid on his own apron that was embroidered with the Murphy's name surrounded by corn, watermelon, and I think potatoes. Above the left part of his chest, his name stood out in gold thread.

"It isn't getting any earlier so here's what we'll do. I'm gonna go back and count the cash drawer and make some journal notes. While I do that, you get the bags off of each of the bins. We'll pull open the windows and roll down the awnings later."

Gerald walked off and clicked on a light bulb in a closet that acted as the office. The gold light fought with the blue light but both died in the middle of the market that felt like a cold cave moist with rotted fruit and vegetables. I reached over to the nearest bin and the sackcloth mounded over it made a lumpy, brown tent. It was rough against my fingertips and tugging at it, I realized the oily burlap was heavier than I expected. Using both hands, I was able to slide the sack off the bin and reveal a mound of potatoes that looked like a dusty cluster of grapes and smelled like rust and mud. Gerald hadn't told me where to put the cover so I folded it in half and lay it on the floor that was a mosaic of green, yellow, and red stains.

I pulled the sack cover off the next bin and a mound of twisted and gnarled sweet potatoes as thick as birch tree roots appeared. Folding up that cover, I lay it on top of the other and continued to uncover the rest of the bins. Pretty soon, I had the whole row of potatoes and onions opened. The bins were a quilt of thin and fat, gray, purple, and brown orbs.

Some machine clicked and ticked as Gerald leaned over it and fluttered his fingertips like he was playing an organ. When I had worked half way down the row of bins that held the fruits and green vegetables, the ticking stopped and Gerald walked out of the office. He stood at the end of the fruit row and looked at the stack of cloths that now looked like hotcakes.

"You move fast, girl. And neat, too. Maybe what we've been needing around here all along is a woman's touch."

I felt proud right then and I thought that maybe I could do anything I tried to. Gerald patted my shoulder as if he could read my mind, and then I felt anxious to get on to the next task, eager to learn it and then to do it.

"I'll be done with the books in about five minutes. Get the rest of these bins done, okay?"

Gerald patted my shoulder again as he turned to walk off, but when he dropped his hand, he grazed my behind. I jumped from his touch but he was now at the doorway of the office, smoothing his white hair over a pink bald spot on the crown of his head.

Later, once we had the front windows of the market open and the pine green awnings rolled up, Gerald and I carried four bins with the fall specials out front: pumpkins, yellow squash, garnet yams, and ears of corn. The November air sucked the trace of warm air right out the front of the market.

"Christ almighty it's cold today."

My eyes must have looked like balloons right then. Gerald snickered.

"Sorry, girl. Sometimes I do take the Lord's name in vain. Come Saturday, I'll go to confession. Just don't tell your mother-in-law."

He broke out into a grin like we were now pals with a special secret. He elbowed my side, waiting for me to respond.

"Okay, I guess."

"Whyn't you stack these bins nice and neat while I check up on our mushroom inventory, okay girl?"

I nodded like I knew what he wanted and even though I showed a little hesitation, he turned and went to the dark corner of the market. So I started working on the yam bin, and what really helped me was remembering how Dad had shingled the garage roof when I was little. I laid the biggest yams at the bottom of the bin, all facing the same way. Then I added a second row of smaller ones on top of those, starting them far enough back to make sort of a stair. Pretty soon, I had a lumpy pyramid of brown and red. The pumpkin and squash bins were easier because they were bigger, but I followed the same pattern as the yam bin. I finally got to the corn bin when Gerald came out and inspected.

"You're fast at this, too, girl. You're a better stock boy than stupid Nilsson. He makes the bins look no neater than quarry reject piles. Nice work, there. Oh, corn's low. Gotta get a call into the Durand Co-Op and get some more. Keep up the good work."

Gerald had me lug a big rusty dial scale that looked like a clock with a nest hanging from it to the front of the market. He hung the scale by its chain over the bins. After he made the phone call to the corn supplier, he made two more calls and then came out and fixed the price amounts on the tomatoes and on the lettuce by sliding an index card with the old price out of the metal card stand and slipping a card with the new price into it.

"Damn market prices change on some items as the season wears on. The scarcer the item becomes, the more we gotta charge."

In a few minutes, the first customers walked in and began to rummage through the bins and drop potatoes, or corn, or lettuce, or onions into brown paper bags that crackled and crunched under the weight. One of the ladies ran in like she was in a relay race, and I noticed she was wearing denim coveralls stained with dirt and oil.

"Where's Gerald, Miss?" she said to me. I saw gray and brown curls, matted with sweat, sticking out from under her denim cap. She was still wearing pancake makeup and eye shadow, though, so no one would mistake her for Ralph the filling station owner, I guess.

"He's in the back. Can I help with something?"

"Price on these tomatoes is too high. I'll pay a nickel a pound, but no more. Go tell him that, please."

"I think he's on the phone right this second. If you wait, I can —"

"I can't wait, Missy. I had to close the filling station to get dinner fixings. I can't be gone all morning. Now scoot."

I turned to get Gerald but he was already on his way out from the office. He rolled his eyes like he was expecting this from her. I stepped back and listened.

"Morning, Madge. Now what's the problem?"

"Nine cents a pound for these puny things here?" she said as she raised a small but plump tomato up to Gerald.

"Madge, a man's gotta earn a living. My supplier just raised the price on me so I —"

"Woman's got to earn a living right now, too, Gerald. I'm not making much over at Ralph's. How's about you help with this?"

"All right," Gerald sighed. "Seven cents a pound for you, Madge."

"Six. I'll pay six."

"All right. But no more than two pounds."

Madge nodded and began to toss tomatoes into a bag. She plopped it into the scale with the nest.

"That'll do her, yah. Oh, yeah. Head of lettuce, too."

Gerald waved me over behind the small, scarred oak counter where a cash register made of shiny brass sat. 'Watch, now,' he said.

He pressed a two on one row, then a two on a row right below. Both numbers popped up in the register's small window. He pointed to a small lever and when I pulled it, the cash register drawer popped open as a small bell chimed.

"Twenty-two cents, Margaret."

She reached into her coverall pocket and pulled out a quarter. She handed it to Gerald.

"Out of two bits," he mumbled, handing back the pennies. He leaned over and wrote '22 cents' on a lined pad.

"Thanks, Gerald," she said and ran out.

"Did you follow what I did just then?" he asked me.

It seemed pretty easy. I nodded.

"And your math is good? Can't afford to come up short in the change drawer."

"It's okay."

"Just make sure you write down the total of each charge. That's the only way I can balance the till at the end of the day."

By lunchtime, I was ringing up every customer and helping anyone who needed assistance. Gerald sat back on a wood chair and watched. At twelve thirty, he stood up.

"Okay, girl, take a half hour for lunch. You earned it. You know, it took stupid Nilsson three days to learn the cash drawer and make change. Maybe we'll get lucky and he'll get killed over in England. Then I'll hire you."

Gerald's joke sent a chill through me because I thought that Nilsson could just as easily be Andrew. I ran toward the front door to take my lunch break and get away from Gerald's joke.

"Be back by one. Got a corn load coming and we'll need to weigh it in."

I didn't really know where to sit on my lunch break so I went outside and leaned against the autumn special bins. Even though it was probably only thirty degrees, as I stood there in my overcoat and ate the biscuit Daisy had packed for me, Minnetonka Avenue was bustling with people. Actually, it was bustling with women; they carried packages, they ducked into shops, and in the shops, women waited on them, women sold the goods, women rang up the cash registers. It looked like Hopkins had become a town of only women and its main street was a stream of feminine energy. I don't know why, but as I chewed the last bit of the sweet and brown crust of Daisy's biscuit, I felt like I was in the flow of something important and that I was part of that stream. Proud, I guess. I felt proud that I could do something and from what Gerald had already said, I could do it well. Would women keep up this stream of energy and occupation even when the war was over, or would we all be going back to our homes, back inside to our children? I don't know why I thought about such crazy things as I stood there. We all belonged inside with our children and only a war or some other disaster would interrupt that, or should as far as I was concerned. It was all well and good that I could paint or ring up a charge or help with the produce market while Andrew was overseas, but what was most important was what Mom said all along: I found a good man, and I'll be making him a good home. For once, I felt right, I felt normal.

The screech of metal brakes broke through my daydream, and I saw Gerald waving at a big truck that looked like a gray pillow bulging at its seams with gold corn silk. I never saw so much corn in my life. Whether or not my lunch break was over, I didn't care. I ran back along the side of

177

the market to see what we were going to do with all that corn.

When I got to the side of the market, Gerald stood at the back of the truck with a wheelbarrow that looked as big as a stagecoach and its worn, grainy gray wood was probably as old as one. A thin man in a straw hat straddled a mound of corn at the open tailgate of the truck as he heaved pitchforks full of the green and yellow ears into the wheelbarrow. Gerald smiled when he saw me.

"Hey, girl, come on over and hold onto the wheelbarrow while he fills it. I'm gonna get the heavy duty scale ready."

I took the handles of the wheelbarrow and they felt like smooth tree branches. The weight wasn't too bad and even as the man in the back of the truck pitched the ears in, the wheelbarrow didn't seem to get heavier to support. When it was full up, Gerald stood behind me with another of the ancient wood wheelbarrows.

"Take that load over to that big metal plate there. Just push the handles forward and move it onto the scale. Watch the dial on the scale and holler out the weight, okay?"

The wheelbarrow moved easily as I pulled it away from the back of the truck, and the ears of corn brushed and thumped as I wheeled it onto the scale. A rusty spring twanged as the metal hand of the scale registered the weight. The needle vibrated a few seconds and I waited till it stopped completely.

"Looks like forty and a half pounds."

"Great!" Gerald yelled as he made a note on a clipboard. "Now wheel the load over to that canvas and dump it over. When you're done, dump it over. Then go back to the truck for a refill."

That's how my day of corn hauling started, and we did the same thing over and over for about three hours, only pausing if a customer rang for us. We were done when Gerald verified that four hundred pounds of corn lay on the canvas, and I was glad because my arms throbbed with pain. Dropping the handles of the wheelbarrow, I rubbed the burning muscles of my upper arms. Gerald came up from behind and slapped my rear end.

"You did a hell of a good job. I'm proud a you, girl. Just wait till we get the pumpkins and squashes in."

He walked back into the market, rolling his white shirtsleeves back down as he did. My rear end actually stung from his slap, but I didn't care just as long as I didn't have to grab the wheelbarrow again. The customer bell chimed and I ran into the market. As I passed by the office door, I heard the clinking of ice against glass and saw Gerald taking a drink from a glass with what had to be whisky. Near the sale bins, I saw Doc Anderson. He grinned at me and met me near the apple bin.

"Daisy said I'd find you here. Hope it's okay I stopped in and all."

178

My chest tightened. He obviously wasn't here to buy potatoes or apples. I plucked a couple of strands of corn silk from my left shoulder.

"Well, Mary, you best hang on to Ernie's baby things. You betch ya gonna need them because the test results came back and guess what?"

I already knew.

"You're gonna be a mama again."

Of all things I could'a' been thinking right then, or should'a been, only one thing popped into my head: 'Can I keep working or do I have to spend the next months in bed?'

"Oh, yah, no problem there this time. You could work I'd say up to your eighth month. Congratulations again there, Mary."

"Congratulations again, girl," Gerald said later as we pulled into the driveway. He laid his hand on my knee.

"You're one helluva worker. We got as much done today as when Andrew and I team up. I'm proud of you." His breath blew in my face and it smelled like stale eucalyptus. As I stepped out of the car, it was dark enough to be midnight but it was only four thirty. Winter was well on its way, and the smell of simmering lamb and tomato drifted out from the kitchen.

Daisy's Irish stew, I thought as my stomach growled. I was tired, sore, and hungry. Daisy met Gerald at the door and handed him a drink. Gerald took a sip, then paused and pointed at me.

"You should'a seen this girl working today. Andrew married himself an honest workhorse. Better looking than Nilsson in her work smock, too."

Daisy's small eyes contracted into darts. Her mouth stretched into a railroad track of tension. "Umm," was all she said.

Gerald walked into the house, chatting about all my accomplishments for the day. Daisy took a drink from a half-filled glass of gin and started to follow him. I heard Ernie giggle and coo and ran to get to him. Daisy turned abruptly and stopped me at the door.

"Another letter from Andrew," she said as she turned and walked into the house.

Ernie was in his playpen in the parlor, his little pink and white hands made fists around the metal bars, and his body was a bouncing dumpling of yellow terry cloth. It kind of got me upset to see that Daisy left him alone. I had been so busy all day and concentrating on my work that I hadn't thought about him much. I squeezed him to me and ran into our room. I dropped him on the middle of the bed and showed him the envelope and the framed photo of Andrew in his uniform we took just before he left.

"It's a letter from Daddy."

179

Ernie reached for the envelope corner and started to pull it toward his mouth that was dewy as a rose. "No, Ernie. Mommy has to read it first." I tore into the envelope. "Listen, Ernie:"

'My Dear Mary,'

Ernie giggled and I kissed him. He grabbed for the letter but I intercepted his hand bit it playfully.

"That's Mommy's, honey. Now listen:"

'Sorry it took so long since my last letter, but we ship out tomorrow and I've been too busy with that. How's my favorite redhead? By the way, bad news: the ship I'm sailing on won't be the Queen Mary after all. She's in New York. I'll be sailing on the Lurline. I won't be able to write from the ship because by the time you get it, you'll have gotten a letter from me at the base in the South Pacific. That's where we're going to be based and I guess we'll be going to a bunch of South Pacific islands to keep the Japs off or get rid of them. They haven't told us much more than that because of security.

'Have you started catechism yet? Mom should be able to help you through a lot of it. She knows church traditions like the back of her hand. It's still seventy-two here in San Francisco. That's the city nearest our base. It's pretty far from Los Angeles and Hollywood and since we'll ship out from here, I guess I won't get to rub elbows with any motion picture stars.

'My stomach hurts a little from the ground pork slop we had for dinner. Food is okay, but you get to have as much as you want so that makes it pretty great. Except for right now. My muscles don't ache like they did at the beginning of basic training. Even though I'm small compared to a lot of the guys, they all respect me because I'm keeping up on everything. I'm thinking about doing some boxing here, too, but I promise I won't let anyone hit me in the face too hard.

'I got a new buddy here who's going to be on the ship with me and everything and you'll never guess what: he's a roller derby star and his last race before he joined up was in Hopkins. On our first date, we missed seeing him by a day. How's that for amazing?

'Jack Bullock -- Wild Jack we all call him 'cause he'll deck you if you call him by his first name, Billy -- is his name and he's done some of the wildest stuff you ever heard. He hopped trains all over the country with a buddy of his so that they could join up with different roller derby outfits. They were almost arrested as hobos once, even. He's teaching me the ins and outs of craps 'cause he beats everyone. He's real sharp about odds and bets and things. I never met anybody like him in Hopkins before and even though he's not Catholic -- he doesn't even believe in God -- I like him a whole lot.

'I miss you and Ernie so much. They don't know how long we'll

180

be fighting down there so it may be a long time before we get to see each other again. That's the last time I'll mention that because it does no good to keep bringing it up. The Lord is watching over me and I pray every night. I just got to think about each day and keep faith that the Lord will bring us back together when it's time.

'My love, I just needed to let you know I was thinking about you as we get ready to get on our way. I will write at the very soonest I can. God bless you and my baby boy.

'I love you.

'Your Andrew.'"

The last paragraph was almost impossible for me to read through the wet veil of my tears. I swelled with pride for the second time today: this time because of the honorable man I married and his acceptance of his duty. Ernie crinkled the corner of the letter with his little hand and I pried it open and spared the page. All of Andrew's letters were keepsakes, and this one was no exception. I lay back on the bed and held Ernie against me and the heaviness of sleep pushed my eyes closed.

"Dinner's on!" Daisy hollered and startled me out of my sleep. Ernie jostled awake and started to cry. Patting his rear to calm him, I tucked the letter from Andrew away, kissed Ernie once more and we went to the dining room.

Gerald talked about my stocking the bins, my loading the corn, and my cashiering through all of dinner, and with every bit of enthusiasm he showed, Daisy nodded and her mouth twisted tighter and tighter till it looked like a red licorice whip. Through the whole dinner, Gerald kept refilling his and Daisy's wine glasses -- I passed on the wine because of my nursing. I was glad that Ernie grew fussy and forced me to leave the table.

When I stood up with Ernie and passed by Gerald, he pinched my rear end. I jumped and Ernie roared into a cry. Daisy was staring at her plate when it happened and looked up only when Ernie cried.

"He never carries on like that with me," she said. "You want me to handle him?"

How would you know how he carries on? I thought. You leave him by himself. Shaking my head, I bolted from the dining room, Gerald's pinch still burning my rear end. In our room, I checked Ernie's diaper just to make sure it was clean, even though I knew the way he was crying he was hungry. Slipping down the shoulder of my work dress, I brought out my breast and Ernie clamped on.

"You miss me, baby boy?" and between his slurps and swallows, his mouth curled into a rose bud of a smile.

Feeling him against me, and smelling the sweetness of his head, tears began to well up. Ernie kept eating, and in a few minutes, his head lolled to the side and his mouth fell away, slightly open and dotted with milk. One deep breath and the hint of a tiny snore and he was out. The light in the room made his sleeping face glow pink and peach. Highlights on his parted lips that suckled as he slept looked like dew drops on a tiny primrose.

'Paint it' my whole body shuddered with the urge.

For so long, tending to Ernie tired me out so much that the urge to paint just hadn't bubbled up inside me. Even though I was tired from work, too, right at this second, I couldn't think of doing anything else.

Paint him. Paint him, now, I thought.

Ernie's breathing was steady so I knew I could set him down without waking him. His little body made a crunching sound against the crib mattress as I set him into it. Someone turned on the radio in the parlor and I was sure the voices that rumbled from it would wake up Ernie. I watched him, breathless. He jerked his curled up fist toward his nose, but his breathing stayed even and deep. Now Daisy and Gerald shouted at each other above the radio, but Ernie kept right on sleeping.

Stepping slowly and softly to my bed, I reached under and pulled out my pad and pencil. I slid a chair up to the side of Ernie's crib and opened the tablet quietly, the cover making a faint scrape against the page. Running my hand across the page to flatten it, the bumps and ridges of the paper tickled my palm. How long had it been since I felt that? And, with another baby on the way, would I ever be feeling it again? 'Do it. Do it now,' a voice said inside me.

I pushed the pencil lead onto the page and as I began to sketch the circle of Ernie's sleeping head, the pencil tip snapped crisply. Ernie's eyes, closed as they had been through the radio and the fighting that was still going on, popped open like the Germans were bombing us.

"Eeeeewaaaaah" erupted from his chest. His fists shook as tears popped from the corners of his eyes.

Tossing aside the pad and the pencil that felt like it betrayed me, I picked up Ernie and began to pat his back. For more than an hour, he cried and when he finally fell asleep in my arms, my own eyelids were heavy. I lay back and let him rest on my chest. He was a warm, sweet smelling pressure and I yielded to a deep sleep.

The next morning, I was able to pump my breast milk much faster. As I stepped out the bedroom door, I kicked the pad with the undone drawing and the pencil with its decapitated tip under the bed. A tension welled up in me and I was almost mad. In the kitchen, Ernie lay on his blanket near the stove. Bending to kiss him, with the floral and caramel smell of baked blueberry muffins belching from the oven, I picked him up and held him close. A paper bag rustled behind me as I set him back down.

Daisy stood near and handed me a paper sack with my lunch in it.

"Dee-yer, there's enough in here for you and Gerald. Try to get him to eat his lunch, do you mind?"

Like I have a choice, I thought. Daisy emphasized 'eat' I guess because Gerald spent his lunchtime the day before drinking. I had a feeling today would be no different. As I turned to go, Ernie flashed a smile and the way his mouth formed the smile, it reminded me of Artie. Again, I saw Artie in his face. Daisy must have seen me pause.

"Something the matter?" she asked.

"Ernie looked so much like Andrew just then. Did you see that?"

"I don't think he looks a thing like him," she snorted.

"Oh." I turned to go. "Daisy. If you could take a second at some point today, would you mind showing Ernie the picture of Andrew on my night stand?"

"Why?"

"I don't want Ernie to go through this part of his life without knowing who his father is." Daisy chuckled and my skin bristled.

"Dee-yer, don't forget tonight is catechism at Hopkins High. Father Haggarty tells me a novitiate from St. Agnes will be teaching."

I shrugged. I couldn't care less about any of it, but since Andrew appointed Daisy as my religious watchdog, and knowing I couldn't get out of it, I wasn't going to give an enthusiastic 'oh boy.' Shrugging made sense right then.

I barely had time later that day to wash my hands and eat dinner. Walking the last block to Hopkins High, which was closer to the Murphy's' than it was to mom and dad's, the aspens lining the sidewalk were naked, black sticks that seemed to disappear into the cloudy night sky. Because they grew on both sides of Minnetonka Avenue, they almost felt like the bars of the jail cells I had seen in the movies. The uncomfortable feeling of realizing time was rushing past me flooded through me all along the walk that was so familiar to me. Did I miss school or something? The second floor windows of the Social Studies and Arts building glowed like yellow eyes on the dark front lawn dotted with dormant grass. The brass handle of the school door was cold as the iceman's cube tongs and made me feel the cold night for the first time the whole walk.

The heavy door creaked under the stress of my tug and the air from inside warmed me up. My worn shoes scratched their ratty soles against the cement steps that looked polished from all the years of student footsteps. Right at the top of the stairs I paused and heard the echoes of a woman's voice speaking fast. From the other side of the hall, I could almost hear the clomping and tapping of the footsteps of all the kids moving back and forth down the hall and my stomach all of a sudden

183

knotted like I was going to upchuck. The urge to run hit me, but I didn't know where: to the Murphy's'?; to Dad and Mom?; to my art classes? Wasn't Mrs. Hogrebe's class just on the other side of the hall? A year had gone by, or more, since I saw her last. Anyway, a voice broke through the confusion, a voice that screeched higher than a scrub jay. I remembered what I was doing there at night and I swallowed my memory and turned away from Mrs. Hogrebe's class and headed toward the chirping voice.

Before I could open the classroom door, it flew open and the woman who had been talking held it open for me.

"Mary Murphy, I take it," she said. But the woman, wearing a black veil that fell down across her shoulders to meet a long black dress, didn't look at me. Her face, a smooth, olive skin drawn tight over high cheekbones that met her thin nose, stayed focused on the full classroom. She raised her arm that looked like a stick under the folds of the black gown and pointed to a vacant desk in front. I crossed quickly to the desk. My face was on fire and I felt so stupid. I saw the class was filled with teenagers around my age except for an old woman and a man wearing a checkered coat. 'Looks as old as Dad,' I thought. As I sat, the woman let the door go and it slammed shut like a hammer clanking against metal.

"We're going to cover all the Commandments, and really dig in to talk about six through ten. Anyone know any of those?"

No one raised his or her hand and I glanced past the woman to read what was written on the chalkboard behind her: 'Sister Maureen Therese.'

"How about you, Mary?" she said.

I said the only Commandment I could remember. "Thou shall not kill."

"Okay. Good. Though it's actually 'murder', not kill. Anybody else?"

Again, no one bothered to answer. Sister Maureen Therese stepped to the left side of the room, but she moved so fast that she skittered like a nervous chicken, making the silver cross she wore around her neck sway like a metronome against her white bib collar.

"Honor thy father and thy mother. That's another important one."

Now everyone sighed like they recognized it. I knew that one, too, and I wondered if that Commandment meant your in-laws, too. I hoped not.

"The Commandments are important when it comes to understanding sin. Understanding sin leads us to the Sacraments. The Sacraments are the reason you're here. They're seven of them, but the ones we're going to study and take part in are the three c's: Confession. Communion. Confirmation. Those are what we're concerned with here in

184

catechism."

Sister Maureen Therese stepped over to her desk and lifted a pile of schoolbooks. She set the first pile of twelve books on the desk two rows down from me.

"Keep one and pass the rest behind you."

When she handed our row the books, I grabbed mine and could smell musty dust as I passed the rest behind. The book was as thick as two schoolbooks and the cover was blue cloth. I read the title: 'The St. Jerome Edition of the Holy Bible and the Catholic Catechism.'

"Like the title says," Sister Maureen Therese said. "We'll be looking at the whole Bible, but we'll spend most time on the New Testament and the teachings of our Lord, Jesus Christ. Let's turn to page five and read the introduction together."

Bindings cracked throughout the room and pages fluttered as fingertips scraped to turn them. When I opened the book, the very first thing I saw was a photo of a painting of Christ praying in a rose garden. A gold halo stood out around his head and cast a glow on a burnt umber and red-blended night sky. And his hands! His folded hands were delicate and perfect in form and proportion. The caption under the painting read, 'Christ at Gethsemane' but didn't say who painted it. By the style and texture, I could tell it was oil. Artie flashed into my head.

"The Catholic Catechism is the principal means by which –" Sister Maureen Therese's screeching voice broke through. I turned to page five to follow but now I was anxious to see what other paintings might be in the book. I knew I was going to be bored with this whole thing, but I could at least enjoy looking at the illustrations. On page fifteen was a photo of a marble statue. It showed a woman in a veil with a dead man lying across her lap. The caption read: 'The Pieta by Michelangelo. The Blessed Virgin Mary accepting the offering of her son, Jesus, as Savior.' The folds of her robe and his loincloth made the statue look so real.

That was how my catechism started, and I had to attend two nights a week for two hours each night, listening to Sister Maureen Therese's frenetic voice and being bored out of my skull. The catechism at night and my work at the market during the day didn't leave much time for anything else. And the time it did leave was spent with Ernie. My life was a tiring routine that only varied with the change of winter's onions and potatoes into spring's flowers and berries at the market. Andrew's letters kept coming and brought more news of the war and his friendship with Wild Jack.

The months of routine in my life were interrupted one day in early spring at the market. I had begun to slow down in my work because my stomach was now ballooning up in the fifth month of pregnancy. Gerald

185

had recently allowed me to order produce from farmers and to help keep the books. He came into the office after lunch and waves of stale whisky burned my nose as he shuffled in, slamming the door behind him. I jumped and thought I was in trouble.

"Help me," he whispered. "Get Doc Anderson. Hurry."

His huge body lay jerking on the office floor. He looked like a giant baby as he heaved and tried to catch any breath made me feel sorry for him. I threw open the office door and ran into the market.

The sharp sound of a fist pounding glass startled me and I saw Margaret at the front door. She peered in at me, her face screwed up with irritation. I ran to the door and threw it open.

"Margaret," I now panted. "Get Doc Anderson. Hurry. It's Gerald!"

Margaret nodded and bolted across Minnetonka Avenue and I heard tires screech and horns honk.

"Maaarrry," Gerald moaned from the office.

Running back to his side, his face was turning red and purple. His eyes seemed to bulge with red and blue veins. 'A dead fish,' I thought.

"Mary, pray with me. Please, girl. Hurry."

I kneeled down next to Gerald and the old wool carpet dug into my knees. Crossing myself like I learned in catechism, I started the only prayer I knew:

"Bless us, oh Lord, and these, thy gifts which we —"

"No, girl. We're not eating. The Lord's Prayer."

I shook my head.

"Our Father," he whispered.

"Our Father," I repeated.

"Who art in Heaven," he said.

"Who art in Heaven."

Gerald's breathing started to lighten and his chest slowed down.

"Forgive me my sins," he whispered. Gerald's body stopped jerking: a final breath rushed out of him. He went still. His hand that had been clutching his chest fell and slapped the floor like a cube steak. Doc Anderson rushed in and fell to the floor, his hand reaching for Gerald's wrist. But I already knew what he was going to find out: Gerald was dead.

Later that afternoon, I closed the market and walked back to the Murphy's. As I turned the corner, cars lined the driveway and the street. People moved in and out of the house and I stepped in and headed for my room, ignoring the mumbling and crying that echoed all around. Ernie lay in his crib. I watched Ernie sleep and a shudder went through me when I thought about Andrew possibly dying overseas. I wanted to tell Andrew everything right there, to look at him and hope he'd forgive me. I was ready to move back home if he didn't forgive me, too. If I couldn't tell him, I knew that I had to tell someone, soon.

Gerald's funeral was a couple of days later and I thought I had the chance to tell my dad how bad I was feeling and why. Mom and Dad came to pay their respects to Daisy and while people chatted in the parlor, Mom sitting right between Daisy and some rich lady in a black dress and pearls from Minneapolis, Dad stepped away and nodded for me to come with him. Ernie was restless in my arms so I knew he could use a break from all the funeral sadness. Dad looked around the house like he was confused and for the first time, I saw his face looked a lot thinner from the last time I saw him. I pointed toward our room.

"Darlin'," he said as he pulled a chair up for me, scraping it across the floor of our room without lifting it.

"I hate like all heck that we're never seeing you, what with you carrying another baby and all." He plopped on the edge of the bed.

Whatever he had to say, I was ready to tell him about all my bad things, which now from catechism I knew were sin: adultery with Artie and Andrew; pregnancy without knowing who the father was; lying that I knew it was Andrew. He would insist that I come home and maybe that's what I needed to do. But he dropped his head and fiddled with the duck feather in the band of his black hat. He really had something to say, too.

"Umpaa, umpaa, umpaa," Ernie said between blowing bubbles of spit from his pursed lips.

"I think he's trying to say 'Grandpa,'" I said. Dad didn't raise his eyes but a slight nod told me he was glad.

"Umpaa, umpaa," Ernie said again and giggled. He reached out and leaned so that he could grab the collar of Dad's black funeral suit. Dad reached up and played with his hand, still not looking up.

"Darlin', Irma's going to be coming home soon."

"She's done that before. He cheating on her again?"

Now Dad raised his face and I saw a look of tired I never had seen on him before. The wrinkles near his eyes were so deep they looked like the tines of a fork.

"No. That ain't it. Ben got injured. We just heard. Stepped on some sort of land bomb, a mine they call it, I think."

"Poor Irma. What happened to him?"

"Well, he lost a leg. And something else, too." Dad lowered his head again and this time I knew he was embarrassed.

"What else, Dad?"

"He's lost all feeling from the waist down. They won't be having any children."

The image of Ben making gestures to me alongside Minnehaha

187

Creek flashed into my mind. I felt sorry for him, and even worse for Irma.

"Irma's gonna have to nurse him for awhile at home because Ben's mom won't permit them to live there."

"Why's that?"

"Ever since Irma lost the baby, Mrs. Augsburg doesn't want to have anything to do with them. She probably thinks Irma trapped Ben or something like that." A surge of guilt flooded through me, and my face felt hot. Did my face look red? Thinking about it only made it feel hotter. I was glad Dad was so intent on telling me about Irma just so he didn't notice my blushing.

"It's gonna be tryin' on us to say the least," he said.

I couldn't talk to Dad right then. He looked miserable and thin enough as it was. Whatever I had going on in my head and heart, he didn't need to hear it, and there was no way I could move back home with Irma and Ben there. My sins are my sins, I thought. I have to bear them.

"Before we get back to sin," Sister Maureen Therese said a couple months later. "I want to start tonight with what I call the Immaculate Misconception about the Blessed Mother, Virgin Mary. Here she is, in all her glory." Sister Maureen Therese held up an art book and pointed to a painting of a woman.

"This is the Annunciation, as painted by Rembrandt."

The painting of the young Mary made her look terrified of the angel Gabriel who looked like a fiend jumping out of shadow. I could sense her fear, that's for sure.

"This one by Rubens shows the Madonna, Mary, with the child, our Lord, Jesus.

Now that face of Mary was almost blank, like she had no personality at all. I wondered why Rubens made her look so lifeless. Sister Maureen Therese fanned the book and this time held it up, making the spine pop and crack. The photograph spread over the two pages.

"Michelangelo's Pieta. I think it's my favorite of all the art depicting the Blessed Mother. Notice that though Christ lay dead on her lap, her face shows solemn and graceful -- she's not a mother mourning, but a saint with heavenly acceptance of the Lord's will."

To me, her face was confused and sad, not graceful and solemn. It stirred up a mix of feelings I wouldn't understand until much later. Sister Maureen Therese slammed the book shut.

"Now, who can tell me anything about the Immaculate Conception?" The little old man in class raised his hand. "Mr. Gunderson."

"Well, Sister, if I can remember from Sunday school, the Immaculate Conception is how Mary came to be Jesus' mother. When the Holy Spirit made her, well, ya' know."

188

"Wrong! Anyone else?"

No one raised his or her hand this time. All I wanted to do was grab the art book from Sister Maureen Therese's desk and look at the Pieta. That expression on Mary's face captivated me.

"Okay, don't all raise your hands at once. What Mr. Gunderson just explained is what I call the Immaculate Misconception." She opened the art book again to the Rembrandt painting.

"The moment Gabriel told Mary the Holy Spirit would make her with child is the Annunciation, the 'announcement', like this painting is called. It's not the Immaculate Conception. Actually, when Mary herself was conceived and born, she was born free of the Original Sin. She was born Immaculate, and ready to be the mother of God. Eve fell from grace with the Original Sin, and Mary was born free of that sin and therefore, full of grace, bringing the hope for all of our souls in Jesus Christ."

I thought about Mary's strangely sad face and I raised my hand. "Murphy."

"Did the angel Gabriel tell Mary what was going to happen to her son?"

"No."

"So she just went along with everything as he was tortured and crucified?"

"Of course she did. She had to allow the Lord's will."

"But she was human -- how could she allow her son to go through with all of it and suffer like he did?"

"She accepted the will of God from the Annunciation forward."

All I could think of was Ernie's little face at home right now with Daisy. Tears clogged the corners of my eyes. "But it was her baby, her son."

"I don't presume to question the Blessed Mother's decisions, Murphy. She is holy. Let's get back to discussing sin."

The sad face of Mary flashed in my head again -- resentment. She must've felt it.

"Excuse me, Sister Maureen Therese?"

"What now, Murphy?"

"If someone was gonna hurt my boy, no matter who it was and whose will it was, I would protect him. I would resent and hate them for it. If Virgin Mary felt like that, wouldn't that be a sin?" Sister Maureen Therese inhaled sharply and crossed herself.

"Mary Murphy," she said between clenched teeth. "You must never compare yourself to the Blessed Virgin Mary. She is beyond human comparison. It is a sin to even think such things."

My face flashed hot and I slumped in my chair. Sister Maureen

189

Therese picked up the catechism book and opened it. "The last sin were going to talk about is mortal sin," she said. "Remember I said that most all sins can be forgiven? In fact, the only ones that can't be are mortal ones -- turning your back against God and his will. An example would be a person who was once a Christian but who then becomes an atheist. Murder is another mortal sin, but recently, a convicted murderer in Sing Sing was granted absolution before being executed in the electric chair. We're waiting for the Pope's opinion on repentant murderers. Another mortal sin is suicide. Can anybody guess why?"

The man who reminded me of Dad raised his hand as he cleared his throat.

"Seems there that if you're dead, you can't confess your sins very easily," he said.

"That's it. So, as you all get ready to do your first confessions, do me a favor. Don't commit any mortal sins!"

The classroom erupted with laughter. But I didn't find much to laugh about because this confession idea was bothering me. I raised my hand.

"Murphy."

"Sister Maureen Therese, who's gonna hear my confession?"

"I was going to get to that, but since you asked, I might as well tell you. Your confession, your absolution, and your penance can be heard and granted only by a holy father." That confused me. All along in catechism class, whenever we'd talk about confession, I thought it was supposed to be to the person we hurt.

"What good does that do?" I asked.

Sister Maureen Therese paused and glared at me. She flitted over and stood right in front of me. "The good that does, Murphy, is gives you forgiveness for your sin."

"Why can't you just tell the person you sinned against that you did it, and you're sorry?"

"Number one, not all sins are committed against people. Two, one layperson is just as big of a sinner as another. Number three, it's not in a sinner's power to grant absolution. Only a holy father can do that."

I saw Father Haggarty's face right then, and how he held and comforted Daisy when she wept after Gerald's funeral. If I told him anything, he would tell her, I knew it. I couldn't risk Daisy having the truth before I had the chance to tell Andrew.

"Your mind wandering, Murphy? You got that dazed look in your eyes."

"Sorry, Sister."

"Is it clear that only a holy father can grant absolution and that the

190

only confession you should do is to him?"

"Yes."

A week later, I kneeled inside the confessional at St. Anthony's. Some sort of wooden panel slid open and a soft shimmer of light appeared through a hazy screen. As my eyes adjusted to the soft light, I could make out the silhouette of Father Haggarty's head and shoulders. Silence followed and I felt him studying me like I was some sort of trapped animal. I felt awkward until he cleared his throat.

"Do you know how to begin?" his voice made me feel less anxious.

"I'm not sure," I whispered. Please, don't recognize me, I thought.

"Repeat. Bless me, Father, for I have sinned."

I repeated the words.

"How have you sinned against the Lord, our God?" he asked.

My heart pounded so hard my throat felt like a tom-tom. My Andrew, I thought. I can't tell him, Andrew. I won't betray you.

"Did you understand the question?" he said.

"Yes," I whispered. Maybe he won't recognize my voice.

"Then you have to answer."

"Yes, Father."

"How have you sinned?" Now he sounded irritated.

"My sin is —" thump-thump my heart now pounded in my ears.

"My sin is —" I can't. I can't do this.

"Speak, child. Please."

"I have been impatient with my baby," I said. It was the first thing I could think of other than the truth. A lie felt better right then.

"The Lord forgives impatient mothers. Is there anything else?"

Did he recognize me?

"No," I said.

"Are you sure?"

What does he mean by that? The air in the confessional began to feel stuffy.

"Yes. That's all I can confess."

Father Haggarty grew quiet and paused a minute as if he was deciding my fate. He leaned toward the screen and spoke softly.

"For your sin, you must recite three Hail Marys. As you do, consider the virtue of the Holy Mother and your responsibility to emulate her."

"Yes, Father."

"Do you know the Act of Contrition yet, or do you want to repeat it after me?"

"After you," I said.

Father Haggarty led me in the prayer. When it was finished, I stepped out of the booth and the hot church felt fresh compared to the stifling darkness of the confessional. I joined the others in the pew who were praying, but I didn't feel relieved. I felt scared, and lost, and dishonest. The baby kicked at me hard.

The baby's movements in my stomach grew worse and worse over the next couple of months, and whenever I had any tension or anxiety, they were even stronger. Since Gerald's death, I was running the market. I even hired a fifteen-year-old boy to help me out. Between the two of us, we managed to get produce ordered, stocked, and sold. Daisy decided that the market would be put up for sale once the second baby came. She said that with Ernie, I had to work, but with two children, I couldn't. I didn't trust her explanation and I knew she wasn't looking out for me. What she was up to, I couldn't guess then.

I really dreaded the end of my job at the market. I felt like I had done a lot to keep it going and had learned a lot about business. Whatever problem that came up, whether it was a late carrot delivery or Margaret demanding a better deal on rutabagas, I knew how to solve the problem and keep everything going. I kind of hoped that Daisy would see fit to keep the market until Andrew got back. After all, he was going to need some sort of job. Maybe I could keep working, too.

But I went into labor on August 12, 1943, while I was weighing a pound of peaches for a customer. This baby, who had been so active through the whole pregnancy, suddenly pushed and felt like it was clawing to get out. I dropped the peaches and they splattered on the market floor as I bent over from the pain. The lady customer knew what was happening and raced to get Doc Anderson.

The next day I opened my eyes and the sun was blaring in through beige Venetian blinds and the smell of rubbing alcohol and camphor didn't help my groggy feeling. My head ached from the ether, and my stomach twisted. I thought I was going to upchuck, but the burning in my privates took my mind off my belly ache. It was ten the next morning when the nurse came in.

"Morning, Mrs. Murphy."

Her voice was soft and soothing but when I glanced up at her, I saw that she had a squat body and was husky as a produce deliveryman, her gray hair cropped close to her head. 'Anyone tell you what you had?' I shook my head.

"At two forty-five this morning, you delivered an eight pound, three ounce girl."

"What's the date?"

"August thirteenth. You want to see her, Mrs. Murphy?"

I nodded, my head still feeling stuffed with dishrags. In a moment, the metal door hinges screeched back open and the nurse carried a white bundle. She paused and propped the door open with her thick calf.

"Look who I found out there, too."

Daisy came in with Ernie, who held her hand tight as he took his timid steps. His shoulders and chest were bare under the denim overalls he wore and they puffed out over his diaper. He had just started walking only a month or so ago and each lumpy step he took caused his head of dark brown curls to bounce. When he saw me, his pink cheeks puffed up over a pumpkin-tooth of a smile.

"Amamma, amamma," he said. He used the word for both Daisy and I so it wasn't always clear which of us he wanted. But what he did next let me know he meant me.

Ernie dropped Daisy's hand and ran to the side of the bed. As the nurse leaned over to hand me the baby, Ernie clutched the edge of the blanket and tried to climb on top of the bed. The mattress I lay on came just above the top of his head and he struggled to life his left leg up to get a hold.

"Up, amamma. Up. Up," he said.

He held his hands up for me to help him but I now held the new baby. Her pink head, covered by a down of pale hair, moved in tiny circles as she slept.

"Up, amamma. Up, up!" Ernie began to whimper. His left leg slid off the bed and he caught himself.

Daisy sat in the visitor's chair with her hands folded and I couldn't figure out why she wasn't helping Ernie. The nurse, realizing Ernie was getting upset, leaned over and set him on the bed. Ernie crawled toward me and the nurse grabbed him to keep him from leaping on the baby and me.

"No, no little guy" the nurse soothed him. "Let me help you."

She carried Ernie around the end of the bed and held him up near the baby and me. His face broke out into a smile and I kissed his soft cheek.

"This is your little sister," the nurse said.

"Sisso. Sisso." Ernie repeated.

I held the new baby out for him to see her and his smile fell from his face as his mouth dropped open. He looked her over, then glanced up at me.

"Amamma, amamma," he said.

He struggled against the nurse. Daisy stood up and joined us and I thought she was going to grab Ernie. Instead, she reached for the baby. Ernie's eyes were turning to wet glass so I knew I had to give the girl up.

When I let Daisy take her, the nurse loosened her grip and Ernie flew to my chest. He hugged and nuzzled me.

"Looks like someone misses his mama," the nurse said.

"Amamma, amamma," he said. He buried his face against my neck.

"Everything's under control here," the nurse said.

The nurse walked out. Ernie twisted his head and when he saw Daisy holding the baby, he crawled across the bed, his hands pumping the bed like they were on fire, rolled his diapered rear end over and dropped down to the floor. He ran to Daisy and the baby, rocking and teetering on his unsteady legs.

"No, amamma. No. No." He held up his hands to Daisy and she glanced at him but then went back to coddling and cooing at the new baby.

"Grandma's angel, yes," she said, softer than I ever heard her speak. She kissed and stroked the baby's hands and head.

She never did that with Ernie, I thought. Probably because he's a boy or something.

"Ernie, come on to Mama," I said. Patting the bed, he gave up and turned back to me. His eyes were glossy with tears, but when he saw my face, his toothless grin erupted again. His wobbly legs pumped and he stepped up to the side of the bed near me and I was able to pick him up without hurting too bad. He buried his face in the nape of my neck.

"So what do I call my grand baby?" Daisy said to the baby. "Your mom's never decided a name."

She was right on that one. Between work and Ernie and all, I hadn't given it anymore thought. Andrew liked 'Louise' but I wasn't sure I did. Without Andrew to run it by, though, I figured I had to call her 'Louise.'

"Louise. Call her Louise."

12.

"Louise!" I hollered.

"Louise. Come, Mama wantses you," I heard Ernie say from the kitchen.

"It's okay, Ernie," I said now that I knew where she was. "I'll come get her. It's almost time for –"

"Shh!" Daisy said. She jumped up and turned the radio up. "Listen."

"Now we go to the Oval Office," the radio announcer's voice rumbled.

"What?" I said, pausing by a chair.

"The President's going to talk. Shh."

"Ernie. Bring Louise out here," I said.

I sat in Gerald's leather chair across from Daisy. I didn't know if the radio was extra hot because of the muggy August afternoon or if one of its tubes was burning out, but I could smell hot glass and wire. The radio had been on a lot the last couple of weeks ever since the atom bombs were dropped on Japan. We were used to special reports breaking in on the Hit Parade or during Amos and Andy, but the last time the President spoke was when Germany surrendered. My heart pounded in my chest -- did this mean Andrew was coming home?

Ernie walked in and at age three, his body was thin and lanky and his dark curls bounced as he led Louise in with an iron grip on her right hand. He was a healthy boy other than the asthma. The medicine Doc Anderson prescribed kept the breathing problem under control for now. Louise's left hand was a soggy fist as usual in her little mouth. Ever since she started teething, she chewed on her closed fist.

"Ladies and Gentlemen, the President of the United States. Mr. Truman," a man with a nasal voice said.

"My fellow Americans," President Truman began.

In a couple of minutes, President Truman explained that the A-bombs brought Japan to surrender. The war was over, and our men were coming home. The President finished and the radio broadcast went back to the Hit Parade and the Andrews Sisters singing 'Rum and Coca Cola.' I looked at Daisy and her face was frozen, a shelf of tears perched on her

195

lower eyelids. Ernie and Louise wrestled with a gray sofa pillow, giggling and pulling.

"My boy's coming home. He made it," Daisy whispered.

'When?' I thought. Tomorrow? Next week? My hands shook with excitement.

But the muggy summer became a crisp fall, and all the aspens were dropping their leaves. The peaches, plums, and nectarines had long sold out at the produce market and we slowly replaced them with squash and potatoes. By Thanksgiving of 1945, a depressing and quiet meal spent with Daisy, Father Haggarty, Mom, Dad, Irma, and Ben in his wheelchair, I still didn't know when Andrew was going to get out or why he was still in. I got two more letters just after Thanksgiving and they were short, excited, and it sounded like he was real tired. Christmas, he wrote. He'd be home by Christmas.

On December third, an unexpected snow flurry blew in and snowed us in. I couldn't get to the produce market for the next two days and all of Hopkins had been choked off under the white blanket. Ernie, Louise, and I sat on the quilt in the kitchen as Daisy clipped a candy thermometer to the side of a pan of boiling sugar syrup that gurgled and rolled. The whole kitchen smelled like warm marshmallows.

"Now remember, dee-yer. Don't stir it anymore or you'll wreck the divinity. If Andrew's home by Christmas, believe me, he'll want lots of his walnut divinity."

This was my second lesson in divinity making in the two days we were stuck in the house together. The first batch Daisy made didn't cook long enough and it turned out to look like a puddle of oily snow and when she tried to roll it into pieces, it pulled up from the wax paper in sticky ropes. The color was right, Daisy said. She felt that the divinity should be white as Hopkins in December and sweet as a spring morning. "Not sticky as tar, though," she added.

"We're cooking this batch long enough this time, you betcha," she said.

The phone in the hall rang, clattering its bells off the wooden walls of the hall. Daisy glanced at me with a sour expression. "Now who could that be? And right now with the divinity boiling and all." The phone rang again.

"All right, I'll be there, just hold your horses. Dee-yer, watch the thermometer and if it gets to one hundred eighty, just pull the pan off the stove." Daisy shuffled out the kitchen door and her heels made that quick clicking sound I had grown so used to for the last four years.

"Yello," Daisy said.

"A - bee - see- dee- elemento - pee," Ernie sang his version of the

196

ABC's.

"Ah - see - dohmen - pee," Louise repeated right after him. She had recently begun to mimic everything Ernie did or said.

"Oh, my Lord. My Lord!" Daisy cried.

"Shh, Ernie. Quiet for a sec," I said.

"Ky-ett sec," Louise repeated. She put her finger up to her mouth then shoved her fist in and started to gnaw it.

"My boy. You're all right. My boy!" Daisy hollered into the phone.

A jolt went through my body and I scooped up Louise and grabbed Ernie's hand. "Come on," I said. My throat had already swollen. By the time we dashed the ten feet next to Daisy, my eyes were gushing.

"My Andrew! My Andrew!"

Daisy kissed the phone and held it in the nape of her neck like it was a baby. I set Louise down and Ernie grabbed her hand and stepped back from us.

"Am I bad boy? Is you crying 'cause of me?" he asked.

"No, Ernie. No. Mommy and Gram are crying because we're happy."

"I can't believe I hear your voice," Daisy went on. "Your dad was so proud of you. He was."

I clenched my hands in order to keep from ripping the phone out of Daisy's hands. She turned her back toward us like this was a private call or something. I tapped her back. She brushed my hand away. I pulled on the receiver cord and she yanked it back toward her.

"Andrew!" I screamed. "Andrew. I'm here! I'm here!"

Daisy spun around and her eyes looked like molten glass. Pursing her lips, she spoke quietly. "Of course, son. Anything you want."

She thrust the phone at me, picked up Louise and went back to the kitchen. The phone receiver was warm and moist from Daisy's tears.

"Andrew?"

"Is this my Mary?" he said. It was so long since I last heard his voice that I almost didn't recognize the nasally pitch.

"Andrew?" was all I could manage. My chest heaved and a sob choked from me. Ernie stood next to me and he broke into a sob.

"My girl, my Mary. It's okay. I'm coming home."

"When?" My throat cracked with the pain of tears.

"I'm in California now. You know what the weather is like here?"

"No."

Ernie grabbed me and sobbed into my skirt.

"Is that one of my kids?" Andrew asked. But his throat now strained and cracked.

"It's Ernie."

"Put him on, Mary. For just a minute."

I pulled Ernie off my skirt and held the phone receiver to him. His face was striped with tears that cascaded over his crooked mouth.

"Here, baby boy," I said. "Say hello."

He pushed the phone away.

"No. Mommy too hurted by phone."

That made me giggle and when I laughed through my tears, Ernie started to crack a smile, too. "Hang on, Andrew." I held the receiver out again.

"Say Hello, Ernie. This is your daddy."

"Hello, Ernie," Ernie said.

"No, baby boy. Say 'hello, Daddy.'"

"Hello, Daddy," he grabbed the receiver and held it to his ear. A smile crept up on his lips. "Uh-huh. Nope. No bad things got us. No monsters, either. Do you like peabutter and namana sandwiches? Okay. Mamma." Ernie handed the phone back up to me and Andrew sobbed and choked.

"I can't believe he's old enough to talk," Andrew said. "Lord, I missed him. My Mary, I missed you so much."

"Andrew, how long before you're home?"

"Well, I'm in San Diego, California. I get on a train tomorrow. Probably take about five or six days."

"Oh, the weather bad there, too?"

"No. It's seventy five degrees out right now."

I almost dropped the phone. How could it be so warm in winter? I didn't want to tell him that it was nineteen outside in Hopkins.

"Get home as soon as you can. There's someone else who misses you, too."

"I love you, Mary. Tell Ernie I love him. I'll be home –"

"I'll tell Louise, too."

"Oh, yeah. My baby girl. I can't wait to meet her."

A week later, Andrew would get his chance. But before that, we had some tense moments waiting for him to get home. I was tense because the last time he called, he was boarding a train in Denver and Colorado was getting as hard hit by the early winter snow as Minnesota. He was due in the next morning to the Hopkins Depot. The train hadn't arrived by three o'clock and all the trains between the Midwest and the Rockies were delayed by the bad weather.

Daisy's tension came less from worrying about his train -- he made it through three and a half years of war, after all -- and more from embarrassment. She planned a huge welcome home party, against my

198

wishes, and as people began to show up for cocktails and hors d'oeuvres at seven, we still hadn't heard from Andrew. Each time the door opened, a 'Welcome Home' sign of purple foil letters and yellow streamers fluttered in the freezing breeze as a jolt shot through me and I leapt up. I finally just sat in one of the chairs in the hall. Ernie sensed my tension and he grabbed his barn puzzle and sat on the floor next to me. Louise was being passed around in the parlor and I could hear kisses and laughter as she was admired.

"Evening, and bless you, Daisy," Father Haggarty said. He closed the hall door behind and I saw a whirlwind of snowflakes try to escape back out into the cold. As he pulled off his overcoat, he nodded cordially to me.

"Mary, good evening."

Right at that moment, with Andrew due home and feeling like I had someone who really cared for me, I realized how much Daisy had excluded me entirely from the family's social circle. So much so that the very priest who heard my first Confession, placed my first Communion wafer on my tongue, and who anointed me as a Christian soldier at my Confirmation, that same priest had a friendship and allegiance to Daisy and a complete coldness to me. I hoped he cared a little more for my soul.

Father Haggarty turned his back to me and put his arm around Daisy. The few people who had arrived before Father Haggarty were busy tinkling ice into tumblers or plopping hors d'oeuvres onto their plates. The parlor was becoming a bee hive of clinking crystal and china and murmuring voices mixed with Louise's constant performance of her version of the ABC's. The air was filled with roasted ham, fresh baked rolls, cinnamon, and rose water perfume.

"Where's our boy?" Father Haggarty said.

"Not home yet. We haven't heard from him since yesterday," Daisy said.

"There, girl. You know the Lord watched over him in the South Pacific. Your boy'll be home safe. You'll see."

With that, he kissed Daisy's cheek and walked into the parlor. Daisy glanced at me then followed behind. 'Not even a wondering how I feel about my husband's return?' I thought. 'How about asking how Ernie's asthma is? Or Louise's talking?' Just like the rest of the guests who had showed so far, everyone was concerned for Daisy and barely nodded at me. The doorbell rang and I went to get it, knowing it wouldn't be Andrew. I pulled it open.

"Mary, girl. How are you?"

My mom's gray eyes smiled from under the fur rim of a green parka hood.

"Mom. What are you doing here?"

"Daisy invited us, girl. Now you step aside before I freeze out here."

As she stepped into the parlor, the thick arms of the green parka rubbed against her sides making her look like a big spruce hedge. Daisy flitted in to see who had arrived and when she saw me helping Mom's parka off, the expression on her face that was a joyful greeting turned into resignation.

"Hi there," she said over her shoulder. She turned and went back into the parlor.

Mom rubbed her arms and I saw that the long sleeves of her pink tea rose dress looked a little tight around her forearms and wrist. She pulled off her black leather winter gloves that were worn gray in spots and underneath she had on her white Easter wrist gloves. I rolled my eyes.

"Where's Dad?"

"He ain't feeling well again. His bladder and all."

"How'd you get here?"

"Your sister's out parking that fancy car of hers. She don't want it to get any dents so she's picking a safe spot on the street."

"Amamma Hellman!" Ernie yelled. He ran right through his wooden puzzle pieces, sending them clattering across the hall floor, and jumped to Mom. She grabbed him up and kissed him.

"There's my big boy! Whatcha got in your hand?"

"Puzzie," Ernie said.

"Looks like a blue rooster to me. Isn't that silly?"

Ernie giggled and Mom tickled and kissed him. All of a sudden, it felt like I was back at home and watching Mom kiss and play with Jimmy. She never did that with me or Irma, but she always did it with him. I felt jealous of Ernie and Mom for a second, and then I felt ashamed. I vowed to myself right then that Louise would always get just as much affection and attention from me as Ernie.

"Wanna come with Grandma and see what's going on in the parlor there?"

"Yeah, Amamma Hellman."

"Say Grand - ma, Ernie."

"Gran-amamma."

"That's close enough."

Mom and Ernie walked into the parlor. I went to pick up the pieces of the puzzle and as I turned my back, the door opened.

"I was wondering what they do with you here."

Irma's voice made me jump and her perfume filled the hall with cake spices and jasmine. At least it wasn't rose water.

"If you're the hired help, they're in trouble. I mean, the way our

200

bedroom always looked! Hi, sis."

When I turned to greet her, I was shocked. She slipped off her mink coat with her thick fingers that sparkled with diamonds and gold and immediately began to adjust a pink tulle wrap that covered the thin straps of the pink satin gown she wore. Through the wrap I could see that the straps dug into her thick shoulders and where the dress met her waist and thighs, she bulged like an overstuffed Wisconsin sausage. She had been battling weight ever since she lost the baby. It had been only two weeks or so since I saw her at Thanksgiving, but she looked even fatter. I almost would have said she was pregnant except for the fact of Ben's injury.

"Hi, Irma. Gosh, you didn't have to get so dressed up."

"You think I'm gonna meet my brother-in-law in a house dress? Not on your life."

Irma clicked open a sequined clutch and pulled out a black stick that looked inlaid with mother-of-pearl. Balancing it between the thumb and index finger of her left hand, she pulled out a gold case and popped it open.

"You're smoking now, Irma?"

Plucking one of the cigarettes from the case, she twisted it onto the end of the black stick. 'Think one of those gentlemen in there will have a light?'

"I guess."

"That and some gin and I'll be all set."

Mom stepped back into the hall. She frowned at the cigarette holder, but then her eyes brightened.

"Irma, you gotta see the spread."

"Definitely, mother. First, the bar."

"Irma, you watch yourself. You're driving and all."

"Yeah, yeah," Irma said.

"Mary, you're really lucky to live here. I mean that Daisy, she's perfectly quaint. Come on, Irma."

Quaint! What kind of a word was that for Mom to use? Every time she put on those white Easter gloves, it seemed like she instantly became a Vanderbilt. And all I could think of as they walked arm-in-arm into the parlor was that Irma looked like a homely Mae West. My mom and sister just didn't make sense and boy did I miss Dad right then.

I turned back toward the front door and froze: a man in a military uniform was leaning over and setting a green canvas duffel bag on the ground. He stood up and set his cap back on his head. Andrew's brown eyes glazed over in surprise.

As if I stepped into a tunnel with Andrew at the other end of it, the wood walls of the hall began to spin like a cyclone around me. Voices from

201

the parlor blurred into a buzz in my ears. Andrew's face. His face. He was here.

"Mary, I'm home."

I couldn't move my feet and as Andrew stepped to me, I could see his arms and shoulders had grown thicker but his face was so thin that his high cheekbones jutted out. Falling into his arms, my chest heaved and explosions of sobs echoed through the hall.

"My Andrew, my Andrew," I whispered into his chest.

Lifting my face to his, he held my cheeks tenderly and stared at my eyes. His eyes began to sparkle with tears and he pulled me to his mouth, his warm, soft mouth. As we kissed, our tears joined to become warm streams down both of our faces.

"My Mary, my Mary," he said through our kiss.

"Andrew!" Daisy screamed as she scurried across the hall.

Daisy threw her left arm between us and pulled Andrew to her.

"My boy," she cried. "My boy."

She kissed his face several times, leaving pink marks of lipstick. His cheeks still glistened from our tears. Daisy burst into a sob and buried her face in the same place on his chest that I had. The party moved from the parlor to the hall. Father Haggarty joined Andrew and Daisy and as Andrew held Daisy with his left arm, he reached out for Father Haggarty with his right hand. Father Haggarty took Andrew's hand in both of his own.

"We've prayed for this moment a long time and the Lord decided to grant our wish. Welcome home."

Andrew nodded then glanced over Father Haggarty and caught my eye again. My breath stopped short and I had the feeling we were standing on New Ulm Street again. His dark eyes penetrated my heart even as more people now joined in greeting him. A sharp slap on Andrew's back from one of the group broke our eye contact.

Mom and Irma stepped into the hall last and Mom walked Louise over and handed her to me. Ernie stood on my left and grabbed my leg, afraid of all the commotion I guess. Irma leaned against the parlor doorway and crossed her legs.

She looks like she's vamping, I thought.

As soon as the loud greetings died down, I took Ernie's hand and made my way toward Andrew. His eyes locked on me for a second, but when he saw Louise in her pale blue dress and the matching blue barrettes in her thin blonde hair, his mouth fell open and his eyes welled up. He nodded toward her as if to be sure and I nodded back. He parted the huddle of guests and his eyes darted down to Ernie. He saw that Ernie was clinging to me and he stepped forward and lowered himself on to his haunches. Daisy, Mom, and the other lady guests in the hall all murmured a soft cry at the same time. As Andrew opened his arms for Ernie, Ernie stepped back behind me.

"Ernie. Member the picture of Daddy we looked at every night?" I said.

"Uh-huh," he answered.

"Well, come say hi to your daddy."

Ernie stepped around and peeked at Andrew. Andrew broke out into a grin and reached out but Ernie stepped behind me again.

"He's shy sometimes," I said.

Louise pumped her legs and broke out into a giggle. Andrew stood up and reached for her and Louise used my body like a springboard to jump into his arms. She put her chubby arm around Andrew's neck and pumped her legs with excitement.

"Dadda, Dadda, Dadda," she said.

When Ernie saw Louise in Andrew's arms, he stepped out from behind me and held up his own arms.

"Daddy. I Ernie."

"You sure are, big boy," Andrew said. He swooped down and pulled Ernie up to his other shoulder. Louise leaned over and kissed his cheek with a loud smack and Ernie followed her. I'll never forget how Andrew buried his head between Ernie and Louise and squeezed them until they giggled.

"My babies. My babies," he said.

"Well that was wonderful. Let's go have some food," Daisy said.

All the guests except Mom and Irma filtered back into the parlor. Mom went up to Andrew and gave him a peck on the cheek.

"Welcome home, Andrew,' she said. She turned to catch up with Daisy like an anxious puppy, saying as she turned the corner into the parlor: 'Daisy. Ain't it just grand that our kids are back together again!"

"Mary, you never told me how handsome my brother-in-law is," Irma said. She stepped away from the wall and walked toward Andrew, her hips swinging back and forth like a clock pendulum. Andrew glanced at me, his eyebrows raised.

"Andrew, this is Irma. Remember, she lived in Wisconsin when we first got married and didn't make it out here to meet you before the war," I said.

Andrew kissed Ernie and Louise once more, and then set them down. Louise ran into the parlor and Ernie sat back down in the hall chair, keeping his eyes on Andrew the whole time. Andrew pulled on the edges of his uniform jacket to straighten them. He held his hand out to Irma.

"You silly. We're family," she said.

She slapped his hand away and leaned forward to kiss him. Andrew turned his cheek and his eyebrows knitted in confusion. I shrugged because I didn't yet know why my sister, my married sister, my big, fat, married sister, was acting like some sort of tramp. As Andrew leaned back from the kiss, Irma threw her arms around him and pressed him into a hug. Andrew patted her back lightly.

"Nice to finally meet you, Irma."

She pulled away from the embrace and Andrew's hands dropped instantly. Irma kept hold of his sides and I could see a pink flush breaking out on Andrew's cheeks.

"Don't be a stranger no more, okay brother-in-law?"

"Yeah, okay."

"Now I'm going to get myself something to eat. Anyone want to join me?"

Andrew and I both shook our heads. Irma sashayed into the parlor.

"I'm sorry. I don't know what's gotten into her," I said.

"I don't care. Come over here."

He pulled me to him again and our mouths met with the force of lost days and years. That kiss spanned the four years of our separation and led to an unbroken chain of love for the next couple of days. We clawed and tore at each other physically and emotionally, opening forgotten sexual channels and baring our intimacies as we got reacquainted. Daisy took charge of Ernie and Louise. A knock at our door announced each of our meals but Daisy kept out of sight. Our bed became a haven from the pain of missing each other and a cocoon from which our marriage would be reborn. Saturday evening rolled around and we lay entwined in each other's arms. As Andrew snored quietly, with my cheek pressing against his chest that had grown a line of downy, black hair while he was gone, I glanced over and saw the time.

My movement disturbed him, but when I saw it was five o'clock in the evening, a pang shot through me: Father Haggarty's hearing confessions right now. Why did that matter? Because it was time for me to tell Andrew the truth.

"What time is it?" he asked like a bomb was exploding. Since he'd been home from the war, that's how he woke up -- real excitable.

"Five o'clock."

"Is something the matter?"

"No. I gotta tell you something. Very important."

Andrew rolled over and rubbed his eyes. He pulled a cigarette out from the case on the side table, tapped it to pack it down, and then lit it. He exhaled the first puff of white smoke that smelled like burning cow

204

dung.

"Go ahead, Mary. I'm listening."

"Okay. But you have to know that this is really hard to say."

"What d'ya mean?"

"Very hard," I answered.

Andrew paused and bit on the tip of his lower lip. Something flashed through his mind, I could see his expression change. "Wait a minute. Did you," he swallowed hard. "Did you have an affair while I was gone?"

"Oh, God, no. No. This happened a long time ago, even before we were married."

"Mary, whatever you did before we were married, that's none of my business."

"But it might be. Andrew, it was real bad. You gotta listen to me."

Andrew sat up and twisted his cigarette out into the ashtray. He blew the last puff he took up into the air, then rolled over and wrapped his arms around me.

"Let me ask you this, Mary. Is whatever you have to tell me a sin?"

"Yes. I guess."

"Don't tell me."

"But Andrew."

"Whatever it is, especially since it happened before we were married, it's between you and the Lord. Remember your first confession?"

"Yeah. I don't think I did that right."

"Doesn't matter. You confess this dark, deep sin," he said that like he thought it was funny or something. 'Confess it and do your penance.'

"Andrew, I think —"

"Shh. Not another word."

"Andrew."

"It's between you and the Lord now. Forget it."

Andrew brought his hand up to my left breast. Did he really understand what he was telling me to do? Confess to Father Haggarty? As I faded into another moment of pleasure, I realized that I had to bury the whole thing. Forget it. No confession, no penance. Our marriage was being reborn over that weekend, but some of the old parts of it were going to stay. By Monday morning, the chrysalis of our new life together burst open. Daisy pounded on our door.

"Wake up, lovebirds. Breakfast is on."

Andrew stood up, startled again and I opened my eyes but couldn't believe it was morning. Nothing but the dimmest orange gray light shined through the windows of our room. Andrew tapped his cigarette and I stood, wrapping the sheet around me.

205

"Seven-thirty!" I cried when I saw the bedroom clock. "We'll be late for work."

Andrew drew a hand through the dark strands of hair that hung like mop strings over his eyes.

"What are you going on about?"

"The market was closed all last week. We better get there in a jiff to open it up and make some money." I scurried past Andrew but he grabbed my arm.

"Andrew. There's no time for that. I gotta get to work."

"Hold it, Mary. Let's take this slow, now."

He pulled me down next to him and I could smell the coffee and pancakes or waffles over his stinky tobacco. My hair now tickled my face and I threw it back.

"You don't get it. In the winter, we gotta open the store whenever the snow lightens up or we won't be able to meet cost. We also gotta get back orders in and weighed," I pleaded.

"Whoa. You sound like some man or something."

I didn't understand what he meant and that hurt me somehow.

"Andrew. I gotta —"

"You don't gotta do anything except for get out there and take care of the kids."

"But I learned a lot and I think I can help you keep things going."

"Mary, that was all fine and good while the war was on. But no wife of mine is gonna work. Now you just relax and let me handle everything. Things are going to get back to normal now that I'm home."

From that day forward, things did get back to something, I don't know if it was normal. Andrew managed the produce market day in and day out. I stayed at home with Ernie and Louise (even though I daydreamed that some catastrophe would happen at the market and Andrew would need me there) and Daisy went back to her most important chore: shopping. She had a small fortune after Gerald's death and now had the time again to pursue whatever collecting whim struck her. Daisy was happy, Andrew seemed happy to work at the market for now (as long as you didn't ask about the war -- he said he'd never talk about it), and the kids were happy that I was home with them.

But for the weeks that followed Andrew's return home, all the way through the holidays and into the first part of 1946, a strange cloud seemed to hover over me. I guess all I was supposed to do was take care of the kids, which wasn't easy, and help keep the house, also not easy. But it was always the same: a dirty diaper here, a load of dishes there. Always the same. Nothing like the thrill of selling out on potatoes or being the Banana Queen. What was wrong with me again? Why wasn't I happy being a mother and a housekeeper? Everyone in Hopkins seemed happy that things were back to the way they were before the war. Any hope I had of maybe helping Andrew again at the market dissolved in February, just before Valentine's day.

"I'd say about seven weeks along, Mary," Doc Anderson said. He leaned back in his leather chair and its hinges squeaked. He was a silhouette against the blowing snow that howled with the wind just outside the wooden shutters of his private office.

"Another baby?" I was beside myself. I had suspected it this time when my cycle was late again. Expected it and feared it. Doc Anderson must have seen the look on my face because his voice softened.

"Have you talked with Andrew about ways of keeping this from happening?"

I felt my cheeks go warm when he asked the question. I shrugged.

"Not really."

"I know you're Catholic and all, so you may run into some problems with this. But you're a real fertile gal. There are some options we could look into."

"What do you mean?"

"To keep this from happening again."

"What does being Catholic have to do with it?"

"You should probably ask Andrew about that."

"They didn't say anything about it in catechism."

"They probably wouldn't. Mary, if you want to slow down with having children, there's one way I think is okay with Catholics. You need to think about changing how you do what you do."

"Huh?"

"The frequency, I mean. Also, pay attention to your cycle. When you're near it, avoid having intercourse."

"That doesn't sound difficult."

"It isn't but it also isn't sure fire. Other ways are a lot more effective. Again, talk to your husband. See what he thinks." I stood to go and Doc Anderson stood up and took my hand.

"Mary, congratulations, anyway. Oh, Mary, how's Ernie doing on the new medication?"

"Okay. Whenever we get a heavy flurry or rain, he breathes like a wounded moose but I calm him down and give him an extra breath of the stuff."

"I don't like that he's having any problems at all. There aren't any medications out there we haven't tried. Get him in here at the beginning of April, before spring hits, and we'll see where he's at." I turned to go again.

"Mary? You want me to talk to Andrew for you?"

"No. It's okay Doc. I'll give him the good news and then tell him what you said."

Andrew was very quiet when I told him later about my pregnancy. He sat on the bed and rubbed his hands, stained by green, red, and brown vegetables splotches. Ernie and Louise played on the floor next to us and Ernie's wheezing stirred up. Frozen rain pelted the bedroom windows.

"I don't know what were gonna do if this keeps happening, Mary," Andrew said. He didn't look up but seemed to stare at a worn spot in the Oriental rug on the floor. "I ain't making enough at the market, you know? We're just lucky right now that Mom's letting us stay here."

"Doc Anderson did say that we should –"

"You no take that, Louise. That mine," Ernie screeched. Louise started to cry and Andrew glanced at them.

"Ernie, don't pull things outta your sister's hand," I said. Ernie kept pulling at the wooden bell and Louise yanked back on it.

"Mama, mama," Louise started to cry.

"Ernie, now come on."

Ernie yanked on the bell and Louise fell back and started to wail. Andrew stood up. "For crying out loud, Mary. Is this what you did while I was gone?" Andrew snarled. "No wonder he doesn't listen."

Andrew yanked the bell from Ernie and handed it back to Louise whose wail turned into a dying sniffle. He pulled Ernie up by his suspender straps and swatted his bottom. Ernie now broke out into a wail.

"You ask once, Mary. Once. If the kids don't listen, then you punish 'em. Otherwise, they're never going to respect you. Now, what was it Doc Anderson said we should do?"

"Hurted Ernie's rump," Ernie cried. He stood up and walked to me while he rubbed his rear end with his hands. I reached for him.

"Cripes, Mary. Don't baby him or he isn't gonna learn the lesson."

"Go sit down and play," I said. But I was as surprised at Andrew's temper as Ernie was.

"Doc, Mary," Andrew said. Now it seemed like he was impatient with me.

"He said we have to find a way to keep this from happening because I'm so fertile." Andrew nodded toward the kids like I said something indecent.

"He said there're some different ways."

"Nothing doing, Mary. It's the Lord's will."

"Doc said that the way for us may be for me to pay attention to my cycle and avoid –" Now I glanced at the children. "Avoid any pleasure contact just before and just after."

"The Pope says we can't interfere at all. If it's meant to be, it's meant to be."

"But Doc said –"

"I don't care what Doc said. Is he gonna be there to keep us from going to Hell?"

"Is the Pope gonna be there to help us feed the kids?"

Andrew jumped off the bed like I set his pants on fire. He stood over me with his hands rolled into fists on his sides. 'You never talk to me like that. Ever.'

He turned and stormed out of the room, his feet pounding. My heart matched his steps, beat for pound, and my hands were ice cold with fear. Why was he so mad? Where did that anger come from?

"On the nest again, huh?" Andrew's brother John said as he slapped me on the back a few weeks later.

"Yeah. Thirteen weeks or so."

"Let me see. It's March tenth today, so thirteen weeks ago," he said. He looked up like he was adding numbers in his head, his full, slightly wild eyebrows pushing together as his sapphire blue eyes rolled back and forth. "September, then. That's it."

"Yeah. I guess."

"Well, good. Andrew, you old cat. You could be in Philly in time for the leaves to change. Baby'll be about a month old, or so."

"What would I go to Philly for?" Andrew asked.

Daisy walked into the dining room with a serving platter loaded with corned beef and steaming cabbage and potatoes. The house had been crackling and gushing all day as the spring thaw began, and right as Daisy set down the platter, ice cracked and exploded like a broken mirror on the front porch.

"That was a doozy," John said. "'Course, in Philly, we get our thaw a lot sooner than Hopkins here. And it's never so loud. So Mom, corned beef and cabbage. What's the occasion?"

"Since you won't be here for St. Patrick's, I figured I'd make it tonight," Daisy said. "Now John, before you pounce on the food, would you say grace for me?" John set his fork back onto his plate, the potato he stabbed still stuck to its tines.

"Sure, Ma," he said. I thought he sounded a little irritated. "Name of the Father, Son, and Holy Spirit."

As soon as he finished grace, he reached out and pulled a big hunk of the corned beef off the platter. The corner of his navy wool suit coat sloshed into the horseradish sauce as he brought his fork back down.

"John, your coat there," Andrew said.

"Honey, I told you shouldn't wear your good suit coat at the table," Daisy said. John shrugged and licked the horseradish off his coat.

"Unca John eats his coat," Ernie said with a giggle. I laughed, too, but for a different reason: a family could eat for a long time on the money his coat must have cost. John stood up and slid his coat off and at thirty-two, he was already working on a pretty serious potbelly. It pushed and bulged through his suspenders and against his white shirt. The edge of his blue and gold silk tie sat like a spoon on his belly.

"So, John, tell us what you're doing in Minneapolis anyway," Daisy said.

"Here to see my little brother, Mom. And to meet his pretty wife."

"You should get one of your own soon," Daisy said under her breath.

"I'm sure that ain't the only reason he's in town."

Andrew said that with the same brooding and quiet attitude he took whenever John came around. When John visited, the house turned loud and boisterous and at the same time, Andrew grew quiet and moody.

"Were also doing some business with Three M. Trying to get them to invest on the ground floor of this plant we're trying to get up and running. If Three M joins in, we'll need someone to run the plant." John glanced at Andrew. "Someone I can trust."

"What's the plant gonna make?" Daisy asked.

"It's a revolutionary thing, Ma. I think it's going to make us all real rich."

"What is it?" Andrew said. He seemed to ask the question just to have something to say. His eyes didn't leave his corned beef.

"What it is, little brother, is something that's going to make the radio obsolete."

"Obso - what?" I said.

"Obsolete. So that it's no longer necessary," John said.

"Mary went to high school—she knows what that means. Anyway, that doesn't sound possible," Andrew said.

"Imagine this," John went on, ignoring Andrew's comment. "A box you can turn on, just like the radio. But instead of just sound, you see a picture, too."

"You mean like a movie picture?" I asked.

"That's it, pretty girl. This box will show you movie stars. Or, you ever want to go to Africa or China? It'll show you those places, too. Even the fights. Right in your own home. They call it television and anyone who wants to make money should get into it now. Like you, Andrew."

"What would I do?"

"You'd manage the first television manufacturing plant. Business will be small for now, but the more we make of them, the more people will be able to afford them. We see a television in every house ten years from now the same way you see a shoe horn in everyone's closet today. Andrew, we couldn't pay you much now, but we'd give you shares in the company."

"What's that?" I asked.

"Andrew would own a piece of the firm," John answered. "If it skyrockets, he'll make a fortune."

"And if it doesn't, I've worked a long time for nothing. Sounds too farfetched, John. I'd rather stay here and keep my hand in the vegetable bin." I nodded and tapped his arm.

"You gotta look ahead, brother. You gotta see the big picture through the little one, if you know what I mean."

"Sounds like a load of crap. Another one of your make it rich in a jiff kind'a deals," Andrew said.

"So you'd rather stay in town here, I suppose. Or maybe go to medical school?"

Andrew threw his napkin in frustration. His eyes flared.

"I just may do that sooner than you think. Just because you lived off pop and me while you went to your fancy Philadelphia school doesn't mean you're the only one with brains."

"With two kids, Andrew, no matter what you wanna try to do, you're gonna need money to do it. Television is a way to get it."

"It sounds pretty good, Andrew," Daisy said.

"Mom, you think everything John says sounds good. Just because he's rich."

"Andrew!" Daisy snorted.

"Sorry, Mom. It just doesn't sound so great to me."

"Andrew, just do me a favor. Think about it, okay? It could mean a lot of opportunities for you," John said. He took a big bite of his corned beef.

Over the next few weeks, Andrew did think about it a lot. He spent so much time thinking about the possibilities John mentioned that he almost never talked at home, to me or the kids. If he did, it was usually to correct the kids or to advise me how to be firmer. At the beginning of April, just before Ernie was due to see Doc Anderson for his asthma check-up, I decided to surprise Andrew at the market. The weather had warmed up enough so that I was able to dress Ernie and Louise in their short pants. We walked along Minnetonka Avenue but Minnehaha Creek and the falls that were roaring with the waters from the spring thaws north of us drowned the horns and occasional car brakes out. Winter's flat, cold smell was giving way to a slight floral, almost gamy earth smell. As we got close to the market, I pointed the aspens out to Ernie and Louise and how they were beginning to explode with soft green buds. As I pointed out the aspen that was leafing in front of the market, we heard screaming.

"No, damnit. I can't give 'em to you for that!" Andrew yelled.

"Daddy's mad. Ernie didn't do it," Ernie said. Since Andrew had been home, Ernie cowered whenever he heard him raise his voice. He cowered and always thought he was in trouble.

"It's not you, Ernie. It's —"

"I'm never coming here again, Andrew Murphy! Your father would be so ashamed!" Margaret hollered as she walked out the door and slammed it behind her. She was so upset she didn't even recognize me but walked right on past. The door flew open again.

"Another thing. Dad cut you —" Andrew stopped dead when he saw us. "Mary? What are you doing here?" I held up a basket.

"Lunch."

Andrew snorted air out his cheeks, releasing whatever frustration Margaret caused him. He ran a hand through his hair, and then scratched the top of his head.

"Come on in. There's my boy and my girl, too. What a surprise!" He seemed excited and surprised to see us, but he also still seemed peeved at Margaret. He leaned over and picked up Louise and rubbed Ernie's head.

When I walked into the market, the smell of the stale apples, old cabbage, and musty potatoes brought me back to those years spent there. I hadn't been to the market since Andrew got home and a wave of sadness pulsed though me.

"Let's eat in the office so I can keep an eye on things," he said.

The office was still crowded with the desk that seemed too big for it, and the oak chair I sat in often as Gerald was teaching me. The clutter of paper, pink and white invoices with the layer of carbon paper between, and the battered and worn black phone felt both familiar and so distant. I suddenly saw Gerald lying on the floor in that awful moment, and Ernie much younger sitting on the quilt next to the desk. Andrew sat in the desk chair that rolled and creaked under his and Louise's weight. He put his feet up on the desk.

"What are you looking around so much for, Mary? You act like you haven't seen this place before."

"Just thinking, that's all."

"Well, let's get the show on the road here. I don't have a lot of time."

As I opened the picnic basket, I noticed that Ernie sat on the floor right where he used to when I was working. 'He remembers, too,' I thought. Pulling out the oranges and cold chicken, I heard Ernie choke on his breath.

"You okay there, Ernie?" Andrew asked.

Ernie nodded but when he inhaled again, I heard a rumble in his chest I hadn't heard before. Louise mimicked the breath and giggled.

"Ernie. You having a problem?" I asked.

"Must be something out in the bins," Andrew said. "Maybe you shouldn't have brought him here."

As if Ernie agreed with Andrew, his next breath sounded like air passing through a straw. I threw open my purse and pulled out his aerator.

"Here, honey. Breathe it in."

His little lips wrapped around the funnel-like metal tube and as he inhaled, his lungs sounded like they were constricting. He almost gulped for breaths.

"Slowly, now, Ernie. Let the medicine work."

"What hurt Ernie?" Louise asked. Her face started to turn pink out of fear, her eyes welling. Andrew held her close.

"Ernie's okay, Louise. Don't be scared," Andrew said.

But as Ernie took in the next couple of breaths, his chest seemed to collapse on itself in a struggle. I pulled the aerator out of his mouth and shook it. The medication sloshed inside so I knew there was enough. I depressed the top and saw the medication mist like a cloud. I turned back to Ernie and as I did, he fell onto the floor. His arms and legs began to flail like he was swimming. He was gasping to death.

"Ernie, Ernie!" I cried.

Andrew fell on the ground next to Ernie. Louise started to wail. Andrew lifted Ernie's head but his neck was a washcloth under his grip.

"Ernie! Ernie!" he cried.

"Get Doc Anderson, Andrew. Go get him!"

Andrew's eyes darted between Ernie and me like he was a bird about to be attacked by a snake. In a second, he was on his feet and out the office door. Louise, now crying in full force, sat down next to Ernie's head and rubbed his dark curls.

"Ernie, up! Ernie, up!" she said.

Ernie now rattled and wheezed with each breath. I opened his yellow-checkered shirt and could see his eyes rolling just under his dark lashes. I rubbed his stomach and kissed his little hand but his breathing still sounded like tearing bed sheets. Louise rubbed his head and I turned my head over my shoulder constantly as we waited for Andrew.

"Come on, pumpkin. Doc Anderson's going to be here soon," I said.

My own tears began to well up. Why weren't his eyes open? What was so wrong with his lungs all of a sudden? The slamming door of the market startled me. Doc Anderson roared into the room, zipping open his bag as he did.

"It's some sort of allergy response triggering his asthma," he said.

He pulled a hypodermic from his black case and a small vial of a clear liquid. "Mary, get his left sleeve up," he said.

I rolled his sleeve and as soon as I did, Doc Anderson inserted the needle and plunged the medicine in. Within seconds, Ernie's ragged, gasping settled down into a quiet rumble. In a minute, his breathing became deep and steady. Doc Anderson placed his palm on Ernie's forehead, and then held his little white wrist while he checked his watch. Ernie's eyes popped open.

"Hi, Doc," he said.

"Hello there, son."

"Are you sure he didn't get stung by a bee or anything like that on the walk over?" Doc Anderson asked Andrew and I later. Ernie and Louise played on the floor in the office.

"No, Doc. Ernie's real scared of flying bugs and he would've screamed if anything got close enough."

"And he didn't eat anything odd?"

"Nope."

"Hmm. Well, that being the case, then he's got acute allergic asthma and it could be anything growing here in Hopkins or in the whole state."

"What can you do about it?" Andrew asked.

"I'll check back through the records and all, but keep in mind I'm fairly certain that we tried everything."

"What then?"

Doc Anderson shrugged.

"Move. It's probably the only choice you got."

"Move? To where?"

"You got to get him into a dry climate, one free of severe winters and where our weeds don't grow."

"What about Philadelphia?" Andrew asked. I was surprised that he even thought about Philadelphia.

"No. Weather there's not much different and the same thing for the weeds."

"Where, then?" I asked.

"Out west. That's probably your best shot. If you don't, I don't know how bad his attacks are going to get and we don't want to keep pumping him full of adrenaline. I'd say get him out of here as soon as possible."

I knew Andrew was upset by the way he plucked a cigarette from his shirt pocket. As he stuck it in his mouth, Doc Anderson grabbed his arm.

214

"Not with this boy's weak lungs you don't. Take it outside, Andrew. You're going to have to give those up if you want to give Ernie's lungs a chance."

Doc Anderson dropped the hypodermic into his doctor's bag, pulled out a red lollipop and handed it to Ernie. He looked back at both of us as he walked toward the market door.

"Get Ernie out west," he said like he was our father.

"California?" Daisy said at dinner that night. "Try Philadelphia. And after all, Louise's got no breathing problem." I wanted to kill her right then.

"Mom, didn't you listen?" Andrew said. "Philadelphia's as bad as we are here. Ernie needs dry weather."

"Well what the heck you think you're gonna do out there?"

"I don't know right now, Mom. But I gotta look into it."

"And what about the market?" she said.

"I guess you can finally sell it."

Daisy slammed a serving of potatoes onto her plate, the silver spoon sounding like a hammer as it struck the porcelain plate.

"I guess I could," she said. Her mouth twisted into a tiny pucker around each word.

"You were planning on selling it someday, weren't you, Mom?" Daisy glared at me.

"I wanted to sell it sometime ago, when it was really worth something. Then I could'a' made a killing. But someone talked me out of it."

"Daisy, I was only looking out for Andrew."

"Hey, it's no time for arguing. You two didn't think I wanted to stay here in Hopkins and be a fruit seller anyway, did you?"

"I had some hopes that you'd continue your father's business." 'And strangle on her apron strings', I thought.

"I'd like to know something," she said.

"What?"

"What are you going to do in California?"

A couple of days later, we got our answer. A letter arrived from a Jack Bullock addressed to Andrew and I remembered Wild Jack from all the stories Andrew told from the war. Andrew got home that day and when he saw the envelope, his face that hung from fatigue and worry perked up.

"Well, I'll be," he said after kissing me. "Let's see what's going on with him."

Andrew's eyes scanned the sheet of loose-leaf paper that was scrawled with black ink. He broke out into a smile at one point, and then his eyebrows knitted. With worry or confusion, I couldn't tell. Flipping the page over quickly, Andrew mouthed the last sentence of the letter. He looked up at me and his face looked puzzled.

"You're not gonna believe this."

"What?"

"Wild Jack's living out in Los Angeles. Got a new wife named Jessie. He's trying to break into radio."

"Oh." It really didn't interest me that much.

"His mother manages a motel and he invited us out."

"We can't afford a vacation, Andrew."

"Not for that. Wild Jack says they're hiring all over Los Angeles right now and they're practically grabbing vets off the trains."

"For radio work? You don't know anything about radio."

"Not radio, Mary. Airplane business. I guess there are a bunch of companies out there that need employees to build planes. Wild Jack says war vets are the first people getting the jobs."

"Okay. So we go to Los Angeles. Where we gonna live?"

"That's what I said before. Wild Jack's mom owns a motel and he says she'll put us up for half what rent costs out there."

"Do you wanna build airplanes, Andrew?"

"I don't know. I guess. But I know for sure that Ernie needs dry weather and Los Angeles is just about a desert."

"Can you really make money doing that?"

"Wild Jack says the pay is darn good and there's a future in airplanes."

"What about medical school?"

"I ain't even gone to college, Mary. Medical school takes even longer than that. The war took away that chance. But now, the Lord has provided us with this opportunity. Can you see how blessed we are?"

I didn't know if the Lord was going to provide for us or not, and even though I had completed my catechism and had been going to church every Sunday since then, I hadn't found much faith. But I found myself praying silently in my head on May 7, 1946, when we had the last of our clothes and belongings packed into Gerald's old car. Daisy had for sure provided for us, or Andrew and Louise at least, by giving us the car to use in California. She didn't drive, anyway, and I don't think the car was worth much. That morning, the sky was a clear blue we hadn't seen in months as it flared out over, above, and around Daisy's gray house. Aspens stuck up like leafy green swords and the sun was a comforting warm.

For the second time in twenty-four hours, my eyes gushed with tears as Andrew squeezed Daisy to his chest one final time. The night before, Daisy had a dinner for Mom, sporting white gloves again, Dad, and us. Dad looked pale and thin from his kidney condition. Mom's hug and kiss was quick like a pat on the back. But as Dad squeezed me to his bony chest, his hands curling tight on my arms, it felt like he would never let go. His tears dropped onto my shoulders and when they did, my own gushed out like a bursting damn. So to see Andrew and Daisy hug one last time, I felt that feeling of separation and a dread of whatever was going to happen to us in California.

'Our Father, who art in Heaven,' repeated through my head.

"Bye, Dee-yer," Daisy said to me when she let go of Andrew. She touched my arm.

"Take care of my boy."

We climbed into the front seat of the car and Ernie and Louise romped in the back seat. Daisy came up to the open window on Louise's side and reached out and held Louise's face. Andrew turned the engine over and the car began to vibrate and I could smell the odor of burning gasoline.

"Bye, Gram's girl."

"Bye, bye," Louise said.

Daisy stepped away from the car and Ernie crawled over Louise and grabbed onto the open window. "Amamma, I love you," he said. He reached his hand out and Daisy touched it lightly.

"Bye, Ernie," she said. She turned and her heels clicked on the front walk and in a moment, she slammed the front door. I glanced over at Andrew as he stuck his arm out the window to signal that he was pulling out. He dropped his face to the left and rubbed his cheek against his extended arm. He flicked away the tear on the right side of his face with his hand.

In a few moments, we drove down Minnetonka Avenue where both men and women now strode along the sidewalk. We passed Doc Anderson's, and then Murphy's Produce Market with its locked door and banner painted in red letters that read 'FOR SALE.' The car rolled to a stop at New Ulm Street and Andrew reached out and took my hand. My stomach began to twist with tightness and then I asked Andrew to pull over.

From my window, I could see the bank of Minnehaha Creek, the green grass of spring overwhelming the brown spots of winter. But from under the grass, I could see the buds of ladyslippers peeking up and a few were open. Throwing open the car door, I ran to pick a few of the flowers.

As I bent over, I realized we had stopped near the Name Tree. Its white bark now looked more like a scribbled pad than the trunk of a tree. I waved to Andrew to come join me for a minute. Running my hand along the waist of the tree, I found my initials: 'MBH.' Had it really been eight years since I scratched them in? Could I really be twenty-one already?

217

"You okay, Mary?" Andrew asked. His voice was choked with concern and he kept glancing back at Ernie and Louise whose little heads stuck out from the back window of the car.

"Look, Andrew." I pointed at the initials.

"What?"

"My initials. Those were my artist's initials. I put them there when I was thirteen." Andrew ran his hand over them. "Hang on a second." He pulled out the stainless steel pocketknife he brought home from the service and swung open the blade.

"Hide your eyes."

I did. I could hear him scratch the bark.

"Okay. Open them."

When I looked at my initials again, they now read: 'MBH + AGM.' They were also now enclosed by a heart. "Now that's some art," he said. "Let's go."

Andrew ran back to the car. I stared at the initials a moment longer and something about how he changed them made me twist with irritation. But the heart he scratched around the initials 'cause me to well with a feeling of warmth, security, and love. Those feelings seemed to drown out the irritation.

As I made my way back to the car, I stopped and looked at the creek once more. The falls still seemed to roar from the spring thaw further down the creek.

"Will I ever be back here again?" I said to no one.

13.

We had only been living at the motel that Andrew's Army buddy, Wild Jack, set us up in for about a week when I got the frantic call from Mom. Dad's kidneys were failing and we had to get home. Wild Jack's mom, Millie, who managed the beach motel in Venice, loaned us the money to take the train home. The train pulled into the Hopkins station a day later. We stepped off the train and Irma stood in the cold May morning in a long coat, her breath sending up a fog. Jimmy stood right next to her in a thick jacket. They waved toward us and I grabbed up Louise. But Irma's face was colorless and flat. She wore no makeup and her eyes were dead and I thought she looked just like the sister I shared a room with all those years.

"Dad's gone, Mary."

Andrew and Ernie stood behind me and my legs started to give out. Andrew rushed for Louise and took her from my arms. I felt like I was inside of a tunnel with no air and a numbness vibrated through my body. I reached for Irma and my arms fell on her shoulders. Jimmy hugged me from behind.

Two days later, we walked into Hopkins Lutheran Church and I saw Dad for the first time in weeks and the last time forever. The church itself was so simple with its two rows of oak pews, an oak pulpit and small cross that hung on the bright white wall. Compared to St. Anthony's with all its sculptures, stained glass windows, and wooden carved crucifix, this church was a blank canvas. Mom sat in the front pew, Irma next to her, Jimmy next to her, and Ben sat in his wheelchair just outside the pew.

Just to the right of the pulpit sat the plain wooden coffin, its lid propped open and two bunches of gardenias and carnations sitting at each end. Dad's nose and forehead just stuck out over the side of the pine box. As we walked up to it, the carnations and gardenias filled my nostrils with their overpowering scents. My heart pounded in my throat because I never had seen a dead person.

"He looks like he's sleeping," Andrew said.

I leaned over the edge of the coffin and now saw Dad's face that in the two weeks or so we had been gone must have shrunk. His cheekbones stood out like boney bridges from either side of his nose. His chin sunk down into the folds of his neck and his skin looked like beeswax. That

219

wasn't his face. I hadn't seen my dad asleep in a long time but that wasn't him. I had to look past his face and I followed the lapel of his dark Sunday suit and there were his hands crossed neatly over each other, just like he would do when he was thinking about some problem. But his hands, like his face, looked like yellow wax, the tips of his nails clean like I never saw them. Even the lines and cracks of his knuckles looked smooth. Footsteps and the crack of a book spine saved me from having to look at Dad anymore; the preacher now stood behind the pulpit.

The preacher cleared his throat and began but what he said and how long he said it, I couldn't say. I just stared at the thin hair on top of Dad's head and imagined this was all a dream. He was going to stand up at any minute and call me Mary girl. Or else tell me about the newest contraption he had dreamed up to 'cause the sun to stay up longer or make the snowfall at his whim. All this and more played through my head, from the church until the graveside.

Later that day, a few neighbors dropped in and brought food. Jimmy went into Dad's workshop and started to clean it up. He had planned on cleaning it up and making it into his room. The Darlana's brought Ernie and Louise over and left a raspberry pie. Around dinnertime, Mom said she was tired and went to bed. Irma, who had eaten more of the dishes that had been left than anyone else, announced that she was going into Hopkins to get something. Ben looked at us when she left, shrugged his shoulders and wheeled himself into their bedroom. The wheelchair's wheels squeaked like rusty bicycle tires and when he reached their bedroom, he shut the door.

Andrew sat on the couch and played with Ernie and Louise. The wind kicked up outside as I plopped down into Dad's chair near the radio. The crocheted quilt that had been stained from all the years of his sitting smelled like him. Burying my face into the yarn, I smelled him: I smelled his garage, his pipe, and his hair oil. Again, the tears flooded my face.

"You okay, Mary?" Andrew asked.

I shook my head because right then, it felt like someone had ripped a hunk of my belly out and threw it away.

"Why's Mama acrying?" Ernie said.

"She's thinking something sad," Andrew said.

I stepped across the room and switched on the radio. Organ music screeched mysteriously and then The Shadow made some sort of discovery. Leaning back against my Dad's chair, I could almost feel him nearby. Toward the end of the program, Irma came back home, a brown paper bag crackling in her hand.

"Anyone want a shot of bourbon?" she said.

"You guys want some dinner?" Andrew asked Ernie and Louise.

"Yeah. Dinner!" they both echoed back.

I had been thinking about Dad so much that I forgot the kids would need to eat dinner. I was so glad Andrew took control of them. 'Let's go in the kitchen.' He took them both by the hand. Irma crossed over and plopped onto the couch.

"You know, he's good looking, that boy. Did I ever tell you that?"

I didn't answer. Irma opened the bag and pulled out the bottle. She held it out to me.

"Jim Beam. Come on, Mary. You'll feel better."

"Dad didn't allow alcohol in the house," I said.

"He got over that once Ben and I moved back home."

"He couldn't have liked it too much, if he did."

Irma twisted the cap off the bottle and slammed it over her head. Bubbles of bourbon gurgled through the neck of the bottle as she drank. Irma lowered the bottle and smacked her lips. "That's some good stuff. You ought'a try it."

"I'm pregnant."

"Oh, yeah," she said. Her eyes went dull for a moment and she looked away.

"Why don't you honor Dad a little today and take that outside?"

Irma glared at me and raised the bottle to her lips again. This time she slurped and sucked air through her teeth to ease the bourbon's burn. Her green eyes bore into me and did not blink.

"I told you already. He understood why I need a little drink now and then."

"A little, Irma?"

I leaned back in dad's chair again and listened to the rest of the Shadow. Irma spread out on the couch, the black silk material of her dress ballooning out from her thighs and rear end that had obviously been growing over the last couple of months. Between the actor's lines, I could hear the bourbon bottle pop as Irma's lips sucked another sip. This went on until well into Fibber McGee and Mollie. By that point, Andrew came back in with the kids.

"Hi, Mama,' Ernie said. "We eated berry pie, too."

Louise repeated Ernie's phrase: "Eatbed pieberry too."

"Time for bed, isn't it Mary?" Andrew asked.

"Oh, yeah. Would you get them into their jammies and then I'll take them into Mom. She asked if they could sleep with her tonight."

"Sleeps with Amammy Hellman. Yea!" Ernie said.

While Andrew got their pajamas on, I stood and stretched. I walked over and switched off the radio. Irma still sat on the couch, clutching the bottle and staring off.

"He never loved me, you know?" she said. The words seemed to garble from her lips.

"Oh, Irma, yes he did." I had no patience for her whining right then.

"How would you know?"

"All he ever did was worry about us. Fine daughters we turned out to be, huh?"

Irma sat up and chopped the air with her hand to shut me up. The bourbon bottle started to slip and she caught it, causing the liquid in the half empty bottle to slosh.

"I don't know about you, but I married well and that made him proud. Just 'cause I lost the baby after Ben went overseas didn't make him less proud."

I wanted to laugh. Getting pregnant and having to marry a playboy. Me. Getting pregnant and not knowing which of the two was the father. His cup of pride must have runneth over, I'm sure. Another thought flashed in my head and that one I shared.

"We probably killed him. Broke his heart because he had such hope for us."

"Damn you, you think you're so –"

Irma slogged back another shot of bourbon as she stood. I ignored her. She walked toward the bedroom door.

"You know, Mary. Everyone ain't as lucky as you. It doesn't matter whether I get up any day or not. There ain't no reason for me to be, except for being there to wipe Ben's rear end. I just want a life that makes sense, like yours. Since I ain't got nothing more to say, please excuse me while I go help my husband do his personal business."

The bedroom door creaked on its hinges as she opened it. She paused like she was going to say something else then shook her head and stepped inside. She slammed the door behind her.

We stayed on for just a few days and in that time, Mom still got up at the crack of dawn and did her chores from then till breakfast, then from breakfast till lunch. She never cried in front of any of us and when she talked about Dad, it was as if he was just outside in his workshop or next door at the Darlana's. We finally decided that there was nothing more for us to do so we caught our train and headed back out to Los Angeles.

"Mama, why you crying?" Ernie asked. Choked by my tears, I didn't know how to answer him.

"Mama, what's the matter?" Ernie said three weeks later. We were on the floor that night playing pick-up sticks when a labor pain wrenched my stomach. I clutched it and it stopped. Jack and Jessie were laughing and talking in the room next to ours where Millie put them.

"Okay, Mary," Andrew said joining the kids and me. He carried a tablet with its first three pages flipped over. He pointed at it.

"We gotta figure something. I won't be due for a raise for about nine months or so. But with all of our eating and clothing expenses, we gotta hope that Millie keeps our rent down. If not, with the new baby and all, we're gonna get into--Mary?" The second wave of labor pains wrenched my stomach and I felt the gush of water ooze onto my legs and the floor. Ernie stood up.

"Mama went pee-pee on the floor!"

"Ernie, knock it off," Andrew hollered. "Take your sister in the other room."

Andrew reached down and helped me onto the bed. My stomach was now contracting and expanding, grinding with pain.

"We gotta hurry, Andrew."

"Okay, hang on."

Andrew ran next door and in a second, Wild Jack and Jessie were in our room.

"I'll drive, Andrew. You take care of Mary," Wild Jack said.

Jessie was already on the floor with Ernie and Louise but she kept her focus on me. "Anything else I can do?" she asked. Andrew and Jack helped me to my feet and led me to the door.

"Honey, just stay here with the kids. That okay with you?" Wild Jack asked.

"Of course. Just hurry up, she doesn't have that long."

As we stepped past Jessie and the kids, I was mad at her and I had the craziest thought: 'You may be good with them, Jessie. But I know how to make them!'

Andrew brought Maureen Therese -- the girl's name we had decided on, in honor of my catechism teacher -- into me the next morning and told me she had been born at ten thirty the night before. As I nuzzled her nearly bald head, soft and moist from baby oil, Andrew explained that she had gotten tangled in the umbilical cord and was choking when she was born. He went on to explain that the doctor said he had never seen a baby fight so hard to survive that kind of thing. She was a natural fighter and would grow up real strong. Even in my foggy state, I could tell that Andrew was covering something up.

"Okay, what's the matter?"

"Mary, what d'ya mean?"

Maureen Therese clawed at my breast and I opened my gown and placed her on my nipple. It had been awhile since Louise had suckled and it felt so good and right to have Maureen there. She ate like I was drying up.

"This one's got a lot of spunk," I said. "So, what's bothering you?"

Andrew sat on the edge of the bed and dropped his head in his hands.

"I think we gotta watch ourselves. I'm not pulling a lot right now and we're just barely making it with the rent and all. What was it Doc Anderson said to you before, about keeping you from getting pregnant again?"

"He said there was a way for us to keep me from getting pregnant. I've heard more about it and I think it's called the Rhythm Method." Andrew exhaled with frustration.

"Gotta be a sin. Just has to be," he said quietly.

"Any other way I think is even worse. But do we have to figure it out now? Just look at this little angel here."

Andrew glanced at Maureen and his eyes softened. He reached over and stroked her head. "She is a beauty. Tough little bugger."

"We can talk about all this later," I said. "It isn't like it's the Depression still, you know?"

Andrew slid onto the bed and wrapped his arms around me. Maureen Therese slurped and suckled.

The screen door of the house creaked open as we stood on the porch, which was really nothing more than two steps of cement that led up to a five foot square of cement protected by a small overhang. As Andrew twisted open the brass doorknob, a light breeze blew the aroma of Jasmine past us.

"Flowers, Mama," Ernie said.

"Flowers," Louise repeated.

"Kind of stuffy in here," Andrew said.

We stepped into the small room that was dark from the shades that were rolled over the windows and right away the clean smell of Jasmine from outside was wiped out by a smell that was like old cigars and dirty, wet towels. Andrew pulled one of the shades up and blue sunlight spilled through the lace shadow of some bush outside the window.

"Could you imagine a house in Hopkins being this hot in January?" Andrew said. As he crossed the room toward the dining area, his steps made the wood floor that looked black as tar creak.

"Mama, can I go outside?" Ernie asked.

"Me, too!" Louise yelled.

"Yeah. Just make sure you go around to the back of the house. Millie said there's a backyard and that's where I want you two to stay."

Ernie and Louise ran back out the front door and I heard them scream and laugh as they ran around the outside of the small house. Their shouting didn't disturb Maureen Therese as she lay in my arms asleep.

"I'm going to check out the two bedrooms," Andrew said.

224

"I'll be in the kitchen."

I walked through the dining area that sat off from the small living room, past the pine table with high back chairs, and stepped into the kitchen. The fridge buzzed and rattled. The white enamel stove sat just across and when I pulled the shade open over the kitchen window, I saw that the enamel on the stove was chipped in places and the chips bloomed with orange rust. The tops and sides of the stove were streaked with burned grease. The faint smell of rancid oil seemed to be everywhere.

'At least there's double sinks,' I said to myself.

"Mary, come here a second."

I crossed back into the living room and through a hall that was no bigger than a large closet. Sunlight passed through a pink shower curtain in the bathroom at the left but I found Andrew standing at a window in a bedroom on the right. He pointed out the window.

"Look at that tree."

I looked out the window at Ernie and Louise wrestling in the shade of a tree that must have been twenty-five feet tall. Its branches were covered with leaves that looked like ferns. I never saw a tree like that before.

"Isn't it something? If you lay in bed here, you're looking right up into it."

I didn't answer because I noticed that a few feet beyond the tree was a chain link fence. Through it I could see the beginnings of a hill that rose right out of the backyard and disappeared beyond the wooden frame of the window. "I don't like that hill out there so much."

"Millie said that hill is called Palos Verdes. Lot of rich people live up there."

"I don't care who lives in that palace place. What if the kids go wandering up there? They could get lost or something."

"They're not going to go back there."

Right as Andrew said that, Ernie ran to the chain link fence and started to climb it. I pushed the window open and it creaked and groaned. Maureen Therese awakened with a start and cried.

"Ernie. Get down from there. You are not allowed to play outside the yard," I hollered.

I turned toward Andrew who still sat on the edge of the bed that I now saw was a bare mattress, striped with blue and black material and splattered with dark and light stains. "You know one of the best parts about us living here in Walteria?" Andrew said. "It's only about fifteen minutes or so to work. Now when I work overtime, I'm not going to be getting home at ten thirty at night. Wasn't it nice of Millie to get us fixed up here?"

I couldn't argue that because even though the furniture and stove in the house were worn and stained, we were spending the same on rent as we did at the St. Charles and now the kids even had a yard to play in. All in all, I guess I was happy.

Andrew seemed happy even though he was now working twelve hours everyday and coming home exhausted. My own days began with getting him his breakfast at six thirty, packing his lunch and sending him out at seven. Breakfast, dishes, Andrew done. Then came Maureen Therese's first feeding at seven thirty, and by then, Ernie and Louise were wide-awake and needed their breakfasts. More dishes. Then laundry. Followed by dusting and mopping. Then lunch, and Maureen Therese's feeding. Each day was filled with these chores until Andrew got home, then dinner, dishes, and a little radio. Days blended more and more. The end of the week with church at our new parish, St. Joan of Arc up Pacific Coast Highway and off Oak in the town of Lomita, was the only punctuation to our lives.

By the end of 1947, right around when Ernie started kindergarten at Walteria School, where he said he fell in love with his teacher, Ms. Bunch, Andrew had been promoted and we were able to buy a Naugahyde couch and a rug for the living room. The cycle of dishes, cleaning, feeding, now watching Louise and Maureen Therese the full day and Ernie for half the day after he got home, was endless. I thought about all the days growing up when my Mom would be up at dawn and in bed, dead on her feet, by eight o'clock and I understood her better. But she never seemed unhappy. I, on the other hand, kept growing more and more bored and my feelings of being tired sometimes felt like moments of deep darkness. Every now and then catch myself doodling on a paper napkin or sketching a figure in the flour on the bread board. That was as close as I could get to doing art of any kind. In that time, Andrew and I began the rhythm method of sexual relations but we were both so exhausted so often, that we often didn't have to worry about it.

Our lives went this way for the first two years in Walteria, until the fall of 1948, just before Louise was ready to start kindergarten and Ernie was ready to start first grade at St. Joan's School. I was making Andrew his breakfast and I had something to tell him. Frying bacon and baking pancakes filled the air in the kitchen and I loaded his plate up and walked it out to the dining room. Andrew was digging the last section of a grapefruit out of the rind and he picked it up and squeezed it like a lemon to get its juice into his spoon. He looked up at me as I came in.

"Mary, what's the matter?"

I set the plate down and sat next to him. Picking up a piece of bacon from his plate, I nibbled on it as I talked to him.

226

"We got a problem, Andrew."

"Ernie acting up again? I can take care of that," he said. He reached down for his belt buckle and my skin prickled. Just after Ernie turned five, Andrew sat him down and told him that any more bad behavior like burning moths with a magnifying glass or lighting the weeds between sidewalk cracks would lead to a spanking with the belt. So far, Ernie had not gotten one.

"That's not it."

I exhaled, my chest tightening. The late hours Andrew had been keeping for so long now began to make him more irritable than I ever saw him. I knew he was under pressure so I guess his anger came from that. I didn't like to rattle him if I didn't have to. Andrew's fork clinked against the plate as he cut into his stack of pancakes. He looked up at me with his mouth full.

"So. What?"

"I missed my cycle."

He dropped his fork and folded his hands.

"How long?"

"Seven days. And I've been feeling like I need to barf for the last three mornings."

"Sure you ain't sick?"

"I'm pretty sure. I'll find a doctor and make an appointment after Ernie and Louise go to school next week."

A neighbor lady suggested a doctor out on Crenshaw Boulevard named Eddie Stevenson so Andrew decided he could go in late the following Monday (he'd be working even later that night, though) and take me to the doctor. We didn't talk on the ten-minute drive and I could tell by the way he tapped the steering wheel with his thumbs that he was tense about the whole thing. The appointment took only a matter of minutes and Dr. Stevenson took some urine and blood.

Eight days later, while I was making Maureen Therese's lunch, Dr. Stevenson called. I had news for Andrew that night. At around nine-thirty, with Ernie, Louise, and Maureen Therese now sleeping in their bunk beds we bought as soon as Maureen Therese out grew the crib, I heard Andrew pull up. I had been dozing on the couch and as I sat up, my arms stuck to the Naugahyde for a second. The back door creaked open and Andrew walked in with his short-sleeved white shirt unbuttoned and his navy blue tie loosened. His eyes looked dull through the horned-rim glasses we had to get for him recently. I kissed him. He collapsed onto the couch and rubbed his hands through his dark hair he was now wearing in a flat top. He looked much older than twenty-five to me and I thought it must be the long hours he was working.

"What's for dinner, Mary? I'm beat."

"I kept steak and biscuits warm in the oven for you. You want some now?"

"In a minute. Let me just sit. It was a hard day."

He just about fell asleep but after five minutes of sitting in silence, he pulled off his shoes and dragged himself to the dining room table. I pulled out a plate and heaped it with two pieces of round steak and brown gravy and scooped two biscuits onto it. The gravy still smelled of mushroom and onion. 'That looks good,' he said. His knife squeaked against his plate as he dug into the round steak.

"Any coffee around here, Mary?"

I nodded and poured him a cup. I sat across from him.

"Andrew, I got something to tell you." ·

He stopped moving his knife and fork and his tired eyes stared at me. "This can't be good news," he said.

"I'm due in April."

Andrew slammed his knife and fork down, making me jump. He dropped his head in his hands and rubbed his scalp like it was on fire. Suddenly, he grabbed his plate and threw it against the wall behind me, spattering gravy on me when he did. I heard Maureen Therese break out into a wail.

"That's just great," Andrew said. He pushed himself up from the table. "Why did you let it happen?"

His yelling scared me so much that I couldn't speak. I guess it was my fault, somehow. He pulled me up from my seat and shook me by the shoulders.

"How did this happen?" he screamed at me.

"Daddy, don't yell at Mommy," Louise cried. She and Ernie stood in the kitchen in their pajamas. Maureen Therese cried from the bedroom. Andrew's grip relaxed and he collapsed onto the chair again.

"I'm sorry, Mary. I'm real sorry. It's just that I found out at work today that we lost a government contract. They started laying people off left and right. I may be one of them." Andrew dropped his head into his hands and I stepped behind him and rubbed his shoulders.

"Ernie, you and Louise get back to bed. Go on now."

They both stood still a second longer, then walked back to bed quietly. Maureen Therese still cried.

"I gotta go see what she needs."

As I stepped away, Andrew stood and grabbed me. This time he threw his arms around me and kissed me. "I'm sorry, Mary. It's obviously the Lord's will. We'll work this out. We have to."

It worked itself out on New Year's Day, 1949. Andrew sat in the living room listening to the Rose Bowl as Northwestern played California. The kids played under the tree that we now knew was a jacaranda that dropped all of its leaves our first April in the house. I thought it was dying until two or three weeks later, when it erupted into a cloud of purple blossoms. I had never seen a tree with flowers like that, let alone in my favorite color. The old tree felt like a member of the family and since the kids played under it so much, I kind of thought of it as the Children's Tree, anyway.

Ernie and Louise were picking up small branches of the tree to make bundles. Maureen Therese was trying to climb the tree but her stubby two-year-old legs wouldn't let her make any head way.

"Oh, balls, they fumbled it again. They're getting wiped!" Andrew hollered.

The ham I was baking for dinner sent an aroma of roasted brown sugar and pineapple all over the house. I peeled the last part of the potato in my hand and dropped it into the pan of cold water in the sink. I bent to open the oven and glaze the ham when my belly erupted with a burning, tearing sensation. I fell to the ground in pain.

"Mary? Mary!" Andrew hollered. He was in the kitchen in a flash but the pain in my stomach caused my eyes to water. Sweat broke out on my forehead.

"My belly. My belly!"

"I'm gonna go call doctor –"

"No! Andrew, help me, the baby's coming!"

My belly wrenched and it hurt so bad I had to push to relieve the pain. It contorted again and I pushed again. I felt fluid and something solid spill into my underpants.

"Mommy!" Ernie screamed. I think Louise and Maureen started to cry as my head began to feel light.

"Ernie! Outside! Now!" Andrew roared. "Oh, Lord! Oh, Jesus! Help us!" he cried.

My head began to swirl and it lolled to the side. As I started to fall into blackness, I saw a bloody lump on the floor and I thought I could see a tiny face with a mouth gasping like a dying fish. Blackness fell over me.

I found myself in an art gallery and as I walked through, I saw a painting of Dad. I seemed to float past another that was Gerald. Now a woman in long robes was guiding me and she stopped in front of a statue and pointed toward it. There was the Pieta by Michelangelo I recognized from my catechism book, but instead of the Virgin Mary, I saw my face.

"No! I'm not you!" I screamed. I ran from the statue and then heard a voice.

"Oh, Maary, you're such funny!"

I turned to see Artie standing in the long gallery, a beret on his head as if he was in France.

"You're such funny, Maary!"

He laughed and laughed and my eyes started to burn. When I squinted from the pain, light burst through and I saw a face. I opened my eyes again and Artie's face melted into Ernie's.

"Mary?" I heard Andrew whisper. "Mary, we're all here."

Ernie sat on the edge of the bed. Louise sat to his left and Maureen Therese lay in the crook of my arm. Sunlight poured through the open window. Andrew leaned over and kissed my forehead.

"How do you feel?"

I didn't know what had happened. I felt a tightness and soreness in my lower stomach. "What happened?"

"Ernie, take your sisters out back and play now. I need to talk to Mommy."

Ernie hopped off the bed and helped Louise and Maureen Therese down. Each of them walked up to my right side and kissed my cheek.

"Love you, Mama," Ernie said.

"Love you," Louise and Maureen Therese said together.

I could smell alcohol and something like sulfur. Andrew sat on the edge of the bed and took my hand. "What happened, Andrew?"

"You lost the baby, Mary."

The little face gasping for breath on the brown tile floor flashed through my mind. But more than that, I felt a sense of shame. I failed. "I'm sorry, Andrew."

"Oh, Mary. Doctor Stevenson said this happens sometimes. He said that you're all right and you just need some rest."

But I knew it was my fault. I did something wrong that caused it. Maybe because I didn't want another baby. I knew it was me. "Oh, Andrew. I did it. It's all my fault."

"Just relax, Mary. You did nothing wrong."

"Where's the baby? What happened to it?"

"We can talk about that later. Just get some sleep, Mary."

My eyes felt heavy. An odd feeling of hollowness now filled my belly. Like my stomach was a birthday balloon. "I love you, my Andrew."

"I love you, my Mary." I fell asleep to the pressure of his lips against my forehead.

Wailing interrupted my sleep. I heard cries coming from the bedroom window, from somewhere in the dark backyard. 'The baby!' I thought. 'The baby needs me!' I jumped up, threw the blankets off, and ran for the backyard. The house was dark and silent in the night but as I stepped into the backyard, the baby's cries grew louder. I ran toward them

230

and when I got to the base of the Children's Tree, the cries were coming from under the ground. I clawed at the dirt.

"I'm coming! I'm coming!" Dig. Cry. Dig. Cry.

"Mary!" Andrew's voice boomed. "Mary! Wake up!"

I was pulled back suddenly and the orange glow of a night lamp stung my eyes. "The baby, Andrew! I gotta get the baby!"

"Mary. You're having a nightmare."

His voice broke through the haze of my dream. When my eyes were fully opened, I felt him holding me. He kissed the side of my face. "It's okay, I'm here, my girl, my Mary," he said.

"Andrew. I had an awful dream. I heard the baby crying. And when I tracked it down, I heard it crying under the Children's Tree."

"Oh, my Mary. It's okay. Go back to sleep."

"Where did the baby end up, Andrew? Tell me."

"I buried it under the tree," his voice cracked. "After Doctor Stevenson examined it, I took it out and buried it under the tree. I prayed over it, and buried it." Andrew's voice was choked with tears.

"The Baby Tree," I said softly.

"Huh?"

"That's not the Children's Tree anymore. It's the Baby Tree."

"Oh, Mary. Go back to sleep."

I did go back to sleep, or back to strange dreams, anyway. Every morning I woke up at that time, I was exhausted from dreams of crying babies and the Virgin Mary. After five days of staying in bed, I wasn't feeling that much better and Andrew had Dr. Stevenson come out to the house. Andrew sat on the edge of the bed as Dr. Stevenson tucked his stethoscope away.

"Well, Mary, your body's fine. I can't find anything wrong. But these dreams and your blues worry me some."

"I can't take anymore vacation time, Doctor, so what do we do?" Andrew said.

Dr. Stevenson was scribbling something on a pad. He tore the sheet off and handed it to Andrew.

"Get these two prescriptions filled. She's to take the one in the morning, and the other at bedtime. They'll help her to relax during the day and to sleep through the night."

What good was I if I couldn't even deliver a healthy baby anymore? Did he have a pill to cure my shame over that?

"I want you up and out of that bed, Mary. You're not going to get any better by staying in bed any longer," Dr. Stevenson said.

I didn't get up till the next day, and the reason I did was that it was Saturday and the kids were noisy in the yard. I could hear Louise and

Maureen Therese playing house. But what woke me up and got me to get up was a popping sound and Ernie's cry. I looked out the window and saw the girls sitting under the Baby Tree, right near the small mound of disturbed soil. My eyes shot past it and on the other side of the tree, I saw Ernie holding up a baseball glove. I was glad to look at anything other than that tree. A flash of a ball flying like a missile hit the glove and Ernie's left hand snapped back with the force of it.

"Ow!" he cried.

"Come on, Ernie," Andrew said impatiently. "You think they're going to throw 'em softer in Little League?"

Ernie yanked the ball out of the mitt and tossed it back. Andrew fired another one to Ernie and again, he cried out.

"That's how my Grandpa taught me to play ball."

I pushed open the window. "Andrew!" I hollered. Andrew looked over at me and his face broke out into a grin.

"Well, if it isn't my Mary, a regular Sleeping Beauty. Come on out. The day's beautiful."

"Mommy!" the girls yelled. They ran to the window.

"Andrew. Can't you go a little easier on him?"

"Tryouts are next month, Mary. I don't want him to embarrass himself. Throw it here, Ernie."

Ernie looked over at me and though I couldn't see his eyes too clearly, I could see that his face was pursed with pain and fear. Of Andrew? Baseball? I didn't know. I smiled at him and he waved the ball toward me and then tossed it to Andrew.

The practice did pay off because in March, he was able to skip past the pee wee league and go right into first division, which for a smaller than average six-year-old was apparently some feat. At least that's the way Andrew made it sound when he talked about it. Throughout that Little League season, Ernie played so well that he was not only the starting first base player but also the lead batter. The team didn't win all the time, but Ernie was always the reason they did when they did. Andrew bragged constantly about Ernie's natural ability and Ernie seemed so proud that Andrew found something special in him. But whenever I sat in the bleachers and watched the games and Ernie was up to bat, he would glance at me with that same fearful look he had that first Saturday morning he played catch with Andrew. When the season ended just before Ernie started second grade, Ernie earned the award for the most valuable player on the Tigers. Andrew beamed with pride when Ernie walked across the field to get his certificate. That pride did not make it past the baseball season.

"Ernie, tell me why you did that," I said. I swallowed the

232

tranquilizer with a cold cup of coffee because I had been nervous ever since St. Joan's School called. It was a week before Halloween and the olive trees in the neighborhood sent a musky scent into the air. Ernie sat on the couch, his arms crossed tightly over his body, and still wearing the white short sleeve shirt and salt and pepper corduroys of his school uniform. He was embarrassed.

"Sister Delores already called. Sister Superior says you are suspended for a week and if it happens again, they won't let you back in. Tell me why you did that." Ernie just shrugged.

"Have you ever seen your Daddy do something like that?" He shook his head.

"It's vulgar, Ernie. It's a sin. Now go to your room and say five Hail Marys."

Ernie slid off the couch and went to his room. Andrew wasn't due home for hours and I didn't know if I should tell him or not. He would be so disappointed. But since Ernie was going to be home for a week -- and still required to do his homework -- I was going to have to tell him.

"Pee on her?" Andrew said flatly at the dinner table later.

"Yes. He took his penis out and told the girl he'd pee on her if she didn't let him have her swing."

Andrew pushed himself away from the table. One meatball lay open like a cut melon and the rest of the meatballs in tomato sauce sat on top of the mashed potatoes.

"Andrew, finish your porcupine balls. It's nine thirty and he's sound asleep. There's nothing to do until the morning, anyway." But Andrew was now standing and pulling his belt off his pants.

"No son of mine is going to be that... that sinful. He's gonna learn."

Andrew barged into the children's bedroom and yanked Ernie out of his bed. Louise and Maureen began to cry so I slid into their bed and lay on my side so they couldn't see past me. I didn't know what Andrew was going to do to Ernie. He rushed out of the bedroom, dragging Ernie along and slammed the door behind him. I patted the girls.

"Shh, go back to sleep, girls."

"Is Daddy gonna hurt Ernie?" Louise cried.

"He was a bad boy. Daddy's taking care of it." But my voice shook and my hands trembled.

"If I ever hear that you did that again —" Andrew yelled.

The belt cracked and Ernie hollered.

"I'm sorry. I'm sorry!" Ernie cried. I wanted to run to him but the girls began to whimper.

Crack!

"No, Daddy, please."

Crack. Crack.

Ernie broke out into a wail. I jumped up from the girls' bed and threw open the bedroom door. Andrew sat on the couch with Ernie lying face down in his lap. Ernie was a quaking, crying lump and when Andrew raised the belt again, I yanked it from him.

"That's enough. He understands!" I screamed.

Andrew's eyes flared at me and his mouth twisted into an ugliness I never saw before. I threw the belt across the room and pulled Ernie away from him. Ernie collapsed in my arms and his tears soaked through my housedress. Andrew stood up and walked across the room. He picked up his belt and Ernie screamed like a wild animal afraid for its life.

"No, Mama! No, don't let him!"

But Andrew set the belt on the table and sat back down to his dinner. I led Ernie back into the bedroom and tucked him in. The girls lay in their bed, the pink blanket pulled up just over their noses, their eyes wide as scared bunnies. Ernie looked with fearful look he always had now turned to panic.

"I'm sorry, Mama. I'll pray. I'll pray hard."

As I closed the children's door, I heard another whimper and I peeked around the corner to see that Andrew held his face in his hands. For the first time since the war, I went to bed without Andrew. We never discussed that incident, but whenever a spanking was required for punishment, we decided that it would be done with both of us in the room and it would always be three lickings.

By February of 1950, just as Joseph McCarthy's voice blared on the radio daily about all the Communists in the government, Ernie had been sent home five more times from St. Joan's. He wasn't listening, he wasn't concentrating, and he wasn't completing his assignments. He also wasn't learning from being spanked, either.

We took him to Doctor Stevenson but he could find nothing wrong with him. Sister Superior had asked us to not bring him back to St. Joan's after this school year finished. When the baseball season came around in April, Ernie went back onto a second division team. His behavior problems seemed to improve a bit. Andrew had another idea about why Ernie had so many problems and on May 5, 1950, Andrew loaded us all in the car and took us for a drive.

A cool breeze blew in from Torrance Beach and the spring day was bright and clear. We drove down Pacific Coast Highway and turned on Crenshaw. A few blocks on the right, I saw a bunch of small flags that marked fields on either side of Two Ninety-Eighth Street. As we turned right, I could hear the red, blue, and green flags flap in the wind. Further

234

down Two Ninety-Eighth Street, as we got to a street called Pennsylvania, an old wooden house that reminded me of mom and dad's sat on the corner, its white wooden clapboards and gray eaves in need of some paint. Andrew slowed the car way down and just past the yard of that house was another, gray and pink with a cement driveway and dirt for a yard. It looked brand new.

"Take a look at the next house just across the little street," Andrew said.

We pulled up to a pale gold and brown house that except for the color looked just like the gray and pink one. It also had dirt for a front yard. When Andrew stopped the car, I saw what looked like a small forest behind a chain link fence where the house's backyard stood.

"Let's get out," he said.

"Andrew. Who lives here?"

But he was already out of the car and opening the back doors for the kids. As I got out of the car, hammering and pounding echoed. I looked around and saw houses across the street, identical to the one we stopped in front of, teeming with workers busy building them. Andrew stood at the edge of a cement path and he waved for me to join him. The house we looked at had windows with crossing wood and individual panes, including a front door with its upper section made in the same window style. Scrolled wood accented the corners of the house and a plant shelf sat underneath double windows in one corner. Andrew stepped up to the door and turned the knob.

"Are you loony? You can't go in here."

I followed him inside and the wood floor of the house, striped oak, was so new that it didn't creak and groan as we walked across it. A sliding glass door right in front of us led from the room we stood in out to a patio. Andrew grabbed my arm. 'Come on this way,' he said. We passed into another room and a red brick fireplace on the wall separated it from the room we were just in. Our shoes squeaked as we stepped onto the yellow and blue speckled linoleum of the kitchen floor. Pine cabinets with copper handles surrounded us. A brand new, brown enamel oven and a brown enamel cook top stove seemed to emerge from the pine cabinets. Three windows let in the sun from the back yard and the patio. Andrew stopped and put his hands on his hips.

"What do you think of this?"

"It's brand new, isn't it?"

"Yep."

"Beautiful."

"Come back this way."

We passed back through the two rooms with the fireplace and into

235

a hallway lined with five doors. Andrew pulled one open. 'Ernie, how would you like to have this room?' Ernie smiled and nodded. Andrew led the girls into the bedroom next door. "Girls. Wouldn't this be a fun room?" The girls ran into the room, their heels clicking on the wood floor.

"Mary, this way."

We crossed the hall and Andrew opened the door to a large bedroom with double closet doors of solid maple. 'Mary, isn't this a room fit for Sleeping Beauty?'

"Andrew, this is all beautiful and everything. But why are we here?"

"You wanna know?"

He looked over his shoulder and closed the door. Lowering his voice, he spoke.

"Mary, I think Ernie's been moved around too much since he was a baby. Also, I think he's too old to be sharing a room with his sisters."

"Andrew, we can't buy this house, if that's what you mean. It must cost a million dollars or something."

"Too late."

Andrew pulled a wad of papers out of his pocket and handed me a set of keys. His smile stretched across his face and made him look as young as when we first met. 'What is this?'

"We own it."

"What? How?"

"Mom loaned me the money for the down payment. Thirty-six hundred dollars." My legs went weak.

"Andrew, what does this house cost?"

"Eighteen thousand dollars. But with my salary now, we can afford the payment on a thirty year mortgage."

"Andrew, I don't know what to say."

Guilt was swirling through me because ever since the miscarriage more than a year ago, we hadn't had full sexual relations; I was too afraid of getting pregnant again and panicked that if I did, I'd lose the baby again. We didn't have to worry about the Rhythm Method or anything like that because Andrew was sensitive to my fears. But he had told me a long time before that when we had intercourse that was the closest he felt to me. It was almost like talking, he said, but it was our souls talking to each other through our bodies. I could feel he missed it, but his worry for my blues I guess kept him from demanding what was his right as a husband to ask of me.

"Welcome home, my Mary."

"Eighteen thousand dollars! Andrew, I'm scared about this."

"Mary, we're gonna be okay. Nothing's gonna happen to us. I'm

236

just glad to get you settled down finally. Get your mind off losing the baby and all."

"Andrew, I'm sorry. I know it's been hard on you, too."

"Well, now we got the rest of our lives here in our home to get better."

I threw my arms around him and cried. A home. That's exactly what we needed and what a surprise that we had one.

We moved in three weeks later, and the day we moved in, I stood in the backyard and looked out through another chain link fence just like the one at the Walteria house except for this time, instead of a hill covered with wild lupines and mustard, I saw what looked like a swamp. It was about half a city block square, and around it grew reeds that could hide ducks and a hairy looking weed that I found out was wild anise. The water itself was a murky, green-brown with fluffs of light green and yellow that looked like egg white along its edges. A dense growth of waxy green bushes grew all the way around the fence and the bushes seemed to be about fifteen feet high, making the whole thing feel like a jungle. Dragonflies buzzed the top of the water and when a breeze whipped through the bushes, I could smell rotted leaves and a musty smell almost like old meat. But with the water and the bushes just beyond our backyard, it felt like we lived near a backwoods instead of a suburb.

"Don't worry, Mary," Andrew said, startling me. I turned to look at him and sweat sparkled on his temples. I reached up and brushed away a bead of sweat that cascaded toward his left eyebrow and noticed a couple of gray hairs in his dark brown flat top.

"Mr. Buhlert said the developer plans to make the whole thing into a park real soon for the neighborhood. For now, though, till they add our street sewers, all the gutters drain into the sump."

"That's what it's called? A *sump*?"

"Yep. That's what Mr. Buhlert said. By the way, he's gonna stop by later today to check out all the finishing details and make sure the house is a-okay. It's sure good that he lives a few houses down, isn't it?"

"Yeah. Hey, Andrew, send the kids out here to play. I know the yard's only dirt and all but we got two bathrooms now and they can clean up. I'll be right out to help unload the truck."

I got Ernie settled in his room next to the front porch that night while Andrew settled Louise and Maureen Therese down in theirs next door and across the hall from our room. As I stepped back into our room, the wood floor was cool against my bare feet but the room was stuffy. I slid open one of the windows that met in the corner and I was surprised. From the sump, which was just a few feet away, crickets chirped wildly and it almost felt like I was home in Hopkins. But above the crickets was

237

another sound I hadn't heard before: a rolling, croaking, almost gurgling sound.

"Bullfrogs," Andrew said as he stepped into the room and shut the door behind him. "How about that, Mary? You ever heard so many? You'd think we were on the bayou or something."

"Sounds like they're welcoming us home," I said.

I rolled over in bed to face the open windows and I could hear Andrew unbutton his shirt and unzip his pants. When he clicked off the lamp, the pale blue light of a waning moon made the leaves of the sump bushes into lace works of silver. I don't know if it was the light going off or just coincidence, but it sounded as though the bullfrogs turned up their cries. Andrew slid in bed next to me, kissed me on the cheek and rolled over. As I had since losing the baby, anxiety caused me to hope that he wouldn't touch me. But just as the night sounds, the quiet of the house, and the warmth of the room began to lull me, I felt a peace and appreciation for him I hadn't felt before. My fear started to subside. I reached over and tapped his shoulder gently.

"Yeah, Honey," he said. His voice already sounded asleep.

"Hold me, Andrew. Hold me and kiss me."

He turned back to me and wove his arms around my middle. He kissed my neck and it felt like a whisper. I took his hand and placed it under my nightgown, between my legs. He jerked it away and I knew it was because he didn't want to force me into anything I didn't feel like doing. He was always taking care of me. Tears began to roll down my face, tears of appreciation and love for him.

"Andrew, please, it's okay."

"No, my Mary. You don't have to."

"Please Andrew. I want you close to me."

As he shifted his arms around, I pulled him on top of me. "Thank you, my Andrew. Thank you."

"I'll thank you for not slamming the back door, young lady," I said to Louise.

School had been out for about a month and the kids were home for summer. The last two months Ernie spent at St. Joan's his behavior, though not greatly improved, didn't result in any more sinful acts. A Mormon family, the Taylors, moved in across the street in the new pink house and the girls were spending a lot of time with two of the daughters. We hadn't met them and Andrew wasn't interested because he thought anyone who wasn't Catholic was a heathen. But I was glad the kids had someone to play with.

I had taken a break from polishing the solid maple coffee and side tables we now had next to the gray Naugahyde couch in the living room. My favorite afternoon radio program, 'Arthur Godfrey Time,' was just finishing as the McGuire Sisters were belting 'The Nearness of You' at the end of it. The screeching of large truck brakes caused me to jump -- I ran for the front window to make sure the kids were safe. They weren't out front but a delivery van with RCA printed on its side was. Two men outfitted in blue shirts yanked on a chain at the rear of the truck and its rear door rattled open. 'Someone's getting something expensive,' I thought.

Andrew pulled up into the driveway a second later and I looked up at the dining room clock to see that it was only two thirty. He shouldn't have been home yet. He slammed the car door and his face was plastered with a wide smile as he rushed to the deliverymen at the back of the van. Just then, I saw them lowering a large wooden crate onto a hand truck. Andrew stood over them, his face now taut with worry. He pointed toward the front door and led the workmen to it.

"Honey, what's this all about?" I said as I threw the door open.

"Mary, have I got a surprise for you."

With that, the deliverymen eased the hand truck up the two steps of the front stoop and they started to roll the hand truck into the living room. "Wait!" I hollered. "Let me get something to protect the floor." I ran into the kitchen and grabbed two clean hand towels. The back door flew open and the three kids ran in.

"Mama, what's going on?" Ernie asked.

Louise and Maureen Therese's bare shoulders rose and fell under their summer dress straps. "I don't know. Daddy's got a surprise so come on out to the living room." I tossed the towels to Andrew and he spread them out. The deliverymen carefully eased the handcart into the living room and paused again.

"Where's it going?" one of them asked.

"Here," Andrew said. He pointed at the front window. "That way I can feed the antenna wire."

"A radio, Andrew? We already have this old Magnavox and it works just fine," I said.

"That's not it, Mary. Stand back with the kids over there."

As the deliverymen centered the crate on the window, my heart began to pound. The kids were as excited as I was. The two deliverymen dug into each side of the crate with crowbars and jerked their arms forward. The front of the crate cracked and popped under their strength, then fell away like an orange peel.

"Oh, Andrew. We can't afford this!" I said.

What stood before all of us was a television, its screen no bigger than a small window. Two amber knobs and a dial like a radio's rose from a

239

maple cabinet. The letters 'RCA' stood out in antiqued brass just above the window. The delivery men cracked the other panels off the crate, handed Andrew a slip of paper to sign along with the instruction book, and then left.

"Mary, welcome to the 1950's. John got us a fifty percent discount. Are you happy, my Mary?"

"I am, Andrew."

"Now we can see 'Howdy Doody.' Everybody talks about him at school," Ernie said.

"What a surprise, huh kids?" Andrew said. A week or two later, I had a surprise for him.

"The baby's due in March," I said. "Dr. Stevenson said everything should go real smooth this time."

"Mary, I'm happy that you're okay again," Andrew said.

I don't think he was too excited about the prospect of another child, but we both had grown to learn that when I was pregnant, I was most happy. I didn't know if it was my body changes, or diet, or just the feeling of being on the nest, but always, when I was due, I was happy.

On March 19, 1951, right when Groucho's duck dropped down from the ceiling with the fifty-dollar bill in its beak because some woman named Gertrude said 'mustard,' my stomach twisted and contracted. Three hours later, Andrew told me, Katherine Lynn was born. At eight pounds, nine ounces, she was the biggest of all the children. Her birth also brought about something else.

The next morning, as I nursed Kathie for the first time, the dark feelings of gloom crept in earlier than they ever had before. Maybe it was because Andrew had been so quiet in his chair next to me.

"Andrew, you haven't said much at all. What's the matter?" I asked. It probably didn't sound too tender but not only was I feeling the blues but my body really ached, too.

"Nothing, Mary. I'm fine."

"You don't sound it. You sound sort of disappointed. Are you?"

"No, I'm thrilled we got Katherine. The Church says that our marriage is meant for children, Mary. So it's the Lord's will that we were blessed again."

"You wanted another boy. That's it, isn't it?"

"You need your rest, Mary. We can talk about this later."

I knew I was right even if Andrew wouldn't admit it. By the way he said it was the Lord's will, I also knew that unless we figured out another way to have relations, the Lord would be smiling on us again.

With Katherine Lynn's birth, the four children took all my energy daily. From Ernie who was age nine and getting ready to go to public school, down to Kathie who was two months and in need of feedings every three hours, I felt awash in dirty diapers, dirty dishes, and dirty faces. One day was just like any other, and with Andrew now working up to twelve hours a day, our new home began to feel like some sort of a stucco and maple-furnished prison. If we weren't exhausted on Saturdays, between changing beds and doing loads of laundry, we tried to take the kids out of the house. Sundays became a real day of rest for me because Andrew took the kids to eight o'clock mass and I stayed in bed and slept in, unless it was a mass near a holiday. Andrew never insisted that I go to church if I was tired, and I almost always was up in time to get breakfast for everybody when they got home. I hadn't picked up a pencil to even doodle in at least five years.

The Lord did smile on us again, on November 1, 1952, just a few days before Andrew rushed to vote for Eisenhower. Martha Joan was born after news came of the first hydrogen bomb explosion over some islands near where Andrew served in the war. It was strange to see the news footage of that bright blast that looked like a blooming flower a few days later--some people called it the birth of a nuclear arms race--while at the same time holding Martha to my breast to eat. There was something wild on the horizon, and dangerous. My children, what would happen to my children if the Communists ever got a hold of a bomb like that? There was something closer to us, in my own body, that was dangerous we came to find out.

In June of 1953, at three months pregnant for the sixth time, I was bent over changing Martha Joan's diaper when I felt a surge of warmth against my thighs. When I looked down, I saw bright red blood. There was no pain, but since Andrew was at work, I didn't know what to do. I dialed Dr. Stevenson and he sent an ambulance immediately. I woke up in the hospital three days later with Andrew at my side.

"Mary? You awake there?"

"Yes," I whispered. "What happened? Where am I?"

"Torrance Memorial Hospital. Everything's okay."

I tried to sit up but my head felt light and the room started to spin. I lie back and as I did, I could feel the pull of a bandage on my pelvis. Adrenaline shot through me.

"Did I lose another baby?"

"Mary, it's okay. You lost the baby because you had a lump in your female organs. It caused the baby to miscarry."

"A lump? You mean cancer or something?"

"No. Dr. Stevenson said it was not cancer. The surgeon got rid of it and you're okay. We just have to be careful for awhile and make sure you don't get pregnant." The gloom and guilt of failure gripped my body.

"How long do we have to wait?"

"Dr. Stevenson says a year or so, maybe. Till your organs heal."

Three years passed before Andrew and I had full intercourse and then at the end of 1956, I was pregnant again. Dr. Stevenson advised that I stay in bed for the first three months. During that time, I relied on Ernie, now 14, and Louise, 13, to help watch and take care of Maureen, Kathie, and Martha. Susan Marie was delivered July 7, 1957, the first of my babies to be born a month before she was due. At six pounds, she was also the smallest. When she was two weeks old, Dr. Stevenson called Andrew and me into his office.

"There's no easy way to say this, but I advise that we remove Mary's uterus," he said.

"What does that mean, doctor?" Andrew asked.

I reached into a jar of jellybeans he kept on his desk. The flavors of lemon, lime, and cherry played on my tongue. Dr. Stevenson held up a pad with a drawing of what looked like an upside down light bulb. He pointed to it. 'This is a normal uterus in place in a woman's body.

Dr. Stevenson dropped the pad onto his desk and began to sketch quickly. He held up the pad again and the drawing from before now looked like a deflated balloon. "This is what's happened to Mary's, probably from the tumor. Her uterus has collapsed. I'm afraid if we leave it in her, there will be the chance she could develop other complications."

"Like what?" Andrew asked.

I don't know why, but all I was thinking about was the sugary crunch of jellybeans in my mouth. It was like the two of them were talking about the Gillette fight last Saturday night. I knew Andrew would make the best decision for me so I didn't feel any need to say anything.

"Well," Dr. Stevenson said. "Let's say she gets pregnant again. If that happens, her uterus could tear or even burst, causing severe hemorrhage, and possibly killing her and the child."

"So you want to keep her from having any more kids," Andrew said.

"For her safety, I think it's advisable."

A licorice jellybean burned my mouth with its acid flavor. I spit it out into my hand. Dr. Stevenson noticed and handed me a tissue.

"What do you think, Mary?" Dr. Stevenson asked.

"It doesn't matter what she thinks, Dr. Stevenson. What matters is the Church says no to any form of birth control and I think in this case, they would even mean this."

"Andrew, think this through. This could mean Mary's life."

My breast suddenly dripped and I knew we had to get home to feed Susan. "Andrew, we gotta go now," I said. I stood up and grabbed another of Dr. Stevenson's tissues and dabbed at the wet spot in my peach colored dress. Andrew stood and offered his hand to Dr. Stevenson.

"Dr. Stevenson, thanks for your time. Whatever the Lord wills it will be and I'm sure he's looking out for us. We don't need any unnecessary operations."

After that meeting and for the first time in our lives, Andrew and I stuck strictly to the schedule of my monthly cycles and each year went by with no more pregnancies. Dr. Stevenson said along the way that it was more than likely that I couldn't become pregnant after all the stress on my womb, anyway.

With the five girls and Ernie, I was too busy to think about much else. First communions, first confessions, first menstruations, these are the things that dominated our lives. Ernie was now a senior in high school, and he had lettered in baseball all four years. He still got into trouble from time to time but we thought his focus on baseball kept him pretty much in line. Louise was starting to date but Andrew turned anyone who wasn't Catholic away at the front door.

By the time Ernie graduated in June of 1960, with a baseball scholarship to UCLA, everyone around was talking about the war in Indochina and the possibility that Communism was spreading more and more. Andrew and I prayed for peace in the area because we didn't want Ernie to have to go to war. Andrew was sure that the ordeals that he had to face in war would destroy Ernie. We didn't know then that something else would destroy him.

On an April night in 1962, the day before we were to go to a conference title game between UCLA and USC with Ernie starting at first base, I had a hard time falling asleep. For the last two weeks or so, the bullfrogs and crickets didn't soothe me but instead seemed to wake me up. Andrew's deep snore that sounded like a rusty zipper didn't help every night, either. But that night, when I finally drifted off, I found myself floating in a dark room. Suddenly, a yellow and blue light flashed and there was the Virgin Mary, her head tilted to the right, as she looked out a small window and prayed. She uncrossed her hands when she noticed me and she pointed at my stomach and nodded.

"No!" I tried to scream but nothing came from my throat.

Virgin Mary smiled and nodded. Suddenly, another flash and she became the creamy marble of the Pieta. A female voice echoed around me:

"Mother, Mary. You're the mother, Mary. Cherish him, for he is holy in you."

My body floated above the statue, pitching and swaying into the darkness.

"Another miracle has been wrought. Another blessing has been brought," the voice hollered.

My eyes popped open and the bullfrogs and crickets screeched in the night. Andrew's breathing settled as I patted his back to make sure he was near me. A cold sweat rolled down my cheek. It was at that moment that I realized I had missed my cycle by over a week. I had dismissed any possibility of becoming pregnant again a long time ago and hadn't given my cycle much thought. But I knew then.

The next day, while sitting on the aluminum bleachers at the game, I turned to Andrew during the inning change. The hot sun had warmed old bubble gum to a strange perfume that mixed with peanut shells and worn asphalt. There was no shade where we sat and the bill of his old baseball cap cast a dark shadow over his face, making his glasses into two tiny mirrors.

"He overthrew him at third, he growled. "He knows better than that."

"Honey, I got something to tell you."

"Whatever it is, Mary. Just what the budget, okay? We gotta keep a roof over the kids heads and food on the table."

"That isn't it at all, Andrew."

"He's batting clean-up. Let's see if his hitting is better than his arm today."

"Andrew."

"What?"

"I got something I need to tell you."

"All right already. What?"

"I'm gonna have another baby."

Andrew's face twisted into the smile he wore whenever he was being a wise guy. He tugged at the collar of his white T-shirt under the short sleeve shirt he wore. "That's a funny one, Mary."

"I mean it. I really am."

"You can't. Dr. Stevenson said so a long time ago."

"I am, Andrew."

"You must got the flu or something."

"Andrew, I'm late on my cycle. And I dreamed about it last night."

"What? You think you're Ruth the Prophet all of a sudden? Dreamed about it. Let's watch the game and quit talking this nonsense."

Two days later, Dr. Stevenson confirmed it. He said that he was shocked and that some sort of miracle must have occurred to help my womb allow the egg to stay. He warned me that I'd have to be careful again and that if I lost this one, it was over beyond a doubt.

During the first few months of the pregnancy, I kept having

dreams about the Virgin Mary, so I decided to read everything I could about her. I started with the Bible but her information was sketchy, so I turned to the Catholic Encyclopedia. It had more information about her and her miraculous destiny. The more I delved into Virgin Mary, the more I began to question my devotion to my faith. Could I offer up one of my children if the Lord willed me to? Could I find solace in Christ and God if I had to lose one of the children? The deeper I questioned these ideas, the more I understood my faith and my lack of devotion.

Toward the end of my pregnancy, I began to pray every day to the Virgin Mary to intercede and protect this baby and all my children. My sleep was fitful with dreams of Her and Her sacrifice and pain. The Pieta became Her in my nights and I became the Pieta. All at once, a sense of grace lifted me beyond my doldrums. Each day I spent washing the clothes or feeding the children reminded me of this grace and Her. I exalted in changing the bedclothes or preparing the meals for my children and for the first time understood why I felt so good whenever I was carrying a baby: I was the vessel of holy life and was a reflection of Her. And with a husband as sinless and noble as Andrew next to me, the meaning of my life became clear.

The great miracle of this pregnancy happened on December 21, 1962. Just three days before Her own pain and holy delivery, my stomach contracted and wrenched as Andrew revved the Impala into fourth and rushed me to Torrance Memorial Hospital. When I awoke the morning of December 22, the pain was terrible and I felt heavy and dark. Again, the mysterious curtain that dropped on me after every birth fell again. Andrew carried in Daniel Thomas -- we named him after Andrew's favorite Catholic TV star -- and I noticed his ears were flattened against his head and his skull was pulled so much that his eyes looked Oriental. His pink, brown skin looked stained and dirty and the black mood made me almost afraid of the baby. Andrew leaned over and handed him to me.

"Mary, he needs you. The little guy -- our second boy -- he went through a lot last night." As I took him, I noticed the large brown spot on his flailing left leg. Had She marked him?

"What's that?"

"The doctor said it's just a birthmark—nothing wrong."

A vibration of a pain started in my right ankle and contracted its way up my leg to my pelvis. I handed the baby back to Andrew. When I reached down, I felt thick bandages. I wanted to go away, to run, and to not hurt. Just then, the door creaked open.

"Well, how's our miracle boy today?" Dr. Stevenson said as his shoes squeaked against the floor.

"Fine, Doctor, looking good," Andrew said.

"Did you get a chance to tell her yet?" he asked.

"No," Andrew said.

"Tell me what?"

"I don't think she's herself yet, Doctor. Maybe you should –"

"Tell me what?" I hated everyone right then.

"You had quite a problem in there. Your uterus tore and we had to do emergency sutures. You lost a lot of blood and the damage to your uterus is irreparable. I don't know how he was able to make it to term at all. This little guy made it through a real ordeal the last six months. He's got a will to live, you can believe that. Okay, I'll let you folks have some time, now."

What the doctor didn't know was that I knew who saved the baby: the Virgin Mary. It had to be Her and Her grace. How could I repay her? When Dr. Stevenson walked out, Andrew turned to me. His eyes were glassy with fear.

"Looks like you gotta stay here about a week or so. I brought you your Bible and your book on Virgin Mary." When Andrew said Her name, a bolt of grace flashed through me again, parting the evil curtain of darkness for just a second. My body contracted and pushed and I began to weep.

"It's the end, Andrew. I'm finished," I cried.

Andrew stepped up and held Danny out to me again. "No, Mary. That's not it. Look at him -- our miracle boy. Danny Thomas. Our seventh baby. He's the beginning. Hold him."

I took Danny in my arms and again the blackness gripped me: I had to fight it and I would by going to church everyday and praying before Her image. She would rescue me and raise me up. Danny cooed as if he knew my thoughts. I kissed his cheek that smelled of baby oil and his skin was soft against my lips. She will raise me up, and you will save me, too, I thought.

14.

Oh shit, Danny thought as he closed the diary. They named me after a TV star! And Dad was making Mom into a baby factory. Was he just super-horny and he could blame it on the Catholic crap? Danny understood being horny for sure, but seven kids just because of it? Plus, there was no way they could give each kid what they needed, come-on. And it was no fucking picnic being the youngest, either. Danny didn't feel close to his brothers and sisters; he hated them and was pretty sure they felt the same. Everybody had to fight for what they could get from Mom and Dad and everybody must have resented each other, too: he for being the baby and having to be bossed around by everyone older, and his sisters because they were forced to give up their teenage years to help take care of him. It was a house full of picking on, sabotaging, or ratting out each other. No god damned 'Waltons' or 'Brady Bunch' that was for sure.

And Christ, all that work to take care of everybody? But Danny now felt ashamed after reading about how hard his parents worked. Being a whore had its risks, but it really was easy work compared to what his mom and dad had to do to survive. He just had to look out for himself and he was doing that the easiest way possible. He had worked hard through school and got grants to make his way through UCLA. He tried hard to sell his screenplays, too. It's just that the few agents or producers who responded seemed to always want to go out on dates. And pretty soon, it was trips to San Francisco, or Palm Springs. He had no time to finish studying at UCLA and besides, he had learned everything they could teach about screenwriting, anyway. He'd get passed from one agent to a producer to another agent and screenwriting became a faint echo in all the lavish nights on the town. Sex for a phone call was just so easy and he had the looks and the body for it.

By twenty-two, the phone stopped ringing and so did the trips. He even thought once that he was falling for a producer, but the morning he walked out his front door onto Nichols Canyon, he thought maybe it was the producer's Jaguar and pool that attracted him more. That day, he walked the mile or so to Santa Monica Boulevard and he never looked back. Yeah, this has been easy work.

Another line in the 'Hail Mary' prayer came into Danny's mind: *Blessed is the fruit of thy womb...* All the kids were more of a curse than fruit, except for maybe me, he thought. At least the fruit part. And he had decided that his mom was a true artist who he for sure took after. But what is blessed about giving up your gift?

That idea made his stomach twist. He had a lot of nerve to judge his mom about that didn't he? What screenplay was he working on to sell right now? And he was their 'miracle boy' with a will to live? He glanced over the bottle of Red Devils and felt a pang of guilt. These ideas kept him awake and prevented any hope of sleep. He gave up trying and continued to read the diary.

15.

"Here. I think it's only right that you should hold your last child as he gets baptized."

Andrew and I stood in the side baptism nave at St. Joan's on a cool Sunday morning. Keith and Gretchen Duncan, friends from the parish, stood with us as Danny's godparents. The girls were pacing anxiously just outside on the front portico of the church. Andrew handed Danny to me and I held his head over the font as Father O'Connor reached in and poured a palm of water over Danny's head. He began to cry as Father O'Connor blessed him and it made us chuckle a bit.

After Danny's baptism, we stayed for the early mass then took the Duncans and the girls out to the Hot n' Tot coffee shop around the corner from the church on Pacific Coast Highway. As we slid into the booth with its Formica and aluminum table and stained turquoise vinyl seating, Maureen and Louise got into it.

"I'll sit next to Dad," Louise said.

"What else is new? You're Dad's kiss butt," Maureen said.

"It's better than being his pain in the butt," Louise answered.

"Girls!" Andrew said. "I don't care who sits next to me. Just knock it off and sit down."

Louise slid in the booth next to Andrew and Maureen slid next to the girls and me. Keith and Gretchen, who now seemed to feel a little awkward, sat in the chairs on the opposite side of the table. The clinking and clanking of glasses and plates filled the silence as much as the smells of frying bacon and pancakes filled our nostrils.

"This is on us," Keith said. Gretchen smiled and nodded.

"No. He's our boy so it's our treat," Andrew answered.

"You got enough mouths to feed, Murphy. This is our present to you all," Keith said.

Andrew shrugged and read his menu.

"Mom, can I have fried eggs?" Kathie asked.

"I want some, too," Martha added.

"Me, too," Susan screamed.

"All right, girls. You can all get some fried eggs."

"So Northrop got in on that moon program -- what's it called again?" Kenny said.

249

"Apollo," Andrew said. "No. We bid for the rocket engineering but Boeing beat us out."

The waitress, wearing a blue and white uniform and a matching small hat that made her look like a nurse, took our orders. As she walked away, I noticed the chestnut brown fall she wore with its three sets of curls.

"That's a pretty fall, Louise. Don't you think?" I said.

"Yeah. We can only wear a simple bun at Bob's, but I like those curls better," she said.

"What's the matter with a pony tail?" Maureen asked.

"That's too tomboyish," Louise said. She glanced at the back of Maureen's hair. "No offense, but you'll figure it out someday."

"What?" Maureen flared. Her temper reminded me of Andrew's.

"A fall just makes a woman look more lady-like. That's what men like," I said.

When we finished breakfast and said goodbye to Keith and Gretchen, Louise followed us home in her light blue Volkswagen Bug. As Andrew opened the side kitchen door, the phone was ringing.

"I'll get it!" Kathie said. She bolted past Andrew and me toward the kitchen phone.

The kitchen still smelled like the pot roast we had the night before because the cold weather made us keep the windows shut. I stepped in with Danny who slept in my arms. I heard Kathie tell whoever it was on the phone to hang on a minute.

"Mom, it's Aunt Irma and she said it's important."

Andrew took Danny from me and I ran to the pine broom closet where we kept the kitchen phone. I picked it up and Irma sounded like she was choking.

"Irma?"

"You gotta come home, Mary. Mom's had a stroke. She didn't make it."

The next day, as the 707 jet airplane touched down at Minneapolis Airport, I was still in shock from the news of Mom's death. But after our first jet airplane flight, I couldn't believe we were really in Minnesota when only five hours before, we left Louise and the younger kids at home. Danny had slept through the whole flight and only stirred a bit during the takeoff and landing. As we stepped off the airplane, the air felt like our electric freezer and the flat silver sky and the blankets of snow made everything look the same, or almost like nothing. I didn't miss this biting cold and colorless landscape. I felt a pang of cold inside.

"Virgin Mary, please look over us in this hour of pain," I prayed.

When the cab turned into the driveway of dad and mom's house, I had another surprise: the driveway, lined by shoveled snow banks, was a black asphalt smooth surface. The yard was covered with snow and Dad's garage looked like a cottage. The house really knocked my socks off: where the two bedroom, ramshackle farm house stood was now a two story replica of a Victorian farmhouse. Orange light glowed from the front windows and a long porch ran the length of the house. I knew from the letters Mom and I had been exchanging over the years that the house was being worked on, but I didn't guess how much. Obviously, Irma and Ben had made it their house once they moved in with Mom. And Mom with all her fancy airs must have felt proud of her house for once.

Unlike the house, Irma looked worn and haggard. She wore a plain house dress and her graying brown hair was piled sloppily on her head. At 41, she looked like a ghost of Mom, and the way she tore Danny out of my arms and began to kiss him reminded me of how she used to kiss a kitten or a duckling. Ben was a shadow of himself, too, his hair gone wispy on the top of his head, his shoulders and arms just strings underneath his gray sweater that ended at his lap. A tattered, crocheted afghan lay across his lap and I recognized as Dad's. 'From Dad's chair to your wheelchair,' I thought. 'What a strange life that afghan has led.'

Andrew and I sat down to a chicken-fried steak dinner with Irma and Ben and the only conversation we had at all centered on the size of my rear end. Irma couldn't believe I had any weight on my body at all -- I could've defended myself with my nine pregnancies, but I didn't want to rub Irma's face in my family. She was most surprised by how big my rump had grown. Ben's only contribution to the conversation was that he thought I still looked good, for being 38. He also told us that my brother Jimmy wouldn't be in for Mom's funeral because he couldn't get out of work.

Andrew and I excused ourselves early so that we could get out to Peterson's funeral home to visit Mom. Irma insisted that I leave Danny with her and I really didn't want to bring him into a funeral home, anyway. I gave him up to Irma.

Riding in one of Irma's three cars, we drove down Minnetonka Avenue and the street was shiny with snow, reflecting the orange street lamps and the blue and red of traffic lights. We drove in silence, and as I looked at the shop fronts that hadn't changed in thirty years, it felt like I never lived in this little town. Peterson's Funeral Home loomed up on the left like some sort of Swiss Chalet and as we got out of the car, I listened for Minnehaha Falls that were just about across the street. Even in the middle of winter, the falls rumbled and swirled.

Inside the funeral home, organ music played 'Amazing Grace' over speakers in the corner of the reception area. Martin Peterson, grandson of the founder of Peterson's, and a classmate at Hopkins High School, led us

251

into a private room where a large, floral curtain hung.

"Your mother's lying in state just behind that drapery," he said and then walked out.

Andrew drew back the drape and behind it sat a copper coffin and a kneeler next to it. I looked in and saw Mom, the dark circles she always had under her eyes still visible under the flesh-colored makeup. Her mouth was pursed into the expression of disapproval I remembered my whole life and her gray hair sat on top of her head like a hornet's nest. The dress she wore was green rayon and I thought it made her look elegant.

She was peaceful there in her casket, but it wasn't natural to see this woman with a mountain of a will and a closed fistful of opinions lying there. I suddenly remembered that it was some twenty-years ago when she first met Andrew and danced with him in the living room and I was now about the age she was then. My eyes began to well up when I thought of that, but looking at Mom lie there was almost like looking at a stranger. Who was she to me really, besides the person who bore me? Why did her letters she sent over the years only ever tell me what Irma was doing to the house, or for herself? What made her so mean to Dad all the time? As I tried in my way to emulate the Virgin Mary, I wondered who Mom tried to be. Her mom? Her grandmother? Mothers are a mystery: attractive and repulsive at the same time, loving and judging, close and aloof. What do we ever really understand them about them?

"Mary, you ready to say the rosary? Mary?"

"Oh. Sorry, Andrew. Yeah."

Andrew's rosary beads clicked as he pulled them from his pocket. I pulled my clear, pink glass beads out, too, but only mechanically followed Andrew as he chanted the prayer on each bead. I vowed as I looked at my mom there that I would never leave my children wondering who I was, or why I did what I did.

"Why are you always like this?" Maureen screamed at me a week later.

Danny was crying for his morning feeding while I pulled Susan's hair into pigtails. The TV blared in the living room, making Susan squirm as I twirled and tucked her first pigtail, twisting it tight with the elastic band and its clear plastic beads that looked like cherries.

"Mommy, hurry, Captain Kangaroo is starting."

"Just hold still, Susie. It's only gonna be a second."

Maureen leaned against the doorframe, her arms folded over her baby blue, quilted robe. She was hardly ready for school.

"Maureen, your father told you already. Now go get ready before you're late again and I hear from the Dean of Discipline."

"Just tell them I'm sick."

"You want me to lie to a holy father?"

"Mommy!" Susan cried.

I twisted Susan's second pigtail and she ran out the kitchen door, leaving three long strands of her red-brown hair between my fingers. Brushing them off against my pink and white nightgown, I stood and went to the ironing board that was set up by the back kitchen door. Already tired from the morning's usual chaos, I reached for my cup of coffee but the olive green Melmac teacup was empty.

"Maureen, can you help me out and pour me another cup?"

"Mom!" Kathie hollered. She rumbled into the kitchen with Martha right behind them.

"Our uniform skirts. We need 'em!" Martha cried.

They both stood in the doorway, their white blouse tails trailing down and covering the tops of their legs. They both already had on their saddle shoes and their white socks rolled down to make donuts at their ankles.

"Hold your horses. I'm just getting to them. Go finish up getting ready and I'll bring them to you."

The iron sizzled under my wet fingertip and I began to press the gray, white, and black plaid of Martha's skirt. Hot wool and steam floated past my nose. Maureen set the teacup and saucer on the edge of the ironing board.

"Doesn't it bother you that the way they teach us to be Christian soldiers at Bishop Mahoney High is only through the nuns' and priests' way of doing it?"

The iron grated against the wool fabric. I took a sip of the coffee that had the metal taste of the dirty percolator.

"Their way of doing it, Maureen, is the way of being a Catholic."

"Then being Catholic is being stupid. Did you know that all they ever said about human reproduction in biology was that if you desired any pleasure with sex, it was a sin? The boys are supposed to say three 'Our Fathers' if they feel they want pleasure and us girls are to say three 'Hail Marys' and wait till we're married"

I blushed -- I didn't have a good answer for that one, not the way my married life began.

"Your father wants it this way, Maureen. As long as you're living at home here, you have to follow his rules. No public school, that's it. Now, go get ready."

Maureen stomped off toward the dining room doorway, and then paused.

"There's more than they're teaching us at Bish. I know there is. I'm going to learn it one way or another."

253

Friday afternoon rolled around and things got even more hectic around the house. Andrew was due home at five instead of seven -- he was willing to skip the two hours of extra overtime if the choir was that important to me, and even miss 'Rawhide' and '77 Sunset Strip' -- so I got the water boiling on the stove for the spaghetti at four o'clock. The sauce was already done and it sat in a pot next to the water, making the kitchen smell like boiled tomato sauce, onions and oregano. Kathie and Martha sat at the kitchen table with their schoolbooks spread out and their blue fountain pens scratching out their homework on loose leaf. Susan held onto Danny for me as I stood at the sink and filled his tub with water for his afternoon bath. As I dipped my elbow in to test the water, I remembered the sheets out on the clothesline.

"Kathie! Martha!"

"You don't have to yell, Mom. We're right here," Kathie said.

"I need you two to go take the sheets down."

"Mom, we're doing our homework," Martha whined.

"It'll take the two of you five minutes. You want clean beds tomorrow night, don't you?"

"I don't care," Kathie said.

"I do. Now get out there before it gets dark and they get mildewy."

Kathie sighed as she stood, her chair sounding like a car horn as it scraped the kitchen floor.

"Come on, Martha."

The back kitchen door slammed making the window made of glass slats rattle in its aluminum frame. Danny's arms flailed and made his tub churn with bubbles as I lowered him into it. His face broke out into a pink, toothless smile. He was the only one of the children that liked his bath. Susan helped me by squeezing the dab of baby shampoo onto his head. As I rubbed his soft head into a foamy mess, I heard the front door slam.

"Oh, no, Maureen," I said.

Susan looked at me with a confused expression. Everything was ready for us to go to the choir tonight: Andrew would be home early; dinner would be ready right when he walked in; he'd have a good hour to relax before we had to go; the girls would have their homework done. I forgot one small thing: I hadn't mentioned to Maureen that she'd be baby-sitting for the couple of hours we'd be gone tonight. Not that it mattered that much, because we didn't go any place very often so we never asked her to sit.

Maureen must have gone straight to her room, which was fine with me as I rinsed Danny's head and finished rubbing his soft body with soap. I lay him on the towel and dried him. While I smoothed baby oil into his

254

head and lotion onto his arms and legs, Kathie and Martha walked in with the sheets that looked like a giant wad. They dropped the wad on the table and sat back down to their work.

"You gotta fold those or they'll wrinkle up."

"Can't we do it after we get our homework done?" Martha asked.

"Okay. You can do it tonight while we're gone to choir."

"The 'Flintstones' are on tonight, Mom. We gotta watch them," Kathie said.

"All right. Fold them after but just make sure they get folded before you go to bed."

By ten to five, the girls had their homework finished and were busy setting the table for dinner. Each of the olive green Melmac plates made a hollow sound as they set them on the brown Formica kitchen table. Susan held onto Danny while I poured the pot of cooked noodles through a colander in the sink. As the steam sent a starchy smell into the kitchen, I jerked the colander out of the sink because I was afraid the steam might somehow warp the copy of the painting of the Annunciation that hung just above. Andrew walked in the side kitchen door.

"I'm home, my Mary," he said.

"Right here, honey. Susie, I'll take him back now. Kathie, get me your Dad's plate, please."

Andrew kissed me as I heaped a pile of spaghetti noodles onto a plate.

"Go sit down, Andrew, and get comfortable. Maureen! Dinner!"

Maureen walked in a few minutes after the rest of us had sat down at the table. She wore a pink angora sweater, jeans, a scarf and her hair was pulled back into a pretty ponytail. Andrew glared at her as she sat, obviously bothered, but I just wondered why she was dressed like that.

"You were holding the rest of the family up," Andrew said.

He crossed his hands and we all followed suit, crossing ourselves along with him. When grace was finished and I opened my eyes, I realized that not only was Maureen dressed up but she also wore powder blue eye shadow and dark eyeliner. She shoved her fork into the middle of her spaghetti and began to twirl it like she was twirling her hair.

"Eye shadow, Maureen?" I said.

"Mary, the garlic bread, please."

"It's Friday night, Mom," she said.

"Watch your tone, Maureen," Andrew said through a mouthful of spaghetti.

Oh, no, I thought. Did she ask to go out tonight? I couldn't remember.

"So. What's that got to do with anything?" I asked. "Andrew.

Your tie. It's in your spaghetti."

"Don't you remember, Mom? I asked you two weeks ago about tonight."

"Maureen, I don't remember." I didn't.

"You gonna eat that or just play with it?" Andrew said to her.

Maureen dropped her fork and folded her arms.

"I was planning on eating tonight at the drive-in."

"Drive-in?" Andrew said.

"Yeah. It's a double feature -- 'The Raven' and 'The Tingler' out at Vermont Drive In."

"Maureen, we've got a problem," I said.

"What?"

"We need you home to baby-sit tonight," I said. "We've got choir try-outs."

"Baby-sit?"

"Just Kathie, Martha, and Susie. Danny'll be with us."

"But you told me two weeks ago I could do this."

"Can you guys reschedule it or something?" I asked.

"It's a special double feature and it's tonight only. That's why I asked about it so far ahead."

"Who are you planning on going with?" Andrew asked.

"Barbara Terrence and Stacy Harrington."

"Have I met these girls?" Andrew asked.

"No. You said before that you don't want to meet any of my Torrance High friends."

"That settles it right there. You'll stay home and baby-sit," Andrew said.

"Andrew, I obviously told her she could and I think --"

"Nothing doing, Mary. It's about time she learned that those Torrance High hooligans aren't the sort of people a good Catholic girl should mess around with. We got choir tonight and that's that."

Maureen pinched her lips together as her eyes began to well up. She pushed her plate away.

"May I be excused?" she said.

"You haven't eaten anything," Andrew said. "I don't put bread on the table just --"

"Andrew, it's okay. The spaghetti will keep. Go head Maureen."

She walked out as her shoulders rolled over and her chin dropped to her chest. If I hadn't forgotten, and then insisted on the choir, none of this would've happened. I set down my fork and patted Danny's bottom a couple of times.

"Blessed Mother, please don't let me keep making these terrible

256

mistakes all the time," I thought.

But the next mistake centered around Maureen wasn't made by me, or Andrew, or anyone else but her. On Monday, June 3, 1963, while I dusted the living room, I had the TV tuned to 'The Secret Storm.' As I rubbed the maple coffee table with Old English lemon polish, the screen went blank and an announcer's voice broke in: "We interrupt this broadcast for a KCBS special report." My stomach sunk because we had a whole bunch of these interruptions during the Missile Crisis and we thought everyone of them was going to be an announcement of nuclear missiles heading our way.

"This is Matthew Benty in the Channel Two Newsroom," the news reporter said as the dead screen now became the news anchor at his desk.

"We have just learned from the Vatican that Pope John the twenty-third passed away a little over thirty minutes ago."

My legs grew weak under me and I had to sit. Pope John with his simple, down-to-earth ways and his fatherly personality was gone? It couldn't be.

"The cause of death has not been determined as of yet. We will break into this broadcast to provide more information as that information becomes available to us. To repeat, Pope John the twenty-third died a half hour ago in Vatican City, Italy."

"We will be joining our correspondent at the White House to hear President Kennedy's reaction in a few moments. Until then, we'll resume the regular broadcast."

The screen flashed and Peter Ames was now having an argument with his son, Jerry Ames in a dark alley somewhere in Woodbridge. I reached over and turned down the set.

"Susan!" I hollered. Susie ran into the living room, her Slinky hanging down like a metal snake behind her.

"Mommy?" she cried.

"Kneel down with me, Susie."

"Why?"

"We have to pray. Come on, kneel down."

Susie dropped her Slinky and kneeled down next to me. I crossed myself and she did, too, folding her hands into a prayer position.

"Say it after me: Our Father ..."

"Our Father," she repeated.

"Who art in Heaven ..."

St. Joan's School took the next three days off for official mourning and all students were required to attend the rosary masses that were held Tuesday and Wednesday morning. It was a good thing that Kathie and Martha had the day off Wednesday to help me because I hadn't had time to

257

dust and vacuum since Monday, what with all the time we were spending at mass. I called Kay, Connie and Agnes--three parish friends who I had started to meet at the Hot 'N' Tot every Wednesday for breakfast-- with the idea of planning some sort of meal in the parish hall after the memorial. They thought it was a great idea. I peeled potatoes and chopped eggs all Wednesday long for a potato salad that had to serve fifty to a hundred people.

The next day, while the other parishioners were attending the memorial mass, Connie, Agnes and I set the food up on the folding tables in the parish hall. As Connie unwrapped the two hams she baked, sending up the smoky, brown sugar smell, Agnes was busy filling the thirty cup coffee dispenser. Danny lay in his playpen shaking his rattle and chewing on his left hand, his six-month old legs beating a rhythm as he shook the pink rattle.

"He's going to be a rock'n'roll star, they way he's shaking, rattling and rolling there," Connie said.

"Jesus, Mary, and Joseph, forbid," I said.

"Mary, the potato salad looks scrumptious. You use mustard in it, too?" Agnes asked.

"Yeah."

"I figured," Connie said. "Just the egg yolks wouldn't get it that yellow. So where the heck is Kay, anyway? Mass'll be over in about forty minutes and we got a lot more to set up."

"I thought she might be in the mass," Agnes said. She placed stacks of Styrofoam cups next to the coffee pot.

"No. She's bringing rolls, cookies, and punch," I said. "She also said she had an idea about how we could repair the roof."

I pointed overhead at the vaulted ceiling that was stained brown and gray from the heavy rains back in January and February.

"I spent half the night making those hams and the relish tray. If she thinks I'm gonna climb a ladder and --"

"Oh, Connie, quit blubbering!" Kay hollered.

She walked through the side door near the stage and set a big, cardboard box on the wooden floor next to the blue velvet curtain.

"Someone wanna give me a hand? I got three more boxes of this stuff in the car."

Agnes walked up to her.

"Sure, I'll help you. But that's an awful lot of rolls, isn't it?"

Kay laughed and pulled open the box.

"It's not rolls, Agnes. Look."

She held up a white mug with a drawing of Pope John in red and gold imprinted on it. Kay and I joined the two of them as she lifted another thing out of the box.

"Look at this."

It was an electrical switch plate with a colored sketch of the Pope in the 'on' position and a line drawing of Satan in the 'off' position.

"So what is all this?" I asked.

"We're gonna sell these mementos of the Pope today. If we can sell it all, we'll raise enough to help get the roof fixed."

"Where'd it all come from?" Agnes asked.

"The Archdiocese store in Los Angeles. I told them what we needed, and why. They verified everything with Father O'Connor and were glad to give it to us."

"Three dollars!" Connie cried. She waived the inverted mug at us and pointed at the price sticker. Kay yanked it from her.

"That's what they wanted for it at the store. We'll sell them for fifty percent off whatever they're marked. Oh, yeah, Mary. I saw something for you in here."

Connie dug around inside the box, and then shook her head.

"Okay, it's in one of the other boxes. I'll show it to you later."

We had just enough time from that moment to get all the food set out and as the parishioners began to file in, their voices echoing off the beige walls of the parish hall, we began to set up the Pope souvenir table. Agnes and I moved Danny's playpen behind and I opened a gray folding chair and set it next to his playpen. Kathie and Martha ran up to the table as they pulled their chapel veils off and rolled them into their hands. I frowned as they both shrugged at me.

"Hi, Mom," Kathie said. "We're hungry."

"Go get a ham sandwich and some potato salad, but don't cut in line. Sit anywhere you guys want, but come back over here in a half hour."

Agnes and I spread mugs, combs, candles, rosary purses, and small pictures of the Pope out on the table. As we emptied the second box, we laid out key chains, chapel veils that had been blessed by Pope John, pencils, pens and rulers. Kay ran up and joined us.

"I found it, Mary. It was in the third box. Look at this."

Kay held up a plaster holy water wall font that was finished to look like blonde marble. It came complete with a finger sponge in its bowl. But what was amazing about it was the figure above the bowl: it was a replica, exact as far as I could tell, of the Pieta. The Virgin Mary and Jesus. I had been adding crucifixes, votives, and copies of religious paintings to the house since Danny was born, but what I had been wanting was a wall font to use at home.

"How much?" I could barely get the question out.

"Twenty-five dollars. So half of that is twelve-fifty."

I dropped into the chair, the cold metal pushing against the small of my back. I couldn't afford twelve fifty. Kay placed her hand on my shoulder.

"Tell you what. If we can manage to sell the rest of this stuff today, I'll buy this as a gift for you. After all, you deserve something for putting this whole luncheon together."

A half hour later, as people who had finished their lunch began to browse key chains or consider mugs, Kathie and Martha ran up. Martha snatched up a key chain.

"Oh, Mom, can I have it?"

"Put that down, Martha."

Martha held the key chain higher and looked at the back of it.

"Martha."

She tossed it a few times in the air and that was it. I stood up and snatched it in midair.

"You better learn to listen better, young lady. I need you two to go pick up your sister from Jackson."

"Why us?" Kathie said.

"I have to stay here to help with the sale. You two walk over to Jackson, pick Susan up and come back."

"Walk all that way? Two times?" Kathie said.

"It's not that far. Just remember, it's for the good of the Church. Now go."

By twelve thirty that day, the last few parishioners finished their coffee and cookies and wandered out of the hall. The girls had been back about a half hour and Susie sat next to Danny and kept an eye on him for me. We propped the doors open on either side of the stage because the day was warming up and all the heat from the parishioners really made the hall stuffy. The girls helped as we gathered up paper plates and plastic forks. We wiped down the tables and finished sweeping.

"Okay," Kay said. "We have one mug, a fountain pen, a chapel veil and two key chains left. I'd say it was a good day."

"There are three girls that helped, you know, Kay," Agnes said.

"Yeah, maybe we could give them a little thank you gift, huh?" Connie chimed in.

"All right. We sold everything we were going to sell. Take what you want, girls."

Martha rushed up first and grabbed a key chain. Kathie picked up the fountain pen, followed by Susan who tore open the plastic cover of the chapel veil and tried it on.

"Look how boss this is," Martha said.

"Really boss," Kathie chimed back.

"Girls, what kind of language is that? You sound like beatniks."

"Oh, almost forgot. Here's for you, Mary," Kay said.

Kay handed me the holy water wall font and my heart pounded.

"Thank you, Kay. Thanks so much. It's going up the second we get home."

"You're gonna put that up at home, Mom?" Kathie asked.

"Yes."

"You gonna use it for a plant or something?" Martha asked.

"No. I'm going to put holy water in it so that every Sunday, every Thursday rosary night, and every holy day in the year, we can bless ourselves."

"With all the stuff you keep putting up, Mom, our house is really starting to look like the church," Kathie said.

"And if our house looks like a house of the Lord, what's the problem with that, young lady?"

"It's just sort of embarrassing when friends come over, that's all."

"Teenagers!" Connie said.

"Let's get going, Mary," Kay said. "I'll give you and the kids a ride home."

Kay drove us home. I couldn't resist so I went to insert the Nat King Cole eight-track tape again, but Kathie stopped me.

"Don't you have any Elvis, Aunt Kay?" Kathie asked.

"I should say not. The way he dances alone is sinful," Kay answered.

"I hope you're not listening to that heathen, Kathie," I added. "Now listen to a real saint of a singer."

I pushed in the tape and by the time we pulled into our driveway, Nat was finishing 'Walking My Baby Back Home,' while Kay and I sang along with him. The girls hopped out of the back seat as soon as the car stopped, dropping their hands from their ears. They didn't much like our singing. Kay's Cadillac rumbled as the girls unloaded the playpen. Danny was wide-awake and kicking in my arms.

"I gotta get this little guy in and feed him."

"See you tomorrow morning, Mary."

I held up the holy water font and waved it toward her.

"Thanks again, Kay."

"Mary, you worked hard pulling the luncheon together. Everyone should be thanking you. Bye."

The girls had run ahead into the house and as Kay's car rolled out of the driveway, I walked into the breezeway and thought I heard Maureen's voice through the open kitchen door. When Danny and I stepped into the kitchen, the other girls surrounded Maureen and were showing her their

261

gifts. Maureen, still in her plaid uniform and white blouse, looked up at me and her eyes looked like I just caught her stealing. I glanced up at the clock as I pulled the door shut behind.

"It's only ten after two. They let you out after the Pope's memorial at Bish?"

"They sent me home."

I held up the holy water font and her eyes scanned it then stared back at me, obviously waiting for my response.

"I've been wanting a font for so long and one with the Blessed Mother is more than I could have prayed for."

"It's nice, I guess."

I stepped past the girls and pulled out one of the kitchen chairs and sat. Opening my blouse, I set Danny on my breast and his six-month-old new teeth clamped on painfully.

"So did they give you tomorrow off, too? The girls got it off from St. Joan's."

"You guys, buzz off. I gotta talk to Mom," Maureen said.

Kathie led the girls out of the kitchen and I heard them clomp across the living room and giggle as they ran down the hall to their bedrooms. I rolled my eyes at the noise.

"One of these days, I'm going to talk your father into getting us wall-to-wall carpeting. The noise in the house is just too much, don't you think? Why don't you sit down?"

Maureen folded her arms and then I knew something was wrong. She leaned against the counter next to the sink.

"You're not going to start in on transferring to Torrance High again, are you?" I asked.

"Mom, they didn't give the whole school the rest of the day off today. Just me."

"What?"

"They sent me home. You have to meet with the Dean of Discipline tomorrow."

"Ouch! Easy, baby boy."

I pulled Danny away from my nipple until he started to fuss. He slurped loudly as he started to eat again.

"Maureen, what did you do?"

"I told the truth."

"About what?"

"Okay, I didn't go to the memorial assembly in the gym for the Pope. When Father Duffy caught me, I was in the corner of the library reading the Bible."

"But you skipped out of the Pope's memorial. Why?"

"I'll tell you what I told him. The Pope was just a fat, little old man. Even though I felt bad in a way for not going to the memorial, I felt I would've been a hypocrite if I did. So I was spending my time reading through the Bible to try to figure out why the Pope matters at all. That's what I was doing when Father Duffy caught me."

"You didn't really call the Pope a fat little man, did you?" I asked, almost out of breath.

"Yes, Mom, I did. When Father Duffy brought me to the Dean of Discipline, the Dean said that he had it with my disrespectful mouth and my calling the Pope a fat little man was beyond forgiveness. So now you have to go see him."

"Maureen, I just spent the last four days with people who are hurting because the Pope is gone -- me included. People who know in their hearts that he is the representative of Christ and St. Peter here on earth now. I can't believe you could be so sinful. I can't look at you--go to your room."

Maureen pushed away from the table and ran to the hall door. Through a voice that sounded weak from tears, she said: "I didn't think you'd stand up for me, anyway."

'Blessed Mother,' I prayed silently. 'Please intercede for Maureen.'

Andrew was home later than usual that night, and when I told him about it as he ate his plate of baked beans and wieners, he dropped his fork and flew out of the kitchen. Danny was sleeping in my arms so I walked slowly to the dining room door. I heard screaming and in a moment, Andrew pulled Maureen by her pony tail into the living room.

"Who taught you to talk like that?" he roared and his hand flew across her face. Her cheek flared bright red and I saw tears slide down her face. I stepped back into the kitchen and shielded Danny's ears.

'Hail Mary, full of grace ...' I prayed silently.

Slap!

'Blessed art thou amongst women ... '

Slap. Cry!

'Blessed Virgin, please intercede ...'

Maureen wailed and I heard the floor creak as she must have been going back to bed. Andrew came around the corner and saw me whispering.

"What the heck are you doing?"

"Praying, honey."

He shook his head and fell back into his chair.

"Discipline, Mary," he said. His voice was cracking. He rubbed his hands together and I could see a tear had caught on the edge of his horned rim glasses.

263

"These girls need more discipline, not just prayer."

The next day, Connie picked Maureen, Danny and me up and we met with the Dean of Discipline at Bishop Mahoney High. The faculty, he was told, had no more patience for Maureen's constant challenges to Catholic theology. With her flagrant disrespect just shown toward the Pope, the school had no choice but to expel her. The Dean left me no opening for arguing, discussing, or begging. He handed me her file with her transcripts and said that by the way, she made straight A's in all classes -- except for religion, which she failed again -- and that her credits should be good enough for whatever school we placed her into. Maureen was silent during the entire meeting, staring straight ahead at the Venetian blinds over the Dean's shoulder.

She was silent on the drive home as Connie and I discussed that the next nearest Catholic high school was thirty miles away and they probably wouldn't take her, anyways. Connie persuaded me, and I already knew what we had to do: Maureen Therese Murphy was to be the first Murphy child to be enrolled in public high school. Connie drove down Carson Avenue and we enrolled Maureen at Torrance High. I was disappointed in Maureen and I felt like she was the worst of my kids, so sinful, so blasphemous. I prayed silently to the Blessed Mother to guide her. I couldn't foresee how much I would need the Blessed Mother to help with another one of our children.

16.

I needed to go check how clean Maureen got the bathroom because in the last month or so, her work around the house had gotten sloppier and sloppier. She was too old to still leave crud stuck to dishes or dust under a table lamp that she didn't care to lift. As I stepped into the hallway, I saw the holy water font sponge looked dry and when I touched it, it was. I decided I'd refill it after checking the bathroom.

Maureen hauled a mop and bucket out the doorway as she yanked the door shut. Her hair was pulled back into her pony tail and her bone-thin arms stuck out from the worn, short-sleeved uniform blouse she wore. The blouse had been white once but it was a shade between yellow and brown now, with blotches of dark spots on it. I went to open the door.

"Mom, you can't go in, the floor's still wet."

I slipped off my sneakers and stepped onto the linoleum that was cold and damp under my feet. I couldn't see any filth but its ochre color with brown, red, and green specks hid dirt well. Looking around the door at the toilet, its white porcelain sparkled. When I lifted the lid, I did see some filthy spots. I ran my hand across the butter cream yellow tile around the sink and could feel grit left from cleanser she must have used. The sink was okay, but the tub had a ring of gray grime that was broken where her rag must have actually scrubbed it.

"Okay," I said.

Maureen was already down the hall putting the mop and bucket away.

"Maureen!" I hollered.

"Hold on!" she hollered back.

When she came back down the hall, her face looked puzzled.

"What's the matter?"

"Take a look at the tub and toilet."

Maureen exhaled with frustration and rolled her eyes. She stepped past me and I heard the lid of the toilet creak up and drop back down. She sighed.

"I'll go get the toilet brush."

"And the cleanser, and your cleaning rag. You missed a lot."

Maureen came back down the hall lugging the bucket and mop.

"Now hang on a second. What if I hadn't come in to check on the

265

bathroom? Would you have just left it like this?"

"I guess."

"It's still filthy."

"Mom, no matter how well I clean it, it just gets dirty again. Why should I worry about it that much?"

"How about because the rest of us will have to live in that filth?"

She shrugged her shoulders and stepped into the bathroom. The toilet brush scraped the porcelain as she cleaned it.

"What about some pride in your work?"

"Cleaning the bathroom is hardly my work, Mom."

"Well, if you ever expect to marry somebody, you better learn how to clean a house."

Oh, how I sounded like my mother again. Maureen grabbed the rag and looked around the bathroom. I pointed to the tile next to the sink and she wiped it.

"Clean a house! You think that's what I'm going to do with my life? Not me. I'm going to be a doctor, or an architect, or a lawyer maybe. Then I'll hire someone to clean my house."

"And to have your babies, too?"

"There's more to life than being a housewife and mother, Mom."

"Is this what they're teaching you at Torrance High?"

"I know you never read or anything, Mom. But there's this book -- The Feminine Mystique -- and as far as I'm concerned, Betty Friedan has got it going on. Women are capable of working and they belong out of the house if they want, just like men. Maybe we can dream, like Martin Luther says, and make better lives for ourselves than women before us ever could have known."

She looked at me to see what was next and I pointed to the tub. Maureen dropped to her knees, spilled cleanser into the tub and started to scrub.

"Look Missy Dreams--you think those are new ideas? Who do you think ran the gas stations, and the banks, and the grocers during the war? We all did."

"Oh, Mom, all you ever did was have kids."

"Maureen, I ran Murphy's Produce, just like this woman named Margaret ran Ralph's filling station in Hopkins. We all had to work and we kept the country going for years."

She stopped and looked at me as she began to rinse the tub. Her eyes looked puzzled again but her resentful expression started to soften.

"Then you understand what I'm talking about," she said.

"But when your Dad came home, I knew what I needed to do. So did every other woman in the country. We needed to get back into our homes and we were happy to let our men take their jobs back. We didn't make any Feminine Mistake--

"Mystique, Mom."

"Whatever. It's nothing new. We all worked but we knew we had to get back to the most important business -- our children and our homes. So don't go getting hoity-toity with me."

I checked the tub and ran my hand along the counter. Maureen stood near the open bathroom window, her arms folded.

"I never knew you worked, Mom. So they forced you all to go back to being housewives?"

"We were glad to be housewives again because it didn't take an Einstein to figure that you couldn't work and keep a good house and be a good mother. You just can't do it all."

Maureen dropped the rag into the bucket and picked up the mop.

"Maybe you couldn't do it all, Mom. But I think I can."

My head was spinning after talking with Maureen and it seemed like somewhere in my early life, I must have thought the same things and wanted more, too. But that was a long time ago. In the confusion that I felt, I turned to prayer, seeking guidance from the Blessed Mother. We would all need it that November, just before Thanksgiving.

"Ladies and gentlemen, we have just been informed that President Kennedy has been shot only moments ago in downtown Dallas. The President and Governor John Connolly of Texas were both injured and have been rushed to Parkland Memorial Hospital in Dallas. We will remain on the air to bring you up to date information as we receive it. Again, to repeat, President Kennedy has been shot and it appears that he is critically wounded. Please stand by for further information as it becomes available."

I couldn't think of what to do so I pulled Danny out of his high chair and held him close to me. Pushing his face against mine, his cheeks, smeared with strained pears, were cool and soft against mine. The gentle odor of the pears was soothing somehow in that awful moment.

"Blessed Mother," I choked between tears. "Please watch over President and Mrs. Kennedy at this time and bring them both through this. Please, Blessed Mother."

The phone screeched over Walter Cronkite's voice. I ran to it.

"Oh, Mary," Connie cried over the phone. "We have to get to the church. We have to pray now for the President and Jacqueline."

"Connie, get Kay to meet us. Agnes is probably at work, but the three of us can hold a vigil."

"I'll be over as soon as I call Kay."

Connie picked Danny and me up about ten minutes later and by eleven that morning, we walked in the back door of the church. Connie stepped to the front pew, genuflected, then slid in and popped down the kneeler. The church was empty and quiet. Danny and I stood in front of the niche that held the Blessed Mother and the blue votive candles. I struck a match which echoed crisply in the nave, then lit one of the candles nearest the edge of the Virgin's pale robe.

"Oh, Blessed Mary, I light this candle for President Kennedy and ask you to intercede to the Lord for him. Amen." I dropped a quarter into the slot in the devotion can.

Danny and I stepped over to the pew, I genuflected and he giggled as I dipped down onto my knee. We slid into the pew next to Connie. I went to my knees after setting Danny against my shoulder and could hear Connie whisper the Lord's Prayer as her rosary beads clicked in her folded hands. Her head was bowed and I saw that she didn't have on her chapel veil and a bolt of anxiety shuddered through me when I realized I had forgotten mine.

"Connie," I whispered. "We forgot our chapel veils."

"The Lord will forgive us this time, I think, Mary."

A shuffling at the altar caused us to both look up and there stood Father O'Connor in his black habit with his purple scapular in his hand. Even though his face looked red like he had been running, he broke into a broad smile.

"It's good to see the Blessed Mother club back here on this terrible day."

"Hello, Father," Connie said. I nodded but wondered what he meant by the 'Blessed Mother Club.'

"Ladies, I needed my scapular to perform prayers for the President," his voice cracked. "I've got the TV on over at the rectory if you care to come and watch the news."

"No, Father, we're gonna stay here and pray for the President," Connie said.

"Pray hard, dear ladies. Oh, here comes Kay."

The church doors scraped closed behind us and Kay's quick steps echoed in the church.

"Hi Father," she said as she dropped to her knee, genuflected, then slid into the pew. Kay did not forget her chapel veil.

"I'll leave you ladies to pray and will let you know if there's any news."

Father O'Connor waved a blessing over us and hustled his plump body down the center aisle, his rubber shoes squeaking all the way down the tile floor.

"Morning again, Mary," Kay said. "I sure didn't think we'd all see each other a second time today."

Kay crossed herself and began to pray.

"So what was Father O'Connor talking about with this Blessed Mother Club?" I whispered.

"With all of the parish events we've been planning and the way we meet at church every morning for early service, I thought we really have formed a club," Kay answered. "And because we all share the veneration of Virgin Mary, I thought it made sense to call us the Blessed Mother Club."

Connie shrugged and I nodded and that was the official beginning of the Blessed Mother Club. And the first official task of the club was to sit and pray for the President and Mrs. Kennedy. Twenty minutes after Connie arrived and in the middle of our rosary, Father O'Connor burst through the back church doors.

"Oh, ladies," his voice cracked. "We lost him. The President has gone to the Lord."

Connie broke out into a wail and dropped her head against Kay's shoulder. Kay's eyes flowed with tears and my chest heaved and rolled. Father O'Connor fell into the back pew and began to moan. Danny lay against me and his little legs bounced. He found something funny, and above all of our collective sobs, Danny giggled.

"Father," Kay said a few minutes later. "We would like to remain and pray today. Is that all right?"

"Yes, ladies. It's all right. I'm going to inform Sister Superior to let school out now and to send all the sisters to the church. We'll hold mass as soon as they're here."

We continued our rosary and twenty minutes later, we heard the school bell ring and the doors of the school slam open. Footsteps and mumbles surrounded us until the school was empty fifteen minutes later. At the end of our rosary, the sisters from St. Joan's School, their heads hanging low in their black habits, filed into the two pews opposite us and kneeled. With their heads bowed, they looked like two lines of black crows gathered at the site of a saint's death.

"Mom, where were you?" Martha hollered later that day.

"Martha, watch your tone. I was at St. Joan's praying for the President."

"Kathie's been in our room crying and screaming for you ever since we got home from school two hours ago."

"Where's Maureen?"

"She's not home. I guess public schools don't care as much about the President as Catholic schools do."

"Why you still in your uniform?"

"'Cause all my regular clothes are in the laundry room hamper.

You haven't done a load of our stuff I guess."

"Martha, take care of your brother for a second. Put him in his high chair and get him started on his carrots and peas, okay? I'll be there in just a couple minutes."

I walked into the girls' room we had painted pink a couple of years back and Kathie was curled up on top of her twin bed. Her black and white plaid uniform skirt stood out against her pine green, chenille bed spread. I stepped over a pile of clothes mixed with school books and when I got to her side, she clutched the framed photo we had of the President that hung in the den Andrew had added on. When she saw it was me, the pale, freckled skin around her eyes that were swollen pink cracked open in wet ovals.

"Oh, Mom," she threw her arms around my waist and dropped her head in my lap.

"It's okay to cry right now, Kathie."

She followed my advice, her thin back and arms heaving and vibrating with her cries.

"Where were you? It's terrible and I was alone."

"I was at the special mass for the President."

"But I needed you, Mom. It hurts so bad."

Kathie rolled over and away from me. She almost sounded mad now.

"They shot him, Mom. He's gone. He's gone. And you weren't here when I got home."

"I told you I was at mass. If you attended more often, you'd understand that you're never alone with the Lord."

"You don't understand."

"I do, Kathie. But you have to remember that he's with the Lord now and that's the best place he could be."

"I don't care. He's not here, that's all I know. And it hurts."

"Don't you think I felt like this before?"

"Just go away, Mom. Go away."

Kathie curled back up with the photograph and began to whimper. I left her and when I stepped through the hallway, I dipped my finger in our holy water font and crossed myself.

For the next four days, until President Kennedy's funeral, the TV was on in the house like it never was before; we saw President Johnson's hand raised as he took the oath; Oswald's mouth cry as he was shot; Jacqueline's hands holding her children; and John-John's hand saluting his father's casket. The TV stayed on through that Sunday when Judy Garland, choking back the tears for her friend, Jack Kennedy, sang 'His Truth is Marching On' at the end of her variety hour. The TV was on until the

270

funeral was over, then it seemed to stay on all the time from then on because there seemed to be one crisis after another in the world and no one was going to be caught off guard like we were with Kennedy's death.

The TV was on the week before Danny's first birthday in December, as I was getting ready to take my driver's test at the DMV. Connie sat on the couch with Danny while I put my shoes on and the CBS Morning News with Mike Wallace was droning on in the background.

"Andrew's going today to pick up the new car," I said. "It's sort of a present for learning to drive."

"What is it?"

"A Triumph Herald. It's red with black leather seats and he said it was a good – "

"Mary, what's the matter?"

"Shh."

My eyes were fixed on the television screen because just after a report on Elizabeth Taylor's most recent marriage, the news was reporting on another marriage: there, standing along side a woman who looked like Sophia Loren, was Artie Janek. "The famed Paris painter whose works were fetching some of the highest prices in the Europe and American art markets," the reporter bellowed, "just exchanged vows with performance artist Lilla Scarletti, one time friend and confidante of our own Andy Warhol."

"Mary, what's the matter?"

I couldn't speak. Artie looked no different than when we were painting together. And that woman he married, her figure alone was half of my own fat, baby-tired body. Artie, Artie, Artie.

"Mary, we're going to be late to the DMV and that won't help you pass your exam."

The news report finished and I looked at Connie.

"My goodness, Mary. You really do look like you just saw a ghost or something."

What Connie didn't know was the ghost I saw was me, in my skirt, painting my lady's slippers next to Artie. As that ghost floated through me, I felt dusty and dirty as a haunted house. And a dark feeling of being hollow grabbed hold of me for the next couple days.

It was a good thing that Connie spent all that time teaching me how to drive and letting me practice in the church parking lot and around the streets because I passed my driver's exam easily and when the holidays hit, the Blessed Mother's Club was in full force putting on the Christmas Festival and carnival on the school grounds, arranging the food drive for St. Anne's Catholic Orphanage, and arranging the after-mass celebrations in the parish hall during all the Christmas holidays. That dark feeling crept up now and again but the constant distractions kept my mind on other things and off Artie's face. During that time, I lugged things in the back seat and trunk of the Herald: boxes of holly hock, or cases of fruit punch, or platters of fudges and divinities the four of us pitched in to make. Danny always sat in his car seat in front. It all lead up to the candlelight Midnight Mass on Christmas Eve, with the choir going around to all the Catholic homes in the parish and singing Christmas carols afterward.

The Wednesday after New Year's 1964, Connie called and asked me if I was watching the morning news. After the report on Artie, I turned the news on every morning hoping to hear about him again, and to see his face. Danny was in his playpen while I dusted the living room table and waited for the washer to finish Andrew's work shirts. Lemon furniture polish floated up my nose and I was glad to grab the phone.

"You watching the morning news?" she said.

"Yeah."

"What's on it?"

"Something about Jack Ruby's trial."

"If they find him guilty, it'll be a crime," Connie said. "He's a saint, killing that Kennedy-killer Oswald. I hope that jury is smart enough to figure that out. Anyway, turn to Channel Seven News, quick."

I rushed to the dial and flipped it. A crowd of people was standing inside a church, near the altar.

"I got it, Connie. What?"

Before Connie could say anything, the camera moved in close on the face of a statue of the Blessed Mother. Some sort of moisture seeped from her face.

"...These witnesses say the statue has been crying since yesterday," a reporter said. "An envoy from the Los Angeles Diocese is on the way to verify the miracle. This is Wayne Saks reporting."

My heart pounded in my throat.

"Connie. What church is that?"

"St. Vincent de Paul Church.'

"Where's that?"

"Downtown L.A. Off Figueroa."

"I gotta see Her."

"Mary, they haven't even confirmed ..."

"Can you go?" I asked.

"No. I got too much —"

"Bye, Connie."

I scratched out a quick note to the girls for when they got home. I snatched up Danny, his diaper bag and two jars of baby food and we ran for the Herald. I hadn't done much freeway driving at all but Danny and I got on to the Harbor Freeway toward Los Angeles and I knew it would take us right into downtown Los Angeles. In twenty minutes, we drove through the shadow of one of the few skyscrapers that loomed over the city and disappeared into the hazy air that felt wet and warm. Right where we were, the freeways flowed over each other in a stack that looked like a woven basket. We slowed down and joined a solid line of cars that stacked up toward the Figueroa exit. I rolled down the window to get some cooler air and the exhaust fumes from the cars around us smelled like burned rubber. My mind started to race with excitement over presenting Danny to Her directly, after she interceded to bring him safely into the world. Could I get a drop or two of her tears and bless his forehead maybe? The same line of cars we were stuck in seemed to drip off the freeway car-by-car. I saw a sign at the end of the exit that had an arrow pointing right to St. Vincent de Paul.

Unfortunately, the line of traffic moved right like a drunk snake and it took us a half hour to go the half mile to the church. A parking lot behind a mud brick wall was jammed solid with cars and someone was waving a flag right in front of the church that said 'parking'. Not that we had the choice, because the flow of the cars carried us like a nasty river and pretty soon, we pulled into a parking lot across the street from the church. It cost fifty cents to park and I was lucky I had brought back a bunch of RC Cola bottles to Takahashi's market a few days back.

Once we got to the front of the church that looked like a huge, old California mission, we had to get into a long line of people waiting to go through the heavy, weathered wood doors into the nave. A flock of newspaper reporters stood on one side of the entrance, their arms fluttering as they flipped their notebooks while men with TV and flash cameras jostled each other on the opposite side. I held Danny on my hip and the diaper bag hung from my other arm and I suddenly realized I hadn't thought to grab his stroller or anything else to set him down in. It wasn't until after twelve thirty, an hour after we had been there, that we even stepped out of the sunlight and onto the front portico of the church. I set Danny down on the orange and brown tiles that were cool from the shade. He plopped down and sat and my right arm trembled as I let it fall into its natural position for a few minutes. Voices echoed all over the porch and the news people still fought to jump ahead of the rest of us.

By two o'clock, I was feeding Danny his jar of bananas as we sat on the hard tile of the stoop just outside the church doors. The last spoon went in and Danny made a slimy banana motorboat engine with his lips. The line of people in front of us suddenly moaned and groaned. I picked up Danny as everyone surged back but the crowd only separated to allow through a priest in a long black robe, and a cardinal or bishop in a red satin

273

robe with a red satin cap. They stood right next to us, and I noticed the bishop or whatever church official he was had cocoa brown skin and chocolate-colored eyes. He smiled at Danny and me, showing his white teeth and purplish gums.

"Parishioners," he said. His voice almost sounded Irish but it was lower and seemed to follow a rhythm as he spoke. "I am Cardinal Dhir from the Los Angeles Diocese. I am afraid to say it but the statue of the Virgin Mary is not an authentic miracle. The church just installed air conditioning and one of the vents blows directly on the statue."

The news reporters on either side of the door stopped their pushing and shoving and walked off toward both ends of the portico. Cardinal Dhir continued.

"Because yesterday and today are so humid here in Los Angeles, her tears were really only condensation. I am so sorry, but the parish fathers tell me they didn't know this until the air conditioning repairman came to inspect the vents today. But we do not need a visual miracle to have faith in Our Lady's presence, now do we?"

With that, the cardinal and parish priest stepped past us and into the dark stoop. People crossed themselves and grumbled behind us and a flow of the faithful emerged from the church.

By two forty-five, Danny and I made it back onto the freeway heading south and it looked like the whole city of Los Angeles was, too. Just as the car would start to roll and get to five or ten miles per hour, we'd stop again and sit a few seconds. We crept like this for a long time and it was almost four o'clock when Danny and I pulled into the driveway. Martha and Kathie ran to the car.

"Where were you, Mom?" Kathie asked. "Dad's home a little early and he was hoping you would have dinner started."

I grabbed Danny who was deep asleep and rushed into the house. Andrew sat at the kitchen table, still in his work shirt but with a loose tie. When I leaned over to kiss him, he turned away.

"I need to talk to you in our room," Andrew said. He could have been talking to one of the girls by the way he said it.

I walked into our bedroom and closed the door behind me. After I placed Danny in his crib, I sat on the edge of the bed next to Andrew. His arms were folded.

"Mary, what the heck did you take off to Los Angeles for?"

"I told you already, Andrew. It was possibly a miracle."

"So you thought it was just fine to make the girls fend for themselves when they got home?"

"Andrew, all I thought about then was the Blessed Mother. You always wanted me to be a devout Catholic, now you're mad that I am."

Andrew ran his hands through his hair and rubbed the moss green high-low carpet we installed last year with the toe of his wing tip work shoe.

"I work thirteen, sometimes fourteen hours a day, Mary. Someone has to be around the house and make sure the girls are okay, and dinner gets made, and all that. That's your job, don't you think?"

"Maureen and Kathie are old enough to take care of themselves. And they can look out for Martha and Susan. Even Danny, sometimes."

"That's not the point. You belong here."

"My first responsibility is to God, Andrew. You know that. And the Blessed Mother who made Him flesh on this earth. She brought the miracle of Danny into my life and I will venerate her and seek her in every moment of my life."

Andrew turned and took me by the shoulders. He looked over his glasses at me without blinking.

"I understand why you did it, okay? It's just that you gotta remember that you're a mother and a wife, too. Even Virgin Mary was Joseph's wife before she became the mother of Christ."

I wanted to scream at Andrew: every dirty diaper, every fight the kids have, every dish that has to be washed, load of laundry or meal that has to be cooked reminds me that I'm a wife and mother. So if sometimes I make a mistake or need to see a miracle, I always remember.

He let go of me and began to undress. I felt a little odd, like I was betraying the Blessed Mother somehow.

The week following Palm Sunday, I was busy with the Blessed Mother Club arranging the Passion Play Pageant and the Easter Carnival at the school. Andrew and I had joined the church choir by this point. We got home early from choir practice and when we walked into the living room, all the lights were off except for the blue glow of the TV and we saw someone hop up and run out the front door. I screamed and Andrew flipped the dining room light on. Kathie and Martha sat on the floor in front of TV in their nightgowns. Maureen was wiping her face with the back of her hand and straightening her dress.

"What the heck's going on here?"

Rod Sterling's voice was echoing from the TV and Andrew went over and switched the television off.

"Kathie. Martha. Bed." The girls knew his tone and jumped up and sped off, leaving two half-eaten chocolate Scooter Pies still in their plastic wrappers on the floor.

"Was that what I think it was?" Andrew thrust his finger toward the TV.

"The Twilight Zone's not that bad, Dad."

"It's of the Devil and it's forbidden to be watched in this house.

Why's it on?"

Maureen shrugged. He stepped closer to her.

"Answer me. Why?"

"I let the girls watch it."

Andrew's hand flew across her face.

"Andrew, she graduates from high school in two weeks. She's too old to be slapped," I said.

"If she's still under this roof, she's not too old to be slapped. Maybe she's needed more smacking around from the beginning. Curb some of that wild behavior."

Maureen started to leave.

"Sit down," Andrew said between his teeth. "We're not finished yet. Don't ever let me catch you turning on Twilight Zone again, you understand?"

Maureen nodded.

"Now. Who the heck was that who ran outta here like a bat outta hell?"

"David."

"David who?"

"David Bluff."

"You let a strange boy in the house while we were at choir practice?"

"He's not a stranger. I've known him all year at school."

"Your mom and I don't know him."

"That's because you won't let me bring home any boy who isn't Catholic."

"Andrew, she's right about that."

"Mary, she had a boy over here. For all I know, she was committing a sin."

Maureen rubbed her cheek and glanced at me, her eyes still full of hurt and anger. I looked away, having no idea how to help.

"I guess I should just tell you now," she said. "I'm sure you'll be glad to know. As soon as I graduate, I start work at Bob's Big Boy. I'll be moving in with a couple of friends to share an apartment over off Arlington while we all go to El Camino. I won't be around much longer to break any more rules."

"Maureen, you don't have to do that. You can stay home as long as you need to," I said.

Andrew slid off his glasses and wiped his eyes.

"You're not moving anywhere till you turn eighteen in November. Before then, don't break any more rules around here."

Andrew stepped away from us and went into the bedroom,

276

shutting the door behind him. Maureen just looked at me.

For the next two weeks leading up to Maureen's graduation, the Blessed Mother Club was hectic with planning a graduation party for all the students in the parish whether they went to Bishop Mahoney High or one of the Torrance public high schools. Connie, Maureen, and I also worked for three days on Maureen's graduation dress, using Connie's portable Singer sewing machine and her seamstress skills. During that time we also held two rosaries, one for Maureen and one for Patrick, Kay's son who was graduating from Bish.

By the time Andrew and I were sitting in the bleachers at the Torrance High football field on an unusually foggy and cold June fourth, with the smell of rotten chewing gum and old popcorn coming up from below the metal bench that pressed hard against my rear end, I was glad the graduation party had gone off without a hitch. Maureen's white rayon dress was done and pretty, and we had a week before Ernie's graduation from UCLA. It would be just enough time to catch up the laundry and get the house dusted and vacuumed before the girls complained anymore.

"Maureen Therese Murphy. Graduating with honors," the principal's voice boomed out.

Maureen strode up to the platform in her burgundy cap and gown and waved the rolled diploma toward us and smiled. I knew she had gotten good grades all throughout school but I was very proud of her when I heard the principal's announcement. A few boys and girls screamed when Maureen crossed the platform and I wondered who her friends were at school.

The crowd of family and friends in the bleachers now overran the parking lot where three school buses were going to take the graduating class down to Disneyland for graduation night. Burgundy gowns fluttered all around us in the cool, misty night air and Andrew clutched my arm as he pushed his way through the crowd to get to where the graduates were exiting the football field.

"Dad! Over here!" Maureen screamed.

We turned and Maureen stood with two thin girls, one of whom looked Italian or Spanish, and a handsome boy with dark, frizzy hair who looked like an athlete. All of them had the front zippers of their gowns open and Maureen's white dress with its low neckline made her graduation gown look like an elegant cape. She waved us over and when Andrew got to her, he threw his arms around her and kissed her cheek. He stepped back awkwardly as I joined the group.

"Congratulations, Maureen. We're real proud of you," I said as she kissed my cheek.

"Mom. Dad. These are my boss friends: Babs -- Barbara --

Terrence. Stacy Harrington and David Bluff."

When David stepped forward to shake Andrew's hand, the side panel of a letterman's jacket stuck out from under his gown. Andrew's eyes flashed down at it.

"What you get your letter in?" Andrew asked.

"Baseball, sir," David answered.

"What position?"

"Shortstop."

"Maureen, you never told me any of your friends play ball."

"Well, the reason I wanted you to meet everyone is because these guys are going to be my roommates when I move out to go to El Camino."

"You better know, now, girls," I said. "Maureen is pretty sloppy."

"Mom!"

"We're already planning on that," David said.

Maureen glared at him and he stepped back.

"Huh?" Andrew said.

"Nothing, Dad. David's just being a goofball. Anyway, we gotta go catch the bus. See you tomorrow morning."

Maureen kissed Andrew's cheek and grabbed her two girlfriends by the arm and David followed behind.

"I guess that David is all right," Andrew said.

I didn't even want to tell him what I suspected: he was going to be one of Maureen's roommates in the fall.

Ernie's graduation a week later had its own surprise, too. Because Ernie had been developing some sort of concentration problem for the last two years, we weren't even sure he'd graduate at all. It's not that it mattered particularly because he was at UCLA to play ball and he was the varsity, first string, first baseman for the last two seasons. As we stood in the center of campus near the twin, brick towers of Royce Hall, Ernie came running at us, holding his pasteboard to his head and dragging a girl along with him. His face was a broad smile under a thin mustache that made him look so much like Artie that it made me jump.

"He got a girl finally?" Andrew said when he saw the two. He sounded relieved.

Andrew had worried about Ernie ever since high school when he didn't date; when he wasn't practicing and playing baseball, he'd sit for hours watching TV with a dazed, far-off expression like he was daydreaming. 'What's he thinking all the time?' Andrew would ask. I didn't know. We thought at one point that maybe he would want to join the seminary but he barely passed his religion exams at Bish.

"Mom! Dad!" he screamed and threw his arms around us. "You're not going to believe it. You just won't believe what's happening. There's

278

this guy. And they want me. But I have to—"

"Slow down, honey," I said. His rapid speech he developed in high school had really sped up during college.

"Who's your friend?"

"This is my English and history tutor the coach set up. Without her, I'd a never gotten my degree in phys-ed. Becky, this is my Mom and Dad."

"Hi, Mr. and Mrs. Murphy. Ernie told me a lot about you. Ernie, I gotta go now 'cause Kirk's waiting for me over by the Pavilion. Nice meeting you!" she said. She ran off and her gold tassel flapped behind her pasteboard.

"Kirk's her fiancée. They're going to get married in awhile."

"Oh," Andrew barely said. "So what's the big news? What's going on?"

Ernie thrust a folded letter into Andrew's hands. Andrew unfolded and read it and his eyes about burst out of his head.

"The Dodgers!"

"What?" I screamed. I knew what this meant.

"The Dodgers. Their scout saw Ernie at a few games and they've invited him to try out!"

"Not till the end of August, though, so maybe you can practice with me to keep me in shape, Dad."

"You betcha!"

On the drive back home, Andrew and Ernie chatted away about the Dodgers, about big games Ernie helped win at UCLA, and about the possibilities of being in professional baseball. It all sounded exciting and Ernie was sure happy, but something in the pit of my stomach made me feel the old darkness, almost a dread.

17.

"Damn Oriental heathens are at it again, Mary," Andrew said. "You think they'd a figured it out after the last two wars that you don't mess with us."

I walked into the living room with a plate of tuna salad and a piece of rye bread smeared with peanut butter and set it on the aluminum TV tray Andrew had set up next to his black recliner. Even though the hall door was closed, I could hear the Beatles' song 'All My Loving' blaring from Kathie's room. I glanced up to see President Johnson making an address with his plodding voice and Texas accent.

"Japan attacking us again or something?" I said.

"No. Some place called Viet Nam. Looks like Congress gave the president thumbs up to attack them back for hitting our ships in the Gulf of Tonkin. More power to him, damn heathen commies."

Andrew scooped up a fork of the tuna salad and I could smell the fish and mayonnaise. I pulled off a piece of the rye bread crust and rolled the oily peanut butter around on my tongue.

"They hit the ships today? I mean, it's August seventh, and it can't be a coincidence that Pearl Harbor was December seventh."

"No, Mary. The ships were hit on Tuesday."

"Is it war?"

"No. Chet Huntley said before that the President thinks we can get in there, help the south part of the country, then get out. Probably no more than a month or two."

My stomach sunk because if Andrew was wrong, I knew that Ernie may go to war. We had only heard from Louise once when the invitation to her wedding arrived. I couldn't live through a separation from another child because of war.

"I hope you're right, Andrew. 'Cause Ernie is registered for the draft and all."

"Ernie's gonna be playing ball for the Dodgers after next week, you watch. This whole thing will blow over before the season even opens."

Ernie ran in to answer the phone the following Monday as I leaned over cotton batting and chicken wire I had spread all over the den floor. With Danny playing next to me, I squeezed Elmer's white glue onto the

280

white batting and pressed it against the chicken wire.

"This is it, Mom! Saturday! I go Saturday."

"Go where?" I said. My finger felt sticky and gritty from the paste that had built up on it.

"Dodger try-outs. I have to be at Dodger stadium at ten in the morning Saturday."

I pinched batting to the chicken wire and my stomach twisted.

"What time?" I asked.

"Ten. That's not too early for you and Dad, is it?"

"Ernie, don't you remember what Saturday is?"

"No. Should I?"

"What kind of a Catholic are you? Why do you think I'm sitting here gluing batting to chicken wire?"

"You're always doing something weird, Mom. How should I know?"

Ernie folded his arms and leaned against the ratty arm of our first couch that was a beat-up bunch of brown and gray.

"Saturday is the Feast of the Assumption. I'm making the clouds that will lift the Virgin Mary to her glorious place next to the Lord."

"Huh?"

"The Assumption Mass and festival after in the parish hall. The Blessed Mother club has been planning it for weeks. Here, pick up that end."

Ernie and I lifted the chicken wire that was half-covered by cotton batting and it sort of looked like the exploded end of a butterfly's cocoon. I stepped back and sighed.

"Mom, does that mean you won't make it to my try-outs?"

I pulled the end of the cloud from Ernie's hand. I stared at him.

"Ernie, I know that they mean a lot to you. But really, I'm obligated to bring about the celebration of Mary's rise into Heaven. Don't you think that kind of means a lot more?"

"Does that mean Dad can't make it either?" His voice broke like a violin string as he said the second syllable of the word 'either'.

"You'll have to discuss that with your father. But he's part of the choir, so remember that."

Ernie left. I continued to work on the cloud until Andrew interrupted me a few minutes later.

"So what about Saturday?" he pressed.

"What about it?"

"You told Ernie I have to sing in the choir."

"I told him you might. But I also told him why."

"Ernie's try-outs are more important to me than singing at the church."

I crossed myself, surprised by his words.

"Andrew. Be careful what you say. You may be bound for purgatory."

"I'm taking care of my son. Remember him too?"

"If you have to go to his try-outs, then go. But I can't let down the Blessed Mother Club. Not to mention the Holy Mother herself."

Andrew grabbed my shoulders and looked back toward the kitchen door. He glanced at the hall door, and then spoke quietly.

"Mary, you and I both know that this try-out is more important for Ernie than anything else. It ain't like he can go take any job, with his problems and all."

"He just doesn't pay attention all the time. So what?"

"If that's what you wanna believe because of the crazy people you got in your family, go ahead. But I know he's not all right and I think playing ball's the only thing he's ever going to do."

My stomach growled with hunger and I really didn't agree with what Andrew was saying, anyway.

"I gotta eat now. If you don't mind."

I pulled away from his grip. He stepped back.

"Mary, what's gotten into you? Ever since you started that club, besides being gone a lot, you been real different with me. I don't like the way you talk to me lately."

His eyes looked misty through his horned rim glasses. Was there something wrong with me? Was he right?

"Andrew, I'm just trying to be faithful to the Lord, and to the Holy Mother. Sometimes I get tired doing all this, so that must be what you're hearing."

He wrapped his arms around me and we kissed in a way that we hadn't in a long time. A shiver went through me and I wanted him then, right then. He kissed my cheek and spoke softly.

"Mary, it's gonna mean a lot to Ernie -- probably make him do better -- if you come on Saturday. Please think about it."

Blessed Mother, I thought. Guide me with this. Lead me in the right direction.

By the end of the week, Connie, Kay and I had the parish hall's tables set up and decorated for Assumption Day. The coffee urn was up next to the punch bowl and the paper plates sat in stacks along side the napkins and plastic forks. All we needed was the food, which wasn't going to be set up until Saturday morning. We had just finished hanging the three clouds of batting from a low scaffold at the top of the stage. The three clouds really looked like they were floating above us as I pulled open a metal ladder and set it right underneath the clouds. I climbed the ladder and its aluminum creaked as I stepped. Kay grabbed the feet of the ladder and steadied them.

"Okay, Connie. Hand me up the statue."

Connie set the plaster sculpture of the Blessed Mother on the floor of the stage, and then climbed up. As she lifted the statue at the bottom of the ladder, she looked at its ivory finish and frowned.

"You know, the Fathers were nice to loan us the statue from the rectory and all. But it sort of looks like its made of Avon soap."

"Connie, it's too late to grouse about it," Kay said. "Just hand it up."

I pulled the statue from Connie's hands and even though it was about three feet tall, it felt light and almost hollow.

"Steady there, Mary," Connie said.

"I got it," I said. I placed it on top of the ladder, and then shifted the clouds around so that they covered the statue's feet.

"Okay."

I climbed down from the ladder just as Connie flipped the switch to the stage lights. Blue and white light made the cotton clouds shimmer. But the most amazing thing was how the light made the statue with its outstretched hands looked more like marble. We stepped back to the end of the parish hall. Except for the ladder, the statue looked like it really was ascending into heaven.

"Mary, you did it," Connie said.

Kay put her arm around my shoulder.

"We appreciate you so much," Kay said. "All that talent and all that time you give."

Kay glanced down at her watch.

"Nine-thirty. I gotta get home. So, who's handling what tomorrow morning?"

"Yeah. We better divvy things up," Connie added.

I stepped away from them and turned. My throat was closing on me and I didn't know how to begin.

"You okay there, Mary?" Kay asked.

"Yeah. I just got a problem."

"Talk. That's what we're here for, too, isn't it?" Connie said.

"I can't make it tomorrow."

"What?" Kay screeched.

"Kay. Easy. Maybe she's not feeling well or something."

"Oh, no. You're not—" Kay moved her hands over her belly.

"No, that's not it. See, Ernie got invited to try out for the Dodgers."

"Mary, that's wonderful," Connie said.

"He still doing okay?" Kay asked.

I cringed every time anyone used that word when they asked about Ernie. It wasn't ever just a casual question but always sounded more like they were waiting for him to explode.

"He's fine. Anyway, the try-outs are at ten tomorrow morning and will probably last until the afternoon. I gotta miss everything."

"Mary, you need to go support Ernie," Kay said. "Connie and I can handle setting out food and throwing away paper plates. You go support your boy."

Tears started to gather at the corners of my eyes.

"It's really okay, Mary. We mean it," Connie added.

"You two are the best friends I ever had."

My throat choked after those words and disappointment wrung through me like dirty water. All that work and I wasn't going to get to see anyone enjoy it.

I didn't enjoy much of the next day either. After our forty-five minute ride in traffic to Los Angeles, during which Ernie, wearing his UCLA baseball cap and top over his gray sweats, sat silent in the back seat of the Impala, his right leg nervously drumming, we walked into Dodger Stadium. The sun blared down on the field. Gray haze in the sky overhead made the stadium feel like the inside of our Kenmore clothes dryer. A man in a Dodger baseball cap waved Ernie over and Andrew and I slid into seats just behind home plate.

"You know how much these seats would cost if there was a game on right now?" Andrew asked.

I shook my head.

On either side of us, there were a few young women who looked no older than Maureen and two couples who must have been middle-aged parents like us. I reached up and pulled the lip of the white sun visor I wore lower over my face because the morning sun already felt like it was burning me. My arms and shoulders that stuck out from my sleeveless, white blouse began to prickle from the heat and my navy blue Capri slacks started to warm up, too. My feet weren't warm but they did bulge out the sides of my white sneakers. I hated the fat I had gained over the last couple of years.

Andrew reached out and wove his thin fingers through the pale, pink sausages that were my own. He didn't care about my fat and it hadn't stopped him from wanting to have sex just as often as ever. And since we had discovered several different ways of having sex without me getting pregnant, we still enjoyed that part of our lives. With as busy as things had been getting over the years, it was the only way we still communicated. So

284

when he grabbed my hand right then just to hold it, shivers of love coursed through me. He caught me thinking about all these things and his eyes narrowed like he was suspicious.

"What're you thinking about?" he said.

"Just how much I love you."

"Well, my Mary, I love you, too and am really proud that you worked things out to be here. He needs us today."

"Murphy!" I heard the man at the pitching mound scream. He was tall and thin and looked a little old to be a ball player. He balanced a clipboard against his Dodger jersey.

"That's Walter Alston!"

"Who?" I asked.

"The manager. I didn't know he'd be running this."

Ernie stood just outside the batter's box and swung three bats with black rings on them. He wore a Dodgers helmet.

"Won't those rings mess up his batting?" I said.

"Those weights are just for warm up. He won't bat with them."

Right then, Walter Alston stepped off the mound and waved toward the dugout just to the right of us. A man in a Dodger jersey and blue jeans ran toward the mound, slapping his hand repeatedly into his brown glove.

When the pitcher turned around and Ernie stepped into the batting box, Andrew grabbed my left arm and squeezed it with excitement.

Ernie crouched into his batting position and the pitcher wound up.

"Blessed Mother, let him –" before I could get my prayer in my head finished, the ball streaked past Ernie and popped into the catcher's glove. Ernie's swing seemed to come after the ball hit the catcher's glove.

The pitcher wound up again and this time, Ernie's bat connected but sent the ball straight up into the air. The pitcher caught it and stepped back up to the mound. He fired three more pitches and Ernie swung and missed each one. Andrew leaned forward, his belly pushing against the top of his pants and his eyes squinting like he was in pain.

The next pitch seemed to crack as Ernie caught it with the bat and the ball soared out toward the back fence. The pitcher glanced at Alston who nodded and held up his fingers to indicate that he should throw four more. Ernie sent the next two on the ground between the pitcher and the second baseman, missed the next one, then sent the final ball again back to the fence. Alston nodded and made some notes on his clipboard.

Ernie stepped out of the batting box and as he pulled off his helmet, I could see his face was red from the heat. He glanced toward us and dropped his eyes. Alston pointed to a bench and he joined a group of young men all wearing jerseys from different college teams.

The rest of the afternoon Ernie spent playing both infield and outfield positions in a rotation as each new player took his turn at bat. I don't know enough about baseball to know how they made their decisions, but Ernie made more hits than any of the other young men trying out. It wasn't until two-thirty that the try-outs were over and everyone was told that they'd hear through the mail. Ernie joined back up with us and Andrew patted his back. Strands of his dark hair, wet with sweat, stuck to his temples. Ernie didn't speak for the whole ride home even though Andrew glowed with pride for him.

For the next few days, Ernie and Andrew practiced every night after Andrew got home from work. Even though the practice wasn't going to make a difference since he already tried out, I think it was a habit of communicating they both had just gotten used to ever since Ernie first showed his talent and interest in baseball. Before that, Andrew hardly looked at Ernie so I couldn't complain that they practiced together so much, now could I? They never talked about anything except baseball, and since part of Andrew had always wanted to play pro ball, he grew closer to Ernie because of it. But when Ernie flew in the front door the following Thursday, Andrew wasn't due home for a few hours.

"It's here, Mom! It's here!" he blurted as he waved an envelope at me.

I set down the load of socks and underwear I just took out from the dryer. Ernie thrust the envelope into my hand and the word 'Dodgers' along with the address stood out in blue ink.

"Aren't you going to open it?"

Ernie sat down on the coffee table and folded his arms. He began to rock back and forth. He jumped back up and paced.

"Mom. I can't. You do it."

I slid my forefinger under the lip of the envelope and pulled out the letter. Some sort of smaller page with pink and yellow carbon pages started to fall but I caught it.

"Dear Ernie," I read.

'We would like to congratulate you on your excellent performance at the try-outs August fifteenth.'

Ernie pursed his lips and blew out the air, making a raspberry.

"Yeah, right," he said.

'Right now,' I read on, 'we feel we have enough depth in your position and in our batting line-up. However, we would like to extend an invitation to you to join our triple A farm team in the minors for the next two years.'

"Oh, jeese," Ernie interrupted again. "I already played minors at UCLA."

286

I read on: 'We will monitor our filled positions and your progress and can guarantee a final decision about your future with the ball club then. I know this is disappointing –'

"Got that right," Ernie said.

'--but we feel strongly about you and as a show of that, wish to extend to you a salary of five thousand dollars for each of the two years. Please let us know by filling in the enclosed engagement form and returning it so that we may process your contract. We look forward to hearing from you. Sincerely, Walter Alston.'

"Five thousand dollars!" I said.

"The minors," Ernie sighed.

"But that's almost as much as your Dad makes in a year. To play baseball. I can't believe it."

"Well, then you can play the minors for them. I'm trying out for someone else."

He fell back onto the couch. I folded the letter.

"No one else invited you, Ernie. It sounds like they're real interested."

He stood up and grabbed the letter out of my hand.

"Let's see what Dad says about this."

When Andrew got home, he read the letter and jumped up and down. I hadn't seen him that happy since he got home from the war. With Andrew's approval, Ernie decided to accept the invitation.

For the rest of the year, nothing happened until just before Christmas when Maureen turned eighteen. She had already been in El Camino Junior College for the semester and the Saturday before Christmas, her three friends, Babs, Stacy, and David, all showed up to help her move into the two bedroom apartment on Arlington Avenue. The best thing about it, they all said, was the built-in swimming pool. They drove off with Maureen's bed and her light blue dresser. When the last of her things were loaded into the black Corvair she bought with the money she saved while she worked at Bob's Big Boy in the summer, Andrew and I stood on the front lawn with her. The low, winter afternoon sunlight made the bottle brush tree on the grass next to the curb cast a long shadow that looked like a pitchfork. A cold breeze blew in from the beach and the Palos Verdes Peninsula loomed like a black whale in the distance.

Maureen stood next to the bottlebrush tree, shifting her weight from foot to foot nervously, making the gaping hole on the right leg of her blue jeans open and close like a screaming mouth. She swung her arms that looked bone thin under her light blue sweater as if she didn't know what to do with them. Did she think she was in trouble or something? Her nervousness made me suspicious.

"You don't have to move you know," I said.

"Oh bee-ess, Mary," Andrew said. "She made the choice and now she has to live up to it."

Maureen glared at him.

"Yeah. Dad's right. So, I guess I'm gonna buzz off."

"Huh?" I said.

"Buzz off. Take off? Leave?"

"I'm never gonna keep up with all these newfangled words," I said.

Maureen had already stepped around to the driver's side door. I glanced at Andrew and his feet were planted into the green and yellow crab grass of the front lawn. I knew I couldn't let her go without hugging her. I went to her.

"Promise me that if you need anything, you'll call or come by?"

"I'll bug you if I need you," she said. A smile creeped up the edges of her mouth. She reached for me and hugged me and I wanted to pull her back into the house and lock the door on her. Instead, I kissed her cheek.

"Hey, at least Ernie'll get his room back, right?" she said. "Bye, Dad."

Maureen paused to let him come to her, but he stood his ground.

"You remember your Catholic faith, Maureen. Let it steer you," he said. He turned and walked into the garage.

"Bye, Mom."

Maureen slid into the car and turned the engine on. I stepped back to the front lawn and waved as she put the car into gear and drove off down the street. Would I ever see her again? I was afraid she'd disappear like Louise. Blessed Mother, please protect her.

When I got back into the house, Martha, Susan, and Danny made a half-circle around Kathie and Ernie. The TV blared as Kukla and Ollie sang with Fran. Kathie's face was red and wet like she had been crying and I thought at first she missed Maureen.

"Why'd you have to come home?" she screamed.

"It was my room first and is always gonna be," Ernie screamed back. "Mom, tell her," he said when he saw me.

"What now?" I said.

"Mom, Maureen's old room is supposed to be mine," Kathie said between sobs. "I'm sick of sharing a room with those two." She waved her hand toward Martha and Susan.

"Kathie, Ernie's been sleeping in the den all the time he's been home. He's the oldest and he's got to have his own room."

"That's so unfair. You're discriminating against me!"

I had no idea what she meant by that.

"Okay, how about this? We'll move Susan in with Danny and that

288

way, it'll just be you and Martha sharing the room."

"That's not what you promised a long time ago."

"That's all I can do now, Kathie. It won't work out any other way."

She wiped her face with the back of her hand and snorted.

"It's so unfair," she said again. "Why did he have to come home? I wish he'd just go away somewhere."

Kathie would be getting her wish sooner than any of us realized.

For the next months, the Blessed Mother Club was in full force for all of the feast days of the Virgin. For Annunciation Day, we even put on reproductions of Passion Plays that started March twenty-first and went through Annunciation Day on the twenty-fifth. A few days before Assumption Day in 1965, while Kay, Connie, and I kneeled in the pew before the Tuesday morning mass, Father O'Connor walked in followed by a younger priest. Father O'Connor's face broke out into a wide grin when he saw us.

"Good morning, ladies," Father O'Connor said. "It's a pleasure to let you be the first in the parish to meet our new pastor. Ladies of the devout Blessed Mother Club, this is Father Crawford."

The younger priest, who looked around my age — forty-one -- bowed his head of wavy brown hair streaked with gray. When he looked back up, his gray-green eyes darted from Connie to Kay, and then seemed to rest on me. He looked like he could be a movie star and goose bumps erupted on my skin.

"Morning, Father," we all said at the same time.

"Now, what the hell -- sorry, Father Crawford -- what the heck is all this about?" Connie asked.

"I'm getting on here, Connie. The Mother Church thinks it's a good time for me to step aside and let a new, ambitious priest take over and lead St. Joan's."

"That mean you're leaving?" Kay asked.

"No. Think of me as sort of a vice-pastor. I'll still be doing services, hearing confessions, and all. It's just that this bright new light -- and he comes to us direct from the Los Angeles Archdiocese -- is going to take St. Joan's into the seventies and beyond."

"Father Crawford, welcome," Kay said. "I'm Kay Smith. This is the club leader, Mary Murphy."

I stood up and pulled my skirt down to straighten it. Father Crawford smiled at me and I again felt uncomfortable. What was wrong with me that a father of the Holy church would make me feel like this? I was always going to be a sinner I realized at that moment.

"Welcome, Father," I said. "We're here every morning and we usually ask Father O'Connor to devote the mass and extra prayer to some concern."

"I think the Lord will hear my prayers, too," Father Crawford said. Father O'Connor broke out into a laugh.

"Well, today, we'd like to devote this mass to our continued effort to pray for an end to the Viet Nam problems. Can we do that?"

"Sure. I'm not saying mass today, though. Father O'Connor will be. I'll just be assisting."

The devotion I asked for was nothing new for the Blessed Mother Club. Once a week we had been devoting prayers to the Viet Nam problems, and especially for the boys in the parish who were starting to get called up for service. None of us could even think about the possibility of sending our sons off over there, and I just hoped that somehow, with Ernie in the minors for the Dodgers, that he would miss out on getting drafted. That was my secret prayer during that mass. The Lord answered it very soon after.

"Hang on, Ernie. You got a letter here that I think you need to hear." I had called Ernie in his motel room in Reno, Nevada where the minors' farm team was paying for his lodging during the season.

"Who from?"

"The Selective Service."

"You mean the draft board?"

"Yeah. I guess."

"Read it to me, please, Mom."

The envelope flapped open easily and crisply and the page the letter was written on felt as soft as cotton as I unfolded. How weird that such an awful thing would be printed on something so soft and smooth.

"Dear Ernest:

'You are hereby ordered, on authority of the President of the United States, to report to Tehachapi Army Base in Tehachapi, California on September 16, 1965 at 12:00 PM. One suitcase or bag of personal effects, not to exceed 25 pounds, is allowed.'

My throat began to constrict and I could hear Ernie breathing into the phone.

'A mandatory, full, free physical will be required prior to your –'

"Mom, your voice dropped out. What was that again?" Ernie asked.

I cleared my throat.

'A mandatory, full, free physical will be required prior to your induction and you are to appear for that exam on September 9, at 10:00 am in the gymnasium at West Torrance High School.

'If you require directions to either site, please contact the West Los Angeles Army Recruitment Center at (213)931-8943.'

"You can't play first base with only one arm. So much for my baseball career."

"Ernie, don't say things like that."

"What else does it say?"

'Failure to appear on either date can subject you to full prosecution for high treason in the United States Federal Court which can result in life imprisonment. Sincerely, General Maxwell D. Taylor, U.S. Army.'

I folded the paper up and could hear the Bozo theme song playing from the TV in the living room. Ernie sighed.

"Well, I guess I get to be in the army like Dad. I always loved army stuff, anyways."

Danny banged the floor with a Tinker Toy triangle he made, following the beat of the Bozo Theme song: ...Always laugh, never frown ... tap, tap, tap, tap, tap, tap, tap ...

"Bozo the clown," Danny sang with his little raspy voice.

"I'll be home tomorrow night and we can talk all about it, Mom. I gotta take a shower now. I really stink."

"You sure you're okay?"

"Yeah, Mom. You know you never gotta worry about me."

Ernie seemed kind of happy after I read him the letter from Washington, not scared at all. He told me about his fouling out in the last game of the series and about making a triple play, and then he hung up. Andrew's reaction that night was a lot different from Ernie's. It didn't help that I really didn't know how to tell him. Also, my cycle was real heavy and crampy that day and each time I started to tell him about Ernie's letter, my voice choked with tears.

I waited until after he broke up the hair-pulling fight between Kathie and Martha (Martha took one of Kathie's blouses and wore it to the Assumption carnival where she dropped a candy apple on it and stained it) and before he sat down to eat. Andrew looked up from his plate after his third helping of spaghetti, the red sauce making an oily, yellow-orange ring around his slight lips. 'He looks like he's seventeen again,' I thought as the lump twisted my throat into a knot.

"What the hell's the matter with you, Mary? You spring a leak or something? Every time I look at you tonight you look like you're ready to bawl or something."

"Nothing, Andrew. You want some more spaghetti?"

"Nah. My belt's pushing hard enough against my gut as it is. So what's wrong anyway?"

I handed him a turquoise paper napkin and gestured over my own mouth. He rolled his eyes and followed my example.

"So, what?"

I heard Danny's raspy cry in the living room. The girls were laughing at 'The Munsters' on TV in the living room.

"Wait a second," I said.

I ran into the living room and picked up Danny. At two and a half years, he was still light and lanky. He flashed his brown eyes into a big smile and I knew if he was next to me, this would be easier -- I'd feel Her presence.

"Oh, come on, Mary. He's getting too big to sit on your lap so much."

"It's just for now."

The kitchen seat burped with air as I sat down. I reached into my apron that was stained with tomato sauce and handed him the letter.

"This came for Ernie today."

Andrew's eyes moved like a typewriter back and forth through his horned-rims. His face, so often now twisted into a sour, almost nasty expression, seemed to fall onto the olive Melmac plate in front of him.

He shook his head and dropped it into his hands. He flicked off his glasses and they clunked onto the Formica table, and his hands with knuckles creased like dry sausages rolled in his weeping eyes.

"My first baseman, my first baseman," he whimpered.

I lay my arm on his shoulder and saw Kathie start to step into the kitchen. I waved her away with my other hand.

"Andrew, he can still play ball," I said to make Andrew think I believed it. "It isn't gonna be forever."

He dropped his hands and the whites of his eyes were pink, making his brown eyes look like a Tootsie Pop center.

"He doesn't got the mind to make it in a war with Orientals," he said.

"If he can play ball under pressure like he's doing, and still be okay, he'll make it." Now I really felt like a liar. Blessed Mother, pray for me.

Andrew grabbed my shoulders and now my eyes started to water again. As his eyes jumped around my face, I could see he was trying to figure out what I thought I knew.

"War isn't baseball, Mary. It's death, and more death, and more suffering at the hands of those heathen slope heads. They're as bad as the crazy jigaboos in Los Angeles." Oh, how he reminded me of his narrow-minded mother Daisy just then. I wanted to remind him that all people are welcome in the house of the Lord so he shouldn't be thinking like that.

"Andrew, the kids are gonna hear you," I said. "And Ernie didn't seem so nearly upset about it."

"What does he know? He wanted to storm Normandy from when he was this high," he answered. He held a shaky hand out and let it

292

collapse to his side.

"Storm morndaby. Storm morndaby!" Danny echoed.

Andrew just shook his head. That night, even though it was Thursday and Andrew was usually so tired, Andrew took me two times. After the second time, he held me close and wept into my shoulder.

18.

Ernie quit the team, or rather took a leave of absence, just before his physical a couple of weeks later. His coach wasn't so sure there'd be a place for him when he got back. While Ernie had his physical at West High, Andrew told me quietly that right then, he half wished Ernie were a fairy. I crossed myself and prayed to the Blessed Mother to forgive him. Andrew told me later that he secretly and privately had hoped that Ernie's attention problems would get caught on the psychological exam, but they didn't. I never told Andrew then that I had secretly hoped that, too. But Ernie made it through the physical and all the basic tests and at nine-thirty the morning of September 16, with the dry Santa Ana winds roaring through Torrance and blowing all the cool, moist ocean air back out to sea, we loaded Ernie's duffel bag into the Impala and I held Danny in my lap as we drove to Tehachapi.

We passed through the town of Lancaster, right on the edge of the Mojave Desert, and right off the side of the road, I saw a gathering of cars and a small group of people looking into the clear sky and pointing. Andrew sped up and I could make out a couple of cameras.

"There's a group of nuts," Andrew said. "Must be a hundred out there."

We pulled up about an hour later to the cinder block guard gate of The Tehachapi Army Base and as we approached the white gate, a young man in a beige uniform with a white helmet approached us.

"An MP," Andrew said.

As the young man leaned against the car, I saw he wore a black armband with the letters 'MP' on the upper area.

"What is it, Andrew?"

"Military Police. Standard procedure, I'll bet," he said.

Danny was asleep and dreaming in my arms until the young man spoke.

"Can I help you folks?" he said with a southern drawl.

Danny's eyes popped open and he started to fuss. The young man glanced down at him and smiled.

"Hey there, little fella," he said. A soft cherry candy smell floated past me.

"Wanna Cert?" he held the gold foil roll out to Danny.

294

"No, I thirsty," Danny said.

"Well, can't help you there, little fella. Now, what is it you all need?"

Andrew glanced down at the soldier's badge before he spoke.

"Corporal, we're bringing our son here for service."

"Oh, a new draftee, huh?"

The corporal grinned and showed his front teeth that were separated like a picket fence.

"Well, sorry folks, but I can't let you all on the base."

"I thirsty," Danny said again.

"Quiet!" Andrew snarled at him. I could tell his anger was building.

"It's just to say goodbye," Andrew waved his hand for emphasis. "I'm a vet of the South Pacific for cripes sake."

"I believe you, sir. But regulations are regulations."

Ernie was already outside the car, brushing off his khaki slacks and straightening his light blue, plaid shirt like a child getting ready for his school photo. He looked so young right then.

"Don't worry about it, Dad. It's quarter till already."

"You can go ahead and pull your car over away from the gate and I'll let you walk on to say your goodbyes. That okay, sir?"

Ernie slid back in and Andrew pulled the car around and we sent up a cloud of dust as Andrew laid on the brakes.

"Let's not make this all teary-eyed or anything," Ernie said. "Dad, come open the trunk."

Once Ernie had his duffel bag slung over his shoulder, he stood and faced Andrew and me. Andrew pulled a small package from his pocket and handed it to Ernie and out the corner of my eye, I saw Danny waving toward us. Ernie opened the package and out came a brown, wooden rosary that was varnished in such a way that it looked like it was flecked with gold dust.

"Father O'Connor blessed it himself, son. I want you to keep it with you, always."

"Won't they take it from me?" Ernie asked.

"They can't. You keep it with you all the time. It'll give you strength."

Andrew pulled his own black onyx rosary, its beads dull from the years of slipping through his fingers, and kissed the crucifix as he held it out to Ernie.

"That one's not really the gift," Andrew said.

He pulled the wooden rosary from Ernie's hand and handed him his own onyx one.

"I had that one with me all the way through the war."

Ernie stared at the black beads and his eyes began to tear. He reached for Andrew, and the paused.

"Dad, you used this the whole time I was growing up, for every rosary we had at home, even. You can't give it up."

"I'm not giving it up. I expect you to bring it back home to me."

Ernie shrugged. He obviously didn't know what to say.

"Keep it close to you, son."

Andrew stepped away and walked toward the car. As he slid in the front seat, I saw the flash of his white handkerchief as he raised it to his eyes.

"A long time ago," my voice cracked. "I watched your grandmother say goodbye to Andrew -- your Dad -- when he was off to the war."

"I know who he is, Mom."

"I was always afraid I'd have to have a day like this, ever since you were born. But I hoped I'd be as strong as Daisy was then. I don't know what to say."

Ernie stepped up to me and hugged me. His Brut cologne drifted up.

"I'll be back, Mom. Sooner than you think."

He pulled away but I grabbed his cheek and pressed my lips to it.

"I love you, my son."

As we pulled away from the rusty, chain-link fence, his words played through my mind again. *Sooner than you think...* 'Blessed Mother,' I prayed. 'Let his words come true.' Less than an hour later, She showed me that his words just might.

'I thirsty, I thirsty,' were the only words spoken between the army base and the small town of Lancaster about an hour away. As we drove toward a liquor store, I saw that the small crowd from before on the side of the road had gotten much bigger. And a priest in his white cassock startled me.

"Andrew, stop."

"Mary, we gotta get this kid something to drink."

"There's a priest out there now, and do you see the TV cameras?"

"Maybe it's a movie being shot or something."

"I thirsty," Danny said.

"Okay, okay, just a second," I said. "They're all looking up. What do they see?'

"Mary, we gotta –"

But I couldn't hear Andrew right then: two Mexican women in white dresses with embroidered collars waved signs over their heads. The

Virgin Mary was painted on both of them. A fat man with a short T-shirt that didn't hide his gut held up a banner that read: 'Bless me, Holy Mother.'

"It's another visitation!" I shouted.

Before Andrew had the car completely stopped, I jumped out the passenger door and ran toward the crowd. I pulled on the priest's sleeve and his soft brown eyes flared at me as if I just woke him up from a nap. His gray brows wove together like a mustache.

"Father, what is it?" I asked.

"The Holy Mother has been sending signs all morning. This is greater than Fatima."

Greater than Fatima! I thought.

"Just look at these photos and you'll see her."

He held up two Polaroid photos and his hand shook. I grabbed it to steady it and his freckled flesh was soft as a baby.

"See, it's the Blessed Mother. She comes to us through the sunshine."

He held up the photograph and all I could see was a white rectangle with sunbeams shooting out from it. I shrugged.

"See. The Gate of Heaven. And right here, the Blessed Mother's veil."

Then, I saw that the rectangle did look like a gate of some kind. My skin crawled with the realization of what I was looking upon. When my eyes followed the dry, cracked tip of the man's finger, I felt my throat constrict with a gasp; there, in the haze of the sun's rays, was the outline of Her. Her veil, her downtrodden face, and a pure, radiant halo. I felt like I was going to faint.

"Take your own," the priest said. "Everyone is."

He pointed his thin arm across the faces of people with Polaroid cameras jutting out from their faces like strange noses. The cameras clicked like crickets and tires kicked up dust in the desert as more onlookers arrived. Three women were doing the rosary, but each time they said 'Hail, Mary,' their voices were locked in unison. 'Hail, Mary' they said as the rest of the prayer followed like a chant. The heat of the sun burned my head, but as the prayers mixed with the light, dry breeze, I felt my head grow light.

My mind began to see the crowd from above, the red, and green, and yellow dresses of the women were poppies against the beige and rocky ground. The blue of the sky grew deep, deep as Lake Minnetonka and the cornflowers that bloomed in summer on its shores. I soared, and felt the breath of heaven's winds. There, there She is, looking down at me, reaching for a blessed embrace.

'Blessed Mother, Blessed Mother, Blessed Mother —'

"Mary?"

Andrew's voice jolted me out of my dream. The sun was hot on my head again and I was dizzy, not sure exactly where I was.

"What the heck's going on here?"

"The Blessed Mother."

"Cripes, Mary. Danny was so thirsty, I had to get him a pop at that store up the road. We've been burning up in the car for a half hour, now. What's gotten into you?"

But my stomach and chest felt like a bird flapped inside them, and a strange lightness in my head reminded me of -- the days with Artie and Gopher Foot? -- I wasn't sure just then.

"Andrew, you have to look at this."

I ran to the priest from before and grabbed two of his photos. When I got back to Andrew, the excitement of sharing this Godly bliss was almost too much for me. I shoved the photos toward him.

"Look at this. A blessed event. A miracle."

His eyebrows cringed as he took the photos from me. He scanned both of them quickly.

"So," he said.

"Don't you see it?"

"What?"

"The Gate of Heaven."

"No. I see a reflection of an open camera shutter. That's what happens when you point a camera toward the sun."

I shoved my finger at the image of Her, Andrew's blasphemy starting to make me mad.

"How about that?" I asked, pointing to her veil.

"Looks like sun rays to me."

"You don't see Her?"

"No."

"Look again. Her veil. You see it now?"

"Mary, I see sunshine. Streaks of sunlight. They're just like clouds. People make them out to be whatever they want. Let's go, Mary."

We let go of Ernie that day but once we got word that he had been shipped over seas, months went by between any sort of word from him. I got to a point where I would switch on the TV so that I could keep up with events in the war. I know it sounds stupid, but I was hoping that I might catch a picture of Ernie. A flash of his face or the sound of his voice. I'd be happy in a jif with anything like that because we hadn't gotten a letter from him since Christmas and I was really worried. Andrew said the military always lets you know if something bad happens right away, so I shouldn't get so worked up. But since Ernie went away in August last year,

I kept the TV on everyday. Maybe today I'd see him and anyway, it made me feel closer to him.

I would change channels to watch General Hospital then back to the news. One particular day, after I had caught Danny mixing flour and water on the kitchen floor and sent him to his room, I was embroiled in an episode where something was happening with Doctor Hardy's wife and Lee Baldwin. Danny tiptoed out from his room after about forty-five minutes and gave me a big hug. He went to sit and I hollered.

"No, Danny. You know better. Come over and sit with me."

We only used the raspberry Naugahyde chairs when company was over, or during Christmas. It had to be a very special reason and I never let the kids sit in them at all. Danny slid next to me on the old, gray couch. Just as the soap opera music faded to a Salvo laundry soap commercial, the mail plopped through the front door slot.

Next to trying to catch a glimpse of Ernie on TV, the mail always made me feel tense; would I hear from Ernie today or wouldn't I? I scooped up the mail and it blasted me with the floral smell of an Avon perfume free sample. The envelopes underneath the gold package were telephone and gas bills. As I stood back up, my lungs pushed out a disappointed breath.

"Mommy, are you doing Jack La Lanne?" Danny asked.

"No, honey, just wanted to know what was in the mail."

"Oh, Doctor Hardy!" the actress's voice blurted from the TV. I sat back down, disappointed again.

A knock on the front door startled me. I pulled it open and a young man stood on the front stoop. He wore a delivery cap but I saw what looked like a ponytail poking out from underneath it. I stepped back.

"Mrs. Murphy?" he said.

"Yeah?"

"A telegram for you."

He handed the goldenrod envelope to me and he must have noticed how I stared at his hair. He lifted his hat as I took the envelope.

"See, Mrs. Murphy? Just like Jesus wore his hair."

I slammed the door. I don't know why the young man scared me so much, but when he took the Lord's name in vain, I couldn't listen to the sinner anymore. I forgot about him in a second, though, because the telegram in my hand gave me the chills. I punched off the TV and Danny looked up at me.

"Mommy, why you shut off our show?"

I sat down on the couch and pulled Danny close to me. I dropped the telegram on the coffee table and stared at it. Danny reached for it.

"Is a birthday card for me?"

299

"No." I pulled it out of his hand. "It's not your birthday, yet."

I felt my heart pounding in my ears. Oh, Blessed Mother, give me strength. My boy, my boy.

I slid my finger under the thin flap of the envelope. As I pulled the folded page out of the envelope, the paper felt like tissue on my thumb. I'll need to cry in it, I thought.

'Mr. and Mrs. Murphy,' the telegram began.

'We regret to inform you –' I threw the telegram aside and burst into tears.

"Mama, no cry." Danny's voice cracked more than usual. "No, cry."

I yanked the telephone receiver off its cradle, its once shiny plastic now dented and marred by years of use. My fingers were icy as I dialed Andrew's office. Each click as the rotary returned was like a machine gun's bullets pelting my heart. Snot met up with my tears and my face felt hot and wet as boiled cabbage.

"Andrew Murphy, please. It's Mrs. Murphy and it's an emergency."

The telegram looked like a yellow stain on our green high-low carpet. Danny curled up next to me, his little hands clutching my arm and shoulder.

"Mary, what? What's going on?" Andrew asked.

"We got a telegram. Ernie's ... Ernie's ..."

"Oh, Lord bless us. Oh, Lord." Andrew's voice became gauze in his throat.

"This can't be right," he said. "It can't be."

"Andrew, the telegram's right here."

"Read it to me," he said.

"But Andrew, I can't look at it –"

"I have to hear it, Mary. Now, read it to me."

I reached for the paper again, wiping the tears onto the back of my chubby hand flecked with brown age spots.

"Dear Mr. and Mrs. Murphy," I read. "We regret to inform you that your son–' my voice began to crack and screech. "--Private Ernest Gerald Murphy has been...court-martialed?"

"What?" Andrew screamed.

My heart skipped a beat. He wasn't dead!

"...Private Murphy was to stand trial for the molestation of a minor Vietnamese girl."

"What the hell?" Andrew said. His tone shifted into surprise, then rage.

"...However, the doctors and staff at post six-five-seven have determined that he is mentally unfit to stand trial. Their diagnosis is

300

schizophrenia."

I dropped the receiver. Aunt Clotine's wild eyes and the straight pins she had stuck in her chin burned my memory.

"Mary? Mary!" Andrew's voice was a crackle in the receiver. I pulled it back up to my ear.

"Mary?"

"Yeah. I'm here."

"What else does the damn thing say?"

"Oh. Sorry. It says: The presiding military judges of the sixth military court have determined that Private Murphy's mental impairment was the cause of his behavior. They have therefore recommended a dishonorable discharge with medical considerations.

"Private Murphy will be transported back to Tehachapi Army Base in Southern California and released into your custody."

"I'll kill him!" Andrew roared.

"He's sick, Andrew, sick."

But my own guilt pulled on my voice, making me feel weak. What had I done to make this happen? Blessed mother, I prayed, but instead of comfort felt the clutch of sin and guilt.

"This is vile to me, disgusting," Andrew whispered. "When's he coming back?"

"Let's see ... " I scanned the letter comfortably now. I didn't care about any of it as long as Ernie was going to be safe at home. Whatever he might have done to the girl was only accusation; without a trial, he was innocent in my book.

"Here it is: Private Murphy will be transferred February twenty-fourth. Our regrets, Captain Mark Christopher, U.S. Army, seventh division."

Andrew didn't speak for what seemed like ten minutes but I knew it was a lot less time than that.

"I gotta get back to work. I'll see you around seven."

"I love you, Andrew. I'm sorry."

I said that into dead air because Andrew had already hung up. I placed the receiver back on its cradle and looked down at Danny. His puffy cheeks were little fleshy crabapples and I kissed the top of his head. The tips of his butch haircut tickled my nostrils.

"My miracle boy," I said softly to him. "Oh Blessed Mother, please let me do the right things for him."

The following Friday was February twenty-fourth. Andrew took the day off. He had slept in and shuffled into the living room to join the kids and me. Kathie was doing squats in front of the TV, following along with Jack La Lanne.

301

"Exhale," Jack said his music from an organ played along. "Use that diaphragm and push it out. Deep and out."

"Don't stretch too much, Kathie. You're liable to snap like a twig," Andrew joked.

Air raid sirens suddenly screeched. Andrew whirled around and then dropped to his knees.

"Andrew?"

He looked up at me and his eyes were wild with fear. He stood up immediately and adjusted his plaid bathrobe. But I noticed his forehead right below his salt-and-pepper flat top shone pink from embarrassment.

"Sorry, Mary. Those air raid sirens just give me the willies, you know?"

The startling screech of the air raid sirens was nothing compared to Ernie. When we got to Tehachapi Army Base, two men in helmets and uniforms with black arm bands marked 'MP' rattled along in a jeep in front of us, leading us to a distant part of the base.

"Just what I wanted to see -- the MP's," Andrew said like he was embarrassed.

The jeep stopped in front of a white brick building. A jail? I thought. The MPs gestured for Andrew to park next to them. As Andrew pulled on the parking brake of the Impala, the two men walked around the car and pulled open our doors.

"Thank you," I said, but the dark-haired boy with the single, bushy black eyebrow just nodded.

My heels tapped sharply against the cement steps of the building and as we got up to the heavy, iron doors, a small sign just above read: 'Infirmary.' I reached for Andrew's hand and as I wove my fingers through his, I could feel the moist coolness of his palm.

He's nervous, I thought.

The two MP escorts opened the doors for us and white uniforms flashed in front of my eyes as the smell of rubbing alcohol and something like sulfur waved past my nose. We walked up to a mahogany reception desk that looked like the judge's bench on 'Perry Mason'. Bushy eyebrow stepped ahead of us.

"Mr. and Mrs. Murphy," he said and stepped aside. A Negro woman in an all-white military uniform picked up an intercom phone and glanced up at us. Her eyes were a silky brown-green, a color I would have loved to have captured in a painting if I still could.

"Captain Cooper, front desk," her voice was as smooth as her dark skin and it had southern warmth to it. "Captain Cooper, front desk."

As she lowered the chrome intercom microphone, her eyes locked with mine and in their sparkling, watery way, her eyes said: "Be strong,

302

woman, I've been there before. You can make it." But her brown lids dropped and she went back to her desk chores.

"Mr. and Mrs. Murphy?" a voice barked like a command. Andrew and I turned toward the voice and a tall man with close-cut, gray hair and steel blue eyes nodded toward us.

"I'm Captain Cooper, army doctor," he said.

Andrew extended his hand.

"Captain, Andrew Murphy. Corporal medic of the twenty-third on Okinawa."

Captain Cooper's eyes softened and he seemed to drop his chin out of respect.

"Good to meet you, sir," he said. "If you'll both follow me, I'll take you to your son."

Captain Cooper stepped around the front desk to a staircase. His footfalls were heavy but his manner became friendly.

"So, those fox holes, huh? You saved a few men, I'll bet," he said.

"Yeah. A few," Andrew answered, but he said it like he regretted it.

"You over on Bougainville, too?"

"No."

"I was all over Europe myself. Hey, how about New Zealand? I heard a lot of guys trained down there, too."

"Captain, if you don't mind, can you just tell me what's wrong with my boy?"

"Of course. I apologize. Captain Cooper stiffened up again. "Your son's suffering from delusions, and paranoia, some disorderly thinking, too."

"Can you treat it?"

As Andrew asked that, we stepped up to a third floor landing and a heavy chain link fence that secured a door just behind it stood in front of us. The only light in the dingy, green hallway came from a narrow window covered with a grating at the other end of the hall. A dim, dusty light made the dirty enamel of the walls shine deceptively. A red and white sign read: 'Restricted entry. Department of Psychiatry.'

"We're doing our best," Captain Cooper said. "But you have to understand, this kind of mental illness is very difficult to treat. We're having some success with Thorazine."

Captain Cooper slipped a key into a heavy pad lock and opened the gate. Behind it was the dark door with a window that was reinforced with chicken wire. This door made me feel like I was sinking; it was dimly lit like a confessional, but the chicken wire made it feel like a cage. With the chain link gate now closed and locked behind us, my head began to lighten with fear.

Captain Cooper's keys jangled again, and as he turned the lock on the dirty, ugly door, he paused.

"Please prepare yourselves."

As soon as he pulled it open, a voice in a high pitch cackled out the lyrics to one of those English rock bands songs:

"....aaahhhh I I I see a window and I want to paint it blaaaaaaack!"

My skin tightened as we followed Captain Cooper into the hall.

"Looks like a prison in here," Andrew said. Captain Cooper didn't respond.

"... I I I seeeee a window and I want to paaaiiint it black!"

Each gray door we passed bore a narrow window lined with chicken wire. A thick smell of something like wine and sweat seeped in from under the locked doors as we walked past. The alcohol and odd clean smell of a hospital were missing from this dark place.

"...I see a window! ... I see a window ... paint it black! black! BLACK!"

"Mamamamama ..." a voice moaned somewhere down the hall.

A barred window narrower than the ones in the doors let in a sliver of gray light at the end of the hall, and orange, bare bulbs overhead made the speckled tile glow like hot coals.

"...Paint it blaaack!"

"Mamamama ..."

"...Black! BLAACK!"

The hall closed in on me like it wanted to crush me. Is this what Aunt Clotine felt when they took her away? My heart pounded with fear. Finally, Captain Cooper paused at a door with rust caked in its corners. Andrew looked down at the floor, silent.

"Again, please prepare yourselves,' Captain Cooper repeated. 'We have had to restrain him, but if his last dose of Thorazine has taken effect, we may be able to loosen the straps a bit."

Andrew nodded. I was too afraid even to do that much. Captain Cooper opened the door and stepped in ahead of us.

"Private Murphy, your mother and father are here to take you home now."

Andrew went in ahead of me, and he threw his hands over his eyes as he passed into the room.

"Oh, dear Lord. Dear Lord," he muttered.

I grabbed the side of the doorway for support and felt a squish under my fingers. As I stepped around Andrew and Captain Cooper, I realized the walls of the room were covered by what looked like thin bed mattresses. My heels stuck in the soft floor.

"...No, no, no, no... I heard Ernie's voice cry. My heart pounded

304

and as I stepped into the room, I felt my heart split and crack: Ernie sat on the floor, his bare feet covered with gray dirt as they stuck out from a pair of dirty green pajama bottoms. But his upper body was wrapped like he was in a cocoon, his arms seeming to hug himself. A madman's hug, I thought.

Ernie's cheeks were hollow holes in his pale face and his eyes, oh, his eyes. Once they were full of child wonder, clear as water, and now they vibrated and shifted in the haze of his unclear thoughts. They were crazy ping pong balls in his head.

"…No, no, no…" he whispered and pushed his face against the crust of the wall behind him. His hair, which had allowed his scalp to show through its thinning strands, stuck to the wall as if it was charged by static.

"Not mother, not mother, no, no, no, no…"

Andrew grabbed my arm, and then ran out of the room. Captain Cooper stared at me, obviously not believing Andrew could be so upset.

"This was my husband's special boy, Captain. They played baseball together."

Captain Cooper nodded. He turned to Ernie.

"Private Murphy," he said as he stepped toward him then turned back toward me. "It's best to talk to him like everything's normal," Ernie jerked back as Captain Cooper got closer to him, his head pushing back against the wall and making a cave around him.

"No, no, no," he whispered. Two pearls of dried spit hung off wires of beard on either side of his mouth.

"Private," Captain Cooper said. "Your mother and father are here to take you home."

A machine gun of a scream echoed from another room. Ernie's eyes, scared by the scream, looked like an alert dog and when they met mine, they stared deeply. Moisture started to seep out from their corners.

"My boy, my boy …" I whispered.

I stepped to him and bent down. He never stopped staring, and now his cheeks began to blush red. I pushed my cheek against the white tumbleweeds of his beard, kissing his face.

"Mama? Mama?"

"Shhh… my boy…"

"Mrs. Murphy," Captain Cooper said from behind. "That's the first time he's connected with anyone in the outside world for weeks."

Something about that really made me mad. I turned on Captain Cooper.

"What do you expect, sending boys off into stinking jungles to fight?"

Blessed Mother, give me strength, I prayed as I turned back to

305

Ernie. For the rest of the day, as Captain Cooper explained the doses of medicine we had to keep in Ernie, the doctor we needed to take him to at Harbor General Hospital, the seriousness of Ernie's army discharge, and through his assurances that we could take care of Ernie at home, I stayed near Ernie. Andrew stayed silent. I did feel relief that I had Ernie home and safe again.

As we pulled into the driveway later, Danny and the girls stood on the lawn. Their faces were a picket fence of squinting, curious expressions.

"What the heck they all out here for?" Andrew asked, his first words since seeing Ernie.

"They miss their brother, that's probably all."

I stepped out of the back seat of the Impala, my cotton dress moist along the part of my back that had been against the hot vinyl seat. Ernie's regular clothes lay in a big clump on the floor of the car. Ernie had fallen asleep and as I jostled him to wake up, Danny ran up from behind and hugged my legs.

"Mama's home. I love Mama."

"Everybody step back," Andrew said as he popped open the trunk.

I eased Ernie out of the back seat and his body was a heavy lump of sweat and dirt. He stood up and Susan, always overreacting, screamed.

"Ouch. Stop pushing me," she said.

Martha had elbowed Susan out of the way so that she could be closer to the car. Susan began to whimper.

"You numbskulls!" Andrew barked at them. "Quiet down already."

Ernie rubbed his eyes and looked at the house. When his eyes stopped on the girls, Kathie gasped and jumped back. Martha pushed Susan back toward Ernie. Danny looked up at him and waved.

"Hi, Erwnie!" he said, drawing out the 'r' because he was having a hard time pronouncing his r's that came out mostly as w's.

Ernie laughed and waved back. As I led him toward the breezeway, Andrew came up on his other side and grabbed his arm to support him. Ernie's feet clopped like he had steam irons strapped to them. Just as we passed into the breezeway, with the other kids standing back on the lawn and staring at him like he was Frankenstein's monster, a car screeched up.

"Mo's here!" Kathie hollered.

Andrew nodded for me to let go and as I joined the kids on the lawn, they all sprinted to the side door of Maureen's Corvair. Maureen jumped out from the car, still wearing the little brown bun fall and work apron with the words: 'Bob's Big Boy' printed in red letters on its front. I was surprised to see her at all; ever since she started at El Camino College,

306

her few visits turned into arguments between her and Andrew. Kathie practically jumped on Maureen to give her a hug.

"How's the skolla molla?" Maureen said to Kathie in the funny language they had invented.

"Awright," Kathie answered. "And the Bob's olla?"

"Awright," Maureen said.

Even though their way of talking was real loony to me, and made the rest of the kids feel like they weren't a part of it, I was glad to see at least a couple of the kids get along. Andrew was always worried about Maureen rubbing too much off onto Kathie, but what he didn't understand was the war zone the house had turned into. No one was getting along with anybody, and every nickname and form of hitting you could think of made the house a jungle. I prayed everyday in church for things to get better between all the kids, but so far, my prayers weren't getting answered. Only when Andrew came home, after eleven hours at work and a fuse shorter than it ever was when we were younger, did the house calm down. So to see Maureen and Kathie getting along made me a little happy.

"Is he home?" Maureen asked.

"We just got back. Dad took him in the house. You wanna see him?"

Maureen pulled the bobby pins from her fall and slipped it and the pins into her apron pocket. Kathie reached into Maureen's apron and retrieved the fall.

"Real boss," she said.

Maureen headed up the cement walk to the front door with Kathie and the rest of the girls trailing her like little chicks.

"Hang on," I yelled. "I gotta open the door."

As I pushed the door open, I could see Ernie sitting on the couch next to Andrew. His eyes still wandered like clouds in the wind. Maureen rushed past me with Kathie tagging along so close she could have been a tail.

"Ernie, it's me."

She threw her arms around Ernie. I slid into one of the raspberry chairs: this was a special occasion, after all. Danny jumped up on my lap and the girls gathered around me, leaning against me and obviously afraid. They kept their eyes on Ernie.

"I can't believe you're home," Kathie said. "I'm so glad they let you out." Ernie patted Maureen's arms but his eyes looked as blank as a stuffed animal's. Was he ever going to be normal again? I wondered.

"Hi there, Mo," Andrew said. His words were welcoming but the way he sighed after he said hello sounded as though he was waiting for another fight with her.

"Hi, Dad. Isn't it far-out that he's home?"

"I guess," Andrew said as he shrugged.

"You sound disappointed or something," Maureen said.

"He wasn't discharged because he's a hero, you know? I mean, there was no good reason for it."

"Just like the war," Maureen said.

"At least he's home, Dad," Kathie added.

"Who are you two -- the Ho Chi Minh twins?" Andrew said.

"Let's not go getting all riled," I said. "Ernie's home. We should be thankful the Blessed Mother protected him and brought him back to us, safe. I think we should do a rosary tonight."

"Mo, mo, mo, mo ..." Ernie blurted.

Maureen leaned back, a little afraid. Kathie clutched her waist.

"The doctor said his medicine will sometimes get him stuck on words. Don't be scared, he's still your brother," I said.

"Mo?" Ernie said. His eyes shifted around like he was looking for her and couldn't see that she was right next to him.

"Yeah?" she answered.

"Where's my Mo?"

"I'm here Ernie. Right next to you."

Ernie's eyes landed on her face and for a second, his eyes were his again and the lost, blank expression was gone.

"How's my Mo?" His words plopped slow as corn syrup. I thought it must've been the medication.

"I'm okay. How about you?"

He shrugged and started whispering to himself, his eyes flat as headstone marble.

"What did they give you?" Maureen asked.

"Medicine for my headison. Medicine for my headison."

Ernie started to whistle.

"Thanks for the Memories?" Andrew asked.

I recognized the Bob Hope song, too, but couldn't say why he was whistling it. Maureen turned toward me.

"Mom, what are they giving him, LSD or something?"

"Thornadine. Thorsosine. Something like that."

"Thorazine?" Maureen's mouth dropped. "He's gotta be bad off, probably psychotic, then."

"Oh, Maureen, spare us the college crap," Andrew said.

"Dad, if he's psychotic, then it's like –"

"He ain't psychotic. He's paranoid schizophrenic," he said.

"Okay. But it's gonna take a lot to help him through this. Did the doctors tell you that?"

308

"We have no choice, Mo," I said. "It's home or a state hospital. I want him here."

"I just hope you know it's gonna be like having another kid at home. I mean, this is real serious, Mom."

"I know that. I pray to the Blessed Mother everyday for strength. We'll get through."

We put Ernie to bed awhile later because his medication made him very tired. Maureen stayed for dinner, which turned into argument after argument between her and Andrew. Whether it was the war, the Watts riots, or JFK's assassination, it didn't matter; Andrew and Maureen agreed on nothing. Ever since Kathie's confirmation a year ago, when she asked Maureen to sponsor her, Andrew and Maureen fought.

After dinner, Maureen needed to go home and study. I forced Andrew to walk with me and her to see her off. The front walk was moist from the fog that had crept in from Torrance Beach. Frogs croaked their ribbits in the sump as Andrew stepped past us and walked to the hood of Maureen's car.

"Want me to take a look under the hood?" he asked.

"No, Dad, the car's running okay."

Andrew shrugged and kicked the front tires.

"Could use a little air in the front tires."

"They're okay, Dad."

Andrew stepped around to the back of the Corvair. He kicked the right back tire, making a dull thud with the toe of his wing tip shoe. He stepped into the street to check the left tire and I just shrugged at Maureen. She rolled her eyes -- 'let Dad do his thing' her eyes said. Reaching up, Maureen plucked a bristled flower from the bottle brush tree that grew next to the street. She pulled the flower through her closed left hand just like she did when she was little.

"What the heck ..."

"What, Dad? What's wrong with the car?"

Maureen walked to the edge of the car and I stood behind her. Andrew was crouching down rubbing her bumper.

"Well what is it?" I asked.

"Get a look at this, will you?"

I leaned forward and Andrew pointed at a white bumper sticker. It read: 'Women - N.O.W.'

"Women, now?" I asked. "What does that mean again?"

"It means Maureen wants to be a man, Mary."

"That is so uncool, Dad."

"Those broads are tearing up the streets for equal rights but they just all want to be men."

"Is that what you think, Mom?"

"She agrees with me, and the Church," Andrew answered. He was right, I guess, so it didn't matter if I answered or not.

"Mom, your generation started it. And now you're just part of the generation gap."

"Gap?" I asked.

"Yeah. You used to tell me that during the war, all the women pitched in and ran the businesses while their husbands were overseas. Things were really boss then."

"Horse feathers, Maureen," Andrew said. "Women are staying home and taking care of their families. Broads are tearing up the streets for equal rights but they really want to be men."

"What's wrong with wanting equal rights?" Maureen asked.

"Those broads are just like the coloreds. They're gonna destroy everything that's sacred."

"No, Dad, that's President Johnson's job -- he's the destroyer. We want more freedom. I mean, look at Mom."

"Your mother's a saint!" Andrew growled.

"What if Mom wanted to keep working after the war? What would've happened then?"

"For one, she wouldn't have had a smart aleck like you. Maybe she should a kept working."

"Andrew!"

"It's okay, Mom. I was going anyway."

Maureen bolted for the driver's side door. She stopped and looked at me.

"Mom, if you need any help with Ernie, let me know. If I can't help you make your life equal, I'll at least try to make it easier."

"Don't come around here with your Commie Pinko ideas!" Andrew screamed behind me.

But Maureen had already turned the car on. She put it into gear and drove off, making the damp asphalt slurp and slap under her tires.

"What's happening, Mary? Is the whole world going crazy?"

19.

A few months later, I started to think that Kathie might have mental illness, too. We had just had a week of rainstorms in the early part of January 1968, and part of the Palos Verdes Peninsula had slid into the ocean. But the side of the broken cliff that faced Torrance Beach showed a clear image of the Blessed Mother in the sandy rock. In fact, a bunch of old clam shells ringed the image in a white halo. At least, that's how Agnes described it to me after she saw it. I hurried that morning to get Danny's raincoat and galoshes.

"You're gonna get to see the Blessed Mother," I told him.

He jumped up and down with excitement, even though I wasn't sure he really knew who She was. I grabbed his hand and we ran for the side kitchen door out to the breezeway. Just as I grabbed the doorknob, the phone inside the broom closet made the varnished, pine door rattle.

"Hold on, honey."

I pulled open the hammered copper handle and grabbed the phone as it began to ring again. The vibrating phone tickled my hand a little.

"Mrs. Murphy?" a woman's voice said. Her throat rattled like she had marbles in it.

"Yes?"

"This is eSister Lupe, Deana of Discipline at Bishop Mahoney." She added an 'e' when she pronounced her name with her Spanish accent.

My chest heaved with a spasm. Now what?

"Hi, Sister," I answered. "What do you need?"

"I'm afraid we're going to have to esit down and talk. Your daughter, Kathie, was found esmoking in the girls' lavatory."

"Smoking?"

"A package of ... let me esee." I heard the cellophane rustle of a cigarette package.

"Pall Mallsth."

"I'll kill her."

"Mrs. Murphy?"

"She musta stole 'em 'cause no one in this house smokes."

"Well, however she came about them, we need to esit down and talk."

"Okay. When?"

"This morning if you're free."

I looked down at Danny in his raincoat and galoshes. I wouldn't be able to see the Blessed Mother's face in Palos Verdes. There's going to be hell to pay, her making me miss that!

"I guess."

"She's right here in my office. I can't let her go back to classes."

Danny and I got to the Deana's office an hour later, and when she walked in, the Deana sat behind a large, oak desk with a cross carved into its front. A photo of Bishop Mahoney hung just behind her. The Deana's face was pursed with an angry expression, her full lips turned over each other. The red and white package of Pall Malls, and a half smoked one, sat on the desk between the Deana and Kathie. Sister Lupe stood and nodded to me.

"Sister Lupe," I said. "This is Danny."

Sister Lupe looked at Danny but didn't smile or even nod to him. I guess she didn't like kids much.

"Hello Missuth Murphy," she said. She nodded toward two worn leather chairs in front of the desk. Danny and I both sat.

"Thisth isth a problem with Kathie and esmoking. We found thith in her locker and she was esmoking thith in the girls' lavatory."

She pushed the package of cigarettes and the half-smoked stub toward me with a brown hand that was purple between its creases. I looked at the box, then over at Kathie who stared at her white and black saddle shoes. Danny reached out and grabbed the pack of cigarettes.

"Oh, boy, bubble gum cigarettes."

"No, those aren't for you, Danny." I grabbed the package from him. "I didn't know that Kathie smokes, Sister. And now I suppose I know she's a thief, too."

Sister Lupe leaned back in her chair, touching her hands together in a way that made a pyramid out of their dry, cracked tips. Her dark eyes looked like Oreo cookies behind thick glasses.

"I'm essorry, Missuth Murphy. But thith ith a seriouth violation of the eschool rules."

"You betcha, Sister Lupe. And we're gonna take care of this in a jif."

Sister Lupe's face tightened like she just sucked on a lemon. She reached back and scratched the top of her black veil, making her wimple bow out over forehead.

"I'm afraid isth too late for that, Missuth Murphy. Kathie is expelled from the high eschool."

Sister Lupe pushed a manila file toward me, and on it sat a typed

312

page that was blank where my signature belonged.

"Just esign there, and we will give you her records to take to another high eschool. That's all."

"Sister Lupe, we brought Kathie here to learn discipline. I got nowhere to take her after this."

"I'm essorry. But Kathie broke a major rule here."

"Kathie is the third Murphy to go to Bishop Mahoney. Could you give us another chance, just because of that?"

Sister Lupe reached out and took my hand. She spoke in a quiet tone that was almost a whisper.

"Missuth Murphy, your family is a good family at St. Joan's Parish. We know that. That's altho why it's hard to do thith for uth. Just esign that form. We will all pray for you and for your family."

The pen scratched as I signed my name on the page and Sister Lupe handed me the file. My face must have been bright red, because it was real hot.

"Kathie's records to take with you. Her marks weren't too bad."

"Thank you, Sister Lupe."

We stood to go and Danny kept his eyes on the cigarette pack as if he expected the cigarettes to somehow change into bubble gum. I tapped Kathie's shoulder -- I didn't want to touch her, I was so embarrassed. How was I going to explain to Andrew? I was so disappointed. I pulled open the door, and Sister Lupe hollered.

"Missuth Murphy?"

"Yes?"

"Say hello to Ernie and Louise. Now there were two good estudents, heh?"

We drove in the Herald, with muggy, tropical warmth making our skin moist, and the sun beating down and heating the car. The day was unusually hot for February, even in Southern California. Right then, I could've used a Minnesota ice field, or a sub-zero gust of wind. The car rumbled to a stop and Kathie, Danny, and I walked up the stairs to Torrance High's administration building. After we re-registered Kathie, Danny and I drove off. We passed Two Thirty-Fifth Street and J.H. Hull Middle School. I thought about Susan's straight A's on her last report card, like a chain of arrows pointing to Heaven. She was doing so well in her first year of middle school that we let her join the archery club. And Martha was doing okay in her first year at Torrance High, too. If she kept it up, we'd let her try out for the drill team. What was going wrong with Kathie? I prayed to the Blessed Mother for an answer.

"Would you two stop yelling so much?" Ernie hollered a few days later.

What had started as an argument at the dinner table over abortion escalated into a screaming match as Kathie followed Andrew into the front room. I knew then Maureen had rubbed off on Kathie, the way Kathie argued with Andrew. Andrew was stunned silent by what Ernie had just said and I had to step in between to keep Andrew under control.

"Sick or not, no one talks to me like that," he said between his teeth.

"Honey, calm down. Kathie's got you all riled up."

"Maybe. But that don't excuse a stinking flannel mouth."

'... The end of the Civil War was near ...' the theme song for 'F Troop', Ernie's new favorite show, blared from the TV.

Kathie had already stomped out of the front room and Ernie hollered at the TV each time the Indians were shown.

"... Where Indian fights are colorful sights ..." the theme song went on.

"Whoopppeee!" Ernie screamed at the TV, just as he had every Monday for the last couple of months. Even though he seemed to love the opening, he never stuck around to watch the show itself. Andrew stood nearby and watched Ernie, but I could tell he realized that correcting Ernie wouldn't do any good.

"I'm gonna go watch wrassling."

Andrew stepped into the den and I heard the buzz of the old black and white Motorola, and then the roar of the crowd at the arena.

"Coming to you from the Pan Pacific Auditorium!" the announcer bellowed. "Freddy Blassey is about to defend his title as the –" I pulled the sliding wood door shut to give Andrew some privacy. I admired Andrew so much then because he sure had the right to send Ernie to the den. But he went himself, which was especially nice because Ernie would be shutting off 'F Troop' any second now, anyways.

After the final bugle sounded, Ernie kept the show on just awhile longer. If it was going to be starting in the Hekawi village, then he might watch a little longer. Susan and Martha clanked dishes in the kitchen, and Danny sat by Ernie's feet and connected two orange strips of Hot Wheels track with the flat, bright pink tab that looked like a tongue. Kathie was now in her room and that, above everything else, made the house peaceful for a minute. It was always peaceful when Kathie stayed in her room, even if most of the time when she did, she was crying over some boy. Between arguing or crying, I'd rather have her crying, anyway.

"No, those idiots," Ernie said. He jumped up and popped the color TV console off. He shuffled down the hall and shut his door. The whoosh of rubber wheels as one of Danny's Hot Wheels raced down the track interrupted the quiet. Rock and roll drum music now completely broke the

314

silence.

"Cherokee People!" the singers screeched as Ernie listened to a forty-five.

"...Cherokee Tribe! ..."

I pulled the hall door closed and the music still rattled it. I dipped my fingers in the holy water and blessed myself as I began to pray. Why did I need to pray? First, Ernie was going to be playing this song over and over again. Second, I asked the Blessed Mother to deliver Ernie from this Indian obsession. Third, ever since Ernie started this Indian craze, I felt odd inside, hollow, and almost dark. I didn't like the feeling, and I didn't know what it meant. I needed help somehow with it.

"Blessed Mother, please don't let it get worse." I don't think she heard my prayer that night, though.

A few days later, I got back from mass and when I creaked open the side kitchen door, I expected to hear the song 'Half Breed' blaring from Ernie's room. The house was silent, though, so quiet that even Danny noticed it was too quiet.

"Erwnie?" he yelled.

There was no answer. I dropped my black vinyl purse on the kitchen table and ran back to Ernie's room. When I saw the door thrown wide open, I got scared. I glanced around the room and the phony Indian blanket Maureen got him from Knott's Berry Farm for his birthday lay wrinkled and useless as a deflated balloon on his bed. The pile of flat rocks he insisted were old arrowheads lay on the floor next to his bed. But the old belt with glued-on crow feathers that hung on his wall as some sort of a decoration was missing.

I ran down the hall hollering for him. Danny walked into each bedroom and called for him. Ernie never answered. I grabbed up Danny and ran into the backyard. The rot and decay of summer blew in from the sump.

"Ernie!" I yelled and the sump echoed back. A crow screeched and flew from one of the treetops.

A feeling of dread gripped me. Louise's face popped into my mind and the last time we saw her as she got up from the table at the Hot 'N' Tot and pulled out her engagement ring from her purse. My chest heaved as if a wrecking ball slammed into it. Danny and I ran and checked with neighbors on all sides but no one had seen him. We ran up Two Ninety-Eighth to Arlington down past Pennsylvania and Crenshaw. We couldn't find him anywhere.

"Blessed Mother, he can't be gone. Bring him back! Bring him back! I can't lose another baby." I prayed inside my head. I didn't know what to do next so I ran inside and called Andrew.

315

"What now, Mary?" he said a few minutes later.

"I can't find Ernie."

"Did you check at the Taylors? You know how he likes to wander sometimes."

"I've been over at every neighbor's house. The Scottos. The Butlers. The Skromedas. He's gone Andrew. He's gone!"

"Mary, now calm down. He's an adult so he knows how to take care of himself."

"He's got problems. He can't help himself. What'll we do?"

"Call Torrance Police, Mary. I'll come home to look for him, too."

I called just after I hung up from Andrew and the police said they'd have to wait forty-eight hours, even if he was mentally ill. They also said that since he was an adult, even if they found him, he'd have to want to come home. Danny and I waited on the couch for Andrew to come home, still as we could be. I don't know what I thought would or wouldn't happen, but I knew I wanted to sit on the couch and wait. The side kitchen door burst open and I heard Andrew come in.

"Mary, what'd the cops say?"

Andrew's chest heaved like he had just run home.

"We gotta wait till the day after tomorrow, I s'pose."

"For crying out loud," he said.

Andrew's head shifted like he was nervous, glancing around the kitchen as if he expected Ernie to just walk in or something.

"What time did you see him last?"

"Around seven-thirty this morning."

"Where?"

"In his room. Listening to his music."

"Oh, that Indian crap again, huh?"

I shrugged and nodded. Andrew turned to go back out to the breezeway, and then stopped again. He kissed me.

"You sure look pretty for being so worried."

I patted the side of my own beehive that I started wearing. Andrew's tone of voice made me think of all the times we used to have relations in the middle of the day. Andrew rubbed my face and my eyes began to close on their own.

"Erwnie?" Danny yelled from the living room.

My heart sunk again and Andrew jerked his hand back like a naughty boy.

"Let's go find Ernie," he said. He bolted out the door, through the breezeway and out to the car.

"Come on, Danny. We gotta find Ernie."

I reached into the pocket of my pink sweater I wore as I slid into

316

the front seat of the Impala. I fondled my rosary beads and that made me start to relax.

"Hail Mary," I said to myself.

We drove for over an hour, making our way up and down each street between Lomita Boulevard and Sepulveda. Andrew held my left hand the whole time, and I clutched my rosary with my right. We didn't find Ernie and by the time we pulled back into the driveway, I knew the girls were all home from school and probably hungry. It was five minutes to dinner time after all, and the sky was losing its light. Susan came screaming out to the driveway, tears pouring down her face.

"Now what?" Andrew grumbled.

"My archery bow, Mom! My bow! Someone took it."

"Come on, Susan," I said as I slid out of the car.

My skirt clung to the back of my legs from sweat, I guess. I patted Susan's shoulder and the rough plaid wool of her school uniform scratched against my palm.

"It's gotta be somewhere around the house, Susan."

"No it isn't. I looked everywhere for it. My arrows are gone, too."

Andrew's footsteps echoed in the breezeway and then I knew.

"Andrew!" I screamed.

Susan stepped back, confused. Andrew stood at the opening of the breezeway, his hands rolled into fists and his arms making triangles on his hips.

"Yeah? What, Mary?"

But when I realized that Ernie had Susan's bow and arrows, my mind raced. I screeched at him.

"Ernie has it!"

"What the hell's the matter with you?"

"Ernie's got the bow and arrows."

"Huh?"

"Susan's bows and arrows! He's got 'em and he's gonna hurt someone."

"That's a knuckleheaded idea," he answered. "How do you know that?"

"He's gonna hurt someone. Or else himself!"

"I want my bow back, Mom. Loony Ernie!"

I didn't know why, but when she said that, I went bonkers. I grabbed her by her shoulders.

"Don't ever call him that!"

Her little shoulders became picket fence stakes in my hands as I shook them.

"Mom!" she cried.

317

"Don't call him that! Ever."

Andrew's hand clenched my arm, tighter than I ever felt before. I pulled my hands away from Susan.

"Mary, calm down already. Susan didn't mean anything. Jees."

My stomach twisted from shouting and my face felt strangely hot and cold at the same time. I looked around at the other kids who were now lined up on the front lawn.

"Kathie made dinner, Mom," Martha said.

The way she said it made me realize she was afraid of me. Kathie's eyes watched me like a scared cat, Susan whimpered from her shaking, and Danny stood behind her and stared. I scared them all, that's what I saw in their faces. Andrew grabbed my elbow.

"Mary, let's go make some dinner."

"Don't worry about it," Kathie said. "I already made tuna salad and rye bread."

"You guys eat?" Andrew asked.

"We didn't know what to do," Kathie said. "So we just waited and watched 'What's My line?'"

Andrew led me into the kitchen and pulled out my chair. He tapped the seat gently. As I sat, the kids scraped and scratched their chairs on the linoleum. I felt frozen.

"Come on, Mary. You gotta eat. There's nothing we can do right now."

I collapsed into the chair and Andrew dug into the stainless steel bowl and dropped the lettuce with shreds of mayonnaise and tuna onto my plate.

"Want some bread, Mommy?" Danny asked. He held out a piece of rye bread that twisted under his grip.

"No thanks, Danny."

"Pass the non-fat," Martha said. Kathie slid the aluminum pitcher of reconstituted milk to her and as Martha poured a glass, it made a bright white stream into her aquamarine, aluminum tumbler. Martha went to take a sip, then paused and looked at me.

"Didya want some milk, Mom?"

I shook my head. I could barely chew the bite of tuna salad in my mouth, and the thought of a gulp of no-fat milk would have made my twisted stomach tighten an extra knot. The kids around the table and Andrew at the head of it, with a forkful of lettuce going into his mouth, formed a tunnel in my mind all of a sudden. Its sides were closing in on me and I pushed back from the table before it swallowed me up.

"I can't eat."

I left Andrew and the kids and I went into the living room. 'To

Tell The Truth' glowed on the TV, with Kitty Carlisle in one of her nutty outfits bantering at Peggy Cass. My eyes wandered to the holy water font by the hall door. Dragging my feet across the carpet, I dipped my fingertips into the cool water, and then touched them to my forehead.

"Blessed Mother," I prayed. "Please protect Ernie and bring him back home."

I kneeled on the carpet, its green, high-low pile pushing into my kneecaps, and began to pray below the crucifix that hung over the fireplace.

I guess the kids finished dinner and got to their homework and I felt Andrew just brush past me at some point on his way to watch TV. When the phone rang, its crisp bell startled me from my prayer and I heard Andrew turn down the TV right as Gomer Pyle said: "Gollll -eee."

"Yello," Andrew answered. "Yeah. This is him. Okay. I understand."

What? What did he understand? Was Ernie --

"We'll be down to see him in about fifteen minutes, chief."

Andrew dropped the phone back onto its cradle without even saying 'goodbye.' He reached behind him and rubbed his neck.

"Ernie?" I urged.

Andrew nodded.

"Is he ..." I could barely breathe.

"He's okay, Mary. They got him at the downtown Torrance Police Station"

"Why? Did he do something? Where was he? Why didn't they –"

"Let's get over there and find out."

"So you'll understand," Detective Barton said a few minutes later as we sat in wooden chairs in the Torrance Police Station. "He'll have to stay in custody at Harbor General for observation."

"How long?" Andrew asked.

"Seventy-two hours," Detective Barton said. He reached up and scratched his dirty blonde, butch haircut.

"He's not a crook," I said.

"We know that, Mrs. Murphy. But with shooting arrows and all at the officers, he's a danger to others and himself. Not to mention that when we found him, he was, well, exposed."

"What?" Andrew growled.

"He was naked. He was naked. Waving his ... manhood at us."

Detective Barton looked at me and I could tell he was uncomfortable with what he had to say next. His voice dropped into a whisper.

"He was fully excited."

"Oh," Andrew said.

"He must have some serious problems, if you know what I mean."

"How long before he can come home?" Andrew asked.

"If the doctors at Harbor General say he's sick, we couldn't make any charges stick anyhow. Just a couple of days. You got any other kids?"

"Yes," I answered.

"Boys?" he said with a hint of hope in his voice.

"Just one. The rest are girls."

"You may want to keep close tabs on him for awhile, if you know what I mean."

"I don't," Andrew said.

"It's just that with my experience, when a guy's a flasher, it sometimes follows with other perversions."

"None of the girls go near him, anyway. They're too afraid of him," Andrew said.

I know Andrew thought about the same thing I did at that second: his discharge from the army for molesting the Vietnamese girl.

"Except Susan," I added.

"Well, you should keep her away from him for now."

"So he didn't really break the law?" Andrew pressed.

"Trespassing at Madrona Marsh. Indecent Exposure. That's it. Except, when he shot the rubber-tipped arrows at the one officer, well, he's just lucky our guys aren't trigger-happy."

"I wanna see him," I said.

"Yeah. Okay, Mrs. Murphy."

Detective Barton led us through a hallway, and as I followed behind his thick shoulders and blonde hair that looked like a scrub brush, all I could feel was relief that Ernie was okay. Det. Barton stopped in front of a cell.

Ernie sat on a bed in the jail cell, shirtless, and it looked like his shirt was now a loincloth wrapped around his middle. When Ernie looked up at me, the mud lines he had painted on his face made the whites of his eyes sparkle brightly. I felt my head lighten as if I were being sucked by a Kirby vacuum cleaner into another moment.

Artie? I thought. I saw Gopher Foot around the fire, and I felt Artie enter me under the lean-to. My heart pounded as Ernie's face became Artie's and back to Ernie's again. A dark gloom descended over me like a curtain.

Ernie was ordered by the court to spend the next month at Norwalk State Mental Hospital. The darkness that fell over me when he was taken there stayed with me like a rain cloud that just wouldn't go away.

'Forty days and forty nights' a voice said in my head. Was it the Blessed Mother? 'You are being tested like Noah, and Job -- do not fear, ' the voice said to me.

The week before Ernie was to come home, I was driving home from church and decided to stop by Maureen's. She had been working the night shift at the Bob's Big Boy and she didn't have classes on Thursdays. As I walked up to her apartment door, I could hear the screeching and scratching of guitar music and then the screaming voice of that Janet Poplin, or whatever her name was.

"...Take another little piece of my heart now baby ... Take it!" Her voice was so hoarse. Thinking about the church choir music, and the singers like Nat and Judy Maureen had heard growing up, I didn't understand how she could like this strange rock and roll.

"Take it!" the voice howled again. Just then, I heard the low rumble of a man's voice. I knocked on the door.

"...I say come on, come on, come on ..." Janet screeched on. The man I heard now laughed. I knocked again.

"Mo?"

The record needle scratched and the music stopped. I heard footsteps and shuffling around just inside.

"Mom?"

"Yeah."

"Hold on!" she said. A little more shuffling happened just before the door creaked open. The smell of burning alfalfa struck a nostalgic chord in me.

"You burning something?" I asked.

"No. Hi, Mom. What're you doing?"

Maureen's voice shook like she was nervous and her eyes were red like she had been reading or something. The hair stood out on the back of my neck.

"I was on my way back from church and just wanted to stop over and say hi."

A boy of about twenty with long, curly brown hair and thick, dark sideburns waved his hands in the air like he was fanning someone. He wasn't wearing a shirt.

"Mom, this is Kirk. Say hi to my mom, Kirk."

"Hi, Mom," he said, snorting a laugh and bobbing his head like a brown mop.

"How do you do?"

When I glanced back at Maureen, her arms were folded and it looked to me like her blouse was on inside-out. I didn't want to know why.

"You cooking alfalfa in here or something?" I asked.

"Huh?" she answered.

"Smells like alfalfa, or burnt peanuts."

Kirk snorted another laugh and Maureen glared at him.

"That smell," I said again, feeling kind of stupid that Maureen hadn't even asked me in yet.

"Just incense, Mom. That's all."

"Why are your eyes so red?"

"Who are you -- Jack Webb or someone? I hope you didn't come here just to give me the third degree."

I stepped back onto the front walk because now I knew Maureen didn't want anymore company. That snorting smart-aleck Kirk was probably enough.

"Maureen, I wanted to talk to you. That's all. Did you know Robert's winning the state? They think he may give his speech in a couple of hours."

"The polls don't close till eight. He can't give any speech till after that. Figure on sometime tonight."

"Wouldn't you like to go to Los Angeles and see him? I mean, a Kennedy right nearby and all."

"Traffic wouldn't be so cool, Mom. It'll get all jammed up around the Ambassador Hotel when he shows up."

"Well, I guess I'll be getting along, then. Just wanted to say hi."

"Where's the holy shadow?" she asked, referring to Danny.

He had lately taken an interest in making an altar by draping bath towels over the clothes hamper. It was so cute how he wore a matching towel as his vestment. Anything that encouraged him to follow his dream to the priesthood was fine by me.

"Danny's out in the car. I wanted to see if you were home first. But since you're busy and all."

"Yeah. Kirk and I are going to study for an astronomy test."

I crossed myself quickly and Maureen scowled.

"What?" she asked.

"Astronomy's bad, Maureen. It's full of that Age of Aquarius song stuff. You better watch your soul."

"Astronomy, Mom. Not astrology. Astronomy's a science. It's what all the Apollo astronauts study before they go into orbit. So they know what they're looking at."

"Well, you just watch out for your soul, anyway."

Maureen shrugged and I saw the inverted seam of her blouse make her shoulder bulge. I tugged on the corner of the seam on her shoulder.

"This a new fad or something?"

"What?"

"Wearing your blouse inside out?"

Maureen's face blushed and Kirk snorted a laugh behind her.

Maureen fumbled to straighten the shoulder out.

"No. I guess I just put it on backwards."

I wished the little bell inside my head that always told me when the kids were lying hadn't just rung. But standing on Maureen's front stoop, talking to her in her doorway, I just knew I had to ignore the bell. Her life was hers.

"Okay, I'll let you two get back to your books then. Bye, Kirk."

"Catch you later, Mom!" he hollered.

As Danny and I drove home, I couldn't explain what I was feeling. Maureen's music, her friend with long hair, her incense, all of it was so strange to me. And I felt real uncomfortable with her, like neither of us knew what to say to each other. Or else, like I didn't belong, or that she for sure didn't belong to us anymore. I raised another stranger, just like Louise. Was that all I could do? Raise strange children, or strangers?

When Ernie was let out of Norwalk State Hospital, Andrew and I picked him up and Andrew was again very patient and kind with Ernie. And Ernie, as usual after a state hospital stay, was in a daze for the next couple of weeks. His doctors tried all kinds of new medicines on him, but mostly he sat around staring off. Andrew never lost patience with him and seemed to always know what was going on with Ernie. Andrew read his medicine bottles, then went to Torrance Library and looked up the chemicals and all their side effects. I admired that he could read those technical books and understand them at all.

By the time the younger kids were back in school in fall, Ernie was starting to act a little more normal. At least he wasn't sitting around everyday staring at the ground. The only effect the last hospital stay seemed to have at all, was that it caused him to be afraid at night. Andrew thought it was maybe all the tests, or shock treatments, or something, so we decided he shouldn't be left alone. Keeping in mind what the doctor said about his sex problems, we didn't want any of the girls to share a room with him. Danny was still afraid of the dark thanks to the girls sitting him down to watch 'Chiller' a few times when Andrew and I were at choir practice. It seemed to solve both of their problems by letting them share the bedroom.

The next couple of months both of the boys seemed to be doing better and as Thanksgiving approached, Ernie became distracted by his Indian hobby again. As the year inched closer to November, Ernie was getting more excited to reenact the first Thanksgiving. I don't know where he got the idea we were going to, but he was always full of crazy ideas so I wasn't surprised.

When we had all the construction paper witches, ghosts, and pumpkins hanging in the front room windows for Halloween, Ernie asked everyday when Thanksgiving was. The Sunday before Halloween, the sky

323

had turned bright clear and the Santa Ana winds blew all the moisture out of the sky and out of our noses. The frogs in the sump must have thought it was summer again, or else were hot from the eighty-degree day, because they croaked and hollered in the middle of the afternoon. Only the long shadows from the sump's trees let us know it was fall. Andrew was working in the garage and I sat at the kitchen table helping Martha sew her Bat Girl Halloween costume. Danny sat next to us drawing a castle and a witch with his Crayolas. He held up his drawing.

"That look like Baby Daphne on her broom?" he asked. Baby Daphne was a witch who hosted a children's TV show that came on after Bozo every day. Danny had drawn a perfect castle with a round tower in the middle. And just off one side of the tower, a shadow in the shape of a witch on a broom hung in the pink and blue sky.

"Yeah. Looks like her to me," I said.

Andrew walked in and cranked on the knobs on the kitchen spigot. He rubbed his hands hard enough to take the skin off.

"Something the matter, Andrew?"

"Damn mower still isn't working right. It's so hot, too."

"Why don't you take a break? Want a Delaware Punch or Bubble Up?" I asked.

Andrew walked over and slipped his arms around my waist. I felt my cheeks blush -- I didn't like the kids to see us get too physical. He shook his head and kissed my cheek.

"I could go for a nap, though, my Mary."

My cheeks flared even more, even though Martha didn't look up as she cut the black felt with pinking shears. I knew what Andrew meant and I couldn't believe he was serious. It had been six months or so since the last time we took that kind of nap and that's when all the kids were at the Spring Carnival at St. Joan's.

"We gotta get Martha's costume done."

"It's okay, Mom. I can finish the pinning and pattern cutting."

Martha being helpful! How many times could I have used her help before and now, she says it's okay.

"Danny's gonna need his nap –"

"Susan'll make sure he takes his nap," Martha said. "Go ahead, Mom."

Andrew kissed my cheek again and I felt my insides turn into butter. The smell of his sweat from working in the yard made my skin tingle. I pushed away from the table.

"We're gonna take a nap," I said. I surrendered.

We got to the bedroom so quickly, I wasn't even sure my feet ever touched the ground between the kitchen and our room. Andrew pushed the doorknob lock with his right hand as he pulled at his belt with his left. The bedroom was hot and a leafy musk blew through the cotton and lace sheers that covered the window overlooking the sump. I closed the window quickly and when I turned, Andrew was already under the blankets, naked, his head resting on his elbow.

"Andrew?" I said, touching the corner of my eye to remind him to take off his glasses. It wasn't just because glasses aren't for bed, but more because I didn't want Andrew to see the plump and lumpy mounds my hips and rear end had become. As he pulled off his horned rims, I looked past his slight double chin, past his graying flat top hair, into those eyes that sparkled eighteen again. Could he also see past my red hair that was becoming rusty gauze, and my rear end that was big as the Impala's back seat, and my legs that were both thicker than the water heater? Did he remember my skinny body and my firm breasts? If he couldn't see past the lumpy wreck I had become, he wasn't letting on.

My house dress seemed to float off me and I slid into the bed next to his comfortable warmth. For the next hour, we were together, alone, one, then two, alone, together, again. I could only hear his sweet breaths and the frogs outside.

"Mommy, come on," Danny whined outside the bedroom door a little while later. "I want to take a nap with you!"

He had just knocked on the door, causing the deep, sawing rhythm of Andrew's snoring to skip a breath. Andrew lay on my pillow and his right arm lay over my breasts. The white sheet that covered us, stained a pale gray-yellow from years and naps past, rose and fell with each of Andrew's breaths.

"Mommy, come on!"

The brass doorknob twisted and scratched as Danny tried to open it.

"Hold on," I said. Again, Andrew's snoring skipped a beat then revved like a rusty zipper. I slid out from under his arm. My house dress tickled my skin as I slipped it back on. When I opened the bedroom door, Danny stood in his Bozo pajamas, staring up at me.

"Okay, come on in."

I lay back down, this time on top of the sheets. I patted the bed between Andrew and me and when Danny tried to slide under the sheets, I pulled them tight. He didn't need to see his father naked.

"No," I said. "Let's sleep on top."

Danny shrugged and lay down between us. He began to nod off, rubbing his eyes. He sat up all of a sudden, jolting Andrew enough to change Andrew's breathing rhythm again. I put my finger to my lips.

"Shh."

"Mommy, it's too hot," he whispered.

It probably was too hot there between us so I patted the bed behind me. As Danny bounced down the bed, Andrew jostled then rolled over. I was now sandwiched between my two loves, my husband and my little priest. After Danny nodded off, I felt my eyelids turn into bricks.

The bed was suddenly vibrating after what couldn't have been more than a few minutes. My eyes popped open and Andrew's back was still toward me and his breath now rumbled evenly. I glanced to my left and knew where the shaking was coming from: Danny lay next to me, but he pumped his legs together, making his knees knock. I realized he was wide awake and it was right then I saw that his jeans were pulled down. I tapped his arm and he jerked his hands from his crotch and looked at me like a cornered bunny.

"What are you doing?"

Danny shook his head, then reached down and pulled up his white underwear. It was obvious he was excited.

"Nothing, Mommy."

"Why were your underpants down?"

Danny yanked his pants up and zipped them.

"Just 'cause."

I guess I had caught him playing with himself. Not only was he too young for that but the very idea of that sin terrified me for his soul.

"That's very vulgar," was all I could think of to say. "You shouldn't touch yourself like that ever again."

Danny rolled over and faced me; he looked so much like Andrew must have looked at that age. One of his missing front teeth made his mouth look like a pumpkin's and the puff of brown-blonde hair on top of his head made him look like an ostrich. His brown eyes began to moisten.

"I'm sorry, Mommy. I won't do again."

I kissed his forehead and pulled him to me. Why was he touching himself that way? How could he even know his privates did anything else other than help him go pee?

A week later, it happened again. It was Halloween day and even though the hot summer temperatures had dropped to seventy-two by then, it was still sticky outside. The rule in our house was that if you were under eleven years old, you had to take a nap before you could go trick-or-treating. Danny lay down at four-thirty, an hour before dinner, his Doctor Smith mask and light blue, polyester uniform that looked just like the character's costume from 'Lost in Space' set up on a chair next to his bed. We had argued in the costume row at Hall's Five-and-Ten because he originally wanted to go as the Flying Nun. It took a lot of convincing to get him to understand that his costume had to be for boys.

326

When I went to wake him up at five-thirty, he was flapping his knees and rubbing his privates again.

"Danny!"

He jumped up so hard that his head slammed against the wall. But I didn't care because I was so scared for his soul.

"Is it time for trick-or-treating?" he asked as if I didn't see him.

"It won't be if you keep doing that!"

"What?"

Blessed mother, I thought, now he's lying, too. Why was he acting like this? What had I done to cause such sinful behavior? Ernie lay in his twin bed across the room. He stuffed his face into his pillow and laughed.

"You wanna go trick-or-treating?"

"Yeah."

Ernie laughed again and muttered into his pillow.

"Ernie, please, this is serious. Promise me something, Danny."

"What?"

"Don't touch yourself anymore. It's gonna become a habit and it's very sinful. You won't grow up to be a priest if you keep sinning like that."

20.

"Hello, Dee-yer," Daisy said through a red, net veil that hung down from a red satin pillbox hat. She stepped in the front door, clutching her white gloves and shifting her gaze between my stomach and my face. I instantly held my breath as a cloud of rose water surrounded me like a stinky halo. Daisy had decided to surprise us for Thanksgiving.

"You look – healthy," she said after giving me the once over.

She jerked her head around to look at the house. Seeing it for the first time, her nose crinkled up as much as mine must have from the burn of her perfume. Andrew stepped in behind her, huffing and puffing as he set down her green plaid suitcase. I wanted to hit him right then; with a dust rag in my hand and fat feet and plump legs sticking out from under the orange and brown moo-moo I wore, I felt naked.

"Surprise, Mary. Look who's here!"

"Well, where are my grandkids I've never met?"

"They're all at school still, except—"

Danny ran out from the hall and when he saw Daisy, he stopped and stood close behind me. Daisy took such a breath that I thought the air had cut her nose; she must have been surprised to see how much Danny looked like Andrew.

"Looks just like him," she said. She lifted the netting from her face, and it was then that I saw the deep lines that had gouged her face from the corners of her eyes. Coke bottle glasses made her eyes bug out of her head. Edges of brown hair that seemed more like brown plastic than soft hair stuck out from under her hat. Could this little, shriveled thing really be proud Daisy? As she leaned toward Danny, I felt bad for her.

"He's the spitting image of my Andrew." She turned with a slow, awkward creak and tapped Andrew's chest with the back of her hand.

"You should a told me how much he takes after you. Come here, boy!"

Danny pressed hard against my side.

"Don't be shy, now. I'm your Gram Murphy."

She reached out for Danny and I saw veins on the back of her hands that looked like brown and purple lightning bolts. I didn't know what to do so I pried Danny's hands from my waist and nudged him toward Daisy.

328

"Go on, honey. It's your grandma who's here to visit."

She grabbed Danny and pulled him to her into a bone-thin hug. Stepping back, she took his face in one of her little hands and it was then I saw the mahogany cane she was using.

"Why aren't you in school? Sick or something?"

"He missed the December cut-off this year, so we decided to let him stay back till next year."

"Lord knows what he's gonna learn staying home, hmm, dee-yer? Unless he wants to learn about being barefoot and pregnant, that is."

Ernie let out one of his Indian howls. It seemed to make the whole house vibrate.

"Whoo-hoo-whoo-hoo!" he howled.

Daisy startled back and jammed her cane into the carpet to keep her balance. Andrew rushed around past her and down the hall.

"You got an animal in the house?"

Daisy glanced around the room again and her mouth twisted as her eyebrow arched. She shifted her weight on her cane.

"Seems like it by the look of things."

"How long we get to have you for company, Daisy?"

"Just till I get affairs settled."

"What affairs?"

"Are you feeble-minded or doesn't Andrew tell you anything? I'm moving out here for the weather. I'm not spending the last few years I got left in an ice box."

"Who-hoo-whoo-hoooooooooooooooooooooooo!" Ernie howled again.

"Shut the hell up!" Andrew growled as he led Ernie out of the hall. I looked past them at my Pieta holy water font and I had the urge to run to it and bless myself but I hadn't gotten a chance to pick up holy water from the rectory. As Andrew got Ernie settled down on the davenport, I could almost hear Daisy's accusing words those years ago: *...He doesn't look much like Andrew to me...* As she turned to face him, my skin tightened and chilled -- was she going to ignore him, laugh at him, or criticize him?

But she didn't say anything. She didn't even look at me and roll her eyes; instead, she reached out and patted Ernie's face.

"Do you remember me? I'm your Gram Murphy," she said, almost whispering it. I guess spending all those years in that ice box Hopkins had chilled her down. When each of the kids got home awhile later, she hugged them, talked to them, even sat and watched 'Here Comes the Brides' with them.

The whole time I chopped celery and made onions sweat for the turkey dressing, Daisy sat with the kids laughing and talking. Mo, who had

329

come over early to help me cook, alternated between peeling potatoes and laughing with Daisy. Even if she still didn't like me, Daisy sure seemed to love the kids. "Right on, Gram Murphy," Kathie said at one point. "You're groovy," Martha added. I always was 'right off' with Kathie and 'so not groovy' according to Martha. The kids were taking to her and I knew then I could put up with anything she would dish out to me as long as she was good to the kids. And if Daisy hadn't shown up right then, there's no telling what permanent damage Danny might have suffered.

"What're you making there, dee-yer?" Daisy asked me the Sunday morning after Thanksgiving. She hobbled into the kitchen, her wig a little crooked over a fringe of her white hair. Her pink, terry cloth slippers scraped on the linoleum as she walked over and to the table and paused.

"Hotcakes.' The thick, white goo plopped in the stainless steel bowl as I mixed it.

"Before mass?" She loosened her quilted, pink satin robe from around her shoulders.

"Just the batter now. Thought we'd whip 'em up when we got home and have a nice sit-down breakfast. It'll be a jif when we get home from mass."

"I'm not sitting at any picnic table," she said, tapping the top of our burgundy-stained, pine dining table. It was a picnic table with benches but that was all we could afford.

"We could set up one of the living room chairs for you."

"Don't bother. I just have arthritis in my legs, not my back. You keep stirring that batter, you're gonna make hockey pucks instead of hotcakes. You gotta leave the batter lumpy and to rest."

I always wondered why my pancakes were so heavy -- maybe Daisy was right about something. Couldn't hurt to go along. I stopped stirring.

"You sleep okay?" I asked.

"Good enough for being arthritic and all. It was a little warm, though. Seventy degrees in November. For crying out loud. You need any help with breakfast?"

"No. If you could go wake the kids up for mass, that'd help."

Daisy shrugged and her little feet shuffled as the bottom of her cane popped against the floor. I watched her almost struggle through the kitchen doorway and saw the slight hump between her shoulders that must have been her spine. In all the time we lived with Daisy before, I never once saw her in a robe and slippers. Daisy was different.

I slid the bowl of batter into the fridge. The stack of plates on the table looked like olive green, plastic hotcakes as I grabbed them to set the table.

"What the --" Daisy screeched from down the hall. "Leave him

330

be!" her voice seemed to rattle the walls and sent a shock through me; I hadn't heard her screech like that since the days of her drunk fights with Gerald. I rounded the kitchen door in a panic.

"For cripes sake!" Andrew yelled as he rounded our bedroom door into the hall.

As I got to the hall door, Danny came running out. He tugged on his underpants to pull them up as he rubbed his left hand against his leg.

"Don't kill me, Mommy. Please don't get mad!" he cried.

Then I saw that his hand sort of shined with something and as he wiped it on his leg, I could smell the foul seed.

"Pee-yew, what smells?" Kathie cried as she ran up from behind Danny.

When I realized what was on Danny's hand and now his leg, my stomach churned and pushed like it was going to force itself up my throat. I grabbed Danny's hand and wiped the rest of the semen from it.

"No, Andrew!" Daisy screamed.

"I'll kill you!" Andrew yelled.

I bolted past Kathie and Danny and the rest of the girls who were now a yawning, confused bunch in the hall. Turning the corner into the boys' room, I saw Andrew, still in his T-shirt and light blue boxers, sitting on top of Ernie. His arms and fists were jackhammers as they beat Ernie. Daisy was flat against the wall, her face bright red.

"Andrew!" I screamed. Ernie wriggled under the attack and I could see the top of his thigh and rear end. He was obviously naked under the gray, wool blanket that he tugged and pulled to keep himself covered.

"A kid!" Andrew snorted through his red face. "A little boy now!"

He punched at Ernie who was now a ball under the blanket. Lunging at Andrew to pry him off, I felt an arm fly into my stomach and I flew against the wall. The impact I made against the wall somehow flipped Ernie's phonograph player on.

"Cherokee People!" the forty-five record blared. "Cherokee tribe!"

The song broke Andrew's rage long enough for him to see me on the floor.

"Oh, my Mary!" he cried as he climbed off Ernie.

He lifted me to my feet. I was dazed, just able to catch my breath as I stood. I noticed him rub his left shoulder and wondered if it was bothering him again. But he reached out and pulled me to him.

"My Mary!" He pulled me closer and he started to shake. Tears rolled down my shoulder.

"...They took the whole Indian nation..." the song played on. Ernie, still under the covers, pulled himself into a ball and began to whimper and I saw blood on the bed. The girls cried in the hall, Daisy

331

stood against the wall sobbing, and I didn't know why I was so calm.

"I'm sorry, Mary. So sorry," Andrew choked between tears.

Two hours after Andrew beat Ernie, three men in white coats showed up at the front door. Armed with papers signed by Dr. Watson and Dr. Stevenson, they grabbed Ernie out of his room, bound his arms in a gray strait jacket, and led him to the back of an ambulance. Following them out to the curb, I felt my body pull and tear like it was being stretched. Ernie kicked and screamed but the three men were stronger. They forced Ernie into the back of the ambulance.

"Noooo! Momma!! Noooo! Please!" he screamed. "Don't let them take me!"

'Blessed Mother,' I prayed, closing my eyes and trying hard to ignore his cries. 'Please let Camarillo State Hospital cure him. Please.'

"Mrs. Murphy?" one of the men in white interrupted my prayer. His voice sounded like tissue paper.

"Hmm?"

"You wanna sign this and get it over with?"

I looked at the paper, and the words 'involuntary, indefinite commitment' stung my eyes like little accusations. I was his mother -- why couldn't I get him through this? What did I do to cause it, and why couldn't I do something to cure it?

"Ma'am?"

"You'll really help him?"

The young man's eyes shifted and he tugged his collar -- I guess he didn't have an answer for me.

"We hope so."

As I scrawled my name on the thin, black line, it felt like I was slicing Ernie's throat and a piece of my heart. When the young man opened the door to get into the cab of the ambulance, Ernie screeched one more time.

"Mommy, don't let them take --" the door slammed shut. The ambulance pulled away and I felt like I'd never see my baby again. My whole body felt stuffed with cotton.

I ran into the house, to the holy water font to bless myself and its bottom scratched dry against my fingertips. That second, the whole world disappeared -- Ernie, Andrew, Daisy, the others kids, all of my life was swallowed up by one worry: I needed more holy water. Running into my room, I grabbed up the glass flask with the cross on top from inside my bra drawer and ran for the Herald. Its engine sputtered to life and I drove off.

When I got to St. Joan's parking lot, it was just after two in the afternoon and the trunks of the palms and pines in the convent garden made long, deep shadows against the asphalt. The sun was at such a low angle that it bore into the stained glass windows of the altar and they reflected the sunlight back with golden sparkles.

"Please, someone, holy water, holy water ..."

Stepping up to the sacristy door, I tugged on it and it was locked. I ran the length of the church to the main doors. One of the stained, oak doors was open, and I swung it wide as I tried to catch my breath. I ran into the foyer. The door closed behind me, its old, wrought iron latch catching and echoing crisply through the empty nave. As I stepped into the nave, I felt my breath suck from my body -- in the very front pew, just off the center aisle, a priest kneeled with his hands folded, obviously praying.

But what was amazing was the hot, fall sun that seemed to cut through the stained glass windows above the altar and beam down to his head. A mosaic of rainbow light floated on either side of the priest, making dust particles dance through the beams like snowflakes in a Hopkins flurry. His bowed head made him look like a sleeping child and the sunshine gave him a halo all around his head and shoulders.

He looked round when he heard me and it was Father Crawford with his face that always seemed worried about something -- like the face of a saint. When he smiled, his eyes still seemed to be narrowed with pain.

"Hello, Mary Murphy."

His voice had a gentle rumble and some sort of a light, eastern accent. I don't know what came over me, but I felt the blood rush to my face and scald it with embarrassment. My knees even started to shake and the only thing I could think to do was to hold the flask out to him.

"You need some holy water?"

I nodded, but I couldn't say anything. It was like I was in the presence of Saint Jerome. Father Crawford's slicked hair and his hands, folded in front of his black shirt and coat, made him look like a man of the Lord. He reached out and took the flask from my hand, and when our fingertips brushed, I felt some sort of an electric spark. My heart began to pound.

"You want to sit while I get the holy water?"

"Yes, Father," my voice squeaked.

"All right," he said and smiled that far-away smile again. He turned and walked to the altar and I was glad he turned away from me.

Crash!

As I slid into a pew, my foot tapped a loose kneeler and it slammed down. Father Crawford had already stepped into the sacristy so he couldn't have been disturbed by my clumsiness. I lifted the kneeler back into position. My eyes fell on the Blessed Mother in her niche to the right of the altar, with the basket of lilies at her feet, and a wave of peace crashed over me. I began to think about Connie, and Kay, and Agnes, too and I felt sad;

I missed the Blessed Mother Club. We hadn't met for coffee in a couple of months and I guess it was all over. I talked to all of them once in awhile, but I couldn't remember why the club ended and right then, I wanted to see them all so bad.

Father Crawford interrupted my reminiscing. He carried the flask of holy water in one hand, and as he stood in front of the altar, with the huge crucifix above, he kneeled and genuflected. He held the flask out from his body, and with his head still bowed, mumbled a blessing. It was spoken so softly, I couldn't tell if it was Latin or English. He genuflected again, and then stepped away from the altar.

"Here you go, Mary."

As I took the flask from his hands, Father Crawford clasped my hand between his two hands.

"Go in peace, Mary Murphy."

I pulled my hand from between his because it felt wrong.

"Thank you," I muttered. I turned and ran down the aisle.

Peace wasn't with me at all for the next few weeks before Christmas. We thought that Ernie being gone and all would return things to normal. It didn't.

The week before Christmas, Andrew and I sat in an auditorium across from Torrance High. Hot lights poured down on us and the rest of the parents who sat in the row of brown, metal folding chairs along with us. A camera on wheels was aimed at a line of students and Susan was up next for the diocese spelling bee. She represented St. Joan's School and was the top speller there. We just knew she could spell anything, and besides that, she had to win: with all her sensitivity, she'd be upset for months. She was the only one of the kids who cried when Ernie was hauled off -- she missed him as much as I did, I think.

"Quarter," the word announcer said.

Susan cleared her throat and straightened the white collar of her uniform blouse that stuck out from under her gray and blue plaid pinafore.

"Quarter. Q-U-A-R-T-E-R. Quarter."

"Correct," the word announcer said.

Andrew caught my hands as I went to clap -- we had been asked not to and I almost forgot. But it was the fourth round, and lots of students from other parish schools had already dropped out.

In the next round, two more students missed. The line of students was now down to just nine. Since it had started with fifty or so, you could tell how important each word was becoming.

"Squirrel," the word announcer said to Susan.

Susan brushed aside a loose bang, tugged at the St. Dominic Savio pin on the left breast of her uniform, cleared her throat, and then spelled it like she was firing machine gun shots. This time, she looked over at us and smiled. I was so proud of her, standing up there by herself, spelling away. I never could do anything special like spelling when I was ten years old. And to think that all the classrooms in the whole diocese would see this on their closed-circuit TV's made me glad that Susan looked so pretty in her uniform. She was the best speller and the prettiest for sure. The line-up of spellers was now just four students. And Susan was still in the group.

"Stationery," the announcer said. Susan stepped up, licked her lips and was about to start.

"The kind you write on," the word announcer added. I didn't know what he meant -- I thought that's what the word meant.

Susan leaned forward and cleared her throat, but I saw her eyebrows wrinkle for the first time during the whole spelling bee.

"Stationery. S-T-A-T-I-O-N -- uhh ..."

"Do you want me to repeat the word?" the announcer said.

Susan shook her head and cleared her throat again. Andrew's chair creaked as he leaned forward.

"Stationery," Susan said again. "S-T-A—"

"I need to caution you, speller. You must repeat the same sequence of letters you already began with. If you change them in any way, you will be disqualified."

Susan bit down on her lower lip and nodded, and I saw a panic in her eyes. I wanted to run to her and tell her she didn't have to win.

"Stationary. S-T-A-T-I-O-N-A-R-Y. Stationary."

A buzzer sliced the air like a power saw.

"That's it," Andrew muttered as he collapsed back against his chair. He always hated it when the kids lost anything.

"Sorry," the announcer said. "You spelled stationary as in standing still."

Susan's eyes shifted in confusion. Her face glazed over red with embarrassment and fear. That was the first, and as the spelling bee went on, only sound-alike word in the competition. Susan stepped away from the microphone and I could see her eyes were two shiny, green marbles, wet with tears.

She didn't talk the whole ride home and didn't want to go to Farrell's for an ice cream treat. I hoped Andrew would say something to cheer her up but he just drove the Herald without saying a thing. Susan must've felt like a loser and I should have told her I felt like that a lot, too, but I didn't think of it then.

Two days later, though, Susan wasn't crying: she was spelling every big word that she heard on TV or the radio. It was almost like she became a spelling machine, and she wouldn't say a thing without spelling

335

something, too. I guess it was better than her worrying about the Watts riots or crying about Ernie all the time. But when Kathie ran in from school that cloudy December day, tears pouring down her face, I wished that Susan had won the spelling bee.

"Chestnuts roasting on an open fire ..." Nat King Cole's velvet voice echoed from the record player. Martha and Danny fought somewhere in the back of the house.

"I like his voice," Susan said. She sat on the rug next to me and tried different pairs of plastic shoes on her Barbie.

"He has a very romantic voice," I said.

That's when the front door burst open. Kathie ran in.

"Mom, Ryan ..." she said between gulps and tears.

"He's not coming for Christmas Eve..."

"Romantic!" Susan yelled. "R-O-M-A-N-T-I-C. Romantic."

Kathie's mouth dropped open and her books dropped out of her hands and clomped onto the floor, their brown paper covers making them look like a pile of mud bricks.

"Shut up!" Kathie roared at Susan. She jumped over her books and ran down the hall.

"...Yuletide carols being sung by a choir ..." Nat sang on.

"Susan, go shut off the record player for now, okay?" I said. I stepped toward the hall and saw that Susan was now starting to cry.

"What?" I roared at her; I had no patience for her easy tears then.

"Kathie yelled at me ... She doesn't like me..."

"Just go shut off the record player."

As I hurried down the hall to Kathie's room, I could now hear Martha and Danny screaming at each other.

"That's my Voice of the Mummy!" Martha screamed.

"Mommy and Daddy got it for my birthday last year!" Danny yelled back.

"Quiet, you two!"

Kathie's door was shut and locked when I finally got to it. I pounded on it with my open palm, and the hollow wood made the fluorescent, pink peace sign decal stuck on it wiggle.

"Kathie, it's me. Open up."

"Go away!"

"Kathie, sometimes boys do funny things and you gotta just –"

"Go away! He was my whole life and nobody cares!"

She must have been crying into her pillow because I could hear her soft whimpers. Her life went bonkers over every boy she ever had a crush on. I worried about that, but I didn't know what to do about it. All I knew right then was I hated Ryan Smith, and if I had a gun, boy would I have let

336

him have it. Susan was now snorting and wheezing through her own tears as she stood behind me.

"Shut up, dog face!" Danny screamed.

"It's better than being a little fairy!" Martha yelled back at him.

I ran into my room and slammed the door. Each child's voice, each child's cry, each child's sound seemed to pull me in all different directions. If it went on much more, I knew it would pull me apart.

"Blessed Mother, guide me now. Give me peace. The family is falling apart."

No answer came and I just kept thinking about Her. This cycle of yelling, and crying, and fighting, and chaos kept up all through the holidays. Daisy, who now lived in a California bungalow in old Torrance, only made things worse whenever she visited that Christmas.

Midnight Mass at St. Joan's on Christmas Eve, I prayed for strength, and I prayed for the family. The church and its prayers didn't seem to stop the war or help the Negroes. No one in church that Christmas in 1968 was happy and I guess only the hippies and dope smokers were. As the choir sang 'Oh Come All Ye Faithful' and parishioners lined up to take Holy Communion, I stayed in the pew a little longer and prayed. I prayed for the Blessed Mother to heal the world, to help make Andrew's shoulder arthritis better, and to watch over the kids. After all, hadn't we all had enough problems? Nothing else could possibly go wrong.

21.

Danny felt creeped out when he closed the diary. To read about his perverted brother, Ernie, molesting him reminded him of the confusion he suffered with his sexuality. No one wants to be gay when they're a teenager, and Danny had tried hard not to be. The only real confusion the molesting caused him was that it gave him something to blame his being gay on. Every time he found himself fantasizing about sex with men, he could blame it on being molested — that was it. The real problem was that he didn't feel any attraction for girls at all, just an urge to *want* to be attracted so that he would be normal. A kind high school psychologist pointed out to him when he was most confused, that being gay was one thing, and being molested was another.

But that was all past, and after reading his mom's words, he felt sorry for his brother. Ernie had a shot at playing pro baseball— something Danny never had any talent for. Could that have saved Ernie? To be focused on something like that? Or maybe crazy was crazy and there was nothing that could be done. He wasn't sure.

Danny was pretty sure that all the praying his mom and dad did never helped. '*Pray for us sinners…*'— that part of the 'Hail Mary' now really made him laugh. He realized years back that praying was just talking to yourself, sort of a way to stop feeling afraid. Now fear was something he understood well, but believing some magic being that was looking out for you was just childish dependence. Just because you want to believe, or need to believe in something doesn't make it real. It wasn't just Catholicism—it was all religions. All the religions, he decided, were an imaginative way to feel less afraid. Just because one million or one billion scared people believe in something doesn't make it the truth. The hard facts of life on Santa Monica Boulevard were enough faith for him. The rest: pure bullshit.

Love was another thing that didn't make sense. He now knew how much his mom and dad loved each other that was for sure. But so what? Would he or could he ever love someone the way his mom and dad loved each other? Even before he was a hustler, he had never met a guy he wanted to date or stay with for much time. He always figured it was because he didn't know how to even begin to love somebody.

338

He shivered as he shut off the light. As he began to fall asleep, he felt something he hadn't felt since he was a kid: very alone.

22.

"...May the light of His love shine through and relieve this sinner of his earthly pain..."

"Amen," Andrew whispered.

I stood back from our bed and watched the gold candlelight splash Father Crawford's fingertips. The fingernails of his right hand sparkled from holy oil as he dipped them into a silver jar and rubbed the oil into Andrew's shoulder. It had been five weeks since the doctors told us he didn't have arthritis, and just over two weeks since they told us that the only thing they knew was the Andrew's joints in his whole body were all inflamed. The oil made the room smell like lilies and turpentine.

"I bless you, in the name of the Father, of the Son, and the Holy Spirit."

Father Crawford reached out and rubbed a small cross on Andrew's forehead, using the side of his skinny thumb. His hands made me think of Artie's in the way they dabbed and rubbed the anointing oil. Father Crawford slipped off his silk scapular, purple and gold in the soft light, kissed it and tucked it into his black doctor's bag.

"Is there anything else, my son?" he asked.

Son? I laughed to myself. Father Crawford must have been younger than either of us.

"Yeah," Andrew answered. "When will the pain stop, Father?"

"Mr. Murphy, that's up to the Lord."

"Ouch. Mary, more aspirin."

"Andrew, you just had some an hour ago. Give it a chance —"

"Balls, Mary! You know I need it. Come on."

"The doctor only gave you aspirin?" Father Crawford asked.

"No. That codeine stuff made Andrew allergic. Doctor Stevenson doesn't want him to have anything else except for the cortisone until we know what's going on," I answered.

Father Crawford nodded as he popped his bag closed. He stood

340

and stretched, his long legs making him look like a giraffe.

"So it's not just arthritis?"

My face must have gone red because it felt hot -- his voice was so smooth, and I couldn't control my embarrassment at liking its sound.

"They're pretty sure it is, but we gotta wait for the tests to come back to be sure."

"Well the anointing should help some," Father Crawford said. "You want me to bless the house before I go?"

"Mary! Aspirin!"

"No. Father Sbaraglia just blessed it a few weeks ago. Thanks, anyhow, Father."

"Aspirin!" Andrew screamed.

"All right already," I said.

I unscrewed the tin cap on the aspirin bottle and sprinkled two tablets into Andrew's hand. He grabbed the blue tin tumbler on the nightstand before I could hand it to him.

"I'll let myself out, Mrs. Murphy."

With Andrew wriggling in pain, it made sense right then for me to let Father Crawford go. But I wasn't making much sense lately and I really wanted to walk him to the front door. So I jumped up from the side of the bed, making Andrew shake and wince a little.

"Mrs. Murphy -- it's –"

"No, Father. I'll get the door for you."

Andrew moaned in the background as I pulled the bedroom door shut. Father Crawford paused at the holy water font just outside the hall door.

"You need some more."

Before I could say anything, a small stream of holy water trickled from the bottle he had just been using for Andrew's anointing. I felt so taken care of and I didn't realize till that second how much I missed that feeling.

"Come by and I'll refill it at the church."

Just as we got to the front door, with the TV in the den blaring 'Scooby Doo,' the doorbell rang. The chime sent a start through me, like a school bell waking up a sound-asleep student.

"That's good timing," Father Crawford said.

The thundering footfalls of Danny, Martha, and Susan, who always had to know who was at the door, rumbled under my feet. I pulled on the doorknob as I said over my shoulder:

"Would you kids please stop run—"

I couldn't finish the sentence as my legs started to give out. Even Father Crawford's strong grip on my shoulders didn't comfort me at that

341

second: Louise stood on the front porch, her gray-green eyes flaring at me.

"Hi, Mary," she said.

"Loulie?" Martha said, stepping past me.

"Martha--you're huge," Louise said.

"Loulie, Loulie, Loulie!" Martha screamed, throwing her arms around her older sister. Louise held her close. She looked right past me. I turned to follow her gaze and Susan and Danny both leaned against the Naugahyde chairs. They looked like they had been caught stealing. Father Crawford's eyes knitted in confusion.

"You must be a Murphy, judging by your looks. But I haven't had the pleasure," Father Crawford said as he extended his hand.

Louise's face lost its color and expression and she didn't reach out to Father Crawford. He dropped his hand after an awkward pause.

"They only said Andrew had something wrong with his arm," Louise said. 'What's the priest doing here?'

"It's okay, Louise," I offered. "Father Crawford just anointed Andrew -- your father. It wasn't Last Rites, if that's what you're thinking."

But that was all I could say. I felt like some invisible thing had grabbed hold of me and my life. Everything felt like a movie all of a sudden.

"Your father's going to be fine, miss?"

"Mrs. Schwartzman."

"Oh," Father Crawford went on. "I thought you were one of the Murphy children."

"She is," I said. "My oldest daughter -- Louise. She's come home."

"Bless you all, then. I'll be going."

Father Crawford nodded once more and stepped past Louise. Martha tugged at Louise's arm. I just watched everything; my muscles were frozen.

"Come on, Loulie. You gotta see our room now. It's really boss."

"Not now, Martha. I don't have that much time."

Louise leaned to look around me.

"Don't be scared, you two," she said to Danny and Susan. "I won't be staying too long."

"Loulie, you got a second, don't you?" Martha asked.

"Go ahead, Martha. I gotta talk to Mom for a minute."

The kids skipped off and Louise still stood on the stoop. I couldn't even think of a thing to say.

"Sorry to surprise you, Mary. But I just found out Andrew's having some problems."

I may have been in shock, but this first name stuff for us was already bugging me.

342

"Since when do you call us by our first names?"

Louise let out a sigh, looked away a second, then folded her arms.

"That's not really all that important right now, is it?"

"Oh. Well..."

"Could I just come in so I can see him?"

"Oh, yeah," I said.

I reached for Louise but she slid past me like some sort of slippery animal. Her bouffant hair sat on her shoulders and from behind, it looked like an orange and brown pumpkin. Her legs were long and full, just like mine used to be. When she stepped and turned back toward me, it was like I was looking in a mirror from twenty years ago.

"Where is he?"

"Our bedroom."

But instead of turning to go into the hall, Louise sat on the couch and waved me over. She looked around like she was waiting for someone to attack.

"Just wanna make sure the kids aren't around."

"There's always someone around," I said.

Louise nodded and smiled for the first time. But her face flattened out again, and she was serious in a way I never remember her being when she was growing up.

"Mary!" Andrew hollered. "Need some water!"

"Just a second, Andrew." I really didn't want to be bothered right then.

"Shouldn't you go say hi to your dad?"

"Not yet. Why haven't you called Murray?"

"No. You know how your father feels about all that."

"Mom- he's your son-in-law. He also happens to be one of the most respected rheumatologists in the field."

"It's just inflammation, Loulie. The doctors have it under control."

Louise reached out and grabbed my hand. She squeezed it tight like she was hugging it, and then I saw a ring with a diamond bigger than a rosary bead and another band below it dotted with diamonds. It was flashier than the ring Irma's husband gave her all those years back. She reached into her purse and handed me card.

"What's this?"

"Murray's card. Give it to dad's doctor and have him send dad's records to him. He'll be able to figure out what's causing the joint inflammation."

I grabbed her left hand and held it a moment. The ring sparkled.

"Was it a nice wedding you had? I don't really know how Jews do that sort of thing."

343

She yanked her hand away and folded both of them into her lap.

"You could have found out if you and Dad had made it. But that's not important now. You gotta get Dad in to see Murray."

"We just did an anointing and I been praying to the Blessed Mother every day. Those doctors don't always know."

She shook her head and sighed.

"The Blessed Mother is with us all the time. She'll take care of us."

"Okay. Well, let's go see Andrew, then."

"Dad?" I said.

"Sure."

"Scooby Dooby Doo, where are you? You're ready and you're willing ..." the TV hollered as the cartoon was ending.

"Danny! Get in here and shut off the set," I yelled. "It's making too much racket."

"Okay!" his scratchy voice echoed down the hall.

As Louise and me stepped through the hall door, I paused and dunked my fingers in the holy water. The water was so cool and familiar. As I crossed myself, I nodded to Louise to bless herself, too. She shook her head.

"No, that's okay."

"It's holy water, for gosh sakes. Been blessed at St. Joan's."

"Let's not worry about it right now," she said.

"I'm not worried. I just want us all to be blessed, that's all."

I pushed the bedroom door open and saw Andrew sitting with his back to us on the edge of the bed. His flattop that had grown too long since being stuck at home spread out from the crown of his head, making a salt and pepper knot out of his messed up hair. Louise grabbed my arm when she saw him.

"Andrew, someone's here to see ya'."

"For crying out loud, Mary," he said over his shoulder. "I don't want to jaw with Agnes."

"It's not Agnes, Andrew."

"Dad, it's me."

Andrew swung his head around and what little pink color was still in his cheeks seemed to just evaporate. His eyes that were glassy now bulged with surprise.

"Louise?" he said.

He stood up and his faded, gray pajamas hung loose from his bony shoulders.

"Mary. Did ya' know about this?"

I shook my head. Andrew started for the end of the bed. He reached for Louise, and then sat down when he held her hand. His

344

shoulders rolled once, and then he started to cry.

"Louise," he said softly. "You came home. You're home."

Louise looked at me but I didn't know what to do. The last time Andrew and me had talked about her, he said he didn't have an oldest daughter. I didn't know why he was crying, and I wondered what to do. At the same time, it bothered me, almost got me mad, to see him cry. But that was all I could feel right then because seeing Louise made me go numb. Louise patted Andrew's head as it lay against her shoulder, and he snorted like a pig.

"I'm sorry...So sorry..." he got out between sobs.

"Shhh," Louise said. "Not now, Dad. Not now. You just need to get better."

"Are you back to stay?" he asked. Andrew jerked back from her shoulder, his eyes flaming with fright.

"I came here because I heard you were sick. I don't want to talk about anything else."

Louise's voice was cool, almost like she had practiced those words a lot. She looked back toward me and I could almost see her swallow her anger at us. She reached around the waist of her camel skirt and tucked in the bright blue, striped blouse she wore.

"Do you need any money or anything?" she asked. She sounded cold.

"I haven't been outta work that long," Andrew snapped back. He pulled the bedspread up and covered himself.

"I'll be back to work soon. We'll be okay."

As soon as we started talking about Andrew's illness, things got comfortable again. Louise relaxed and sat back on the bed. She patted it for me to come sit next to her and I felt like President Nixon had just called me -- I mean, I was excited and surprised and all.

"I don't know if you'll be back to work as soon as you think," she said. 'Murray's going to take a look at your tests and x-rays and then I want you to go see him.'

Andrew looked around the room, almost wildly. I patted the bedspread.

"At his office," Louise said. "That's all I mean. Murray will be able to figure out if you have an autoimmune disease and then what to do about it."

"What the criminy is that?" Andrew asked.

"Sort of like allergies. But only they make you real sick when they flare up."

"I've never had an allergy in my life."

"Yeah. That's right, Louise. How could he be allergic all a sudden?"

345

I added.

"It's not an allergy. It's just the closest thing I could think of to compare to an autoimmune disease."

Louise walked over to the bedroom window, pulled back the curtains, and took a deep breath.

"Frogs will be back soon, huh?"

She sounded so sad when she said that, but I just shrugged.

"If it's an autoimmune disease," she said, "they're going to have to try a lot of different things."

Louise walked back over and sat next to me, touching my leg as she sat. I hadn't felt her touch in so long, my head felt light.

"Maybe they should just leave it be," I said.

"Yeah," Andrew said. "If it started up out of nowhere, maybe it'll just go away."

"It just happened to show up because of your shoulder," Louise said. "You probably have had the disease a long time before. Maybe your whole life. It's good they caught it now."

He eased himself back on the bed and as he pushed back against the wall, his pajama pant leg bunched up enough so that I could see more of the purple spots. Like little blackberries on his skin.

"Well, Doctor Stevenson's my doctor. Anybody else, especially a Jew, I don't listen to," Andrew said. "When Doctor Stevenson tells me I gotta worry, then I will."

"Loulie, how long you gonna be in there?" Martha whined at the closed bedroom door. "I got some really boss stuff for you to see."

Louise stood and straightened her skirt. I couldn't believe how tight the skirt fit over her small thighs. Mine were that small once, I thought.

"I'm gonna go see Martha's room. I'll take off after that."

Andrew's eyes flared and he pushed himself to his feet.

"You gotta stick around, Louise. We ain't seen you in forever," his voice cracked.

"I gotta get back down to Orange County. Beat the traffic and all."

"Stay for supper at least," I said. "I'm making porcupine balls and you know how much you love them."

"I really have to go."

"Come on, Loulie!" Martha cried.

"We got stuff to talk about. Lots of stuff," Andrew said.

I really didn't know what stuff he meant. We hadn't talked about Louise in so long, I couldn't figure out what he meant.

"There's lots of time. I'll be around," she said.

A week later, two days before Valentine's Day, Andrew, Louise,

346

and I sat with Dr. Stevenson in his office, waiting for Dr. Schwartzman to show up. I stared up at two red construction paper hearts that hung next to Dr. Stevenson's diplomas. The words: 'To Grandpa' was written in black crayon. The hearts made me think of all the mother's day cards made in school by the kids over the years. The intercom on Dr. Stevenson's desk interrupted my daze.

"Doctor Stevenson, Doctor Schwartzman is here."

"Mr. Murphy, I'm Doctor Murray Schwartzman. Nice to meet you. Finally."

His short arm, covered by a thick, navy and beige, cable-knit sweater pumped like he was hammering something. I noticed the burgundy tie and white shirt he wore under the sweater. His hair was darker than Andrew's and his blue-green eyes made him look like a movie star.

"You must be Mrs. Murphy."

"Yes." I held out my hand, still wearing my white wrist gloves.

"Oh. I'm sorry." I pulled my hand away and went to slide off the glove.

"You shouldn't worry," Murray said.

He stepped past me and kissed Louise. I looked away because it wasn't just a friendly kiss. Louise's eyes were flat and her face was frozen and tight. Only the salmon rouge on her cheeks and the light blue eye shadow over her eyes created any color. Otherwise, she was white with nerves.

"Andrew, Mary," Dr. Stevenson said with a serious voice. "I've asked Doctor Schwartzman here so that we can go over the diagnosis and figure out a treatment plan together."

"What treatment plan?" Andrew asked. "I thought it was just some sort of inflammation I got."

Murray's bushy, black eyebrows arched as he looked at Dr. Stevenson. They made a mustache over his eyes.

"That's what we thought before, Andrew," Dr. Stevenson said. "That's changed some."

"Mr. Murphy, if I could," Murray said. "You have necrotizing vasculitis. It's part of a group of diseases known as autoimmune disorders. An autoimmune disease makes the body attack itself. That's the simplest way to understand it."

"How'd I get it?"

"It's probably in your family line, Andrew," Dr. Stevenson said. "Genetic."

"Huh?"

"You've had it since the time you were born."

"Is it cancer?" I asked. I couldn't think of anything else to say.

"No, Mary, don't be afraid of that," Dr. Stevenson said. "It's not as serious as all that."

Murray's nose wrinkled to meet his eyebrows, and I knew Dr. Stevenson was either lying or had it wrong. He leaned forward in his chair.

"We have to treat this condition quickly and powerfully," he said.

"Is it gonna kill me?" Andrew asked.

"No, Andrew, you're not going to –"

"Doctor Stevenson, I understand you're trying to help. But don't paint a rosy picture here," Murray said. "We have to keep it from rapidly damaging your internal organs."

"What the ham-n-eggs does that mean?" Andrew asked.

"This disease attacks your blood vessels--makes them real thick," Murray said. "The thicker they get, the less blood flows to tissues. The tissue dies from lack of blood and nutrients.'

I don't know why, but right then, I remembered Artie's crystal ball. Raspberries, too, I could almost smell the raspberries outside my window and hear the wind rustle the vines. Louise's face as a baby, then Daisy's as I lay bedridden. Hopkins to Torrance, Millie in Venice, my mind raced and raced with memories flashing like slides in a Kodak projector. 'How will this movie end?' my sister Irma said somewhere.

"Mary!" Andrew's voice sliced through my nostalgia.

"You feelin' okay?"

I looked around and saw Dr. Stevenson, Murray, and Louise all staring at me. I knew I had a daze moment and couldn't figure out why.

"I gotta check in at Torrance Memorial so they can run some other tests and get me on some special medications," Andrew said. "Get hold of yourself."

The time between Andrew's diagnosis that day and his first surgery a July morning a few months later was lost to me. About the only things I could remember were: Andrew's insistence that Louise could never bring Murray over and my own desire to get to know him; Father Crawford's frequent visits while Andrew slept; and the hole in Andrew's left leg that wouldn't heal. Like some sort of slimy, yellow and red eye, it seemed to watch us try every medicine and procedure we could.

But when I said goodbye to Andrew, I started to think the Blessed Mother had forgotten about me. After a light kiss on Andrew's forehead, they wheeled him away to the blue and white operating room. The surgeon stopped just out side the double doors and looked back at Danny and me.

"We'll leave as much as we can and he'll be okay," the surgeon said, talking about Andrew's stomach that was half dead from the vasculitis. Three nurses in blue outfits, looking like astronauts, pushed the gurney Andrew lay on into the operating room at Torrance Memorial.

348

The last bead of my rosary popped through my fingers as I finished praying some hours later. Blessed Mother, I thought. If you can get those men to the moon tonight, can't you do something for Andrew? Louise kept her promise and stayed with me in the waiting room. She sat next to the window and read.

"Look here--my two dee-yers. How about that?"

It was such a relief to hear Daisy's voice. That was a first for me. I stood up.

"Daisy, come on in," I said. "He's been in surgery for a few hours."

Daisy's eyebrows wrinkled up over her rhinestone, cat-eye glasses. She took a step around me and stood over Louise, her wrists like little sticks poking out from under her ratty, rabbit fur coat. Her rose water scent couldn't hide the moth balls that smelled like an odd mix of mint and pine.

"The prodigal heretic daughter returns, huh?" she said.

Louise's jaw dropped and her book slid off her lap. Daisy turned and stepped around me. She pulled her coat tight around her shoulders and sat.

"I'm here for Andrew, anyway. Not a bunch of Bohunk drama. How is the Hebe, anyway? You married him, right?" Daisy asked.

I couldn't say anything. Out came my rosary beads and I began to fondle them as I tried to make sense of what I was hearing.

'Blessed Mother,' I prayed. 'Please make this turn out okay.'

Louise stood up and it looked like her eyes were going to pop out of their sockets. Daisy just looked her up and down and shrugged.

"Well, Grandmother," Louise said, accenting the word 'grand' as she straightened her skirt. "I'm married to Doctor Murray Schwartzman. We're even planning on having children at some point, too."

"Oh, sit back down. Your story bores me," Daisy said.

As I watched Louise deal with Daisy, I suddenly saw myself back with my Mom and Dad, making the terrible choice between Artie and Andrew. That moment when my heart first pulled in two directions, then folded in on itself--that choking, thick, awful second. I reached to pull Louise to me, to let her know that I felt what she was going through. She stepped away from me. It didn't matter. She loved this man, and it would have to be okay if we wanted to keep her in the family. I wasn't going to lose her again.

"Louise," I said. "Let's just knock it off for now. Your dad's got a lot to get through. With surgery and all."

Louise nodded towards me and picked up her book. She shook the pages toward Daisy who raised her hand and fanned the air. She sat again and began to read.

A couple hours later, just before Andrew was wheeled out of the operating room, the waiting room TV was on. I looked up at the silvery-blue picture of the man stepping onto the moon. The moon!

"...One small step for man, one giant leap for mankind ..." came over the TV.

Please, Blessed Mother, I thought. If they can do that, they can make Andrew better. And please, Blessed Mother, let him understand what Louise needs. I prayed about many things that night.

About a week later, Andrew came home. With only half his stomach and none of his normal color, he was looking like a stick. His arms were now just two Ticonderoga pencils sticking out from his pajamas. The cut on the back of his leg still gaped like an evil eye, but the doctor said all this was pretty normal for this disease and the kind of medicine he was on.

A few days later, his spirit was sort of returning and I was glad because Louise was on her way over to talk things over. As he raised a Melmac teacup to his lips and began to slurp the tea, the doorbell rang. He set down the cup and took a bite of buttered toast.

"That's not Agnes again is it, honey?"

"No. I told her not to come by for a couple a weeks."

"I just don't want anymore of that tuna casserole with the potato chips on top. Just go see who it is already."

Andrew was getting a lot more irritable and bossy ever since he came down with this disease. I wondered if his becoming bossy had anything to do with him losing control of his body. That idea was keeping me patient. When I got to the door and opened it, Louise stood there.

"Hi, Mom. He feeling okay today?"

"Yeah."

"All right. Can I come in and talk to him for a minute?"

I was surprised at how chipper she was as she stepped ahead of me. Just as she turned into our bedroom door, I dunked my fingers into the holy water font and felt the cool, blessed water. I touched my forehead. I knew I was going to need a blessing to deal with this. I turned the corner into the room as Louise finished kissing Andrew on the forehead.

"Hi, Louise," he said.

He propped himself up and his face was suddenly rosy. He had more color to him than I had seen in the last three weeks.

'Please, Blessed Mother. Let the redness in his cheeks be a blessing of His Blood and let him hear what Louise's gotta say' I prayed.

Louise straightened the chenille bedspread and sat down. Her sleeveless, light summer dress with huge daisies on the pattern stood out against her skin that looked like brown sugar. She must've been spending a lot of time laying out at Huntington Beach lately.

"You feeling okay, Dad? They treating you all right?"

"Yeah, I guess. So, you really here to visit or you got some more bad news?"

"Murray can do that," Louise said quietly. "He did ask me to make sure you're getting your medicine on time."

"Yes, he is," I said.

"Okay. Anyway. Murray has offered to stop by once or twice a week to check in on you. Save you some time from having to make an appointment and all that."

I was thrilled to hear that. It would make things a lot easier. Andrew folded his arms and sighed. Louise noticed that and I saw her deflate.

"You know, he just wants to help as part of the family. We even thought maybe we could come together and bring dinner on those visits."

My heart soared when I heard that. But Andrew adjusted his blanket and shook his head.

"We're Catholics in this house. The only reason you're allowed in is because you're still Catholic because you can't undo your baptism and confirmation. We'll just keep our appointments at the office. You gettin' all this, Mary?"

I nodded because even though Andrew was sick and frail, his voice was cold and mean.

"I wish you wouldn't make it like this," she said. She stood up.

"You're gonna be another Christ-killer burning in hell. Is that what you want?"

"Andrew," I just had to say something right then. "Don't you think—"

"No, Mary. Butt out."

"Dad," she said, but there was no fight in her at all. She must've hurt with that.

"Andrew, you don't mean that. Please say you're sorry."

'No, Mom. He very much means that. I just wanted to let you know Murray is willing to come by the house. That's all."

"I'm not having any kike in my house, either. Get that doctor on the phone, Mary. I don't want him touching me again."

"Andrew, please."

"Dial him up, Mary. I'll tell him myself."

"Andrew, he's the best doctor for your disease. You gotta—"

"Someone else can treat me. Get Doctor Stevenson on the phone, then."

"Dad, Murray is the top expert on autoimmune diseases on the west coast. He's a clinical professor at UCLA and Stanford."

"I don't care if he could raise Lazarus. He's a Jew and he stole my daughter's faith. I don't want anything more to do with him. Mary, get Doctor Stevenson, please."

Louise's eyes began to tear up, and for the first time since she had come back to be with us during Andrew's sickness, I saw her get hurt. She stared at Andrew for a second, and then looked at me.

"If that's the way everyone feels..."

She turned to walk and Andrew shooed at her back. She twisted her wedding ring as she walked past me. It was then I felt something pull, stretch, then tear inside me. I ran to follow Louise, but she bolted out the front door and ran to her car. I tried to keep us from leaving this way.

"Louise, please don't--Louise!"

Just before she slid into the front seat, she clutched the top of the car and glared at me. Her eyes swelled with tears.

"You can stand up to him, Mom, but you never do. Even when he's mean and miserable, you should find a backbone."

She slid into the car and slammed the door. As she revved the engine of her Cadillac, all I could think was that she didn't understand that I wasn't a modern woman like her. But Louise had made up her mind right there that I was just as much to blame about everything as her dad. I guess she was right. I watched her drive up Two Ninety-Eighth Street towards Arlington, and this time, I knew I had lost her forever. If I was ever going to get her back into the family again, it was going to take a miracle.

"Mary!" Agnes said in the phone one October afternoon. "You just gotta see it! You won't believe it!"

"What, Agnes?"

"The Blessed Virgin," she said, her words trailing on a weak breath.

"What?"

"She's appeared at Madrona Marsh. Right by Del Amo Boulevard. Cameras are there. Priests. Father Crawford himself."

"You been already?"

"Yes and my body feels like a feather, I'm so moved by it."

"Can you do me a favor, Agnes?"

"What?"

"Come stay with Andrew for awhile. I know it's a lot to ask, but it'll give me a chance to see the Blessed Mother."

What I didn't say was that with Danny now in first grade, being home by myself with Andrew sick and so demanding was getting to me. I almost felt the Blessed Mother came just for me. And it would be nice to see Father Crawford.

"Is there anything special I gotta do?" she asked.

352

"No. You can sit and watch your stories. Just keep an ear out, that's all."

"I can do that."

"Thanks. 'Bye, Agnes."

I went into the bedroom and the smell of old sweat and dirty clothes clung to the air. Even the dry October wind only seemed to stir up the bad smells. As I stepped further into the room, Andrew glanced up at me over his horned-rims. His dark eyes were little cloves in the red-blotched, pale of his skin.

"Mary, I need some water."

"Okay."

I poured the water into the aluminum cup and as I tilted it for him, I saw that his fingers were so thin they looked transparent and blue as he held onto the cup. The water moistened his cracked lips so that they sparkled.

"Andrew, the Blessed Mother has been seen again."

"Oh, jeez. Where this time—at the Hot 'n' Tot on a piece of toast?"

"No. Madrona Marsh. I want to go. I want to ask her to bless you."

"And leave me by myself? Come on, Mary, you can pray here."

"Agnes is on her way over. She's gonna look out for you for awhile."

He grabbed my hand. His grip was weak and shaky.

"What if something happens?"

The way he said 'something' made a chill pass through me.

"Nothing's gonna happen, Andrew. I gotta get to her so I can pray."

Andrew let loose of my hand. His eyelids drooped. He struggled to keep them open a moment longer, but they fell closed; the new medicine they were trying made him so tired. His breath began to rumble and I knew he was asleep again. The side kitchen door creaked open a few minutes later when Agnes arrived. Once she settled herself in a chair and turned on 'One Life to Live', I hopped into turned the Herald and drove down Two Ninety-Eighth Street toward Crenshaw.

As I got to the corner of Crenshaw and Del Amo, I saw cars lining the street in both directions next to the field that became Madrona Marsh. Just before I found a parking spot, I noticed bottles and beer cans in the field and I just knew that Protestant or Jewish teenagers must have been to the marsh to do sinful things.

Pulling up to the curb, I saw Father Crawford immediately, standing with a few ladies from our parish. Kay Hojec, who I hadn't seen in forever, stood off to his right and was the only one I recognized. The group stood in a ring around the edge of the marsh. I had to wade through gold and red spearheads of dry grass, made sharp by the October sun. Grass blades stabbed and scratched at my ankles as I made my way to join the circle.

Foxtails stuck to the hem of my dress like gold tassels, but when I got to the group, I saw what they were all looking at: the dry marsh reeds were flat, and where they were flat, they formed a perfect outline of the Madonna and child. And when Kay bent over and tried to mess up the design, the reeds fell back into position to form the Blessed Mother. A holy thing *was* happening.

I stared at the Holy Mother, and she even had a halo around her where the sun glinted on the gold weeds. The gamy odor of mud and rotted weeds mixed with tar smelled strong as church incense. I pulled my rosary out of my house dress pocket and began to pray. Father Crawford walked up and interrupted me by touching my elbow. I jumped.

"Hello, Mary Murphy. How are you today?"

"Okay, Father." I reached up and smoothed my hair over my right ear.

"And Andrew?"

"He's doing best as he can with his condition."

"Is he here with you?"

"No, no, he's home in bed. The medicine they give him now makes him get tired real easy."

"You didn't leave him alone, did you?"

"No. Agnes came out to the house to stay with him."

"That Agnes. There's a blessed one."

"She helps out a lot, that's for sure."

"She and the other ladies are still keeping up the Blessed Mother Club you put together before I was with the parish."

Right when he said that, I felt a rock hit my heart: I missed those mornings in church and the hot coffee and fresh doughnuts at the Hot 'n' Tot.

"It's too bad I can't join them anymore -- with Andrew sick and all."

I knew it wasn't just because Andrew was sick, but also because of all the other things happening in my life with the kids.

"Do you need me to come by and pray with you? Andrew could probably use another anointing right now."

"Yes, Father, that would be a nice thing."

I really just wanted him to leave me alone. I couldn't explain it then, but there was something he made me feel that I didn't like. When I saw his face, all I could think about was those strange dreams I had awhile ago: we were naked in the sacristy, committing awful sins. Seeing him now in person made me feel like such a sinner.

"Why don't you break off one of these reeds?" he asked.

"Huh?"

"Yes, these reeds are almost holy, sort of like Palm Sunday, don't you think?"

"Yeah, I guess so, Father."

He bent over to pick a reed and when he did, I saw his leg muscles bulge like tree trunks under his pant legs. Strong, powerful -- Andrew's skinny, blotchy little legs flashed into my mind. They were so unsightly now. Father Crawford snapped the reed and waved it under my nose.

"Licorice?" I said.

"Anise. It grows wild all over here."

"Anise?"

"Yes, Mary. It's an herb Italians use. The Holy Father himself has a dish he likes made from its bulb. It's simmered with cream and butter with some parmesan cheese thrown in at the end."

"Sounds so ... exotic," I said.

"Yes, and made from the same weed that grows wild here in Torrance."

Father Crawford kept looking at me and I didn't know what to say. My face felt hot and all of sudden, I felt like a flirty girl who didn't know how to handle the situation. I was fifteen again.

"I'd like to try that stuff some day."

"Come out to the rectory. Mrs. Fracciola, our cook, makes that dish and a good bunch of others, too."

Was he inviting me for a date? How weird, I thought. 'Sinner!' My mind flung back at me.

"Mary?"

"I was just thinking about what you said."

"You're welcome anytime. Here's your reed."

He handed the reed to me and as his hand brushed against my palm, a shiver shot up my spine. I knew I was going to Hell right then.

I pulled out my rosary, Father Crawford blessed it, and I stepped over to the reeds that made the Virgin's head. Praying, I could feel the dry Santa Ana wind rumple my hair. I thought about the days when my hair flowed over my shoulders and I thought about those nights with Artie. The prayers rumbled around me at the marsh but my mind flew back to the Indian chants among the naked aspens. Time, my whole life, seemed like the smoke from church incense. It was all there once, but all that remained was the haunting scent.

355

"Yeah, the Madrona Marsh Indians used to get their water here," a familiar voice pulled me out of my nostalgic blues. "They trapped a lot of the birds here for food, too."

I turned in the direction of the woman's voice and saw Connie talking to a negro man. Her chapel veil was a gauze crown on her head.

"Mary!" she shouted. "I haven't seen you forever!" she cried as she ran up to me. "Have you even been to church? What about Andrew? He doing okay?"

"Yeah, he's okay. How are the kids, Connie?"

"All fine." She crossed herself and looked up. "It's so good to see you, Mary."

Connie turned back to the negro man and talked about the marsh Indians some more, but as she spoke, I could see flames and dancers like black ghosts in front of them. The dry Santa Ana was now a crisp Hopkins wind that whispered through the tops of the aspens. With Father Crawford and his invitation, and Connie reminding me of the Blessed Mother Club, I just had to go. My head was light and I had to step away from Connie. Clutching my holy reed and closing my eyes, I began to pray.

I finished my prayers and as I opened my eyes, I saw that the sun had sunken low. I didn't know how long I had been at the marsh, but I knew I had to get home. I drove the Herald faster than the thirty-five-mile speed limit until I got to Two Ninety-Eighth Street. I turned right and slowed down, and each house I passed reminded me of each year of my life that was lost since the fire meetings next to Minnehaha Creek. I wanted to go back to those times; I wanted lady's slippers in bloom, and aspens burning with gold. Pulling into the driveway, I thought of icicles and raspberries.

Agnes rushed out the front door and waved for me. My heart thudded and I felt electric.

"Mary, come quick!" she said and turned on her heels and ran back into the house.

I rushed behind her, and when she got to the bedroom door, she stepped aside. Glancing in, I saw the back of a man in a light blue uniform.

"Andrew?" I screamed.

The man turned quickly and I stopped: Ernie stared at me with a wandering look in his eyes. He rubbed his nose and a hospital bracelet slid down his wrist.

"Ernie?" I said, but I felt my legs start to give way.

"It's okay, Mary," Andrew whispered.

But it wasn't okay for me. We hadn't seen Ernie in months, and the last time his doctor talked to us it was to let us know that Ernie was never going to get better. Why was he here? How did he get here?

356

"You want some fruit cocktail?" was all I could think of to say.

"Mary, do you need me to hang around?" Agnes asked.

I shrugged and nodded.

"Fruit cocktail, fruit of the vine, bottle of wine, huh Mom?"

"Yeah. Let's go to the kitchen and get some," I said.

Ernie stood up and his arms flopped to his sides. I could see that his blonde-brown hair was wispy at his temples and flecked with gray.

"I'll get the fruit cocktail," Agnes said. "You sit here with Andrew."

"Hey, Mom!" Ernie said. "I ran all the way home," he sang. "Just to say I'm sorry ..."

"Okay, honey, let's go." Agnes took Ernie's elbow and guided him out. Andrew shook his head and his eyes dropped closed and he sat still as a statue.

"Andrew?" I panicked.

"I'm okay, Mary. It's just that kid. What did we do to him, huh? What did we do to that boy?" he said through clenched teeth.

"I gotta go call the police I guess. He can't stay here."

"This is his home, Mary. Why don'tcha give him a couple hours?"

"Danny and the girls are due home--I don't want anywhere near them."

"Mary, come here a second," he said as his chest rattled. He coughed.

"How long you been coughing?" I asked.

"Don't worry about that right now. Come over here and listen to me."

I slid on the bed next to him, and then lay down and put my arms around him. I needed to hold him.

"Mary, you gotta sit up and look at me while I tell you." He coughed again.

"What, Andrew? What?"

"Ernie never stopped talking about baseball with me. He's not completely off his trolley. I mean, he knew he was talking to me."

"Yeah? And if Danny was home right now, what do you think he'd been doing to him?"

Andrew grabbed my hand and his felt cool and thin. He held on and looked over his glasses at me.

"There's nothing you gotta hide anymore. I know, Mary. I know."

A chill shot up my back--what did he think he knew?

"You know what?"

"Who Ernie's dad really is."

A vice seemed to loosen in my belly and I felt my head inflate like a balloon. I was dizzy.

357

"Mary, listen to me. I think the Lord's gonna call me home soon."

But my head was still somewhere up against the ceiling about Ernie. Andrew knew all this time--he knew. How come he was saying this now? Why? Maybe he really thought he wasn't going to make it, but the Blessed Mother was on my side and I knew better.

"Andrew, stop talking about all this. There's all kinds a medicines they can still try. Surgery has helped you, too."

"Mary," he said on the tail of a cough. "My body's not working this out. I can feel it giving way."

"You can't think like that. You just can't think like that."

"Mary, let me finish what I was gonna say--my problems don't matter right this second."

"Andrew, my Andrew."

"Stop and listen to me."

He grabbed my shoulders and I was surprised at how much strength he had.

"I've known about Ernie for a long time."

"How'd you find out?"

"Somehow Mom figured it out. She told me a couple years back."

My head was spinning and I looked away from him. The frogs screamed from the sump and I felt like running to the backyard fence and throwing myself in the mucky water. I folded my arms, and I felt naked.

"You could'a' had our marriage annulled when you found out," I whispered.

"Look at me," he said. "You're my Mary. I wanted you ever since I saw you spying on me in the raspberry field."

"You knew that, too?"

"See, I'm a sinner, too. We're all sinners. It's what we're supposed to be. It doesn't matter if you admit your sin right away or years later. The Lord doesn't keep that kind of account. And besides, you been the best wife I could'a' dreamed of. You got nothing to feel ashamed about in front of me."

"Andrew, my love. I'm so sorry –"

"Shh. Let's forget about it, okay? Besides, my oldest boy is out there with Agnes having his fruit cocktail. My baseball star. He was everything I could'a' ever wanted in a son--everything I never was with a bat and a mitt. What's happened to him since is something the Lord has planned. I gotta accept the Lord's choice for him and leave it at that."

As Andrew was saying all that, I felt myself sitting in the living room in Hopkins, listening to Mom and Dad talk about my problem, who I had to choose for a husband and all. I said 'Andrew' again, like Mom wanted. Right at this second, I knew I chose right.

"It's okay, my Mary. Don't worry about a thing. You're gonna have a lot more to worry about soon. And that's--"

He coughed again.

"That's what you gotta be keeping your mind on now. Let's just have Agnes help you get Ernie back to where he belongs. Take care of things--" he coughed harder. "The way they need to be taken care of."

The police showed up about an hour and a half later, followed by an ambulance. As they hauled Ernie away, I saw little bits of fruit cocktail still stuck on his face. I reached to brush off the bits of pear and peach from around his mouth, but he was rushed past me and I didn't get the chance. He flailed and fought against the strait jacket as they shoved him into the back of the ambulance, screaming crazy things that made no sense.

"You know," the police officer who was in charge said. "Your boy's not any dummy. He was able to break out of the state hospital because he's so clever. They'll probably have to relocate him to the higher maintenance ward at the hospital."

The ambulance doors slammed shut and the metallic grit of their locks felt like a hacksaw going right through my heart. As the ambulance pulled away, I almost felt dragged behind it.

Blessed Mother, what a mess I made of everything, I thought. Please bless Andrew and my sinful soul.

The next few months, Andrew's lungs grew weak, and then his liver was acting funny at Christmas. So much so that he had to spend the whole holiday in bed. Danny was the only one he felt like seeing Christmas Eve, and it was only long enough so Danny could show him his Lost In Space robot Santa had brought him. Andrew could barely smile.

An early morning in March 1970, it was the fifth or sixth day of rain we had. Those gray clouds just hung overhead, dirty as the greasy ceiling at Hot 'n' Tot. Some news guy had been talking about warm ocean water and all the rain, but when they came and took Andrew away in that ambulance, it seemed like it never was going to stop raining. Those dark clouds were a shadow at first, then a dark cave in my heart after that. The Blessed Mother couldn't get rid of the hole in my heart, and neither could church, or the rosary or anything else. I was feeling trapped in a big, gray, wet box.

I clutched my rosary a couple weeks later as Andrew lay in his bed back at home. Paramedics surrounded him.

"Andrew!" I screamed.

One of the paramedics turned and grabbed me. He pushed me toward the bedroom door.

"We're taking care of him--stay back."

I caught a glance over his shoulder and saw Andrew's face looking a dirty, ugly blue. His mouth hung open but his eyes were pinned shut.

"Back up, ma'am," the paramedic said as he pushed me to the bedroom door. He ran back and joined the others.

I heard hollow, thudding sounds and I saw Andrew's legs jerk from the pounding on his chest.

"We got a pulse!" one of them cried.

The paramedic who had stopped me now shoved a tube that looked like aquarium tubing into Andrew's mouth. The other paramedic grabbed a red, rubber thing that looked like an inflated water bottle. He attached it to the tube in Andrew's mouth and squeezed it. Andrew's chest rose and fell as the paramedic pumped the thing.

"Okay. Mrs. Murphy?"

"Yeah?"

"Your husband's stabilized. He was in cardiac arrest. We're taking him to Torrance Memorial."

They loaded Andrew onto one of those collapsing beds with wheels and as they pushed past me, I kissed his forehead. It was freezing cold.

"Andrew?"

"He's not conscious right now, Mrs. Murphy."

I held Andrew's hand that was an ice cube, but I could feel a faint thump as we bumped along Pennsylvania Avenue a few minutes later. The ambulance's siren sounded like a woman moaning, and the red light it flashed lit up each house we passed on the way a blood red. Torrance Memorial, only three miles away, might as well have been in Minneapolis with how long the ride was taking.

Hurry, I thought. "My Andrew," I whispered. "My Andrew."

"Blessed Mother," I prayed. "Help him. Help us, please."

We finally pulled into Torrance Memorial's parking lot and in a second, the ambulance flew open and Andrew was yanked from me. I ran behind as they wheeled him into the emergency room. A big, Mexican nurse stopped me at the door.

"Jue'll gotta wait, missuth," she said.

"You don't understand. I gotta go in," I cried.

"I understand. Jue gotta stay ow here."

She folded her flabby, brown arms over her blue operating room blouse. I didn't know what else to do, so I slid into a black vinyl chair just across from the doors. Pulling my rosary from my pocket, I began to pray.

Rubber soles slapped the tile floor just behind the doors—"Hail, Mary," I concentrated. POP! a soda can opened?—"...The Lord is with thee—" "*Come on!*" a voice shouted. "Blessed art thou," I prayed harder.

"*The Lord is with us,*" I thought I heard a voice say over the hospital's public address speaker. *"Pray, Mary Murphy,"* it said. *"The Lord is with us!"*

I don't know how long I prayed, or how many times those doors flew open and slammed shut.

"Mom?" I heard Louise's voice.

I looked up and there was Louise, wearing a pink, satin dress. Dr. Schwartzman followed her. Dr. Schwartzman nodded at me as he stepped with the Mexican nurse past us and into the emergency room.

"Mom, I just heard," Louise said. "I called Maureen and she's staying with the kids. He's gonna be fine."

I shook my head. I couldn't believe Louise was with me. I could feel nothing but a golf ball in my throat. Looking at how simple and pretty Louise looked, my eyes clouded up with tears.

"Mom?" she said.

"Oh Louise, Louise. What did I do?"

"Nothing, Mom. Don't worry. We're here for you and Dad."

My body began to rumble with pain and my head fell on Louise's shoulder.

"I'm sorry. I'm no good. I don't know what I'm gonna do if——"

"Shh. Don't think that," Louise soothed me. Her voice cracked with sadness. She stroked my head and I couldn't handle it anymore. I heaved and sighed and covered her pink, satin shoulder with wet, almost red blotches of tears. The next few hours went by in a stale blink--one minute was a vinyl and alcohol blur that slithered into the next.

When the emergency room doctor finally came out, he didn't look much older than twenty-five. Dr. Schwartzman stood behind him and I felt Louise grab my arm like a vise.

"Mrs. Murphy," he said. "Your husband is stabilized."

Louise sighed and patted my arm. I felt my stomach relax.

"I'm afraid you need to prepare for the worst."

"What? What's the matter?" the words scratched and clawed their way from my throat.

"Your husband has a severe case of pneumonia. His lungs are weakened from the vasculitis. He's on a breathing machine right now."

"Let me see him," I jumped up. Dr. Schwartzman stepped to my side and patted my shoulder.

"They're doing all they can do in there," he said.

"Just prepare yourself, Mrs. Murphy," the emergency doctor said again.

"Should I call Father Crawford?" I asked.

"That would be advisable, Mrs. Murphy. Why don't we have one of the nurses do that for you?"

361

The lights in the hospital suddenly seemed to dim. I jerked my head around, expecting to see an electric pulse or flash. At that second, I felt my head tighten and my throat close.

"Mom?" Louise said, but it sounded like she was yelling through a cave.

"Why don't you sit down, Mrs. Murphy?" the young doctor's voice echoed the same way.

"What's the matter with the lights?" I choked out.

Louise and Dr. Schwartzman shrugged and shook their heads.

"Isn't it dark in here?" I asked.

"I think she could use a sedative," Dr. Schwartzman said.

"Nurse, get me a hundred milligrams of phenobarb," the young doctor said.

"Just sit, Mom, it's okay," Louise said.

That was the second the darkness fell on me, and I didn't know what hell was just ahead of me. In what was either a couple of hours, or a couple of minutes--time wasn't making sense right then--Father Crawford came bounding down the hall. From the cave in my mind, he seemed to blend into the darkness. The white tab of his collar seemed to be the only part of his body that was clear. When he got up close to me, I could see his purple scapular around his neck and his doctor's bag in his hand.

"Well, here come the judge! Here come the judge!" burst out of my mouth like Flip Wilson.

"Mom?" Louise said.

"You get all dressed up for me?"

"Mrs. Murphy?" he said quietly.

"Mom's not feeling well, Father," I heard Louise say as if I were out of the room. "The doctor gave her a sedative awhile ago."

"Yep, you betcha. Feels like I been tipping the communion cup."

I don't know why I felt like making jokes. I couldn't help it and I was pretty sure it was because of the tranquilizer. The darkness still hung around me, but I didn't care--I felt drunk. A drunk in a closet: that was me.

"Where's Mr. Murphy?" Father Crawford asked.

"This way, Father," Louise led us into the room. As I followed behind Father Crawford, even the horror and fear I felt just a little bit ago wasn't there anymore. It was like I had coffee and booze in me at he same time. I heard a whooshing sound as we stood around Andrew. Each time I heard the odd sound, I could see Andrew's chest rise and fall in rhythm to it.

Even though he lay there with blue and white tubes like drinking straws sticking out of his mouth, arms, and other unmentionable places, the whooshing sound really got to me. 'Whoosh' it went, and I felt myself start to shake. 'Whoosh' it went again and I couldn't help myself. It sounded just like someone passing gas. 'Whoosh!' it went and I started to giggle. Didn't anyone else hear how funny it was?

Louise slipped her arm around me and I think she thought I was starting to cry. Father Crawford kneeled next to the side of the bed, his scapular looking like two purple tongues hanging from his neck.

'Whoosh!' I bit my lip to stop the giggle. Louise and Dr. Schwartzman stood behind me.

Father Crawford mumbled something in Latin and pulled a small vial from his doctor's bag. He shook some gold drops onto his fingertip, rubbed his thumb over the drops, and then moved his thumb over Andrew's forehead. Andrew's eyes were pinched closed like he was in pain. Father Crawford made a small cross and mumbled a blessing in Latin.

Right then, I saw how flat Andrew's hair had become. It looked sort of like the crown they put on Miss America's head.

'There he is...' I heard Bert Parks sing in my head. 'Mister America...' When I thought of that, I had to hold onto a laugh again.

"Mom," Louise said quietly. I guess she could tell I was holding back a giggle.

"Sorry, honey. Sorry," I said.

As Father Crawford began to say the benediction in the Last Rites, he said, "Bless us and forgive us our sins."

"Sock it to me!" I said. I can't say why, but it made me laugh out loud.

"Mary!" Father Crawford said as mean as an old school marm. "Do you understand what's happening?"

I was still stifling my laugh and my eyes teared up as I held it back.

"Yes," I squeaked out. "I understand."

Whoosh! Whoosh!

I had to bite my lip again to keep from laughing.

Blessed Mother of flatulence, I thought. Fart for us sinners.

As the uncontrollable laugh swelled up again, I felt myself slip further and further from the room. It was like I was suddenly watching a movie.

I reached for Andrew's hand to make me feel a part of it all. I saw Louise with tears rolling down her face. There was Dr. Schwartzman behind her with his hand cupped over her shoulder. Just what Andrew needed right then -- the family Jews! Father Crawford was praying next to the bed. I guess they all understood what was going on--why couldn't I? Why did I want to laugh so badly?

Andrew's cool hand at least linked me into what was taking place. Each of his heartbeats registered a faint thump against my fingers, and it seemed like a minute between each one. Those weak thumps calmed my need to laugh.

Father Crawford went on with each part of the Last Rites. Andrew's eyes stayed shut the whole time and the 'whooshing' just kept going. As we got to the last part of the benediction, Father Crawford rubbed Andrew's head with holy oil.

"Mrs. Murphy, is there anything else you need?" he asked.

"No, Father, I guess I'm fine."

Father Crawford left a few minutes later and the doctor who had been taking care of Andrew must have seen Father Crawford leave because he walked in with a nurse.

"Mrs. Murphy, the last test results are in and I'm afraid there's nothing more we can do."

The whooshing sound of the breathing machine was accented by a raspy breath every now and then. It sounded like Andrew was gurgling and fighting for breath.

"What's next, doctor?" I asked.

"Your husband's lungs are filled with fluid. His kidneys have just about shut down."

Louise let out a snort and buried her head into Dr. Schwartzman's shoulder.

"Is the machine helping him now?" I asked.

"It's probably hurting him now. The best idea is to take him off, let him rest comfortably, and see what happens."

"Mrs. Murphy," Dr. Schwartzman said. "Mary. You have to let him go."

Louise's head shook and her brown bouffant bounced as she cried. Dr. Schwartzman lowered his eyes, and then kissed the top of her head. Was I in a movie again?

"Mrs. Murphy, what do you want to do?" the doctor asked again.

Andrew gasped and wheezed as the machine whooshed on. I went to Andrew, picked up his hand, and felt a light squeeze. Was he hugging me goodbye?

"Okay," I said. "Do what has to be done."

The doctor reached over and switched off the machine. It popped off like it was a lamp switch, nothing more important than that. The nurse pulled a tube from Andrew's mouth. Andrew's breathing sped up.

"He's gasping!" I cried.

Louise gripped my arm and I held Andrew's hand, watching his mouth open and close like a beached gold fish. I suddenly saw Andrew carrying the raspberry crates from the Darlana's. I watched as he bent over and handed me my books again.

Andrew gagged and wheezed, and I felt his heart tapping like two infant fingers against my palm. His breathing slowed and his mouth closed again as it evened out. The only other sound in the room was the beep from the heart machine.

"Whyn't you go ahead and go home, Louise," I said. "You look dead tired." I chuckled at those words.

"She doesn't want to leave," Dr. Schwartzman said. It was the first thing he'd said in hours.

"No, Mom, I want to stay."

She didn't have to stay long. At about ten fifteen, with Dean Martin crooning 'That's Amore' from a TV set in another room somewhere down the hall, Andrew let out a tiny cry. I squeezed his hand and his eyes popped open. They were dark and deep as outer space and his expression looked even farther away.

"Mom?" Louise said in a panic.

Andrew let out one deep breath, like a sigh, and his eyelids fell as gently as two aspen leaves in fall. The soft thump of his heart stopped and his body collapsed like a deflated balloon. The ping of the heart monitor changed to a single tone that pulled me into a dark tunnel. A darkness that was black as madness swallowed me. Louise's sobbing was a distant echo and quietly beneath her sobs, I heard Dean Martin once more: "...*That's amore...*"

The days after Andrew's death, the house swarmed with people. Everyone from the church to a whole load of Andrew's cousins, aunts, and uncles filled up the house. Daisy brought over a bunch of people she needed -- friends from Hopkins and other places -- who helped her deal with Andrew's death. She'd stick around late and even spent the night after Andrew's rosary.

The kids had all become very quiet, and Danny was the only one who got involved with the strangers. He set up an altar on the clothes hamper and made a tabernacle with a crown of loose leaf paper that said 'Andrew Murphy.' Our Catholic family and friends egged Danny on to pray in front of his altar.

Andrew's rosary was at Gordon's Mortuary and that was the first time I'd seen him since the hospital. We were led down a long, carpeted hall with open doorways. Jasmine, honeysuckle, carnations, and lilies filled the air with a sick-sweet odor. Organ music drifted over some sort of speaker system. I didn't know what to expect because of all the years we'd driven past Gordon's on the way to church, I never set foot in it.

"Mrs. Murphy," the man in a black suit who led us down the hall said when he stopped by one of the doorways. He nodded for me to enter. My knees shook a little and I had to grab the doorjamb to keep from falling over. I walked around the corner and saw Andrew.

His face almost glowed a yellowish-blue, and his eyelids were pinched shut. His head made a dent in the white, satin pillow and the white satin on the casket lid looked like the rays of the sun the way it burst from the center of the lid. Carnations and lilies filled my nostrils as I stepped up to the kneeler at the side of the oak casket. The flowers that surrounded him looked like a jungle--I didn't know who had sent them all. An American flag was bunched at the open end of the casket, the rest of it draped over the top and sides. I could hear everyone mumbling and sniffling behind me.

"He looks like he's sleeping" someone whispered. No, Andrew snored like a chain saw, I wanted to say.

"They did a good job on him" someone else said. Andrew always had a bit of a suntan, he was never blue and yellow I almost said.

I really didn't know how to feel at all as I looked at him laying there in his black church suit. My eyes landed on his folded hands. The nails looked waxy and his fingers pale, but his black rosary had been woven through them. Its crucifix hung from it but was caught on one of Andrew's jacket buttons, making it stand up and face me. I didn't pray the rosary the night before and I couldn't pray now--that crucifix standing up and pointing at me made me wonder. How, Blessed Mother? How? How could you let this happen?

I didn't take my eyes off his hands. I knew those hands for so many years, and those hands knew how to touch me. Even if they looked like wax now, it didn't matter. I loved them, I loved their strength, and I loved their devotion. And there they now were, as I had seen them so many times, wrapped in a rosary.

His hands came into my mind again the next day at St. Joan's. The church was filled up to the choir loft and I guess I knew some of the people. The oak casket sat on a cart in the center of the nave. I felt odd as I sat with the kids in the front pew. The girls and Danny were sniffling, but I couldn't help them. I mean, I didn't feel like I could reach them because I felt like I was caught in some sort of bizarre dream. It was almost like the kids were strangers, and the church was a strange place, and that oak box was even stranger.

"...and Andrew Murphy was a man of great faith ..." I heard Father Crawford say. "He walked in the path of the Lord, *and that path was a path of shit...*"

What did he just say? I thought. A bubble started to grow in my chest.

"...*He was a fart. An old fart...*" I heard now. The bubble in my chest became like a burp I couldn't hold back. Why was he saying this

366

stuff? The light in the church dimmed, and I began to giggle.

"*...and what about the little farts? Who's taking care of the little farts?*" I swear I heard him say that, too.

I giggled and giggled I don't know for how long. I don't know what else Father Crawford said. I laughed out loud now. Pretty soon, I felt hands on my arms and shoulders, but it was too late for them to join the fun. My eyes turned hazy with tears as I laughed and laughed. I felt someone lift my body as tears of laughter rolled down my face.

23.

This is what crazy feels like.

The Blessed Mother sits on the hill that rolls down to Minnehaha Creek and the lady's slippers dance for her.

"Blessed Mother," I say. "All my trouble started on this bank with lust and blood."

"Hail, Mary," she says with that Mona Lisa smile of hers. "You should be the Madonna, not me. You are the blessed, holy one."

I laugh at this, meaning no disrespect to her. The aspens stir up like yellow dust devils, spilling their leaves and pulling the night down on top of me.

--Who's touching me? Prodding me? Stinging me with wet?

"Maaary," I hear from behind and it's Artie. He presses up against me and I feel the swelling of his personal area against my leg.

"Maaary, I love you. I love you and you can fly!"

And I fly. I follow the sparks of fire and I spit down on Gopher Foot--she can't feel it because it's raining. It's raining and pouring but Gopher Foot won't go whoring with my Artie.

"He's mine!" and I spit. "He's mine!" and I spit again.

Miss Hogrebe calls from the edge of the falls.

"Create!" she screams at me. "Create! You can create like God!"

"And the Blessed Mother? Like her too?" I answer as I run down the school hall to the art room. My paints, my pens, my pads, all jiggle, shake, and vibrate like pretty bells. The Bells of Saint Mary!

Miss Hogrebe plucks out her eye and it drips like a wet pearl.

"Beauty of art is all! Beauty of art is in the eye of the beholder," she hollers.

I run away from her, to the Darlana's field. The raspberry vines scratch my legs but I keep running.

"I'm the Madonna?" I ask the Blessed Mother who floats along side me.

"You are full of grace, blessed Mary. The Lord is with thee!"

The raspberries are in flower and the green leaves make my skin itch.

"Where's the one with the arms?" the Blessed Mother asks. "And the hands?"

--Hands touch me again and I hate how they tickle my skin. And wetness -- is it oil?

"Oil!" Mom screams.

"You can't be sinking no oil well and make money from it in Hopkins, Ernest, you old sinner!" she laughs at Dad. "Mom?" I say. "Dad?" They're not dead anymore. We stand together in the kitchen as Jimmy makes fireflies dance and Irma sings a Cole Porter song: "...You're the top!..." They're not surprised to see me but I want to tell them something. What? Dad smiles at me at first, but then his face screws up into a scowl. He grimaces like Frankenstein's monster.

"You know who I wanted! You know who I wanted you to marry!"

"Don't listen," the Blessed Mother whispers. "Blessed art thou amongst women. You are the Madonna."

Before any sound can squeeze from my mouth, I am covered in thick goo. Why? What is it? Thick, purple...paint! It sticks inside my elbow as I bend it. It pulls at my skin, making purple rat tails as it starts to dry.

Miss Hogrebe laughs at me. Her arms jiggle on her hips as she laughs.

"You're an artist first! You're an artist!"

My pads, paint, and pens are sucked from my hands -- is there a vacuum somewhere near?

I'm pulled into the woods, near the creek, and I feel him enter me as I watch my portfolio and my drawings float up to the night sky. They make a silhouette against the moon. My stomach burns and explodes like a firecracker and it balloons up. As I struggle against the stretch and pull of my skin, the Blessed Mother appears in front of me. Her face glows like a candle flame and I can't see her eyes or mouth.

"He you carry is damned. Out of wedlock you conceived, and from that sin only evil will come. Damned is the fruit of thy womb."

My skin chills with those words.

"Bless me, I have sinned. Bless me, please, bless me."

My stomach churns and rips and in the middle of the Darlana's field, Andrew grabs my hand. My Andrew! My Andrew is whole again! He holds my hand and out from my loins spills each child, tied together by one umbilical chord, making a flesh and blood rosary. Ernie, then Louise, and each child on down until the flesh rosary stops. A child screams as it hangs from my loins. It turns its head, chokes a second, and shrinks into a black rosary bead. The next children pop out and all of them stand in the raspberry field, tied together by the one umbilical chord.

Daisy steps from behind a raspberry vine, and she gathers up the baby rosary and twists it around her hands. The babies scream but Daisy

369

laughs.

"You Bohunk! They don't love you! They're gonna stay with me!"

"No!" I scream. But my throat slams shut like a wine bottle cork.

--What are those hands on my chest doing there? They're cold and dry -- get them off!

Andrew pulls my arm and then Artie holds out the crystal ball (but didn't he pawn it?). I look into the clear, pure glass and see the Eiffel Tower. Artie waves me toward him, but Andrew pulls me back. My muscles burn against the pressure.

An apple falls on the ground at Murphy's Grocery and frogs bellow far away -- where are the frogs I hear? Father Crawford bends over and picks up the apple, taking a bite that pops the red skin as his teeth sink into its flesh. He drops the apple, throws open his arms and his white and green cassock falls to the floor. Heat rises from my feet to my head as his member begins to rise.

I squeeze my eyes closed as he pulls me to him and his skin smells like cloves.

"Oh, Father. No, Father!"

I scream and scream at him but want him at the same time.

"Yeah, Bohunk, just what I'd expect of you," Daisy says from somewhere. "There's a word for you and you know, dee-yer, I'm the only one who's got the guts to say it!"

Father Crawford shakes and shudders, bobbing his head like a puppet. He starts to turn to goop -- like wax? His head collapses into his shoulders like a melting candle and all of a sudden, Danny's standing in front of his altar in the hall.

"Let's say mass, Mommy."

He folds his hands from under the green, terry towel.

"Let's pray for Daddy, okay?"

I can't say anything, though, it's like the cat, or Saran wrap, or something else has my tongue. It's frozen and my body is trapped. Danny turns away from me, genuflects to the towel-covered altar, and turns back around. He waves a pink candy wafer-- those Necco thingamabobs, I think they're called--at me and says, "Body of Christ."

"Is he already a priest?" I wonder. I lean down to accept the candy Host and I hear: "Raindrops Are Falling on my Head" off in another direction.

"Come on," Martha screams and runs in front of Danny. "Let's sing your favorite song, Mom."

The kids lead me like a dumb lamb out to the living room and push me to sit on the coffee table. Danny, Martha, and Susan sit around me and we all start to sing along with Andy Williams.

"...I'm never gonna stop the rain by complaining ..."

Susan and Martha clap along and rock on either side of me. But I can't sing; I can't even move. I just look at the tattered corner of the green living room drapes and pretend I'm in some salon in Paris. The kids bounce against me.

"...and I said I didn't like the way he got things done..." they sing on and on.

I feel my shoulders sway a little to their music.

"Gotta get yourself a good man," Mom says. Is her voice coming from the den? It sounds so young and full of energy.

A jolt sends my body into a fit and I feel my face being slapped. Did lightning strike me like it did Grandma while she was hanging up the wash by Lake Minnetonka?

I'm on my back and I fly through a dark tunnel, but I'm not by myself. Angels in light blue float over me. Metal screeches somewhere and now I float still. My mouth is clogged with something that tastes like a dirty rubber band. The angels move around me and all of a sudden, one of them pulls the dirty rubber band out of my mouth.

"...Angels we have heard on high..." echoes from another dark corner.

"...Glooooooria!" I sing.

My mouth is filled with the dirty rubber band again and the angels lean away from me.

"...Glooooooria!..."

Lightning shudders through me again and my fingers and toes curl up like dead claws. I fall through a black tunnel and when I hit the bottom, I see him.

"Holy Mary, mother of God ..." I hear whispered. "Mary, Madonna. Mary, Madonna with child. Mary, the Pieta," I hear the Blessed Mother say. "As you have been the Madonna, so you shall be the Pieta."

"Me? The Pieta?" I ask her.

Ernie is crouched in a corner of a room with cushions on the walls. He moves his arms like he's stabbing something. He leaps around on his haunches when he sees me and I think that he looks like a bullfrog.

"...Jeremiah was a bullfrog!..." plays in the dark. "...Was a good friend of mine!..."

Ernie keeps waving his arms and I can't see anything in his hand. But I float to him and pull his arms back and see an awful thing: a little girl, covered with blood, flailing her arms like she's swimming. She rolls over onto her back and when I see who it is, ice water shoots through my mouth: it's Gopher Foot. I laugh when I see it's her, and Ernie keeps hopping around her.

371

How did she get bloody? Ernie doesn't have a knife and I can't figure it out. But I keep laughing, anyway.

"You stole my Artie!" I scream. "You look like a dead gopher, now!" I laugh more. My body rises above Ernie and Gopher Foot. A chant echoes through my chest.

"Pray for us sinners...pray for us sinners..." the voices rumble together.

--Who's touching me? The hands are rough. Who's touching me?

Kathie, Martha, and Susan stare at me with tears in their eyes. I feel the gentle scratch of terry bath towels as I raise my arms. The towels surround my head and shoulders, too.

"Why are you acting like this, Mom?" Kathie screams. She grabs Martha and Susan's hands and runs down the hall. I run into my bedroom to the mirror on top of my dresser. I see green and turquoise towels draped around my head and shoulders -- how'd they get there? They do make me look like the Blessed Mother, though.

I'm on my back again. I see a haze floating in the black. It floats above me and in the white haze, I see Andrew's face.

"Andrew! Come to me!" I yell. My heart races out of my chest.

"Andrew, my Andrew" I scream. His face slides back into the haze, and I feel a darkness wrap around me. My nipples harden and I feel a rush in my privates. Is he here to touch me?

"...Now and at the hour of our death..." the chanters chant again.

"Now and at the hour of our death..."

My brain is electric with panic. My legs kick and my hands swing but I'm not doing it.

"Andrew! Andrew! Andrew!"

The haze swirls up again.

"Andrew! You're back. You're—"

This time, it isn't Andrew. Father Crawford stands near me, surrounded by frankincense smoke. He waves the incense burner toward me and its chain creaks like it needs oil. Father Crawford is naked again, except for a trail of the smoke that winds around his body like a scarf.

"Bless me, Father. I'm gonna sin!" I say out loud. He smiles at me and waves his arm, making a wreath of smoke around me. It smells like burning lilies and makes my skin tingle. Father Crawford keeps walking around me, laughing, and the smoke starts to tighten around me. I see the head of a snake as Father Crawford steps up to me. He grabs hold of my arms and I feel my nipples turn to rocks. My heart pounds.

"Mary, Mary Murphy?" a warm voice calls me from the dark. I float toward it, but I start to feel those hands on me again.

--Who's touching me? What's going on?--

372

"Mary, are you awake?"

My eyes pry open and I see Father Crawford leaning over my bed, his hands on my shoulders. The sheers over my bedroom window billow in and out from the wind. Frogs roar and cackle in the sump and I know I'm in my bedroom.

Was I dreaming?

"Mary, the Lord has healed you," Father Crawford said.

The kids bounded into the bedroom, led by Maureen.

"Mom!" Kathie cried. "We heard your voice and you finally sounded normal."

Danny hopped up on the end of the bed, making the pink chenille bedspread vibrate.

"What's going on'" I asked.

"Rest, Mary. It's okay. You've been through some terrible things."

"That's right," a voice cracked through the room like lightning. "Rest, dee-yer, I'm here to help."

Daisy stood at the end of the bed, with Kathie and Martha at her side. I didn't know what day it was, what time it was, or why I was in bed. No matter how crazy I was, I knew I didn't want Daisy near.

24.

"Mom, are you schizo??" Maureen asked a few days later.

Since I woke up from the crazy place, I just hadn't felt the same at all. I wanted to get up, I thought, but then I'd see the kids needed something to eat or a skirt needed to be hemmed and I just didn't know how to care about anything. My body was full of sand and my head was light as a balloon. Nothing was right, nothing was okay. That's when the psychiatrist suggested I should start this diary. Write everything down about my life I could remember to help him understand me I guess. Some days, it was the only thing I could manage to do.

'The Secret Storm' blared on the TV on the nightstand. Maureen sat on the edge of the bed, picking at the chenille bedspread.

"It must've been that, Mom, don't you think?"

I shrugged but I felt so tired just from doing that. An aluminum platter jangled.

"She had a plain old nervous breakdown, dee-yer," Daisy said.

She set the tray on the end of the bed and I saw the gray and lumpy bowl of oatmeal. Daisy's eyes, bugging out from behind her thick glasses, were beady dots in the swirl of lines on her face. Her hair was still brown and she wore it short -- probably to hide her age. Was Daisy here to stay? I shook when I thought that.

"Eat your lunch, dee-yer."

"Some lunch," Maureen said.

Daisy turned on her heels and pointed at Maureen.

"What did you say, Missy?"

Maureen rolled her eyes and kept picking at the bedspread.

"It's just that all she's had the whole week is oatmeal. I could bring her a burger or tuna Sandwich from Bob's."

"I think I know what's best for her," Daisy snarled. "I know for sure I don't need lip from you."

"Oh, Gram," Maureen said. "I——"

Danny screamed in the living room. Daisy sighed, shifted her eyes back and forth between Maureen and me, and then shuffled out the door. I didn't like that Daisy was treating Maureen that way, but I was too tired to do anything about it.

"I told you once, little man," Daisy yelled from the living room.

Her screaming made my skin tense up to goose flesh. "No 'Sheriff John'. That's it!"

"Please, Gram, I'll be good," he pleaded with her.

Martha's laugh pierced the air.

"No 'Sheriff John'. Get to your room."

"Want me to see what it's all about, Mom?" Maureen asked.

"No," I heard myself whisper. Maybe the kids do need discipline, I thought. I was glad she was here for it--I wouldn't have had the strength for it.

"Mom!" Maureen startled me. "You're gazing off again."

The doctor told us that my medicine would make me so relaxed that sometimes, I might just stare off like I used to when I was younger. Only now, I wouldn't be able to control as well as I did then. He told the kids to just tell me when it happened and I'd be able to control it better. I wasn't doing very well with that yet.

"I hate you, Gram!" Danny hollered. His bedroom door slammed shut and Daisy's little feet scampered past my open door. Maureen jumped up.

"I'll be back."

"No, he can come with me," Maureen yelled a minute later.

"Just like your mother!" Daisy screamed.

Maureen dragged Danny into the bedroom and pushed him down on the bed.

"Just stay with us for a little bit," she said.

"Is it okay, Momma?" His voice was scratchier than usual and his brown hair was matted at his temples from sweat. I nodded at him.

"I'm kind'a hot," he said.

It was probably eighty-five outside and real muggy. Usually in September, crisp, dry Santa Anas started to blow.

"I'll open the other window," Maureen said. "It's kind'a stuffy."

As she stepped to the window, it felt like I was watching a movie. My head felt either stuffed or empty like a balloon. Maureen pushed and pulled but couldn't get it to budge. A wave of sadness rolled over me-- Andrew was the only one who could ever get that window to open.

"I'll try," Danny said. He jumped up and stood at Maureen's side.

"Danny, you're seven and I'm twenty-three. Who do you think—" SHRIEK!

The window slid on its frame and a little muggy breeze filtered through the dirty metal screen.

"Now how'd you get it to open?" Maureen said, standing back with her hands on her hips. Danny just shrugged.

"It's still too hot in here," he said.

He plopped back on the bed.

"Icicles," I said.

"What?" Maureen asked.

"You guys think the heat is bad?" I said, but my throat squeezed it into a whisper. "You outta see the icicles in Hopkins at winter. They make your house into a big, frozen jail cell the way they hang from the roof."

"You lived in jail cells in Hopkins?" Danny asked. His eyes were big as coat buttons.

I shook my head.

"Come on, Danny," Maureen said. "I think Mom needs a little nap."

She grabbed Danny's hand and he pulled away from her.

"I wanna bless her."

He ran out of the room and then darted back in with his pink and brown fingers dripping with water. He rubbed his fingers on my forehead, making the sign of the cross on it.

"I bless you with our holy water. Okay, now you can take a nap."

When they left the room, I rolled over onto my side. As my eyes started to fall closed, I reached my arm out but it landed on the empty side of the bed.

"Andrew," I whispered. "Andrew, what's happened? Where are you? What's going on?"

"Jesus, Mary and Joseph, what's going on?" Daisy yelled a couple weeks later. A dry, cold wind blew outside, making the bottlebrush trees bend and look like bloody brooms. September's heat blew away in this first week of October.

"Oh, this is never gonna come off!" she hollered.

Danny and I had been coloring pumpkins, ghosts, black cats, and a witch to hang in the living room windows. In between smelling his sixty-four box of crayons, that is--he kept making me smell them but all they smelled like to me was raisins and wax. The weird music of the show 'Dark Shadows' played in the background, making our Halloween decorating more fun.

RIP!

Daisy shook an orange, construction paper pumpkin at Danny and me.

"Don't you have any sense left? Why are you letting him hang this crap up with Scotch tape on your purple walls?"

She set down the bags of groceries she had just bought and cocked her head from side to side.

Danny crawled behind me, sandwiching himself between the back of the couch and my back. I looked past Daisy and saw the pumpkins and

376

the black cat on the wall. I didn't notice anything except for how fun all the decorations looked.

"There's glue everywhere," she went on, her sunglasses making her eyes dark caves. "Look at the couch here."

She pointed to a thick smear of glue on the black, Naugahyde couch arm.

"Let me see your hands—"

"Don't make me come out, Gram," he pleaded. "I'll be good."

"Too late. Your gooey handprints are all over the walls, the couch, and the table. For crying out loud."

I shrugged. I didn't know what to say.

"I was only gone to Foods Company for an hour. I guess you can't even take care of your own son."

But I wasn't really hearing Daisy anymore because the TV was close on Barnabas Collins's face as he opened his mouth to bite someone. All of a sudden, John Schubek the newsman came on.

"Coming up at four o'clock, the details on President Nixon's leg surgery."

Daisy turned and punched the TV off.

"Enough of that noise."

"But I love my news," I said.

"Too noisy. Danny, go get a Handi Wipe from under the sink. Bring the Four-oh-nine, too. You got some cleaning up to do."

"Gram, my hands are too sticky."

"Go wash and get back out here."

Daisy picked up the grocery bags from the porch and shuffled into the kitchen. I was by myself in the living room now and I looked at our decorations and loved them. Danny was getting so good at art. But the longer I looked at the pumpkins with their big smiles, the more I thought about Andrew. He loved Halloween like I did. The weather, the night-blooming Jasmine, the ghosts and goblins, he loved them all. My chest squeezed like an accordion and I shoved a wad of red construction paper in my mouth to keep Daisy from hearing me cry.

"You whimpering again?" Daisy said a week later. "You keep blubbering all the time, I'll call Doctor Stevenson."

I lay in bed, trying to help Susan sew her Lily Munster costume. I was tired, but I was getting more tired from doing nothing. Daisy was cooking, Daisy was cleaning, and Daisy was taking care of the kids mostly. I should have been appreciating it but every time I tried to do anything at all for the kids, she'd step in and take it over. 'You need your rest' she'd say. The words sounded nice and loving, but the way she said them, with her mean little smile, made them more like accusations. So sitting here pinning a hem on the gray chiffon with Susan helped me feel like I was doing something.

"The hem's a little uneven on that side, Mom," Susan said.

She plucked the straight pins out of the hem.

"Never mind, I'll do it," she sighed.

"Mommy!" Danny yelled from the living room. "I'm hot again."

"Why don't you——"

"Leave your mom be, mister," Daisy snarled. "She needs her rest."

"Why doesn't she ever call us by our names?" Susan whispered.

"Makes her more unusual and special, I guess," I whispered back.

We had all started to whisper lately whenever Daisy was around -- I think the whole family was scared of her. As I smoothed a wrinkle in one part of the material, I suddenly thought of the Blessed Mother. It seemed like I had almost forgotten her. But when I saw her in my mind's eye, with her flowing robe and soft, peaceful, all-knowing face, I felt a lump build in my throat.

"I'm gonna have the best costume at school. I'm so glad Mrs. Conroy brought this leftover material for me," Susan said.

But my ears were clogged and my eyes were fuzzy with tears.

"Mmm-hmm" was all I could say.

Danny ran into the room and when I looked up, he stopped. His eyebrows crinkled.

"Wait, Mommy," he said.

He darted out of the room and in a second was back in with a box of Kleenex. He dropped it on the bed next to me. Susan wrinkled her nose at it.

"What's that for?" she asked.

"Mom's sad again," he said. "I know why, too."

"Why?" Susan asked without looking up from her material. She had just begun to sew and she yanked the white thread tightly.

"She misses Daddy," he said softly. "Do you want me to make an altar?"

I grabbed a Kleenex and shook my head.

"Looks like the Social Security check's got here on time," Daisy hollered from the living room.

I blew my nose and wiped my eyes quickly, afraid Daisy would see me. As Daisy rounded the corner into the bedroom, Danny jumped behind the open door.

"Oh, no, for crying out loud," Daisy said. She slapped a brown envelope with her left hand. "You blubbering again? Why? More money's coming in now than when Andrew was working. You got nothing to cry about."

"I don't know," I said. "Sometimes I just feel bad."

"You been crying too much again. I'll call Doctor Stevenson and see if there's something else he can give you besides that anti-loony stuff."

"Maybe I need to get back to church," I said. "It's been a long time."

"No. I'll call Father Crawford and see if he'll come out here and do a mass. Anyway, I'm gonna get this into the bank."

Daisy turned and left. Was Dr. Stevenson going to come and shoot me full of something else? Was I ever going to get back to church?

"Mom, can I go to Hall's Five and Ten to get my costume today?" Danny asked as he stepped out from behind the door. He kept an eye out for Daisy. When the back door slammed shut, he stepped back into the middle of the room.

"Gram's going out to Crocker Bank. Why don't you see if she'll bring you?"

"I want you to take me, Mommy."

Susan stopped sewing and looked up.

"Yeah, Mom. Why don't you and Danny go for a walk to Halls? Gram's gonna be gone for awhile and I'm okay here."

"Please, Mommy," Danny said, pulling on my arm to get me out of bed.

I didn't know if I could even get up. My legs felt like toothpicks stuck in lard. My head was still a balloon, too. But Danny's brown eyes were almost begging. I suddenly thought about how awful the last six months had been for him since Andrew died and I'd gone nuts. His brown eyes looked old and sad even as they sparkled and pleaded for a Halloween costume.

"Okay. Let me see what I got to wear."

A few minutes later, Danny and I walked down the front walk and onto the sidewalk. Each step I took felt like ground glass and shot spikes of pain up my legs. I guess it was because I hadn't been out of bed for so long, and not outside since they brought me back from Harbor General. As we walked toward Arlington Avenue, the shadows of the bottlebrush trees stretched out onto the asphalt of Two Ninety-Eighth Street. The shadows were long from the October sun and were only interrupted by the explosions of shade made by the Brazilian pepper trees. Cool wind tickled my face and the sun warmed my back. The air was good.

"We gotta turn right up here," Danny said. He ran ahead of me and kicked up dust where the sidewalk ended just before Arlington. He stood at the corner waiting for me as I dragged my feet over the dry dirt and pebbles.

"Mom, can we stop at Takahashi's for a Bubble Up? I'm thirsty."

379

"Okay."

By the time we got to the glass door at Takahashi's, my faded pink and blue housedress stuck to my skin from sweat. Danny creaked the door open, stopped at the nickel peanut machine and rocked its handle back and forth only to get one small peanut. He popped it into his mouth then raced to the back wall of the store.

"Grab me a Fresca!" I hollered, but didn't know if he heard or not.

I pulled my pink coin purse from my dress pocket and could feel the breeze from the ceiling fan tickle my neck. Stale gum, old fruit, and cherry tobacco mixed in the air.

"Meesus Murphy" a friendly male voice said from around a corner. "How you are?"

Mr. Takahashi broke out into a grin, flashing his gold front tooth that sparkled.

"You okay these day?" he asked.

"Yeah, Mister Takahashi. I'm all right."

He rubbed his hand on his beige apron as he limped toward me. (No one could ever ask Mr. Takahashi why he limped from a war wound, and Andrew told me I could never talk to him, anyway.) He grabbed my hand and shook it.

"Good you up and round."

"Thank you."

Danny ran up, clutching the two green soda bottles like they were logs. I popped open my coin purse.

"No, Meesus Murphy," Mr. Takahashi said. "You have feel better treat I give."

"Thanks, Mister Takahashi. It's real warm outside."

He nodded and smiled. He turned toward Danny and the smile dropped from his face like a bomb.

"You no steal no candy?"

Danny shook his head.

"No Boston Bake Bean or Jugi Fruits?"

Danny shook his head again. Mr. Takahashi's eyes turned to slits like he didn't believe Danny. Then he nodded.

"Okay. You go. Take care of mother, Murphy. She good mother."

"Thank you again, Mister Takahashi."

We pried open our pop bottles by the side door, paused just long enough for Danny to check the bubble gum and toy machines, then started back down Arlington. All the shadows from bottle brush trees and Brazilian peppers were swallowed up in the looming shadows of the eucalyptus trees. The musky odor of the trees swirled around us. My mouth burned with the grapefruit flavor of Fresca.

"Know what I'm gonna be for Halloween?" Danny asked after he swallowed a gulp of Bubble Up.

"What?"

"The Devil."

Fresca spurted up my nose when he said that, making my nostrils burn. I coughed.

"Why?"

"You ain't supposed to sniff Fresca, Mommy. You supposed to drink it."

"Real funny, smart alek. Why the Devil?"

"'Cause he's the scariest thing there is. In my catechism book, he's all green and blue with red eyes and fangs with blood on them."

I thought of Andrew as he went on about the Devil, and I hoped he was looking down on us right then--I knew he couldn't be looking up at us. He's with you, isn't he, Blessed Mother? I thought.

"There's H & H!" Danny said. He ran ahead of me to the big feed and pet store that looked like an old, brown barn. I could smell the stale celery odor of rabbit pellets mixed with the peanut smell of alfalfa and hay as I walked up behind Danny. For just a second, the smells transported me back to Hopkins and Minnehaha Falls. But the barn doors of the feed store reminded me of where I was. You could buy everything from sunflower seeds for birds to hay for horses. The rich people up in Rolling Hills were the only ones who bought the hay, I guess.

"Ooh, it always stinks here," Danny said.

"That's what my hometown Hopkins smelled like."

"Hopkins must'a' stunk."

We got to Halls Five and Ten about five minutes later and as we walked in, a small bell on the door rang. An ancient lady with curly, white hair and wearing a dingy, pink sweater looked from around an aisle.

"Hello," she said.

Before I could answer, Danny thrust his bottle of Bubble Up at me and ran for a row of bins down the center of the store. He pulled candy out from the bins like he was plucking feathers.

"Look!" he hollered. "Candy cigarettes. Ooh, wax lips! And Kits!"

The bins of candy made the small store, that usually smelled like mothballs, smell like a trick-or-treat bag.

"Hot Tamales! Candy lipstick!"

"Don't go messin' up the bins now, youngster," the old lady said.

"Mom? Can't I get some? They're only a penny each."

"Costumes first. We'll see after that."

Danny nodded and dropped two cellophane packages of miniature malt balls that looked like caterpillars back into the bin. A cardboard skeleton with a big smile hung above the candy and pointed down the aisle. His other hand balanced an orange sign marked with felt tip pen that read: 'Costumes. This way.' Danny jerked his head up long enough to read the sign, then ran down the aisle. As I rounded the corner, I could hear his tennis shoes scratch against the floor.

"Look at this mask, Mommy."

Danny pulled a mask from a shelf lined with costume boxes that were the same size as the five pound See's candy nuts and chews Daisy brought for Christmas. Danny held the mask up and it was painted with those new, bright colors--fluorescents, I think they're called--all around the eyes and cheeks. On top of the mask sat a coiled snake with its mouth open to strike.

"I like this mask," Danny said.

"What is it?"

"I don't know. It's just spooky, isn't it?" he said.

I pulled down another box.

"Don't be too hasty. What about this one?"

"I don't like Casper."

I slid the box back. Grabbing another, I glanced in the box as Danny leaned against me.

"What's that one?" he asked.

I showed him the costume box.

"A doo-bee from Romper Room? Mommy, that's not very scary at all."

He held the cobra man mask very tightly.

"Danny, that one doesn't have a costume. I think it's just the mask."

Danny looked through the whole shelf, his hands pulling out costume boxes like they were dresser drawers, sliding them back into place each time with a frustrated sigh. All the time, he held onto that wacky, strange mask.

"How about an Agent Eighty-Seven costume?"

"'Get Smart's not scary."

"Look at this Barnabas Collins costume--don't tell me 'Dark Shadows' isn't scary."

"It's real scary but I don't wanna be a vampire."

I knew what he was hunting for and between the cobra man and Lucifer, I preferred he'd be the ugly cobra man.

"Don't mess up the aisle there!" the old lady hollered.

Danny stopped pulling out the boxes. He leaned against the wall and studied the cobra man mask.

"I guess I want to be this one," he said.

"Okay. Just let me check how much."

The mask was marked a dollar-fifty. The rest of the costumes were two seventy-nine, so I guessed we would save some money anyway. I nodded and took the mask from Danny.

"Can I get some penny candies now?"

"A quarter's worth--but that's it."

"Oh, boss!"

We paid for the candy and mask, and the old lady never smiled or said thank you. I couldn't believe how rude people were getting. When we stepped out the door, we stopped at the window display that looked like a miniature graveyard with Popsicle sticks for headstones and angel hair for fog around the stones. Traffic whirred behind us.

"I could make this at our house," Danny said.

He was right--he was so good with arts and crafts and all. Danny turned quickly.

"I'll go press the cross walk."

"Wait."

I don't know how to explain it, but I felt like I wanted to go to St. Joan's right then. It was only a few blocks further, and the temperature was fine for a longer walk. Besides, I hadn't been to mass since Andrew's funeral in April. Six months. I needed to go.

"We're gonna walk a little further, Danny."

Right where Hall's Five and Ten sits, Arlington Street turns into Narbonne Avenue, marking the beginning of the city of Lomita. The street grew wider and busier right after Lomita Boulevard. We walked along past Hank's Garage, where Andrew used to take the red Herald for repairs. Engine oil and dirty metal smells floated across the street and hit our nostrils. My body tensed up -- how many times Andrew and I brought the car to Hanks and then walked on to confession, I couldn't say.

"Hank's scares me," Danny said.

"Why's that?"

"That big thing that raises the cars up--it's real loud and scary."

Danny was afraid of a lot since Andrew died and it was starting to worry me. All I ever heard him talk about lately was something he was afraid of. I didn't know what to tell him.

"You know who to pray to when you're scared, don't you, Danny?"

"Little Nellie?"

"No. That's only when you lose something. Can't you think of who?"

"Daddy?"

My stomach clenched like he slugged me--yeah, when I was afraid lately, I felt like praying to Andrew, too. I missed his strength.

"You can pray to your Dad if you want. But there's someone better even to pray to."

"Who? Jesus?"

"No. Pray to Virgin Mary."

I pulled out my coin purse and opened it. Inside was a little relic. I held it up to Danny.

"See this?"

"Looks like a Valentimes heart."

I flipped the red felt heart over and it did look like a valentine.

"Read what it says, Danny."

He steadied my hand, then read: "Place thy heart in the hands of Mary, Mother of God, and fear nothing."

"You read well."

Danny jerked his hand away.

"Do I have to pull my heart out and give it to Mary?"

"No. It's just a reminder, Danny. It helps me—"

I stopped. I forgot that in order to get to the street St. Joan's was on, you had to stay on Narbonne past Gordon's Mortuary. I couldn't look at the mortuary or its small steeple.

"What's a matter?" Danny asked.

"Let's walk on the other side of the street."

"There's no crosswalk here. Up where the small church is we can cross."

"No. We'll cross here."

I grabbed Danny's hand and looked both ways. No traffic was coming and we ran across the street. Danny laughed the whole way across.

"That was fun, Mommy."

We kept walking and I looked straight ahead. I didn't even want to see the mortuary out the corner of my eye.

"Is that place where Daddy was when he was dead?"

I wished he hadn't recognized the mortuary.

"Yeah."

"Why you walking so fast, Mommy?"

"Just want to get to the church."

By the time we turned left on Two Eighty-Fifth Street, my temples were sopping with sweat. Danny's hand was a warm washcloth in mine. He pulled his hand away as I slowed our pace. We had walked thirteen blocks from home by that point and I'm sure he was feeling as tired as me.

"My hand's too sweaty."

The late afternoon sun played hide 'n' seek with the maples on Two Eighty-Fifth, leaving long, October shadows wherever it blazed through. It seemed like years -- not months --since I traveled down this street. Most of the time then, Andrew's hand was wrapped around mine as we drove the kids to Sunday mass. My heart pounded as we walked closer to Fleming Avenue and the church. A silk screen of tears clogged my eyes and my throat felt like I swallowed a lump of charcoal.

The gold, stucco steeple now loomed ahead of us, its red tile roof just under the cross looking like bloody tears. When Danny and I stood at the edge of the front portico of the church, I couldn't lift my foot to climb the four stairs. The Spanish arches of the portico made me see that day again, and the oak box that took Andrew away. My head felt like it was going to float off my body.

"Is church open now?" Danny asked.

"I think so."

"Let's go in then."

"I can't."

"Oh. Need me to bless you so you can go in?"

I shot my arm out to balance myself. My whole body felt like it was about to collapse and I rolled my head to the side so Danny couldn't see me.

"You gonna barf, Mommy?"

I shook my head as my legs began to give out. I pressed so hard against the stucco that its jagged, little points gouged into my thick palm. As I started to let my rear end settle onto the step, the church door creaked open.

"Mary Murphy?"

Father Crawford stood at the door, his hands on his hips and his face knitted with surprise or confusion--I wasn't sure. His voice sent a jolt through me and I jumped up like a guilty kitten.

"Hello, Father Crawford."

"Well what do you know? I wasn't expecting to see you back here for awhile yet."

When he spoke, I felt my body sort of sigh, then relax. All the pain I was just having over Andrew seemed to just disappear. I shrugged.

"You come for confession?"

Before I could answer him, he jumped to my side because I started to fall over. Before they hauled me off and I stopped making it to confession, I always made it to Father Sbaraglia--I felt awkward and guilty around Father Crawford.

"Why don't you two come on in and have a seat in one of the pews?"

Father Crawford put his arm around my waist and my skin broke out into goose bumps--I'm going to burn in hell for sure, I thought. A priest shouldn't make you feel excited. But it had been over a year since Andrew could put his arm around me and Father Crawford's felt so good.

Danny walked ahead of us and opened the door. As Father Crawford and I passed through, the smell of dry carnations and stale water made my head spin; St. Joan's always smelled like that. My eyes scanned the familiar, mahogany pews, moved up to the ochre wood crucifix, then over to the niche where She stood above the blue devotional candles. My heart pounded as images of Andrew's flag-draped casket flashed in my mind like a slide show. His face, tight and asleep, his yellow hands, his onyx rosary.

"Mary?" Father Crawford said. "Have a seat."

But as I sat, I felt a rumble through my body and I started to shake. My throat slammed closed and my eyes exploded with tears.

"No!" I screamed. "No, no, no..."

"Mama?" Danny cried.

Father Crawford must have been right next to me because I felt his arms clamp my shoulders. He pulled me to him and I my body heaved and pumped with pain and tears. I couldn't stop and I wanted to jump up but my mouth rolled and boiled with spit and tears.

"Oh, Father, oh, why..."

My body twitched and jerked and there in the huge, quiet nave of St. Joan's, I couldn't hold it back any longer and I screamed with anger, with pain, and with loneliness. I don't know how long my fit lasted, but I felt Father Crawford's voice vibrating in his chest as he spoke.

"Mary? Mary?"

Pulling my face away, I could feel strands of my hair sticking to my wet, hot face like postage stamps.

"Mary, I've got to hear confessions in a few minutes."

"We have to go, Father."

"Why don't you rest over at the rectory and we can talk after that. You shouldn't be driving in this state you're in."

"It's okay, Father. We walked here. We'll go now."

"Finally," Danny said. He popped up from behind a pew where he must have been laying.

"I wanna go home and make my costume."

"Okay."

I stood up but I felt heavy and dead. Father Crawford grabbed my hand.

"You can go now. But I'm coming out to the house Monday."

"Okay."

"We'll pray the rosary. Mary, think about this till then."

"What?"

386

"It's understandable that you're in pain. Let yourself cry or scream whenever you need."

You don't live with Daisy Murphy, I thought.

"Thank you, Father. I'm sorry we bothered you. Monday rosary sounds good."

"Mommy, would you hold my mask?" Danny said a few minutes later as we turned back onto Narbonne Avenue. "My hand's getting sweaty from the coke bottles."

I took the mask from Danny and he shifted the Bubble Up and Fresca bottles to both hands now. The mask was moist from his sweat.

"Can we cash these in for two nickels?" he asked.

We were just a block away from Takahashi's as we made our way down Arlington. I didn't see any problem with that--I wasn't all that anxious about getting home, anyway.

"Okay."

Danny walked out of Takahashi's with a Snickers candy bar a few minutes later. He screamed: I was wearing the mask and I jumped at him.

"You scared me, Mommy."

"Oh, you're okay. I was just having a little Halloween fun. (I did it more for me than for him--I had to stop thinking about how embarrassed I was from crying in front of Father Crawford.)

The rubber band on the mask pulled up on the hair at my temples, making them sting. I rubbed them and let the mask rest on the top of my head for a second. Danny laughed.

"Funny hat, Mommy!"

I shrugged and grabbed his hand and he laughed again.

"You gonna leave my mask on your head?"

"I just might, so there."

It was getting onto four-thirty as Danny and I rounded the corner of Vine and Two Ninety-Eighth Streets.

"Mommy, put on the mask, and we'll scare Susan."

"She's at drill team practice. I gotta better idea."

I slipped the mask over my face and the plastic was cool against my cheeks. The little nose holes in the mask barely let in air.

"Let's surprise Gram!"

Danny ran ahead of me but just as I got past the Butler's front lawn, I saw an ambulance in front of our house.

"There! There she is!" I heard Daisy scream.

Before I could pull up the mask, two paramedics fell on me and grabbed my shoulders.

"See! Look how nuts she is in that mask!"

"Momma!" Danny screamed but I saw Daisy grab his arm and

yank him back.

"They're gonna help her," Daisy said.

The paramedics wrapped my hands with some sort of tape and pushed me into the back of the ambulance. One of them pulled the mask off my head, searing my temples as hair ripped out with the band.

"Don't fight us!" the other paramedic said.

"Why are you doing this—"

"It's for your safety. Now just relax."

The back of the ambulance slammed shut and one of the paramedics pulled a thick strap over me and tightened it down.

"Stop!" I screamed. "I'm okay! Help!"

Before I could holler again, I felt a needle poke my arm. My head twirled like a carousel and then everything went black.

I woke up to feel silver-blue light shining in my face. Something buzzed near my head and I thought a fly was about to land on my nose. I went to swat the fly, but I couldn't move my arm. Then I realized where I was: in a hospital. I could turn my head enough to see leather straps that bound my hands. My heart pounded.

Eighth-wing west, that's where I must've been. My mouth was dry and tasted as bitter as burnt walnuts. I didn't know what time it was, whether it was day or night, either. Someone moaned like a wolf somewhere down the hall.

"Why am I here?" I said out loud.

"Oooooooowwwwwwww..." the voice seemed to moan an answer.

"Nurse?" I said a little louder. "Nurse?"

"Oooooooooowwwwwwww..."

I wasn't crazy, I knew that much. How I got here, why I was here, I couldn't remember, not then. Another person with a high-pitched voice giggled over to my left. A low, mumbling sound, just like someone praying, seemed to be coming from the foot of my bed.

"Oooooooowwwwwwww..."

I turned my head to see the bed next to me, to see if I could make out the moaning person--it was just a little old man, his face screwed up and pursed like he just bit a lemon. His lips made a perfect circle as he moaned. On my left, a woman with blonde hair matted to her head like a broken spider web lay on her side and giggled. The praying person must have been in the bed across from the foot of mine because I could just see the steel bars of the headboard.

"Nurse!" I screamed again.

"Mary?" a warm voice called my name. A figure passed by the mumbler. It made some sort of gesture over the mumbler and when it stepped into the blue-white circle of my bed light, I could see who it was.

Father Crawford stood next to my bed, with his black doctor's bag hanging from his left hand. He got to the foot of my bed and smiled. He waved his hand over me and blessed me. All I could think about was whether my hair looked flat and greasy or not--I didn't want him to see me like this.

"Did I miss our rosary?" I asked.

"I'm surprised you thought of that. It was set for two days ago, but since your condition started and all, well, we missed it. Can I stay a minute?"

"Why not. I'm not going anywhere."

Father Crawford pulled a chair up, raking its metal legs against the hard floor. He popped open his bag, pulled out his purpled scapular, and draped it around his neck.

"Do you want to pray?" he asked. "Or do you just want communion?"

"I want to go home."

"You can't just yet, Mary. You've had another episode."

"When?"

"Saturday. I guess after you visited with me. Do you remember that?"

The leather straps twisted and gouged into the skin of my wrists.

"My Lord, I didn't do anything crazy to the kids did I?"

"No."

"I could never live with myself if I did anything to any of them."

"They're fine, Mary."

"Who's with them?"

"Your mother-in-law."

"Father, please loosen my arms. These straps really hurt."

"Mary, they said you might hurt yourself if I do."

"Father, there's nothing wrong with me this time, I swear."

"That's not what the doctor says."

My mouth turned into slimy cotton suddenly. I licked my lips quickly.

"Water, please, Father."

Father Crawford reached over and held a metal tumbler with a straw in it up to my mouth. The cool water sparked in my mouth then slid down my dry throat. I sucked on the straw with all my strength.

"Did I seem okay when I saw you on Saturday?"

"Other than being upset, you seemed fine."

"Nothing happened after that--ouch. Father, please loosen these."

"Mary—"

"Father Crawford, please!"

Father Crawford looked around at the mumbler, the giggler, and the moaner. He looked back at me and his lips rolled around like he was trying to decide if he should loosen them or not. Could he tell that I was okay?

"Your mother-in-law said she had to call the paramedics," he whispered. He slowly loosened the straps and my wrists began to move free again. I slipped my hands out of the straps.

"She said your medicine must not have been working because you wandered off with Danny and no one knew where you were."

"We went for a walk to get his Halloween costume. And then, oh, yeah, we stopped by the church. You were there."

"That took two hours?"

"Father, I hadn't been out in forever. When I felt the sun and fresh air, it just felt so good to be out. I mean, I was embarrassed that I cried and all with you. But I'm not crazy."

"Why did Mrs. Murphy have you hauled off then?"

If I ever had heard the 64,000 dollar question, that was it.

"My mother-in-law thinks I'm not good for anything but having babies and crying. She thinks her way is the only way to do anything. I guess you can't understand."

"Ooooooowwwwwww..."

Father Crawford shifted his head to look at the moaner. He raised his right hand and blessed him. I could smell cloves as he did it--or was that Bay Rum?

"I gotta get back to the kids, Father. Daisy's just scaring the hell--sorry -- heck out of 'em."

"Mary, you don't sound unstable to me."

"Father, I can't say I haven't been loony before--I mean, visions of the Blessed Mother, and her talking to me and all."

"Maybe you did have some sort of miracle visited on you."

"But Daisy just did what she always does--she over reacted. I didn't have time to say anything before they hauled me off."

Father Crawford reached out and slipped his hand around mine. It was warm, dry, and strong. Right then I noticed that the left side of his gray hair, right by the part, was messed so much that it looked a little like a bale of hay. I reached out and fixed it--I don't know why I did. Father Crawford jerked his hand from mine.

"Uhh, thank you."

He cleared his throat and I started to feel odd. Somewhere between guilty and missing Andrew.

"I'll see what I can do to help you," he said.

An hour later, Father Crawford vouched responsibility for me. I had slipped into the same dress I was wearing when they brought me in, and as Father Crawford's pen scratched his signature on the last piece of paper on the nurses' counter, I glanced up at the black enamel letters on the wall: 'Psychiatric Ward' -- the eighth floor of the west wing. I swore as he finished signing the last page that I was never going to be back here again. I was so mad at Daisy.

Father Crawford drove me home in the church's VW wagon. A three-inch statue of the Blessed Mother rattled on the edge of the black dashboard that had been cracked by the sun. Father Crawford's Bay Rum mixed with old cigarettes and the heat of the day made my dress stick to my skin. When we pulled up to the front of the house, he shut the engine off. It made me nervous and I started to twist my hair between my fingers.

"It's been almost ninety the last couple of days," he said. "Sorry I had no air conditioning for you."

"I hate October heat," I said.

"Mary, Mrs. O'Toole has quit as the housekeeper. She's retiring."

"Yes, Father?"

"I know the kids are all in school now--Danny's practically grown up. Did you ever think about working?"

"Work? I spend every day washing clothes, dusting the coffee table, making beds, everything."

"I know how hard you work, Mary. I meant outside the house."

"You mean a job?"

"Yes."

"I haven't worked since the war. I don't know if I can."

"Well, think about it. The church pays decently enough, and if you could use the extra money around the house, we could sure use you."

"I'll think about it, Father."

But right then, all I could think about was how mad I was at Daisy. I wanted her out of the house.

"Father, would you come inside a second--just while I talk to Daisy. I think it's time for her to go and I could sure use your support."

"Sure, Mary. I can stay a minute."

It was two o'clock and the nasty heat that strangled my breath seemed to now pull all of my energy away. My housedress stuck to me like candle wax as I walked up to the front door. The kids wouldn't be home from school for another hour and I knew now was the best time to get rid of Daisy. I waited for Father Crawford to shut the car doors and join me on the porch.

As I stood waiting for him, I couldn't take my eyes off the black construction paper witch flying in front of the yellow paper moon that hung in the middle pane of the front door glass. To our left, where the skinny living room window lay open, a black construction paper tail twisted like a spring from a cat with red, half-moon-shaped eyes. Danny did it all and I was so proud of his artistic talent. He got it from me. Maybe he'd pursue art while he ran a parish, I hoped.

"Oh, this heat," Father Crawford said as he stepped up behind me.

I twisted the stained, tin knob of the front door and heard the organ music of 'One Life to Live' trumpeting from the den. She's even taken over watching my stories, I thought. My feet sunk into the high-low carpet just outside the den--I didn't know when I would be able to get the hole patched. Father Crawford dipped his fingers in the Pieta holy water font next to the hall.

"What the heck you doing here?" Daisy shrieked.

She leapt up from the couch, throwing a pile of saltines from her lap.

"You scared the hell—" she stopped as soon as she saw Father Crawford.

"Sorry, Father. What're you doing here? You're supposed to be in the hospital another week."

I stepped toward the couch and a saltine crackled under my foot.

"Don't go making any messes I'll have to clean up," she said.

"You won't be doing anymore cleaning up around here."

I felt my face flush and my throat choked on my words.

"You don't know what you're saying," Daisy hissed. "Father, she's gotta get back to Harbor General."

"Mrs. Murphy," he said. "If I can speak on Mary's behalf."

"Just...go!" I screamed.

"Mary, let me say it," he said.

But I lunged toward Daisy and she scampered back and fell on the couch, her little legs flipping up in the air like a Can-Can dancer.

"You saw that, Father. She's loony. She's dangerous!"

"Mrs. Murphy, that's where you made a mistake. Mary's as sane as you or me."

"Ha!" she bellowed.

"We don't need you anymore, Daisy. You're too mean. We don't want you here."

"Father, she's crazy," Daisy said. "She doesn't know what she's saying."

Vicki/Nicki, the split personality character on 'One Life to Live,' laughed crazily on the TV as the organ music chimed up to a commercial. It almost felt like the music was for us, not the TV show.

"Ladies, let's just sit down," Father Crawford said.

"No. I want her to buzz off!" I said.

"I'm not leaving my grandchildren with a feeb. She can't even take

392

care of herself."

"They're my kids, you nasty old bitch!"

"Mary, please," Father Crawford said.

I felt bad for saying that in front of Father Crawford, but it felt so good to say it to Daisy.

"I'd expect that kind of talk from a Bohunk."

"Ladies, please. We're all good Catholics now, aren't we?"

Daisy snorted and crossed her arms. I stepped across the room and sat down on an end table. The smell of licorice blew in through the open back window that faced the sump. Anise was blossoming everywhere.

"Father, are you really behind this whole thing?' Daisy asked.

"Yes, I am."

"Then you're gonna burn in hell right along with her."

Daisy jumped up and her little feet rattled across the floor. She turned at the den door and glared at Father Crawford, her eyes tight as two knitting needles.

"I'd never act against the Church.'

She spun toward me. "I'll never forgive you if any of my grand kids--and I mean blood grandchildren--grow up screwy. It's gonna be because of you and your gypsy, Bohunk blood."

She spun back toward Father Crawford. "These kids won't be safe with her, Father. I hope the Church steps in when she screws it all up."

But I didn't screw anything up, at least not then. According to Father Crawford a couple of weeks later, I was the best housekeeper the rectory ever had. I had just flushed the toilet and as it swirled and gurgled, the pine and disinfectant smell spun up into my face.

"You actually disinfected in there, too? Father Crawford said. He leaned against the doorway in his shirtsleeves and I reached out quickly.

"Father, I haven't dusted the doorway yet."

He stepped back and I rubbed the pitted, cherry wood doorway with a dust cloth. Father Crawford laughed, and the kaleidoscope of light that shined through the stained glass window highlighted his silver hair, making it reflect a soft rainbow.

"'Course I disinfect. Otherwise, why bother?"

The way Father Crawford smiled at me made me feel funny. As I bent to pick up the bucket, one of my barrettes popped out of my hair and rattled as it hit the tile floor of the hall. Strands of red and gray hair fell in front of my eyes like spaghetti. Father Crawford bent and snatched up the tortoise shell clip.

I stood up and pulled my hair back into place. Father Crawford slid the clip back into my hair and snapped it into place. Feeling his hand near my hair made my throat suddenly close--I missed Andrew, I missed how

393

he'd stroke my hair. My eyes hazed over with tears.

"Mary, you all right?"

I snorted back my tears and cleared my throat. Wiping the tears away, my hand felt bloated from the cleaners. Father Crawford rubbed my hair gently and I leaned into his touch. He must've thought I was acting like a dog the way I leaned into his hand.

"Mary, anytime you need to talk, you let me know. I'm always here for you."

"Yeah, that's what Andrew used to say."

"Oh, I almost forgot."

He pulled an envelope out of his pocket. Handing it to me, he smiled again. I noticed the tiny gold cross in the left corner of the envelope and the words 'St. Joan's' just below it.

"What is this?" I asked.

"Your paycheck."

"Oh."

"You get one every two weeks."

I held the envelope for a second, then opened it and pulled out the check. I stared at it. What was I supposed to do with it, anyhow? He must've seen again the confused look on my face.

"What's the matter, Mary? Is the check wrong? I can call the archdiocese payroll department and make sure they re-cut you a correct one."

"It's not that."

"What, then?"

My face warmed up and I knew I was blushing--how could I tell him what was wrong?

"Mary?"

"It's just that Andrew--he--he took care of stuff like this."

"I don't understand."

"Bank stuff. Checks, and deposits, and all of it. I just used to sit in the car and wait for him."

"Did you ever write checks for bills?"

"Andrew did. Then Daisy took care of that stuff when I was sick and all."

"You never made a bank deposit?"

"Nope."

"What about groceries?"

"Andrew gave me the cash from the food budget each week. I never spent more than he allowed."

"Mary, he's been gone for six months. How have you been living?"

394

"Daisy took care of everything--she has a head for figures. I'm just a numb skull. Father, can the church just give me cash?"

"Why don't you knock off a little early today? We'll take a ride to the bank and I'll show you what you need to do."

Father Crawford drove me to Crocker Bank. I made my first deposit and my heart fluttered like a butterfly in my chest. I sort of knew how to write checks from watching Andrew, and now I knew how to get my own paychecks into the bank.

"And when it's time to reconcile your statement, I'll help you."

"Susan, Martha, get a move on!" I yelled a few weeks later. "Father Crawford is gonna be here to help me with the bank statement in about an hour. Hurry up!"

Susan and Danny were already kneeling on either side of me. We all faced the fireplace that we had just used the Saturday after Thanksgiving. The temperature had warmed up in the past two days so that we didn't need it, but it still smelled like burnt wood and charcoal.

"...I wanna make it with you..." the boy's voice sang on the radio.

"And turn off your radio, Martha. We don't need to listen to KHJ during the rosary."

"...I really think that we can—" the boy's voice stopped. I didn't mind those boys in that singing group--Loaf or Bread, I think they're called--their voices made me think of Perry and Nat.

Susan and Martha stepped out of the hall, their rosaries swinging in their hands.

"It's Susan's fault, Mom. They're playing Bread on KHJ and she didn't want to miss them."

'Shut up, Martha!' Susan yelled. 'You're the one who broke my forty-five.'

'Let's go, girls. I don't want the rosary to hold up Father Crawford.'

Martha scratched a match against the red fireplace brick just below the mantle and lit the blue and red glass candles on top of it. Andrew's face, smiling in his medic uniform from the war, glowed yellow from the candles. He looked more handsome than I could remember, his slight overbite making his whole face into one big smile.

"You sure you don't want me to lead the rosary?" Susan asked.

As well as she was doing in her catechism class, I still felt like I wanted to lead this first rosary since Andrew's death. I wasn't real sure I'd get it right, but I really wanted to try. Before we started, I looked at the kids kneeling on either side of me, each of their rosaries like some sort of pull chain. Wasn't that what rosaries really were? A pull chain to God?

"In the name of the Father..." the kids followed my genuflection and repeated the words. We were a holy drill team.

The rosary went off without a hitch--it's like Andrew was there, whispering every prayer in my ear. I didn't forget anything. It was almost like we sang through it.

"Mom, you did it just like class," Susan said. I knew it must've been okay if Susan said so.

As Danny and Susan stood up to go, I heard Martha sob. When I looked over, I saw her face sparkled with candlelit tears. Maybe she was the only one old enough to understand this important rosary.

"Martha?"

Her hands popped up to her face and swiped away the tears as if she thought she'd get in trouble for having them. I wanted to make sure she was okay, but I didn't know what to say so I said nothing. She stood up right away and I followed, but tiny jolts of pain shot up my legs.

"Legs are asleep," I said.

"Mom, can we make the Whip 'n' Chill for Father Crawford now?" Susan asked.

"Yeah. Go head. He's gonna be here in about fifteen minutes. A few minutes later, as I stood in front of my bedroom mirror running my hands through my hair to fix it, the electric hand mixer buzzed into life. Bowls clinked and clanked and the kids talked and laughed over all of the sounds.

"You're old," I said to my reflection in the mirror.

My short hair was looking more like a gray Brillo pad than the orange chrysanthemum it looked like months ago. My hand was a swollen, pink balloon with breakfast sausage for fingers. Even with all that, though, hearing the kids laugh as they made dessert made me feel warm. Could we all really be okay?

Out of nowhere, the image of Father Crawford standing at my bed with an erect private part flashed into my mind. Why was I picturing that?

"It's gotta go in the fridge awhile,' Susan's voice broke my fantasy. "No, you can't eat it now."

I looked down at my bulging breasts under the gingham collar of my blue housedress. Pulling on the waist to make them stick out more only made the dress stick to my chunky gut. Why did I even care? I let go of the fabric, sighed and headed toward the hall door.

The doorbell clanged and my stomach somersaulted as I stepped to answer it.

'Blessed Mother, please take these vulgar thoughts away,' I prayed.

Father Crawford stood on the stoop, the white glow of the front porch light making his hair into polished silver. He straightened his shoulders under his habit jacket.

"Evening, Mary."

"Hi, Father," my knees shook under me.

"I brought you a little something."

He held out a flat package wrapped in polka dot paper and white curling ribbon dripping off the top.

"Father, I should be giving you a gift for coming by to help. Oh, sorry, come on in."

"Are you going to open it?" he asked, anxious as a little boy on Christmas morning.

"Okay."

I pulled off the wrapping paper and in it was an envelope addressed to 'Mrs. Murphy.' Inside the envelope was a check for one hundred dollars!

"Father?"

"Sister Superior and I decided to refund the last six months of tuition for St. Joan's School. With the flag from Mr. Murphy's casket you donated to replace the torn one at the school, we felt you deserved this."

"I don't know what to say."

"Well, since it's a check, I figured it would give you practice with your checking account, too."

"Father, thank you. Thank Sister Superior, too, will you?"

Father Crawford stayed till nine-thirty that night and when we got to the end of balancing the checking account, he stayed for dessert. I understood the math it took to reconcile better than he understood Whip 'n' Chill--it was a mystery to him how one cup of cold milk could whip up into such a fancy dessert. He insisted that I put Whip 'n' Chill on the rectory menu. Father Crawford left just after Kathie, who was now in her first year at El Camino College and knew everything, argued with him about Viet Nam and Cambodia, and right when Danny held his hands up to make two peace signs like President Nixon did. I think it was that night when I had the awful dream.

Andrew and I sat on the bank next to Minnehaha Creek, and he looked young again, so handsome in his short sleeves. The lady's slippers surrounded us and the sun filtered through the aspens. We leaned to kiss when all of a sudden, a bunch of soldiers appeared.

"No!" I screamed as I pulled on his arm.

The soldiers were now dressed like priests and pulled and ripped Andrew from my arms. They ran off and I couldn't see Andrew anymore.

"Nooo! Nooo!!" I screamed. I kicked and woke up with sweat pouring down my face. The moon's silver light cut into the dark bedroom and my chest heaved from fear. There was nothing romantic in that moonlight and I couldn't catch my breath.

"Mommy?" I heard Danny's scratchy voice in the dark. I flipped on the night lamp and saw Danny crawl up from just outside the bedroom door. It looked like he had been sleeping by the bedroom door because his right cheek looked like a Tollhouse cookie where the high-low carpet had gouged into his young skin.

"Mommy, you okay?"

I coughed and took a deep breath. Running a hand through my hair, I tried to look okay even though it felt like I was cut in two.

"Yeah. Were you sleeping down there?"

He looked around, then down to the ground, obviously embarrassed.

"It's okay," I said.

"Yeah. I been ascared in my room by myself a lot."

"Too many monster movies on Sunday?"

"No. I'm not scared of monsters."

"What, then?"

"Why were you yelling?"

"I had a bad dream."

He stepped up and sat on the edge of the bed. His Roadrunner cartoon pajamas bunched up around his rear end. He looked at my face and his little forehead wrinkled. Placing his index finger under my eye, he wiped away a tear.

"Here, Mommy," he said.

He plucked a Kleenex from a box on the nightstand.

"I know why you been crying."

"Why?"

"You miss Daddy again. I do, too."

My throat closed and I could barely hold back my tears. He knew. I guess all the kids must've known I hurt. I blew my nose and the sound made me come back to my senses.

"What are you scared of?" I asked.

"A ghost."

"A ghost?"

"Yeah."

"You got nothing to be scared of, then. We got no ghosts."

"Yeah, huh. I heard Martha tell Susan there was a ghost here."

"Even if there was, remember. The Blessed Mother and Jesus would always take care of you. You been saying your prayers before bed?"

"Yup."

"Then you got nothing to be worried about. Jesus will watch out for you."

"Even if the ghost is Daddy?"

398

"What?"

"Martha said she saw his ghost in the bathroom and in the den."

"Martha's a little nutty, then. I never have seen your dad. Don't you think he'd come see me before Martha, anyway?"

"I guess."

"Well, he hasn't. Now go ahead and get to bed."

"But I'm still scared."

I got up and looked down the hall to see if anyone was up. The house was quiet and still. Only the frogs in the sump mumbled and croaked.

"Okay," I said. "You can sleep with me. Just till you're not scared anymore."

Danny climbed into the bed, right to Andrew's side, pulled the covers up, and in less than a minute, his breathing turned quiet and steady as he fell asleep. But as I got back under the covers, still feeling angry and odd over my dream, I felt my body finally relax again. With Danny's warmth and steady breathing, I felt calmer somehow. Oh well, I guess he wasn't going to be scared anymore and I suppose having him next to me helped me, too.

I helped take care of things again the week before Christmas. Martha, Susan, and I drove back from Christmas shopping at Sears in the Herald when it sputtered, spurted, then squealed like a tea kettle.

"What's the matter with the car, Mom?" Martha asked.

I shrugged and glanced at the gauges like Andrew used to. The needle on the temperature gauge crept up like a spider on the wall. A dull smell, like old oranges, started coming through the air vents.

"Roll down your windows!" I hollered. "I don't know if that smell is poisonous."

The car was still lurching ahead so I stepped on the gas and I saw the red eye of a stop light as I swerved to turn right onto Arlington.

"We gotta get to Hank's," I said. My heart was pounding as the temperature gauge stopped in the red, hot area of the dial.

"Why don't we stop at Mr. Smith's Shell station?" Susan asked.

"No. Your dad always said—" the car jerked and chugged and steam blew from under the hood—"he always said service stations charged too much for things. He said even though Hank is a Methodist, he still was the only mechanic he trusted."

We pulled into Hank's and the car was struggling like a caterpillar on a dandelion. It hissed like a snake was under the hood and now the smell was rotten oranges and isopropyl. Even with the windows completely rolled down, we were almost gagging from the smell.

The car inched up Hank's driveway that was stained black and brown from all the cars that must've died on it. Hank saw me and his eyes bugged out of his head. We jumped out of the car because we were sure it was going to explode as the steam screamed from under the hood.

"Mary Murphy," Hank yelled with his Texas accent. "What in the world?"

He ran one of his hands, cracked, brown, and stained with oil, through his slicked-back gray hair, then pulled up his navy blue pants and tucked in his navy blue uniform shirt over his belly.

"Hank, something's the matter with the car."

"Yeah, Darlin', I can see that. Hello girls."

"Hi Mr. Fremont," they answered together.

"Mary, whyn't you and the girls step back while I open the hood. I think I know what the problem is."

Instead of stepping back with the girls, I stood still as an idea hit me: whatever was wrong with the car, I needed to know and understand myself. I wasn't going to be able to rely on anybody else.

"Hank, if it's all the same to you, I'd like to watch you check out the car."

He stepped back and his face twisted into a bunch of irritated folds.

"Mary Murphy, you don't trust me or something after all these years?"

"Hank, that's not it, golly, no. I just figure I ought a be learning about this kind'a stuff from now on."

Hank rolled his tongue against his cheek as he thought about it, making it bulge thick as if he was holding a hard-boiled egg in it.

"Fine with me. Suit yourself. But stand back when I twist off the radiator cap 'cause it could explode all over us."

Hank reached under the Herald's hood, popped the latch and raised it up. The way the steam puffed out, you would have thought it was a Halloween cauldron. He pointed to a flat, silver cap.

"That's the radiator cap."

"Okay."

"See how it's boiling and hissing from underneath?"

"Yeah."

"You're losing a heap of water and coolant--the green stuff. Hey, look here, I think I found the problem."

He pulled a ball-point pen from his pocket and tapped a thick, black hose that shined like tar.

"Look at this here. See all that coming out the side?"

"Yeah."

The hose looked like someone had stabbed it and water shot out

400

from the gash like a fountain.

"That's your problem, Mary. Hose is cracked and it's leaking all your radiator fluid out. You're overheating because of it."

"Okay."

"It'll take ten minutes, fifteen tops to fix you up."

"That's great, Hank. What do you call the hose that's busted?"

"A heater hose. They bust open sometimes. This old girl's got a lot of miles on her and the hose just wore through."

The girls sat on a burgundy-stained bench Hank kept against the wall. They just chit-chatted away while I watched Hank. It was good to see them smile and carry on like that; I remembered how sometimes Irma and I got to do that when we were young.

I looked back in time to see Hank unclamp the hose and pull it off, making water run out the end. Hank brought out a new hose, cut it down to fit, then slid the clamps over it and tightened them. All the time he worked, I looked at the cables and metal parts that hooked one to the other under the hood. Andrew used to send me out of the garage if he worked on the car because he didn't want any distraction and was sure I wouldn't be interested in the whole thing, anyway. But right now, all the shiny and grimy parts of the engine fascinated me.

Just after Hank ran a garden hose into the radiator a few minutes, he popped open a glass cider jug filled with bright green liquid. Propping a funnel up with his left thumb, he poured the green goo into the radiator.

"Whenever you overheat again and have to add water," he said. "Be sure to add this stuff, too."

"Well, what is it, Hank?"

"Coolant/anti-freeze. Gotta add it with the water. If you just put in water, you'll get yourself bushwhacked for sure."

Whatever bushwhacked meant I knew I didn't want to be that. A few minutes later, Hank handed me what looked like a plastic jug of Clorox.

"Keep this coolant in the trunk, okay, Mary?"

I nodded. As I reached for my purse, Hank turned away, picked up some sort of tool, and started tightening a bolt on another car.

"Hank, you forgot something."

He kept on tightening the bolt.

"Nope," he said over his shoulder.

"How much do I owe you for fixing the car?"

"Nothing, Mary."

"Hank, you took care of it. Let me give you a few dollars."

"Nope, you just make sure the next time a hose blows, you don't run outta coolant. That'll kill the radiator for sure."

"Thank you, Hank."

401

"Oh. Mary?"

"Yeah?"

"Bring the Herald back in a month or two. It's been a long time since its last tune-up and oil change."

"I'll remember that."

"Mary?"

"Yeah?"

"You doin' okay with this whole thing and all?"

I knew what he meant by 'whole thing'--he wasn't talking about the car.

"Yeah, Hank. I guess we're doing all right, thank the Lord and the Church."

For the first time since Andrew died, things did seem fine. I really wanted to tell Hank about my job that I never thought I'd be able to get. About how good the kids were doing in school, and about how I could write checks and reconcile the register. Daisy was out of my hair even. Things were pretty good. If I could just stop feeling like my heart was ripped in two, things would probably be as normal as always.

"Come on, Louise, pick up the phone," the telephone sputtered with its annoying ring. "Come on."

I was talking to myself two days before Christmas. The sky was liquid lead as its feeble light made the windowpanes silver. This was the fifth time I had called Louise in four days and she still wasn't answering. I was really missing her and hoping that even though she had become a Jew, she and Murray would come and spend this one very hard Christmas with us. I saw her last next to Andrew's coffin at St. Joan's. The phone just rang in my ear.

Martha walked in as I clanked the receiver back onto the cradle.

"No luck, huh?" she sighed. She still looked up to her big sister. "But the day after tomorrow is Christmas Eve."

"I know."

And I also knew that we were going have to forget about Louise again this year. Death wasn't going to bring forgiveness, I thought. At least not where Louise was concerned.

But I had already made up my mind that this first Christmas without Andrew was going to have to be more special than Christmases before if I was going to make it through.

"That's it," I said and stood up. Kathie stepped back.

"What?"

"We haven't visited your brother in over a year. Tomorrow, we're going out to Camarillo."

Kathie's face screwed up, and I didn't care why: Ernie was still my son and a piece of my heart felt like it was rotting out at the state hospital.

"Will you come with me, Kathie? And wish him a Merry Christmas?"

"No, Mom. He's crazy and that place is full of nuts."

"If he's crazy, it's because of me!"

My face felt warm when I said that--I had never said it out loud before. Kathie turned to go down the hall and I grabbed her arm.

"Kathie?"

"What, Mother?"

"Please come with me."

"I don't know."

I didn't want to force anybody to come, but I really was too afraid to go alone. After my times in the loony bin and all. Maybe I'd just take Danny along -- at eight years old, he wouldn't be afraid of all the loonies. And I'm sure he didn't remember anything about Ernie's vulgar touching. At least, I hoped so. Then I thought better of the idea.

"Maybe I'll ask Father Crawford if he's not busy."

"Sound like a good idea. I'll watch Danny, too, 'cause he shouldn't go out there."

She was probably right, and probably afraid of becoming loony herself. Did I pass it on to her, too? My heart twisted when I thought of that.

"Yeah, I'll just ask Father Crawford."

Kathie was already down the hall when I said that.

Father Crawford did decide to come with me. He even volunteered to drive, too. There we were the next day, riding in the black Volkswagen wagon.

"You sure you want to do this?" he said.

He shifted the car into fourth gear as we rolled along. He slipped his hand off the shift knob that looked like a little bowling ball and grabbed my hand. A tingle shot up my back and I knew I was going deeper into Hell.

"Your hand's ice cold."

"I know, Father. It's just that it's been over a year since I've seen him. It's kind'a tough."

My stomach felt twisted like a wet rag. The last time we visited, it was Andrew and me and that made this whole thing that much harder. Feeling Father Crawford's hand wrapped around mine felt comforting. We drove a little farther before he spoke again.

"He is your son, Mary, and he's got a disease. That's all you have to think about right now."

"I know, Father. I guess part of it is that I don't want to have to be around any crazy people, you know?"

Father Crawford's eyebrows shot up and I figured he knew that I was talking about my visits to the nut house.

"You want to turn around then, Mary?"

I stared down at the plate of fudge in my lap. It didn't look like nice, neat cubes but more like shards of chocolate on the olive green plate.

"No. I gotta see my son and give him this batch of fudge the girls made him."

"Fudge? Yum."

"You don't really want it, Father. It tastes like chocolate sand paper. The girls never get the syrup boiled right, but Ernie's always loved it just the way it is. They were so sweet to think of him, I just have to give it to him."

We pulled up to the gate at Camarillo State Hospital about an hour later. A guard at the gate, who wore a gun in a holster on his side, looked down at us through half-mast eyes. After asking us who we were there to see, he opened the gate that was crowned by curling barbed wire. The weird thing about the gate was that it had holly garland draped across its bars. Barbed wire on top, holly running through its bars -- I guess it made sense for Christmas at the nut house.

In the couple times Andrew and I had visited before, it was sunny, and we saw patients milling around in the thick grass yard. But it was cloudy and cold today as we drove the asphalt driveway to the main building. The yard was an empty, green carpet dulled by the clouds and dew.

When we got to the main building and into the waiting room, I couldn't help but look at the honeycomb wires running through the windows on the left side of the room. The white light that made it through made the dirty yellow walls look like unwashed wax beans, and the bars on the outside of the windows made the room feel like a jail cell. As Father Crawford and I took a seat on metal folding chairs, another family was chatting with a young woman, their daughter from what I could hear them say. But the young woman was just staring at the wall while the father and mother who looked my age chatted away about Christmas presents and divinity that wouldn't whip up right. Cellophane crackled and I saw the mother offer the young woman a plate of goodies.

The young woman, with hair looking as scraggly as a robin's nest, didn't reach for any candy. She couldn't have been much older than Kathie. Did her mother make her crazy, too?

"Oh, God, Judy, not again!" the mother screamed and jumped up.

"What? Oh, for crying out loud!" the father mumbled.

404

I peeked over and saw that 'Judy' had passed water down her hospital gown and onto the floor, making a clear, yellow puddle between her slippers.

"Nurse!" the mother hollered.

"Blessed Mother, please pray for me," I whispered quietly.

"What did you say?" Father Crawford asked.

"Nothing, Father."

I rubbed my nose and my left hand smelled slightly like Bay Rum from Father Crawford and my mind drifted away. We suddenly sit together in sand that is fine and white as sugar. A palm sways next to us as Father Crawford stands up and pulls off his shirt. His firm body shines with oil and the smells of cocoa butter and coconut swirl around me. He reaches down and grabs my --

"Mary!" he spoke loudly as he shook my shoulder. "Ernie's at the door."

I jerked out of my daydream to see two burly men--both as big as Freddie Blassie the wrestler--dragging Ernie towards me. Their hairy arms stuck out from the white shirts they both wore. Milkmen, I thought, as I saw their white pants.

"Didya' come to bring me home?" Ernie asked.

His face was dusted with a few days of light brown whiskers. Two hollow dents made his cheeks look deep as two mattress buttons and his dark eyes stared at me without blinking. He looked like I just caught him stealing or something.

I set down the plate of fudge and rushed to him. My throat was too tight to say anything, and my heart pounded like a deer mouse caught in a trap. I pulled him to me and squeezed. I was so happy to just hold him. Reaching to kiss him, he jerked his mouth away and my lips caught his wiry cheek. Whiskers stuck my lips. He pulled away.

"No more mushy crap. Let's go," he said.

"Well, first, Merry Christmas, Ernie."

"Oh yeah, did you bring me somethin'?"

His voice was hoarse and his eyes darted about the room.

"Your favorite."

"Fruit cocktail?"

"No. Your sisters' fudge. A batch made special just for you."

"Oh."

His eyes stopped on Father Crawford.

"Who are you?"

"I'm Father Crawford. Nice to meet you, Ernie."

"That ain't my name."

"Don't be a goof," I said. I felt my cheeks flare up.

"I'm Jesus now, Mom. That's who I am."

The two guards who had brought him had stepped back a few feet but stood next to each other, both of their arms folded, keeping their eyes on us. One of them sniggered.

"How 'bout some of that fudge?" Ernie said.

"Oh, sure."

As I slid back onto my chair, I placed the plate back on my lap. Father Crawford sat back down next to me, and I kept the corner of my eye on the guards. They made me nervous.

"You getting catechism here?" Father Crawford asked.

"Nope. Don't need it. Told you already, I'm Jesus."

Father Crawford nodded, raising his eyebrows. As I passed the plate of fudge to Ernie, his arm shot out and snatched up a piece. Shoving the whole hunk into his mouth, he ignored a chunk of it that fell out of his mouth and onto his turquoise hospital uniform. I plucked the chunk off his shirt as Ernie grabbed another piece of fudge. He crossed his legs, which were clothed in the same turquoise uniform, and you would've almost thought he was a surgeon.

"Kind'a gritty," he said.

"That's how the girls make the fudge."

"I miss my little buddy, Danny."

A chill shot down my spine. My heart skipped a beat and Father Crawford must have seen my shoulders jerk back because I felt his strong grip on my left shoulder.

"Mary?" he said.

"Heard you played a lot of baseball," he said to Ernie.

"Used to."

"Looks like there's a diamond outside. You get to play much here?"

"Nope. Don't let me outta my room."

He slurped on another piece of fudge and licked his fingers with a smacking sound. His mouth sounds calmed me down somehow.

"Hey, so Kathie's getting good grades at El Camino College", I said. "Martha's doing good at Torrance High, too."

"Can I have more, please, Mama?"

The boy he was flashed in his eyes when he said that. The softness and shy nature I always knew passed through, but as soon as I recognized my normal Ernie, his eyes turned dark as tar again. Was the real world just a swirl of dust to him? A passing breeze? I gave him another piece of fudge.

"The damn Orioles shouldn't a won the Pennant and series," Ernie said. "I could'a' hit better'n most of 'em."

Ernie folded his arms and lurched forward like his stomach ached. He rocked back and forth.

"Ernie? You okay?" I asked.

"Yeah."

He rocked another second, then stopped, raised his head, and shifted his eyes from Father Crawford to me, then back to Father Crawford. His eyebrows screwed up.

"You dating or something?"

My face sizzled with embarrassment and Father Crawford squeezed my shoulder again. He chuckled quietly behind me.

"No, Ernie, I can't do that," he said.

Ernie's eyes looked like ping pong balls as they shifted. He crossed his legs again and huddled up, looking like a turtle with its legs pulled into shell.

"Okay, so you taking me home or what?"

Again, Father Crawford squeezed my shoulder.

"I came to wish you Merry Christmas, Ernie."

My throat felt like it was jammed with a wad of cotton.

"Just for a bunch of crappy fudge?"

"Ernie, do you want to pray with us?" Father Crawford asked.

"I'm Lucifer. I don't pray!"

"I thought you were Jesus," Father Crawford said.

Ernie dropped to the floor and grabbed hold of my legs. The guards lunged at him but Ernie just began to sob like he was four years old again. My throat seized up and my gut twisted.

"Take me home, Mama! Take me home! It's a trap here!"

There was nothing I could do for him, so I just kissed the top of his head. I noticed a little bald spot as I pulled away. A stream of his tears dripped down my leg and the guards paused.

"Please, Mama, please don't leave me!"

The two guards pried Ernie off my legs. His fingernails snagged my knee-highs as they ripped him away from me.

"Don't hurt him!" I cried.

"Mama! ... Pleeeeeease..."

He screamed as they pulled him out the door. I hurried to follow them, but when I got to the door, they were gone.

"Oh, Father, what did I do? What did I do?"

My face flared with tears and heat.

"Let's go, Mary. Come on."

I bent over and picked up the plate of fudge. I had to leave Ernie something, and I couldn't hurt the girls' feelings, either.

"Let me see if a nurse or someone can keep this for him."

Father Crawford nodded. He held the door for me and as I passed into the hall with its green, fluorescent light, and grimy, stained beige walls, I wondered if I could ever come out to see Ernie again. If it got him riled up, and it hurt so much to see him dragged off, it might be better for both of us if I didn't.

Two women sat at a gray, metal desk and I figured they were nurses. As I stepped over to them, I saw a doctor in a white coat walking up to the desk, too. One of the nurses smacked on a piece of gum. She looked up at me.

"Yes?" she said.

I wiped a tear off my cheek.

"Excuse me. But could you be sure that Ernie Murphy gets this?"

The nurse glanced down at the plate and her eyebrows wrinkled like a caterpillar.

"What is it?"

"Fudge. Home made."

The doctor joined us at the desk. He cleared his throat--probably to interrupt us--but the nurse ignored him.

"Sure. Who's it go to again?"

"Ernie Murphy. He really loves his sisters."

"Excuse me, Ma'am," the doctor said to me. "I'm Doctor Phillipson. Are you a relative of Ernest Murphy?"

The doctor's mustache twitched on the right side like he had some sort of itch.

"Yes. I'm his mother, Mary Murphy. This is Father Crawford."

"Father," Dr. Phillipson said with a nod. "Do you have a moment to talk?"

I looked to Father Crawford and he shrugged and nodded.

"I guess," I answered.

Dr. Phillipson lead us to a small waiting area just on the other side of the nurse's desk. Is that where you wait while your son gets a lobotomy? I thought. We all sat and Dr. Phillipson's mustache twitched again.

"Mrs. Murphy. I've just been assigned to supervise your son's psychiatric treatment. Now while the lithium is serving to stabilize his mood swings, I'm afraid we're not having any success with the delusions or the obsessive/compulsive disorder."

"I don't understand all that mumbo jumbo, doctor," I said.

Dr. Phillipson nodded, brought his hands together like he was going to pray, touched them to his lips and then spoke again.

"Ernest is probably going to have to stay on medication the rest of his life. But until we can find the right combination, I'm afraid he'll have to stay here."

Father Crawford stroked my shoulder.

"You mean he can never come home?"

"I don't see that as an option right now."

"But wouldn't he get better if he was at home, with me, his sisters and brother? His family?"

Dr. Phillipson leaned forward and his eyes shifted as he checked to make sure we were alone in the waiting area I guess. His mustache twitched so much now lit looked like a caterpillar on a hot griddle.

"Ernest can never be near children."

My face flushed. I knew what he was getting at.

"Isn't there some sort of medicine you can give him for that?"

"No. I'm sorry, Mrs. Murphy. He's always going to be a pedophile. He's always going to have unhealthy feelings for children he can't control, especially with this schizophrenia. He's a lost young man. Lost."

Whatever else Dr. Phillipson said from then on, or what Father Crawford said on the ride home, I couldn't say. My head felt like it was stuffed in a jar and all I could think of was that awful word--lost. What had I done to Ernie? What could I do to save him?

I couldn't stop thinking about Ernie even into the new year, and I decided one day to get my mind off him, I'd finally clean out Andrew's side of our closet. I didn't know what I might save or what I might get rid of. But as I ran my hands over his gray work slacks, I could see Andrew on his black recliner, his feet in black socks stained with white patches of Dr. Scholl's foot powder. There on the floor of the closet his Sunday shoes-- brown wing tips--the same shoes I'd nag him about not matching his black suit. I slammed the closet door.

Down the hall, I stepped into the front bathroom. The butter cream-colored tile felt cool under my feet as I crept to the medicine cabinet. I didn't look at the fat monster of my reflection. Rusty hinges creaked as I pulled open the medicine cabinet, and I saw those prescription labels again, with expiration dates for 1972, a full year from now. How I had hoped we would have refilled those prescriptions then, or maybe not even needed the medicine anymore by then. How I had hoped to never need the cortisone, the prednisone, and the darvon filled a week or so before... The bottle was still three-quarters full.

"Mom?" Martha's voice screeched.

I slammed the medicine cabinet shut. I couldn't get rid of any of it.

"Did I startle you?" she asked. A murmur of female voices rolled down the hall

"Who's here?"

"Come out and see, Mom."

"I gotta get to Dr. Stevenson's. Is it that chatterbox Kirby Vacuum salesman again?"

"Come on."

As I got to the hall door, I recognized Connie's laugh. And Agnes was giggling. I walked into the living room and there was Kay holding a box, looking still as a piece of porcelain.

"Mary!" they hollered.

I ran into their arms. It had been so long since we all sat at the Hot 'n' Tot. I hadn't even seen anybody in church in awhile.

"Well, the Blessed Mother Club's finally doing something more than just drinking coffee or selling cakes," Agnes said. "Here."

She pushed a cardboard box into my arms and inside was two loaves of Weber's bread, cans of Campbell's soup, and vegetables, and a red, net bag of delicious apples.

"What is this?" I asked.

"Mary, the sisters have donated some of their excess food to you and the kids," Connie said.

"Food?"

Martha, Susan, and Danny ran out to join us in the living room. Kay sat in one of the raspberry vinyl chairs.

"It's not much, we know," Kay said. "But Sister Delores said the convent always has surplus they save for the O'Briens over on Two Thirty-Seventh, but we should bring some of it to you and the kids this week."

"Is it candy or Cracker Jacks?" Danny asked.

I shook my head and the kids walked off. It was such a sweet thing that the Blessed Mother Club reunited just to help me. But at the same time, I felt embarrassed taking the food.

"Don't just stand there gawkin' at it, Mary," Agnes said. "Set it down and tell us what's been going on."

"I'll go get some coffee going," Connie said. "You still have your Sunbeam percolator from the Blue Chip Redemption Center, Mary?"

I nodded and set the box on the coffee table. I took the other raspberry chair next to Kay. Agnes sat on the black couch. They both wore dresses with flower prints and it felt like spring even though it was the end of January.

"I feel awful," I said.

"What's been happening?" Connie asked, poking her head around the kitchen door.

"Kids okay?" Agnes asked.

"Nothing like that. I just gotta get to the doctor's in a bit."

"What's the matter, Mary?" Kay asked.

"Nothing. Ever since my crazy fits, I take medication and Doctor Stevenson checks me every few months. Just gotta make sure everything's okay."

"You really all right?" Kay asked.

"You know, with my job at the rectory, and the kids doing okay in school, what do I got to complain about?"

"You missing Andrew?" Agnes asked.

"Nice going, big mouth," Connie yelled from the kitchen. "How stupid can you be, Agnes?"

"It's okay. I miss Andrew an awful lot. Sometimes I feel like straight pins are stuck in me and someone's pushing on them. Being by myself is the worst of it. Least I got Danny sleeping with me every night, 'cause otherwise, I don't know how I could make it through the night."

"You outta be careful about that," Kay said. "He's too old for that."

"If it makes her feel better, it's okay," Connie fired back. "I guess we better not keep you from the doctor's--there'll be a fresh pot of coffee for you when you get back."

Agnes stood up, then Kay and Connie followed. Kay reached out and patted my elbow.

"We're praying the rosary today after we deliver the other donation to the O'Briens. Father Crawford's gonna let us in the church. If you're done with your appointment by three o'clock, stop by."

"I'll try."

As the ladies marched out the front door, I felt a pang like a ribbon being pulled on my heart. Connie stopped at the end of the front walk.

"We'll be back with more stuff next week. You know, that Gladys O'Brien lost her husband and was left with twelve kids at home. You're doing okay compared to that. Anyways, don't forget, Mary. We'll be here for you, always."

I thought about that a little later as I sat in Dr. Stevenson's private office. My eyes moved around the room to the book case that stood behind his desk, jammed full of brown books with gold labels. The sun painted stripes of shadow through the Venetian blinds and against the wall where his certificates hung. University of Pennsylvania one read, and another said Johns Hopkins. A peppermint scent came from a dish of pillow mints on the edge of his desk. The red leather chair, bigger than Andrew's recliner, had a big dent where his head must have rested. Except for the tick of a clock on a side table, the room was pretty quiet, other than the occasional traffic noise from Crenshaw Boulevard. His door creaked open.

"Okay, Mary, here are the results."

Dr. Stevenson, in his white uniform that buttoned between his neck and shoulder, plopped a manila folder onto his desk. His slid into the leather chair, rolled up to the desk, and opened the folder. His bushy eyebrows were wire above his bifocals, and as he read, he nodded every now and then. A car's brakes squealed.

"Well, the news is good, Mary."

He turned a page in the folder, and then looked up at me.

"This is Doctor Thompson's note." He read it and smiled. "Okay. All right. Mary, the medications you've been on haven't affected your body too badly. And it says here that Doctor Thompson is recommending that they're no longer necessary."

"What?"

"Yes. He believes your nervous breakdown was entirely trauma-related. Stress from Andrew's death. You don't have a diagnosable mental illness."

"So, I'm not nuts then?"

"No, I don't think so. There's no reason for you to stay on the anti-depressants. Doctor Thompson agrees."

"I'm not crazy!" I jumped up.

"No, Mary. You're healthy as a horse. You can stop the medication today."

"Doctor Stevenson, I have been feeling good. I really have. I think the kids and me are going to be okay."

"That's it, Mary. You can go now."

I stood up and my heart was pounding so hard that I thought it would blow the top of my head off. Things were really going to be all right. Thank you, Blessed Mother, I thought. Thank you.

"Now, Mary, you need to be careful, though," Dr. Stevenson added. "Don't get overworked and if you feel overwhelmed, call me, okay? We can always put you on a tranquilizer before things get out of hand."

"I understand, Doctor. I'll be careful and I'll call if I have any crazy thoughts."

The Herald sputtered and coughed as I drove down Crenshaw. I don't think Dr. Stevenson knew how important it was for me to hear everything was okay with my head. I wasn't just another Aunt Clotine! As I pulled into the driveway, I could hear Danny screaming from the kitchen. Here's the first test of my mental health, I thought. Help me, Blessed Mother.

Walking through the kitchen door, I saw Danny standing on one side of the kitchen table, his face bright red with anger and tears. Martha and Susan jumped up from the other end when they saw me. They both waved loose-leaf paper at me.

"Look at what the little sissy weirdo's doing now, Mom. Look," Martha said as she shoved the paper toward me.

I grabbed the sheet of paper from her hands. I looked down at the white page with blue lines and on it I saw a house, a mansion with three pillars over its porch, drawn with black and brown crayons. The windows of the house glowed yellow, and in the yellow, I saw silhouettes. The mansion could have been drawn by an architect, it was so exact and life-like. Martha reached over and yanked on the page.

"That's not it, Mom. It's the weird ones, look."

"Mommy, don't look at them!" Danny cried. "Please, Martha and stupid Susan stole them from my room. They're thiefs!"

"Shut up, little weirdo!" Martha hollered.

"Stop with the name calling, Martha," I said. "You watch your flannel mouth!"

Even though Danny pleaded with me, I wanted to see what else he drew. Turning the page over, I saw two women in what looked like matching evening dresses standing across from two men who wore matching suits. Behind them was a fancy fireplace with a pointed opening and a big mantle. Two of those candle holders stood on either side of the fireplace, and fancy tie-back drapes surrounded two windows. It all looked like 'Dark Shadows' or 'Beverly Hillbillies.' Above the mantle hung what was a painting, I guess, with a woman on it. Underneath, the words 'Ye Mother' were printed.

"Why's he drawing such spaced-out stuff?" Susan asked.

"Susan, Martha. Why did you take these from Danny's room?"

"Yeah, you stealing pigs!" Danny hollered.

"Danny--no name calling goes for you, too."

"He's in there with the door shut so much, Mom," Martha said. "He never goes out to play kickball or hide-n-seek. He's such a freak."

"We needed to know what he was doing in case he was getting himself in trouble," Susan chimed in.

"Both of you--go to your room."

"Mom, we thought—"

"Just get, now. You shouldn't've touched his stuff."

The girls rolled their eyes and stomped off. I sat on the raspberry chair and its soft surface was cool.

"Sit next to me, Danny."

He sat, his short-sleeved, yellow checkered shirt untucked from his faded blue jeans and his little brown strings that were his arms lay on his lap. He kept his eyes down as he swung his feet.

"Danny, can I look at the rest of these?"

I picked up a pile of loose leaf pages from the coffee table.

"Okay, I guess."

As I flipped through the pages, the same four people in the first drawings now held babies. In another drawing, the same two ladies pushed a fancy carriage with four babies' heads sticking out. Everyone was always dressed identical.

"Who are these people, Danny?"

"Just some people I made up."

"Why they all dressed the same all the time?"

"'Cause they're all twins."

"Huh?"

"See, the rich twin men live in this mansion." He held up the house drawing again.

"Then these two twin ladies met them one day."

He held up the fireplace drawing.

"Pretty soon, they all got married and they had twin babies."

"What's happening here?"

I held up another drawing of the mansion with what looked like flames jumping from its windows.

"Then this old witch--she's on the other side."

I turned the page over and there was a witch on a broom--but just her shadow, flying around the top of a castle. Each stone on the castle was highlighted and shaded to show up.

"Then she put a spell on the rich people, and took their babies, and made their house burn up. And then the ladies and men all cried."

He held up another page and there the four adults sat on a fancy, antique couch, rubbing their faces and holding each other.

"What happened next?"

"Well, I started to draw that, but that's when Martha busted in and grabbed all my pictures."

"How come everybody's a twin, Danny?"

"'Cause twin's always have a brother or sister all to themselves."

"Have you been drawing like this a long time?"

"Ever since I got my own room when Ernie left. I like to shut the door and pull out my crayons. Then I make my drawings and know what else?"

"What?"

He looked around like he was afraid the girls might be near. He spoke real soft and quiet.

"I make them talk while I'm drawing. Just like on TV."

"Do you have anymore like this?"

"Promise you won't tell?"

"I promise."

"I'll show you, Mommy."

Danny led me into his bedroom and pushed me to sit on his bed.

414

As always, the orange bedspread that looked like corduroy pants was neat and perfect. Creaking open his closet door, he pulled out Andrew's old, leather briefcase I gave him when Andrew died.

He popped it open and there was a pile as thick as the church missal of crayon drawings. Men, women, children, and always, big houses and evil monsters that would destroy them.

"Each pile has a different story," Danny said.

Why the mansions, I thought. And all the families--Danny had a fantasy family I never knew about until right then.

"TV helps me think of what to draw," he said.

"Danny, you're a good artist. But you know what else?"

"What?"

"You tell stories, too."

"Uh-huh. Some day maybe I'll draw a story just about you."

"You wanna see something secret I have, too?" I asked him.

"You mean your art?"

"Sort of. Let's go to my room."

I led Danny into the bedroom, peeked down the hall one more time, and when I could only hear the girls mumbling as KHJ played in the background, I knew it was safe. I shut the door and locked it.

"Must be a big secret!" Danny said.

"Go sit on the bed and I'll show you."

Danny crawled up on the bed and I opened the closet door. Reaching behind Andrew's slacks, I grabbed a bristol board pad I had kept since high school. I carried the pad with its light blue cover and brown, frayed edges to the bed.

"Before I show you this, you gotta promise me something."

"I promise. Let me see, Mommy."

"You don't know what you're promising yet."

"Okay. Tell me."

"You can't tell about this. Now, promise."

"Not even Susan?"

"No. Not Martha, either."

"I hate Martha. I wouldn't tell her nothing."

"Danny, you don't hate your sister."

"She's mean. I do."

"Promise you won't tell anybody."

"I promise."

"Okay."

I turned the blue cover sheet and Danny looked at the dark gray and light gray lines of the pencil drawing.

"That looks like somebody," he said.

415

"Who?"

"Uh. I think..."

Danny chewed on his lower lip, using the tips of his teeth that were coming in large, and were now sticking out buck like his father's. The way he chewed his lower lip made me yearn for Andrew right then. Danny blew air out through his mouth and I felt my heart speed up as I hoped he would be able to guess.

"Father Crawford?"

"Yes!"

I still had it, I knew, right in that second. I could still draw.

"It's not done yet," I said.

"How come it's a secret?"

That was a harder question, and I had been praying to the Blessed Mother for an answer to it. An hour hadn't gone by in months when I didn't think about Father Crawford. All that affection I felt for him I was putting into the drawing.

"How come, Mommy?"

"'Cause it's gonna be a surprise," I lied. "I'm gonna finish it for his birthday."

"Oh. You sure draw good, Mommy. Can I have that picture if Father Crawford doesn't like it?"

"You can have it if he doesn't like it, I promise. Now I want you to make me another promise."

"What?"

"That you'll always draw, or someday maybe even write. Everyday. Never let anything stop you."

"You gonna cry Mommy?"

I wiped a tear from my eye.

"No. I'm no big baby, Danny. I'm gonna put this away now."

As I stood up, my face flushed with heat. Why was I so embarrassed? Or, was I ashamed?

I startled awake about five-thirty in the morning two weeks later, feeling as though my time of the month had finally arrived. Danny tossed a little in bed, and I pulled the blanket up to his neck. Tiptoeing down the hall, the cold air pricked my legs and arms. Light shocked my eyes as I flipped the switch on and pulled up my night gown. My underwear was clean and I dropped my nightgown and slid onto the toilet seat. My cycle was due January twenty-third and I'm always right on time to the day unless--

It was such a crazy thought. Just because it was February sixth, and I was two weeks overdue...But then I wondered if somehow, some way, something special, something holy was happening to me. I fell onto my knees and began to pray.

"Blessed Mother, have I been chosen to bring a savior into the world?" The heresy of my words made my mouth dry up.

"Blessed Mother, please send a sign. I need to know if my vile thoughts for Father Crawford somehow have caused this condition..." I closed my eyes and dropped my head back and I was ready to see a bright light, a ray from Heaven, from the Lord. When I opened my eyes, all I could see was the glass ceiling fixture, caked with dust and dead moths. My heart raced -- why else would my cycle be late? I had to be pregnant. Had to be.

"Blessed Mother, I beg you..."

The floor under my knees began to vibrate. I threw my arms wide.

"Blessed Mother, I feel your sign!"

The walls of the bathroom vibrated like Jello. I shielded myself from the crackling glass of the mirror and now the room rumbled and rolled like thunder.

"Mom!" I heard one of the girls shriek. What was happening?

Throwing open the bathroom door, I saw the girls huddled in their doorway. Danny screamed as he ran down the hall toward me, and the floor heaved like the ocean and threw him side to side like he was a pinball. I ran for him and held him close.

"Get back in the doorway, Mom! It's an earthquake!" Kathie screamed.

The walls of the hall now buckled and bent, looking like snare drums. Glass rattled somewhere, dogs barked outside, and over all of it was the terrible rumble. I was terrified, but at the same time, light as a cloud. This was the Blessed Mother's sign. I knew it must be. I rubbed my stomach as the rolls and jolts began to end. Danny's face was pressed against my side and he whimpered. The girls cried, too.

"We're okay, everybody," I said. "It was a miracle and we're okay."

It was a miracle--this was the Blessed Mother telling me. It had to be.

"There could be a bigger earthquake coming," Kathie said. Susan and Martha screamed out, and then started sobbing with fright.

The hall shook again and the girls screamed again but it stopped in a few seconds. I thought about what it might all mean for me, about this special child I must be carrying, and how holy I was now. But the phone rang a couple hours later. I had forgotten about my pregnancy but was still worrying about Louise and Ernie. I hadn't been able to get through to Louise or to Camarillo State Hospital. Maureen had called earlier to let me know she was okay.

"Mrs. Murphy, you've seen the news?" the woman's voice said.

She was so cold as she spoke.

"Yeah. We've been watching John Schubek on Eyewitness News."

My knees shook more than when the earthquake happened. I glanced over at the girls and Danny, all huddled on the couch in their pj's. The news reporter was bellowing on TV from a collapsed building at Camarillo State Hospital.

"We're unable to locate your son right now."

A bolt of pain shot through me.

"What?"

"Two of our main buildings have collapsed. There are several patients still not accounted for."

"He's gotta be there!" I screamed.

"Mrs. Murphy, we're doing our best. It's dangerous for the rescue workers because we keep having aftershocks."

"What'll we do?"

"Mrs. Murphy, prepare for the worst. We'll let you know as soon as we know."

"Thank you."

I hung up the phone and felt like a boulder was pressing my chest. Is this what the Blessed Mother had in mind? I had to give up Ernie for the miracle I was carrying?

"Quick, everybody!" I hollered.

Kathie, Susan, and Martha jumped up like another quake was starting. Danny dove under the coffee table.

"We gotta do a rosary now."

"Mom, don't you want to watch the news to see if they pull Ernie out?" Kathie asked.

"If he's dead, it's the Lord's will," I heard myself say.

I guess I meant it. Another part of me felt that he was better off dead rather than suffering, anyway.

"So why do we gotta do a rosary?" Susan asked.

"Come on, we're gonna pray for Ernie, whether he's dead or alive. Let's go."

The girls rolled their eyes and stood up. They were a drill team of resignation as they walked past me to get their rosaries. Danny just stared at me from under the coffee table.

"You, too, Danny. Go get your rosary."

When were all kneeling a few minutes later, with the TV sound off, I was about to start when I looked down at Danny's rosary.

"Don't you remember the loop?" I asked.

"I can't do it, Mommy."

"Watch me. It's like I showed you before. Loop it over your right hand like this. See, as you go round, you'll be able to tell where you're at by your thumb."

"Okay," he said.

"Let's pray. In the name of the Father, and of the Son, and..."

When we were about half way through the rosary, the front door rattled with a knock. Martha jumped up and ran for the hall.

"Jees, Martha, it's just the door," Kathie said.

Kathie stood up and opened it.

"Hi, Father. Come on in."

Father Crawford stepped into the living room and I suddenly remembered I was still in my robe. He wore a loose, black shirt, but not his collar.

"I came as soon as I heard about the state hospital. You all okay?"

The girls nodded. Danny stood next to me.

"We're okay, Father. We were just saying a rosary," I said.

"Have you heard any more from the hospital?"

"An hour ago. They said they'd call when they knew."

"I'm stopping to check on a few other families right now, Mary. I'll go ahead, but I'll come back later to check with you--unless you need me to join you for your rosary?"

"No, it's all right, Father. Come back later."

We finished the rosary after Father Crawford left, and I told the kids they'd still have to go to school. I pulled the TV sound back on and the reporter was back at the state hospital. I wasn't paying attention to what he was saying because the camera moved past the reporter and showed the pile of rubble that had been one of the wards. The main building where we visited Ernie before Christmas was all jagged concrete and shards of wood. Firemen in suspenders scurried over the chunky pile like ants on a hill.

"We'll be pre-empting regular programming as we continue our coverage at this scene of nature's devastation," the reporter said.

I held tight to my rosary and watched the TV for the next hour. The girls and Danny were busy getting ready for school. The TV stayed on Eyewitness News the whole day and I never even got up to change. I had been through the rosary two more times and it felt like my rear end had melted into the davenport. All my stories never came on because of the earthquake reports and I think it was about two-thirty in the afternoon when the phone rang again.

"Mrs. Murphy?" a man's voice said this time.

"Yes."

My heart pounded in my chest and I felt light-headed. My face flared like I was embarrassed.

"This is Sergeant Boyle. I'm the supervisor of the rescue operation

419

at Camarillo State Hospital."

"Did you find Ernie?"

"We haven't been able to find your son. We think we've located all the survivors and most of the victims, too. We're going to keep looking, but we may not have any news for another day or two."

"Why?"

"There's a lot of rubble and we have to be careful because of aftershocks and all. We're hoping we'll know something soon."

"I'm praying for everyone."

"Thank you, Mrs. Murphy. We can use the prayers right now. We'll talk to you soon, ma'am. Good bye."

My body was thick from sitting, and my head was dull. But when he said it could be a day or two and said the word 'victims', I felt my body twist and tighten like a spring. I hung up the phone and collapsed back onto the couch. Could I take anymore before I'd crack again? I couldn't tell if it was clouds in the sky or tears in my eyes that made the afternoon light tarnish. All this because of my pregnancy? Why?

When the doorbell rang awhile later, it woke me from a nap. The kids were due home pretty soon so I was glad the doorbell chimed. Right as I turned the doorknob, I felt that odd heat in my face again. Father Crawford stood on the stoop. His spicy Hai Karate cologne tickled my nose awake.

"Father. Come in."

"Everything still okay, Mary?"

"Yeah. You want some coffee, Father? I got a fresh can of Folgers."

"No. I'm only going to be a minute."

I slid into one of the raspberry chairs and pointed to the black davenport.

"Can you just sit a minute with me? I've got some special news."

"They found Ernie?"

"No. Not yet."

"What then?"

I stood up and went to the front window. I wanted to make sure the kids weren't nearby. We were safe right then. I sat back down and leaned toward Father Crawford. His eyes shifted like he was confused.

"Father. I have a surprise."

"What?"

"There's going to be a blessed event around here."

Father Crawford stood up like the couch had caught fire. His eyes flared behind his glasses.

"Don't panic, Mary. We can contact the sisters at St. Anne. Now which one of the girls is it?"

"Father, it's not one of the girls."

His brow wrinkled and he let himself fall back onto the couch, his trousers making a scraping sound.

"Who, then, Mary?"

"Father," I said. I looked down at my stomach.

Father Crawford's face drained of color. His brows were now check marks over his eyes.

"Mary, have you been sinful?"

"What?"

"Who did this to you?"

"Father, that's not it."

The way he stood up, folded his arms looked down at me, it could have been Andrew I was talking to.

"Loneliness is no excuse, Mary."

"Father, can I—"

"You're a good Catholic, Mary. You need to confess. You need to see Father Sbaraglia."

"No, Father, it's not like that. Please sit down. You're acting like a jealous husband."

"What do you expect? Andrew hasn't been with the Lord for a year and you're already in this condition."

My father's face flashed in my mind and the same kind of disappointment was in Father Crawford's eyes. Now I knew what he thought and I jumped up.

"It's not what you're thinking, Father. Believe me, I learned a long time ago about the price for adultery."

"What are you talking about then, Mary?"

"Conception by the Holy Spirit."

"What?"

"Father, this is gonna sound kooky, but I am with child by holy means."

Father Crawford sat back and his eyebrows wrinkled again.

"Mary, please explain."

Father Crawford made me think of my dad again and that terrible day when I lied about Andrew. This was all so different but it still made me think of Dad.

"I will tell you now, Father."

"You are feeling okay, right?" he asked.

"I'm not feeling crazy, Father, if that's what you mean."

As a matter of fact, except for feeling hot a lot, I was feeling healthier than ever before. Even with Ernie being missing and all.

"Are you sure you're pregnant?"

"I'm sure of it, Father. Right when I got up this morning and prayed to the Blessed Mother for a sign, the earthquake happened. It had to be a sign."

"This is California, Mary. Earthquakes are prone to happen-- usually without the birth of a savior."

"It's not only that, Father," I snarled at him. He was making me mad. "There's something else."

"What?"

"I'm overdue on my cycle by two weeks."

His eyebrows wrinkled up again. Leaning back in the chair, he exhaled through his mouth. Why was he acting so exhausted?

"How old are you now, Mary?"

I felt my face blush.

"I can't answer that, Father. You shouldn't ask."

"Mary, don't be coy. How old?"

"I'll be forty-four at the end of the month."

I dropped my head because I felt like I had just confessed to murdering Christ.

"Have you felt any different at all recently?"

"Different how?"

"Your body. Anything else odd happening?"

I hadn't been sleeping well. But even worse was how I feeling hot out of nowhere sometimes. I admitted to that.

"I seem to get embarrassed a lot more now. My face feels hot a lot during the day. But it's just being embarrassed."

Father Crawford leaned forward and by the look on his face and his slight smile, I guess there was more to my embarrassment. He looked relieved as he reached out and took my hand. His was so warm and dry as usual.

"You need to see your doctor. I think you're going through the change."

"What change?"

Father Crawford stood up.

"I need to go check on the O'Briens now, Mary. Talk to your doctor, okay?"

"What do I tell him?"

"Just what you told me. See you in mass on Sunday."

As Father Crawford walked down the front path, I couldn't help but feel he was wrong. I'd go to Dr. Stevenson but I couldn't wait to tell Father Crawford how wrong he was about this 'change.' I turned the TV back on to see if there was any update on Camarillo State.

"Don't touch the dial!" I screamed three weeks later. "Hang on, Agnes," I said into the phone.

"Mom, can't we ever watch anything but the news?" Martha asked.

"You can watch 'Brady Bunch' tonight. But leave it on the news today."

"It's been three weeks since the earthquake, Mom. Someone will call us if they ever find Ernie."

"Go do your homework and leave the set alone."

"Mary?' Agnes said again"

"Oh. Sorry. I'm a little tired over Ernie and all."

"You still not sleeping?"

"Could you if you didn't know where Patrick was?"

"No, I couldn't. But anyway, what'd do you think about helping us in the snack booth at the Annunciation Carnival?"

"I guess I could."

"It'll take your mind off of things for awhile."

"I'm praying we'll hear about Ernie by then, anyways."

"Mary, they're pretty much through with the rubble at Camarillo. He must've wandered off or something. Now I pray everyday for the police to just find Ernie and bring him back safe to Camarillo."

"Thanks, Agnes. I ask the Blessed Mother to protect him wherever he is."

"Come help us at the carnival, Mary. Get your mind off it."

"The girls haven't stopped talking about it, Agnes. They're going even if I don't. There's something I'm working on and I could sure use that afternoon."

"Mary, you can't let us down."

"I really need the quiet time."

"Maureen still in that apartment on Arlington?"

"Yeah."

"Let the kids spend the night with her after the carnival, come help us, then have the night all to yourself."

"That's not a bad idea."

"Father Pia's hearing confessions after the carnival so you could give confession, say your penance and still have a whole night to yourself. What do you say, Mary?"

"They could use some extra fun after all we been through. Spending the night with Maureen will probably be as fun as the carnival."

"Carnival?" Danny suddenly said behind me. "When is it? When?"

"I'll talk to you later, Agnes. Danny's just heard and now he's all excited."

"I'll pray for you, Mary."

"Thanks, Agnes. Good bye."

I hung up the phone and before I could say a thing, Danny was yelling.

"Will I be able to win a gold fish with the ping pong ball toss?"

I shrugged.

"Or maybe a stuffed Snoopy? I love Snoopy."

"Maybe."

"Can I get cotton candy and a candy apple, too?"

"Danny, the carnival's not till the Saturday after next Saturday. I don't know yet."

"We're going? For sure?"

"Probably."

The phone jangled again and Danny ran off down the hall.

"A cold front seems to be..." Dr. George Fishbeck said on TV about the weather.

I grabbed up the phone before it rang again.

"Hello?"

"Mary. Doctor Stevenson."

"Oh. Doctor. Hi."

"Just wanted to let you know that you're fine--nothing wrong with you."

"I didn't think being pregnant was wrong, doctor. Not the number of times I been."

"You're not pregnant."

"You sure?"

"Very sure."

"Then why'd I miss my cycle?"

"You're going through the change, Mary--menopause."

"I don't understand--is it a disease?"

"No. It's a natural part of a woman's aging process."

"Do I have to take anything for it?"

"It's very gradual, Mary. We'll talk about it each step of the way, and how we'll treat it for you."

He might as well have been calling me to say Ernie was dead. I was so disappointed.

"Okay, doctor."

"Mary, you sound a little upset."

"No, I'm fine, doctor. It's okay."

"You set up an appointment with my receptionist so we can go over all this. Hang on."

I saw the doctor the next Wednesday and he explained all kinds of different things I'd have to be thinking about with menopause. I

424

understood some things, like mood swings, I didn't understand other things like estrogen and progesterone. As for not being pregnant, I guess there was some relief because I wasn't going to have another child. But there was also the feeling that I failed again, that nothing special like being an artist, or being visited by the Blessed Mother, or having a savior was ever going to happen to me. I felt like that pretty much till yesterday--Friday, March eleventh.

Danny and I just got home from Foods Company and I set the paper bag filled with Dixie cups and paper napkins on the table. I switched on the TV news right away, and then started putting stuff away.

"Where's my little tube of Colgate for tomorrow?" Danny asked.

I pulled the small tube of toothpaste out and handed it to him. He started off and I stopped him.

"You don't use it till tomorrow night at Maureen's."

He nodded.

"I'm gonna go draw."

His foot falls pounded against the kitchen linoleum and into the living room. When I didn't hear his bedroom door shut, I peeked around the corner. He stood staring at the TV.

"What is it--they find Ernie?" My heart pounded.

Danny shook his head. John Schubek sat at the reporter's desk and behind him was a school photo of a girl, about Danny's age, with blonde hair and brown eyes like a fawn.

"...the youngster's partially nude body was found by a horseback rider just off Rolling Hills Boulevard in an undeveloped hillside on the Palos Verdes Peninsula..."

"Danny, in your room, now!" I pushed him down the hall.

"...There was evidence of molestation and rape before her death of apparent strangulation..."

"Danny, you better close that bedroom door!" I roared.

His bedroom door slammed shut and I ran back to the TV.

"...details are pending further police investigation. Tonya Lynn Phelps was last seen skipping rope in her front yard on Two-Thirty-Ninth Street in Torrance. The police are looking for the jump rope they suspect was the murder weapon, and a gold neck chain the young girl wore with her initials. Torrance Police are asking the public for any information to solve this brutal attack..."

That was yesterday. Today, at the Annunciation carnival, all anybody was talking about was the little Phelps girl. How she was found, how she was sexually attacked, all of the awful details. No matter where you looked on the school grounds, parents were right next to their kids. If the parents came to the snack booth, they talked about the murder real quietly.

Kids listened, you could tell, and they must have known something awful had happened.

Other than the mood, the carnival was okay. The school's playground has that sweet, stinky smell blacktop gets when candy and gum get stuck to it and the sun warms it all up. As a matter of fact, just before it all happened, Danny came up to me and asked for some cotton candy.

"Agnes, can you handle it while I take him over for some cotton candy?"

"Sure, Mary."

We went across the schoolyard to where Mrs. Farrington was making and selling the cotton candy. We stood off from the machine that looked like a clothes washer drum and was as loud as a Electrolux vacuum. Mrs. Farrington pulled out one of those paper cones and started to twirl it around the edge of the drum. Webs of pink cotton candy gobbed onto the cone and I could smell warm sugar. I glanced up over Mrs. Farrington's shoulder and my heart stopped.

Ernie stood just outside the chain link fence and he seemed to be watching the whole carnival. His eyes were a little glazed over but I didn't care. I ran toward him and saw that he still wore the light blue hospital uniform that was dirty and dingy.

"Ernie! Ernie!"

He looked toward me and a shiver went through me--he had no more personality in his eyes than a dead trout. I figured it must have been because he had been off his medication for so long.

"It's me, Ernie. Mom!" I yelled to him.

He shook his head as if he didn't recognize me and I knew I had a problem. I needed to get him away from the carnival and home so that I could call Dr. Stevenson. Fortunately, the carnival was in full swing, so I would be able to get to him and bring him home without anybody noticing. I was so embarrassed that he was sick, and I didn't want anyone to know what was going on. I yelled for Kathie and Martha who were just getting ready to throw baseballs at the dunk tank. Dell Farmington, who sat on the dunk tank trigger bench, smiled with relief when Kathie and Martha left.

When the girls walked up to Danny and me, they saw Ernie and their mouths fell open. They stared at him.

"Okay, girls, don't worry about anything. I'm gonna go take Ernie home--thanks be to the Blessed Mother and the Lord. I'm gonna take care of him. You guys stick around here and have your fun, then head over to Maureen's. Be home by seven tomorrow morning so we can make eight o'clock mass."

They nodded. I snuck away from the carnival with Ernie and didn't run into anyone as I loaded him into the Herald. As we turned down Two

Ninety-Eighth Street, I could hear Ernie mumble to himself.

"I'm sorry. I'm in trouble. I'm sorry."

"Ernie?"

"I'm sorry. I'm sorry."

He kept his hands in the front pockets of his uniform and his right fist seemed to open and close around something bulky.

"What's in your pocket?"

"No! No! I'm sorry!... Shh! Shh!"

Once we got home and went into the kitchen through the side door, he stood in the kitchen and his eyes shifted and widened like a deer caught in a trap.

"I'm sorry! I'm sorry!"

He pulled his right hand out of his pocket and dropped something. I looked down as pink and white jump rope thumped to the floor, its pink handles clanking on the linoleum.

"Sorry...sorry...sorry..."

His hand reached back in and plucked out a small gold chain and as it hit the floor next to the jump rope, I saw the letters 'TLP.'

I knew right then what happened. My heart pounded and my stomach twisted. Ernie fell to the floor next to the jump rope and chain and his fingertips stroked both gently, as if he were touching a child. That child. That poor little girl.

It's my fault. I didn't deserve Andrew, or the kids. Daisy was always right about me--I ruined them all. If I had gone to Paris with Artie, this wouldn't have happened. Maybe Ernie needed his real father all along and I took him from him. I'm a sinner, just like the Blessed Mother was, too. I know her sin, now; I know the sin of the Virgin Mary. I don't know what to do, what I should do.

Danny read the final words in the diary once more: *I don't know what to do. What I should do?* He closed the diary and held it to his heart. Five days had passed since he began reading the diary and it was as if his life made no sense at all now. She did abandon him to fend for himself in this life, his sisters, too. But he was beginning to understand why. It wasn't because she was selfish. His face grew warm and his eyes blurry. No, it couldn't be. He rubbed his hand across his right cheek and felt the tear. Then another. I can't be crying, he thought. Not since he was a kid, not since *then,* had he cried about anything. But his lips began to quiver and his throat tightened.

The image of his mother and Ernie dead in the car now flashed into his mind. He heard the Herald's muffler popping and saw again the smoke as they opened the garage door. He and his sister Susan walking through the smoke and crap and seeing one of his mom's legs sticking out all white and blue. Looking around the open car door, he saw Ernie lying across her lap and his mom's head bowed down. Just like the holy water font that hung on the wall at home that was a replica of Michelangelo's Pieta he now used as an ashtray. Susan ran out screaming. He stayed long enough to notice his mom's pink rosary. It was looped over her right thumb, just like she had taught him to keep track of his place as he prayed. She had to have been praying all the way to the end. *Now and at the hour of our death,* the final phrase of the 'Hail Mary', he thought.

Danny stood, shaking as his body convulsed with spasms of forgotten pain. He felt his breath leave him as he remembered the cop saying 'We got the bastard that killed Tonya', and another policeman saying 'good riddance to bad trash'. One of them said: 'All right, kid, your mom's a hero.' That was right when another cop came out from the back door. He wore rubber gloves and he slid an open can of fruit cocktail, a spoon, and one of his dad's medicine bottles into a plastic bag. 'She must have knocked him out with a bunch of this.'

"Poor mom, poor, poor mom," he heard himself say through the haze of tears. He looked around his cluttered room at the YMCA, his wrenching and crying now subsiding. Something he had never felt before now overwhelmed him. He wasn't just crying for himself, for the years of pain and feeling lost he had always blamed on his mother. He realized he was crying for her, all of her screwed up choices, her lost chances, her losing herself, all her pain for all those years. He cried as he thought about his sister Louise who never came back to the family, and Susan, who lost her mind not long after they found their mom in the car. And for Ernie, who must have suffered constantly with all the crazy shit in his head. For once, Danny wasn't pissed and feeling sorry for himself when he thought about his mom and family. This was about *her*. These new thoughts plagued him as the room suddenly felt small and claustrophobic. He grabbed the bottle of Red Devils and walked out.

As he walked down the hall, he could hear snoring coming from one of the other hustler's rooms, and through the door of Leo the Latino hustler he could hear some sort of Spanish TV show. What the hell did their moms, or dads do to make them so screwed up like him? And what about all the sad tricks they all shared—what they hell happened to them to make them so pathetic? He shook his head and wondered why the hell he had never thought about these things before.

He walked out of the doors of the YMCA. Dawn's rays burned his eyes with a violet light, a morning light he hadn't seen in years. He rubbed his burning eyes. Santa Monica Boulevard roared and clanked with the morning rush as Danny looked east. He felt the warmth on his face and lightness in his chest. The light pulled the words from his mouth, and through the tears of years that strained his voice, he whispered:

"Mom, I understand. I forgive you. I'm so sorry for you."

The sun burst its golden rays and Danny let himself drop to the curb. He opened the bottle of barbiturates and poured them down a storm drain and threw the bottle in after them. He closed his eyes and raised his face to the sun briefly, then glanced west down Santa Monica Boulevard. He barely recognized it in the morning light. He stood up and pulled what was left of the four hundred dollars the priest had given him from his jean pocket and counted it—three hundred sixty and change. He tucked the bills back into his pocket and turned to make his way back to the YMCA. But his feet felt frozen to the sidewalk and for a second he couldn't move. Too many questions, too many new feelings swirled in his brain. "Okay, Daniel Thomas Murphy," he said out loud. "Now what?" He paused a moment longer. He sighed, turned away from the YMCA toward the west, and started walking.

9 780692 202241